Haiti and the Revolution Unseen

SERIES EDITORS
Brandon Byrd, *Vanderbilt University*
Zandria F. Robinson, *Rhodes College*
Christopher Cameron, *University of North Carolina, Charlotte*

BLACK LIVES MATTER. What began as a Twitter hashtag after the 2013 acquittal of George Zimmerman for the murder of Trayvon Martin has since become a widely recognized rallying cry for black being and resistance. The series aims are twofold: 1) to explore social justice and activism by black individuals and communities throughout history to the present, including the Black Lives Matter movement and the evolving ways it is being articulated and practiced across the African Diaspora; and 2) to examine everyday life and culture, rectifying well-worn "histories" that have excluded or denied the contributions of black individuals and communities or recast them as entirely white endeavors. Projects draw from a range of disciplines in the humanities and social sciences and will first and foremost be informed by "peopled" analyses, focusing on everyday actors and community folks.

In the Shadow of Powers: Dantes Bellegarde in Haitian Social Thought,
by Patrick Bellegarde-Smith

Race, Religion, and Black Lives Matter: Essays on a Moment and a Movement,
edited by Christopher Cameron and Phillip L. Sinitiere

Continually Working: Black Women, Community Intellectualism, and Economic Justice in Postwar Milwaukee, by Crystal M. Moten

From Rights to Lives: The Evolution of the Black Freedom Struggle, edited by Charles W. McKinney and Françoise N. Hamlin

Black Gurl Reliable: Pedagogies of Vulnerability and Transgression,
by Dominique C. Hill

Haiti and the Revolution Unseen

The Persistence of the Decolonial Imagination

Natalie Marie Léger

VANDERBILT UNIVERSITY PRESS
Nashville, Tennessee

Copyright 2025 by Vanderbilt University Press.
Published 2025.
All rights reserved.

Library of Congress Cataloging-in-Publication Data

Names: Léger, Natalie M., author.
Title: Haiti and the revolution unseen : the persistence of the decolonial imagination / Natalie Marie Léger.
Description: Nashville, Tennessee : Vanderbilt University Press, [2025] | Series: Black lives and liberation | Includes bibliographical references and index.
Identifiers: LCCN 2024056863 (print) | LCCN 2024056864 (ebook) | ISBN 9780826507884 (hardcover) | ISBN 9780826507877 (paperback) | ISBN 9780826507891 (epub) | ISBN 9780826507907 (pdf)
Subjects: LCSH: Caribbean literature--20th century--History and criticism. | Haiti--In literature. | Haitians in literature. | Slave rebellions in literature. | Decolonization in literature. | Haiti--History--Revolution, 1843--Historiography.
Classification: LCC PN849.C3 L44 2025 (print) | LCC PN849.C3 (ebook) | DDC 809.89729--dc23/eng/20250117
LC record available at https://lccn.loc.gov/2024056863
LC ebook record available at https://lccn.loc.gov/2024056864

This book will be made open access within three years of publication to Path to Open, a program developed in partnership between JSTOR, the American Council of Learned Societies (ACLS), University of Michigan Press, and the University of North Carolina Press to bring about equitable access and impact for the entire scholarly community, including authors, researchers, libraries, and university presses around the world. Learn more at https://about.jstor.org/path-to-open/.

Front cover image: *Sous le regard des Ancetres*, artwork by Gina Samson. Used with permission of the artist.

For my Mother,
Yseult Marie Paul Châtelain Léger,
my heart and my light
(July 19, 1955–February 14, 2025)

Contents

Acknowledgments	*ix*
Preface	*xi*
Introduction. *Ayiti Ginen*	1
1. Dead Conversations	52
2. Seen/Unseen	98
3. Not This!	146
4. *Défilez!*	202
Conclusion. *Ayiti Ginen+*	249
Appendix. Ancestral Homage for Revolutionaries	261
Notes	267
Bibliography	329
Index	351

Acknowledgments

My mother, Yseult Marie Paul Chatelain Léger, and my dear friend, Danielle Heard Mollel, both passed just before this book was to be published. Each played key parts in its composition. Danielle proofread the work that inspired this book and became a cherished friend in the years after graduate school. My mother served as this book's guide, as the stories of Haiti she would regale me with are why I chose to be a Caribbeanist. I count myself lucky to have loved them both and to be able to bear witness to the fruits of their love in this book. My sister, Lynn Léger, father, Yves Léger, and grandmother Jeanine Chatelain, were also key interlocutors, whose encouragement and care were matched by the enthusiasm of Wehti Wotorson Blackledge, Amy Gather, Armando García, Kavita Singh, Eziaku Atuma Nwokocha, Nicole McFarlane, Kellie Carter Jackson, Mary Frances Philips, Beth Bouloukos, and Jennifer Yusin. I would be remiss to not thank Crystal Martin, Janean Beckham, Tashia Davis Fraser, Lindsay Cato, Jessica John, Belinda Rincon, Anthony Reed, Tsitsi Ella Jaji, Krupa Shandilya, Sarah Senk, Deirdre Cooper Owens, Dennis Tyler, Laurie Lambert, Mariana F. Past, Philip Kaisary, and Raj Chetty, whose support, conversations, and advice contributed to this book's existence.

The support of the Andrew W. Mellon foundation and the Ford Foundation were instrumental to this book's composition, as were the fellowship and mentorship I received during my respective tenures as a Mellon scholar and a Ford fellow from Marlene Daut, Kimberly Jaunita Brown, Sandy Alexandre, Christina Sharpe, Faith Smith, Jonathan Wilson, Modhumita Roy, Rebekah Ahrendt, Margareta Ingrid Christian,

Yoon H. Choi, and the Dark Room Collective. I am also thankful for the support of the Research Foundation at City University of New York (CUNY) and my colleagues at Queens College, CUNY. François Pierre-Louis, Miles P. Grier, William Orchard, Jason Tougaw, Annmarie Drury, Duncan Faherty, Glenn Burger, Karen Weingarten, Steve Kruger, Ryan Black, and Régine Isabelle Joseph provided invaluable assistance. Kaiama L. Glover, Kelly Baker Josephs, and Vanessa Valdes also offered fellowship that contributed to this book's existence. Many thanks to Yomaira C. Figueroa-Vásquez for this book's title and for the opportunity to grow through the Writer's Lab, whose participants helped me through the paralysis of perfectionism; thank you, Treva Lindsay, Tacuma Peters, Sarah Bruno, Adom Philogene Heron, Aurora Santiago Ortiz, and Nadejda I. Webb. My colleagues at Temple helped me rethink this book, and I am grateful to Roland L. Williams, Carissa Harris, James Salazar, Joyce A. Joyce, Casarae Abdul-Ghani, and Gabriel Wettach for their time and good humor. I would also like to thank Alex Gil Fuentes, whose generosity came at the right time.

Cheryl Wall, William H. Galperin, Brent Hayes Edwards, and Daphne Lamothe were my undergraduate professors at Rutgers University. Their instruction and scholarship inspired my decision to pursue a doctoral degree at Cornell University, where Natalie Melas, Carole Boyce Davies, Elizabeth DeLoughrey, Jonathan B. Monroe, Biodun Jefiyo, Gerard Aching, and Paul Sawyer provided the guidance I needed to conceive this book. I thank them for pushing me to think deeply. I am grateful for the individuals who reviewed this book, as their feedback helped me to write with greater clarity and precision. Additional thanks goes to the editorial team at Vanderbilt, Gianna F. Mosser, Joell M. Smith-Borne, and Patrick Samuel. I would also like to thank Carol Lawes, Tessa Hauglid, Joseph Stuart, Johanne Castera, and Brian Lee for their assistance and Gina Samson for her amazing art.

I thank my son, Aa'ran, finally, who taught me more about dinosaurs then I could possibly ever want to know and who loves it when I teach him about Haiti.

Preface

Pride and anger necessitated the course I have chosen here to write Haiti into presence. Yet it is a course I felt ill equipped to pursue because of my diasporic experience of the country, which I know mostly through my family, notwithstanding sporadic visits here and there. My parents insisted, however, that I am Haitian. They never wanted to emigrate and their perpetual grief about having done so compounded the sense of communal betrayal that subtends Haitian migration for Haitians. I, like other children born of Haitian migrants, have inherited this grief and the resistant cultural self on which it is predicated. This resistance is embodied in how we make sense of each other as insiders or outsiders, as Haitians or *dyasporas*, the name for Haitians in exile. Haitians in Haiti refer to Haitians born abroad or who have relocated abroad as *dyaspora*, an appellation that denotes the ambiguities of one's Haitian-ness. The moniker's existence underscores the extent to which Haitian cultural identity is resistantly insular. It is so firmly rooted in the singularity of a history of successful self-determination that the reclamation of difference, of personhood, and of life on one's own terms not only defines group identity but it constitutes this identity as driven by the continuing fight to author oneself, for oneself. To leave is to abandon the fight; to be born elsewhere is to be of questionable resolve for the fight.

I bring the sum of my dubious Haitian-ness to this study and write with awareness of how I am of Haiti and also removed from it. The outsider position I occupy directed my focus to Haiti's significations for others and furnished the material content that I read in *Haiti and the Revolution Unseen*. The insider position I hold produced a reading of Caribbean Haitian Revolutionist literature authored outside of Haiti guided by one sentiment, *"mwen pas moun pou ou?"* This rhetorical question is stated when one encounters insolence and is philosophically rooted in Haiti's resistant sense of self, as it directly translates as "I'm not a person to you?" Outsiders and insiders will find aspects of their Haiti in the pages that follow, where I offer my praise and misgivings on a body of twentieth-century Haitian Revolutionist literatures that double as foundational treatises of Caribbean anticolonial thought. The work I offer here is not recuperative but extends a generative handling of how Haiti indexes fears and qualms about revolutionary possibility and becomes a trope on which to write desires. No more than a canvas for sentiment and thought, Haiti is denuded of its specificities and meanings, and so too is the Revolution in the Haitian Revolutionist literatures of Caribbean thinkers writing outside of Haiti.

In studying Haiti's reduction to significations, this book enacts an ethics of relation that resists an easy understanding of relation: sitting with others and imagining with and through others causes friction that is sensational and complicated, wonderful and offensive, reparative and violent. No effort is made to ignore the messy bigotry present in the texts I study, or to renounce the writers. No effort is made to minimize the feat that is striving to envision beyond the long colonial present with Haitian Revolutionary writing. In these pages, the very act of trying to engage and thereafter imagine with a history of those who have overturned colonial power is held as sacrosanct; as doing so not only calls for greater scrutiny of radical histories, inviting attention to the absented (here Haiti and Haitians), but it also helps anticolonialists envision the distinct possibilities for life that remain in reach. I write with these possibilities in mind and invite you to resist requiring Haiti to be a blank canvas for fears of freedom and dreams of freedom. Instead, I ask that you come to know it as it is, a world onto itself, one that knows that everything in existence can be reinvented for the better should humans forget that *tout moun se moun men tout moun pas menm* (all persons are persons even if we are not the same).

Introduction

Ayiti Ginen

> Agwe Tawoyo, gen yon tan ya we nou.
>
> —"Sou Lamnè"

In 2016 Haiti was admitted into the African Union (AU), or so claimed many Haitian and US news outlets. Had the reports been true, Haiti would have been the first non-African member of the Union. For Haiti's High Commissioner to South Africa, it would have assumed its rightful place upon entry. Jacques Junior Baril stated, "It's not something we decided, it's a place that we earned after we fought for our independence 212 years ago." He continued, "We paved the way for every other African nation to be free today, so historically speaking Haiti should have been in the AU already."[1] Hubristic or prideful, however one receives Baril's contention, what is certain is his understanding of Haiti as an African space and of Haitians as Africans. Haitians are African, he implies, because they successfully fought to remain African. They are African because they showed Africans what it takes to remain African. Baril's words intimate a distinctly Haitian sense of being African, which begs the question: on what ground can Haitians claim to know themselves as Africans and Haiti as an African nation?

Their claim is their rebelling ancestors. More than "two-thirds of the roughly half a million slaves" in the French colony of Saint Domingue (now Haiti) "were African born" by 1789 writes historian Carolyn E. Fick.[2] More than "two-thirds" were unacculturated with the norms of

Europeans and creole (hemispheric American born) peoples on the eve of the Haitian Revolution (1791–1804), and they did not need to be since they were not meant to survive enslavement. The "slave population never reproduced" in Saint Domingue.[3] Instead, African captives (known as *bossales* in the colony) were worked to death and replaced by new arrivals who would be murdered for their labor soon thereafter.[4] And yet despite the immensity of the violence they faced, *bossales* managed to politicize their resistance and were so successful in doing so that they made identification with resistant Africans the bedrock of antislavery and anticolonial contestation in the colony. How did this happen?

Anthropologist Michel-Rolph Trouillot credits the creation of Kreyòl and Vodou, which he argues was the first contest Haitians won against their colonizers.[5] Although colonists tried to "force their own ideas and their own language into the heads of Saint-Domingue's African slaves" by separating *bossales* from their cultures and countrymen, Trouillot contends that *bossales* managed to "outsmart the slave owners."[6] With Kreyòl, they "folded . . . into [the colonists' language] a bunch of African languages" and with Vodou, they "took the colonists' religion [and] folded it into their own religion."[7] Because *bossales* made the language their own and reformulated Catholicism to their Vodouizan worldview, they immersed all captives and their allies among the free into the community they were forging on the fly. Black studies scholar Crystal Eddins argues that this community was possible because of the "web of networks [*bossales*] built through rituals and marronage."[8] Eddins and historian Jean Fouchard both view marronage as especially important in building communality because it fostered "native pride" among maroons and captives.[9] This esteem was "key . . . to building an emerging sense of racial solidarity" among Saint Domingue's captive populace notes Eddins, and central to the innovations in thought that decolonial sociologist Jean Casimir argues bore "the counter-plantation system."[10] This system refers to the cultural institutions created by *bossales* (like the *lakou* or communal yard) that challenged the colonial order in Saint Domingue and Haiti thereafter.[11] The largesse of African self-pride in the colony, coupled with the cultural institutions *bossale* ingenuity bore, attests to how successfully *bossales* had created an oppositional cultural framework in Saint Domingue; through this framework all captives could know themselves outside of French colonial norms. Trouillot thus writes that as captives "**learned to fight**" their "native-born culture" was "**learning to breathe**."¹²

This culture's first breath gave all captives a model for resistance in the rebellious African, whose defiance was so notorious in the colony that Fouchard writes that Saint Domingue had "the problem of Africans difficult to contain."¹³ This position was also supported by the colony's famous chronicler, the French colonist Moreau de Saint-Méry. His "well-known, now-classic chart of [African] 'nations'" reveals that "almost all the Africans imported to Saint Domingue were by nature quick to rebellion" and those who colonists deemed more amenable to servitude, like Congos, constituted the majority of the maroon population, belying the lie of their docility.¹⁴ Africans not only set the standard for resistance in the colony but as the model to follow, they bore a cultural ethos of resistance that allowed creoles, free and captive alike, to resistantly reclaim themselves as Africans irrespective of their place of birth. The white-skinned Haitian revolutionist, renowned nineteenth-century antislavery essayist, and influential political scribe of early Haiti, Jean Louis Vastey, is an apt example. He writes in his 1816 book, *Réflexions sur une lettre de Mazères*, "having been given life by an African woman, I very much identify with being African," notwithstanding that his mother was a free woman of color from Saint Domingue and his father was a white colonist from France.¹⁵ Today Haitians call themselves *Ginens* (African Haitians) and proudly reference Haiti as *Ayiti Ginen* (Africa Haiti) because of the immense influence of Africans in Saint Domingue.

With this book, I foreground their influence and situate readers in a revolution forged by African defiance. Rather than describe the persons held in bondage in Saint Domingue as "enslaved/slave," I choose to refer to them as "captives." This choice acknowledges how *bossales* saw themselves as "free people" before and after their arrival to Saint Domingue.¹⁶ Eddins writes that "resistance among potential [African] captives was a regular occurrence, since . . . most individuals taken to the Americas were victims of some other financial crisis [versus debt], or were either kidnapped or prisoners of war. These were free people who were losing their original liberty, personal dignity, familial and community networks, and connections to their homeland and ancestral deities due to the [slave] trade."[17] I showcase the revolutionary importance of *bossales'* self-conception as "free people" through this book's decolonial framework. This framework draws from the decolonial scholarship of Casimir, Anibal Quijano, Catherine E. Walsh, María Lugones, Walter Mignolo, Nelson Maldonado-Torres, and Sylvia Wynter. Their writings challenge how colonial modernity, and its racist system of classification, have made understandings of power, knowledge, space/place, and being knowable through a Eurocentric perspective alone. Furthermore, their works stress that this perspective overdetermines and obscures other modes of thought and ways of being that exist within trivialized and/or demonized spaces populated by *les damnés de la terre* as defined by Frantz Fanon.[18]

Following Wynter's theorization of culture, place, and colonial knowledge, I understand Haiti as among these spaces and address Haiti's existence as a "demonic ground" in the West, as that which lies "outside of our present governing system of meaning, or theory/ontology."[19] Haiti's existence as a place beyond the West is why I write the decolonial as an inventive process of becoming, which accords with ethnic studies scholar Laura E. Pérez's idea of the decolonial as a process of self "reclamation."[20] Pérez's meaning captures the imaginative self-possessed nature of *bossale* cultural praxis and aligns with how decolonial activist and scholar Catherine E. Walsh consigns the decolonial to persons and "communities" from "below" who "challenge, interrupt, and transgress the matrices of colonial power in their practices of being, action, existence, creation, and thought."[21] I treat *bossales* and their communities of relation as critical and resourceful to express the decolonial nature of their revolutionary efforts; and I make extensive use of Casimir's research throughout the book to establish the criticality of their thoughts, actions, and distinct cultural horizon. I also use Casimir's scholarship because his work has set the standard for writing the revolutionary history of Haitians decolonially. In addition to Casimir, I draw from the populist historiography of Fick, Trouillot, Fouchard, and Eddins to write the Revolution "on its own terms," that is, with cognizance of *bossale* self-knowledge and the widespread resistant mentality it bore among all captives and their descendants.

This mentality is evident in the speech of present-day Haitians, who can express incredulity by saying, *Kisa* (what?), but often choose to say, *Sa blan dit?* (What did the white say?) This expression reveals how their *bossale* ancestors made questioning the sense and racist implications of white colonial speech and action a collective practice. Rather than inquiring with "what" to understand the colonizer's reason, their captive forebears said "what" and refused to internalize hate masquerading as reason. They said "what" and refused to see reason in hate, which safeguarded their distinct individual and cultural sense of self. They reasoned, in other words, without considering French colonial power and taught their descendants that to be African meant critically navigating existence on one's own terms. This instruction made the Revolution possible and is the reason why I invite readers to see the "Black" in Haiti's famous Black uprising as expansive, as telling of a political African-ness that emerged outside the territorial continent of Africa and that manifested from the networks of relations culturally distinct Africans, forged with each other and with non-Africans, in particular, captive and free Black and mixed-race creoles. These relations made Haitians into a people long before Haiti's emergence as a sovereign state, which is to say, the defiance of Africans emboldened captives against French colonial rule; but their way of thinking gave captives and their allies among the free an epistemological framework for being that was not oriented by French colonists.

Should scholars of the nation and its revolution peruse the anthology of Haiti, *The Haiti Reader: History, Culture, Politics*, and turn their attention to the traditional Vodou song "Sou Lamné," composed by *bossales*, what should be apparent is not only the existence of an Africanist knowledge system among captives that supported their grievances, but also how this system legitimated their desire to dis-identify with their abusers. Religious studies scholar Eziaku Atuama Nwokocha defines "Haitian Vodou [as] a system of beliefs and rituals that mines the experiences of everyday people for reflection, healing and inspiration."[22] It is a faith that is tailored to the needs of the folk and in that capacity, it "supplies basic knowledge on how to operate in the world."[23] For the composers of "Sou Lamné," "operat[ing] in the world" meant recognizing the fact of their racialization as chattel. The song cites the hold of the slave ship as their first point of unification as a people with the lines, "In the bottom of the ship/We are all one."[24] This utterance acknowledges that the colonizer set the terms for their initial beginnings. But rather than view the hold as an incubator of chattel and thus of peoples who are born to be slaves because of their black skin, the hold was reimagined against the biological racialisms of colonial modernity, or what Wynter describes as its biocentrism.[25] Instead, the hold was engaged as a primordial battleground. There *bossales* reconceived themselves in solidarity with each other on terms greater than the commonality of flesh. To unite through flesh alone would have meant uniting within the knowledge system and cultural framework of the colonizer. But to unite because persons are similarly imperiled ("They took our feet / They chained our wrists / They dropped us in the bottom"), indeed, to unite because they are firm in their sense of self ("There's a time when they'll see us") is to articulate an onto-epistemic difference from the colonizer.[26] I read foundational twentieth-century Caribbean writings of the Revolution authored outside of Haiti with cognizance of this difference, and I study the canonical writings featured here from the epistemic and cultural perspective of *Ginens*.

G. W. F. Hegel famously said the master knows herself through the slave and the slave through the master, and a body of anticolonial thought has agreed. The *Ginen* says, "I see that you need me to be you, but I do not need you to be me." To the master demanding recognition, to the apologists writing to support the master's demand for recognition, and to the anticolonial radical whose rebellion necessitates recognizing the master's request for recognition, the *Ginen* says, *Sa blan dit?* She reflects, refuses, and keeps it moving. This is the basic praxis of *Ginen* culture and thought, which in *Haiti and the Revolution Unseen* is key to the story of the Revolution. The fundamental importance of this praxis is barely noted, however, in Caribbean classics of the Revolution and scholarly studies of these classics. In other words, canonical Caribbean writing of the Revolution is largely composed with little to no attention to the Haitian revolutionist as African or Africanized. Instead, they are peopled with "mad Haitian rebel[s]," to borrow from Saint Lucia's famed poet-playwright, Derek Walcott. These rebels reference creole revolutionists who are indistinct from the white colonists they fought against or creole revolutionists whose condition of being has remained that of a slave during and after the Revolution.[27]

Walcott conceives of the Haitian revolutionist as a creole alone in the 1958 pageant, *Drums and Colours*, and likely does so because of how readily the Revolution is associated with the *affranchi* generals who governed Saint Domingue independently (without French oversight) and later Haiti. Most commonly known revolutionaries are from Saint Domingue's class of freed peoples who were liberated before the onset of the Revolution in 1791. The *affranchi* class of wealthy slave-owning planters and impoverished skilled laborers included emancipated Africans, emancipated or born-free Black creoles, and emancipated or born-free mixed-race creoles. Most in this populace, which numbered "twenty-seven thousand" and "nearly equaled" the white population in numbers, were mixed-race and Caribbean born.[28] The racially mixed majority were known as *gens du couleur libre* or free people of color, and they held a higher class position than their emancipated peers, being wealthy and/or generationally free (i.e., they and their forebears had never experienced slavery).[29] As "the leaders of the emancipated slaves," *gens du couleurs* established how to conduct oneself when free.[30] Their conduct, Fick notes, entailed miming "white manners," being educated in France and working to ensure that their children were sent "abroad to be educated."[31] Casimir suggests that their colonial comportment resulted from being made to live indebted to the French colonial administration, which not only secured but safeguarded the freedom of all *affranchis*.[32] As a result of this protection, *affranchis* were required to navigate a world that was French and that necessitated that they become French as a matter of survival. In other words, they were forcibly creolized because of the conditions attached to their liberation.

Creolized, as used here, is derived from the origins and meanings of the word, "creole," which as Kavita Ashana Singh writes, "*was* the colonies as opposed to Europe, and [referenced] the people who inhabited the colonies."[33] "Creole," in this sense, "is and expresses the Atlantic crossing and colonization," explains Carolyn Allen.[34] Persons described as "creole" were regarded as social intermediaries or "colonial, 'Other[s],'" and seen as having "one identity by blood and another by place of birth, being simultaneously the same and different [from their Old World parents].... Originally then, 'Creole' [described] an intermediary category, defined primarily by its relationship to others, rather than by an essence."[35] *Affranchis* were collectively regarded as creoles, regardless of their place of birth, because their free status and the majority's "color," asserts Fick, cast them as "an intermediary caste between the whites and the slaves."[36] Casimir adds that their "intermediary" role in Saint Domingue rested primarily with the servicing component attached to their liberation. He writes that "the reproduction of slavery depended on the activity of the slave trade" but "the production and reproduction of the captive as a slave depended on the work of free people of color and emancipated slaves."[37] Both were made to labor "in the defense of the colony" via "an ordinance of 1768," which, Fick reveals, condemned "all free mulattoes and free blacks between the ages of fifteen and fifty-five" to active duty in the *maréchaussée* (police) and the militias.[38] Through these roles, Casimir asserts that both "took charge of subjugating the captives and putting in place the measures needed to contain them in their role as enslaved workers," which for *gens du couleurs* specifically, writes Fick, "reinforce[d]... contempt... for [their] own black origins and at the same time exploit[ed] affinities to a white slave society" that excluded them.[39] Emancipated Black and racially mixed creoles and the African-born *affranchi* "often maintained connections to the enslaved population through family, ethnic identity bonds, and work relations" stresses Eddins, and were less likely to be self-alienated and anti-Black.[40] Likewise, Trouillot argues that as generals in the Haitian Revolutionary army, these individuals were bolder in their actions than the more moneyed *affranchi* (*gens de couleur*) because they "owed nothing to France" and were less likely to cede their sense of selves to France.[41] Still, philosopher Paul C. Mocombe writes that all *affranchis* "shared the same European practical consciousness."[42] Furthermore, Casimir contends that they all were complicit in "containing" the captive "in their role as enslaved worker," since their freedom was inseparable from the work of administering the colony.[43] Because their freedom meant laboring for the colony, their existence as a class entailed being acculturated, creolized, or (as Mocombe writes) "embourgeoised" into the colonial order as an upholder of the order.[44] The class (and the debt of service to one's emancipator or ancestor that allowed one to be in it) was indoctrinating. Indeed, the class's very existence was symptomatic of how "the Atlantic crossing and colonization" created relations meant to sustain the colony at all costs.[45]

Many important leadership roles in the Haitian army (*armée indigène*) would be occupied by members of the *affranchi*. The famous Caribbean-born generals, Toussaint Louverture (1743-1803), Henry Christophe (1767–1820), and Alexandre Pétion (1770–1818) were *affranchi*; Pétion, specifically, was a *gens de couleur*. They (and their classmates) who survived the Revolution would constitute Haiti's first political elite, alongside the politically powerful former captive "black officers . . . from the indigenous army" (e.g., Jean Jacques Dessalines, 1758–1806).[46] The latter captive-born generals were not creoles in the sense of the *affranchi* but their formation into a class united with former *affranchis* after the Revolution, and their close association as vanguards of the Revolution, has invited writers to wrongly conceive of them as similarly creolized. This is especially true of Dessalines who Walcott explicitly references in *Drums and Colours*.

The play pointedly presents Haitian revolutionists as creoles in the manner of *affranchis*, persons who are predominantly Caribbean born and who have been forcibly creolized. Walcott writes in the pageant's maroon scene, "O God, but is hard sometimes to love one another, if he get on like a beast bind him hand and foot. I can't have no ruction in this place. He getting on like some mad Haitian rebel."[47] Emmanuel Mano, a "multicoloured" maroon leader, issues this utterance when a new Black recruit (a runaway captive) attempts to assault another new recruit (a white planter) because of the latter's race.[48] Mano wants no part of racial separatism and accepts the white recruit into his band of Black, East Indian, and Chinese maroons because "the times" prevented self-reflection. He states, "Sometimes the times so bad a man don't have time to think properly."[49] But his Black recruit now has the "time" to think as a member of his multi-racial army; yet the novice maroon still chooses retributive Black power, a choice that, for Walcott, mirrors the revolutionary conduct of Haiti's first rulers, the Saint Domingue–born Dessalines and the Grenada-born Christophe. In the preceding scene, Christophe (less certainly) and Dessalines (more enthusiastically) await the start of "a new age, the black man's turn to kill."[50]

Surely Dessalines and Christophe were more than colonial mimics, as neither could have led armies of liberation and a nascent nation if they aspired to be bloodthirsty colonists. Surely the Haitian revolutionist is more than white colonial power in blackface. Yet within Walcott's framing, neither has a political or cultural antecedent outside of the colonizing West, which is to say, if Dessalines and Christophe are like colonizers and if "the Haitian rebel" by association is also like colonizers, then they are like them because colonizers are the sole source of political knowledge and cultural conduct in Walcott's imagining of the eighteenth-century Caribbean, no matter that Africans exist in his dramatization of the period.[51] Mano is recognizable as an important maroon leader because he is from Accompong, a Jamaican maroon community begun by Africans and maintained by the equitable relations of Africans, Indigenous peoples, and Black and mixed-race creoles. He calls to mind the Africans relegated to part one of the pageant, titled "CONQUEST," who, along with Indigenous peoples are annexed from part two of the pageant, titled "REBELLION," which is set exclusively in the Caribbean.[52] Mano names an African presence in Haiti and the Caribbean that is important to note, but that is ultimately insignificant to Haiti and the Caribbean post-independence. And yet without Africans specifically in one's imagining of post-independent nineteenth-century Haiti, which was primarily peopled with Africans and Africanized persons, the fiction of Dessalines and Christophe's colonial blood lust will logically yield another fiction with respect to Haiti: Haitians as condemned eternal slaves, notwithstanding their self-liberation. Haitians, Walcott suggests, will passively accept victimization and they will do so because they are creoles and therefore "mad."[53] They are crazed because contact with the colonizer and existence in Caribbean plantation society has overdetermined their relations. Haiti's first leaders want to be like the colonizer and will subjugate their constituents to out-best the colonizer's self-aggrandizing violence. Their constituents, in turn, only know themselves through their past conditioning and will accept subjugation once more.

This idea of the "mad Haitian rebel," as a creole who signifies resistance and resigned defeat is rampant within classic Caribbean writing of the Revolution. It even appears in Édouard Glissant's 1961 play,

Monsieur Toussaint, notwithstanding Glissant's cognizance of the Haitian revolutionist as culturally African.[54] The play dramatizes the impending death and imprisonment of Haiti's best-known revolutionist, Toussaint Louverture, and does so deliberately engaging how Caribbean writers have portrayed Louverture as a tragic Western figure. Glissant cites two writers, his countryman Martinique's famed poet-playwright Aimé Césaire, who authored the book *Toussaint Louverture: The French Revolution and the Colonial Problem* in 1961, and the renowned Trinidadian cultural theorist C. L. R. James, who wrote the history *The Black Jacobins: Toussaint L'Ouverture and the San Domingo Revolution* in 1938.[55] Both James and Césaire write Louverture as Westernized because of his French republican sensibility. James argues that his vacillations at key moments in the Revolution are tied to his enlightenment as evidenced by his knowledge of Western literature and politics. His enlightenment prompted his radicalization but limited how far he could act against France. Césaire argues that his dedication to French republicanism caused him to become a hero who tragically sacrifices himself for the future of Haiti. Glissant responds to these readings by subjecting an acculturated Louverture to the haunting inquisition of a chorus of the Dead (among other figures), who critique and/or lament his investment in French culture and the West, more broadly.

The African Vodou priestess Mama Dio cautions Louverture against identifying with the French who see him as an enemy notwithstanding his identification: "Do not take the Acacia Way . . . the sentry . . . dreams of beast at gunpoint; that beast is you."[56] The "Way" had already been taken by this point as Louverture is in prison, but the warning condemns Louverture's choice to ignore the cultural knowledge of his people in favor of French culture. So when the pre-Haitian revolutionary maroon rebel François Makandal lovingly foretells Louverture's rise to power in the collectivist framework of Vodou spiritualism—which believes that the dead and the unborn are sentient beings who can make their presence felt in the world of the living—readers are once again reminded of Louverture's immersion in and rejection of his African cultural roots. Glissant writes in Makandal's voice, "You were not yet born, but we felt your kindness at our shoulder, where the heavy hoe leaves its mark."[57] Glissant wants readers to see that Louverture is imprisoned because of his acculturation, but he also wants them to see that even with his acculturation he remains culturally African. For why else would he see and acknowledge these spirits and why else would they lovingly haunt him, if he were not of them and still like them? In this respect, Louverture is a creole revolutionist not only because he is Saint Dominguan-born, but he is a creole revolutionist because he is creolized—ideologically of the West while remaining immersed in the African cultures of Saint Domingue. He mimes the colonist ("There is no Legba. There is no Ogoun") as much as he proclaims his dedication to the captives' liberation ("I must go to the hills for the freedom of all.").[58]

Glissant writes Mama Dio and Makandal as unable to register Louverture's creole-ness. They still see him as like them and, because they do, they will be there with him when he transitions from life to death. How beautiful and how woefully un-*Ginen*. Mama Dio and Makandal's fixation with aiding Louverture, indeed, the manner in which their haunting is in service of Louverture, is the direct consequence of Glissant's dedication to composing him in accordance with a Caribbean tradition of writing the general. Both characters must correlate to the characterization Glissant is responding to and because of that, they remain tangential to the Revolution and to the making of Haiti. They are resigned to being the unenlightened subjects saved by Louverture's sacrificial leadership (Césaire's reading) or, more generously, safeguarded by it (James's reading). *Ginens* would not have asked Louverture to see the legitimacy of their counsel. They would not have pleaded for recognition—to be seen as worthy of being listened to and as ancestrally connected to one who refuses to reciprocate that connection. They would have moved with the surety of self that knows their vision will be realized with or without Louverture, which is what they did during the Revolution and which is what the Louverture of historic fact conveys to the Directory, the governmental body leading France in 1797, when it considers re-instituting slavery in Saint Domingue.[59]

Glissant knows the captive African as a person who is ardently anti-Western, antislavery, and anticolonial like the African/Africanized Haitian revolutionist. His maroon character, the African revolutionist of historic fact, Macaïa, a Congo, conveys this.[60] Macaïa refuses to be deferential to Louverture even in death, but Glissant is not leading with

Macaïa; which is to say, he did not write a play titled *Monsieur Macaïa* or more aptly, *Neg Macaïa*.⁶¹ He wrote a play that continues (albeit with a twist) a Caribbean tradition of writing Louverture as the Revolution, which causally writes the Revolution as a Western European happening. Thus, it should be of no surprise that Mama Dio and Makandal are more emblematic of the vanquished than empowered self-actualized humans (e.g., *Ginens*). Like Dessalines and Christophe's imagined future constituents in Walcott's *Drums and Colours*, Mama Dio and Makandal remain as they are imagined by colonists and conquistadors: they are envisioned, in other words, as dubiously human presences who exist to serve a superior other.

If the creole revolutionist is a creation of the colonial project, being a revolutionary who is born in the Americas, then the creole revolutionist is also a simulacrum of power and conveyable as such by artists and critics of the Revolution. In this framework, Louverture is a creole revolutionist because of his birth and his way of thinking, through which he embodies a way of being that he resists but remains determined by. Mama Dio and Makandal are not creoles by birth but by signification, by their servile relation to a power that aspires to be like the colonizer in culture and thought. But to maintain this colonial signification, to leave un-interrogated and unthought how Mama Dio and Makandal's haunting of Louverture in Glissant's play replicates and naturalizes the social categories of conquest (the enlightened colonizer versus the simple colonized) is to absent from the reader's purview not only the African Haitian rebel and her distinct decolonial horizon for being; but it is to also absent the very possibility of a life beyond the colony. Enthusiasts of the Revolution, be they artists or scholars, jeopardize their ability to name *and* see colonial power as detestable when they fail to see African/Africanized peoples in the Revolution. With their absence, they lose the ability to see the political and ethical importance of moving in a colonial world without taking the colonizer into consideration. What's more, they lose sight of how the decision to determine oneself and to thereafter stand in solidarity with others who are similarly oriented can produce potent political praxis. The failure to see all this, and engage resistant peoples on their own terms, results in artistic and critical engagements with the Revolution that are defeatist at conception and fundamentally unable to nurture the reader's decolonial imagination as intended. Indeed, what happens is the opposite: the slow rotting of the decolonial imagination and with it the conviction that another world is possible.

With this book, I posit that Caribbean writers of the Revolution fail to capture the richness of Haitian cultural thought or *Ginen* thought. They ignore the conditions of difference that inspired the captive populace's dreams of freedom from colonial rule and replicate the forms of colonial power that they sought to vilify with their Haitian Revolutionist texts. The canonical writer-theorists studied include the aforementioned Black writers James, Césaire, and Glissant and the white Cuban writer and essayist Alejo Carpentier. Given this book's investment in the decolonial nature of *Ginen* cultural praxis and showcasing this praxis's fundamental importance to the Revolution, I write against a biocentric understanding of Black politics. This means that I approach Black decolonial politics as a relational and coalitionist thinking through and working toward new ways of being human outside of whiteness, which is distinct from the disciplinary practice of "studying black people" and Black politics within colonial modernity.[62]

Black studies scholar Katherine McKittrick explains that the study of Black peoples in colonial modernity is often an "intricate Malthusian project [that describes] black ... politics as only and always authentically emerging from, blood-identity."[63] Black decolonial politics, in the sense used here, concerns the lived experiences and knowledge practices of Black people, whose existence demands learning and unlearning their lives and communities outside of colonial modernity. It has its roots in *Ginen* culture, whose critical modalities of resistance say *Ginen yo tout koulé* (*Ginen*, here ancestor spirits come in all colors).[64] This saying counters how colonial modernity's privileging of "blood-identity" politics denies Black peoples the agency to be their own knowledge producers. In other words, it denies them the ability to be active participants in the deconstruction of colonial knowledge practices that damn them as "only and always poor, oppressed, abject, dead, extinct" because their identity is their flesh and their flesh is aberrant being Black.[65] McKittrick writes, "Identity has biologic traces. Identity is corporeal. Studying identity so often involves demonstrating that biology is socially constructed, *not displacing biology* but, rather, empowering biology—the flesh—as the primary way to study identity."66 Black decolonial politics, as treated here, regards identity as dynamic, and as the product of deliberated political choices. This understanding of Black politics displaces biology since it conceives of Black politics as a praxis that embraces solidarities (in group and out) and repeated self-invention. Black decolonial politics privileges how Black peoples have creatively and thoughtfully navigated existence, and it will think alongside marginalized others who have also made the choice to be critical and innovative in their resistance against the colonial project because the point of the politic is to create a new world.67

The influential Black and white Caribbean writers studied here aspire toward a new world. They engaged Haiti as an exemplar of anticolonial liberation and did so with such innovation that their Haitian Revolutionary writings are as canonical as they are to the fields of Caribbean studies, Black studies, and postcolonial studies. Furthermore, their writings of the Revolution are so significant that each of these writers has impacted the field of Haitian studies and its conception of Haiti and Haitian people. I analyze James's history *The Black Jacobins*, Carpentier's novella *The Kingdom of This World*, Césaire's play *The Tragedy of King Christophe*, and Glissant's drama *Monsieur Toussaint*, and show how the authors fail to write the lives of Haitians into presence because each reifies Haiti. They denude the nation of its cultural context and truly unique contributions to the hemispheric Americas to refashion Haiti in their own colonial making, even as their impulses and hopes for their arguments go in the opposite direction. This book foregrounds the tension between the decolonial orientation of their writerly instincts and aspirations and their abstract rendering of Haiti to hold space for both their masterful critiques of slavery, colonialism and white colonial power and their woefully inadequate treatment of Haiti/Haitians.

I composed this book with the decolonial tenor of their writings in mind, and have brought the lesser studied Haitian Revolutionary art of the Black, Haiti-born (US resident) writer and essayist Edwidge Danticat ("Nineteen Thirty- Seven" and "A Wall of Fire Rising") and the white Italian neo-realist filmmaker Gillo Pontecorvo (*Queimada!*) in dialogue with them to author a decolonial literary history of the Revolution that centers Haiti. Pontecorvo's film is used to showcase how Césaire's Haitian writings are *Ginen* in thought despite their anti-*Ginen* point of origin; he extends the decolonial conversations Césaire's Haitian Revolutionist work ignites. Danticat's work showcases Haiti's unique culture of resistant self-authorship and is closely read because it immerses readers in a Haitian cultural sensibility absented from the Caribbean classics of the Revolution foregrounded here. Her writings are included because it is not enough to simply write about this sensibility; it is imperative that readers feel it and come to know it. Indeed, it is imperative that readers come to know Haiti and Haitians.

This book extends the scholarly project of literary historian Marlene L. Daut, who writes the Revolution cognizant of how Haitian people are active agents of their own history. Daut writes, "Haitians, like all human beings, are and have always been the agents of their own destinies."[68] She states the latter in response to how "Haiti seems to matter only insofar as it affected American lives, American slavery, American politics, American history, and American literature" in US-based studies of the Revolution.[69] Her statement is applicable to the canonical Caribbean treatments of the Revolution analyzed here, where Haiti "matters" as a deracinated, Haiti and Haitian-less, idea. I examine the particular ways this rhetorical deracination or absenting operates in the depiction of historical actors in canonical texts, and I open up the possibility for readers to see beyond each text's critical acclaim to address how a happening that shook the world could actually ever happen in the first place.

Ginen

This book insists that its readers know Haiti as *Ayiti Ginen* and Haitians as *Ginens*, as doing so avails them of the fact that African and Africanized captives were the political force behind the Revolution's success. I establish this reading to give readers the bearings needed to comprehend why knowing Haitians as *Ginens* demands a distinct understanding of the Revolution; and it also demands a reevaluation of the stories of it told by canonical Caribbean writers and supported, in turn, by scholars of Caribbean studies, Black studies, and postcolonial studies, who teach and write about influential Caribbean classics of the Revolution.

Indeed, knowing Haitians as *Ginens* equally demands an interrogation of how Haitian studies uses these Caribbean stories of the Revolution to engage its disciplinary focus, Haiti and Haitians. Before turning to what *Ginen* is and means, an overview of the Revolution is in order.[70]

HISTORICAL OVERVIEW

On August 22, 1791, *bossale* and creole captives began their attack on French colonial power, marking what Fick notes as "the beginning to the end of one of the greatest wealth-producing slave colonies the world had ever known."[71] They set fire to "manufacturing installations, sugar mills, [and] tools [as well as] farming equipment," obliterating how the colony came to be "the pearl of the Antilles."[72] Seven days prior to the Revolution's opening, captives from neighboring plantations met at a clearing (*Bwa Kayïman*) to formulate their plans and conduct a Vodou ceremony. The ceremony was said to be led by either a creole priestess of mixed ancestry, Cécile Fatiman, or an unnamed older African woman and one of the Revolution's first leaders, the Jamaican creole and frequent maroon Boukman Dutty.[73] The other initial leaders include Jeannot Bullet, the Africa-born Jean-Francois, and Georges Biassou. Most in attendance at *Bwa Kayïman* were *commandeurs* (slave drivers) or "coachmen, domestics, and other slaves" most trusted by white planters.[74] The majority were not *bossales*, but they were overwhelmingly Africanized as Boukman's famous prayer attests. It invokes the ancestral spirits of Vodou (*lwa* of *Ginen*) and expresses a collective refusal of "the colonial state's version of God's truth," which aligns with *bossale* resistance.[75] Boukman would be executed two months after the Revolution's onset. *Ginens* continued without him.

Within a year of the revolutionary struggle, they had succeeded in liberating themselves. They controlled two-thirds of the colony and by 1792 slavery was abolished in Saint Domingue. Freedom no longer required service to the colonial administration, and because it was now predicated on the desires and interests of captives, white colonists saw their power diminishing in real time. In desperation, they invited the British to join their fight in 1792. Spain joined the war on the "side" of the captives in the same year, using Boukman's compatriots, Jean François and Biassou, and later Louverture, to further its ultimately unsuccessful aims to seize the colony. Trouillot writes that "after March 1796, French whites lost their remaining power in Saint Domingue," which did not bode well for other aspiring white rulers of the colony.[76] Spain would lose all footing on the island when Louverture formally abolished slavery in what is now the Dominican Republic in 1800. The English were driven out two years earlier in 1798 by the allied forces of *gens de couleur* André Rigaud's militaries in the south of Saint Domingue (the armies of Pétion and Jean-Pierre Boyer, among others) and Louverture's in the north (the armies of Dessalines, Christophe, and many of the Africanized creoles at *Bwa Kayiman*).[77] The military presence of the English and Spanish would teach the self-liberated that their enemies were not just the French but a larger global order of white colonizers eager to enslave them for profit. They fought tenaciously as a result.

Louverture's military skill and diplomacy ostensibly safeguarded former captives from colonialism's administrative return by the French, the Spanish, and the British. Yet what proved to be his greatest power was the people's scorched earth tactics. The captives' willingness to burn everything in the name of their freedom created a collective apparatus of monumental power that Louverture would leverage to secure his political ascendance.[78] Their example, and the consistency as well as fervor of their fighting, would lead Christophe to burn Le Cap upon seeing the French expedition approaching Saint Domingue in 1802. Louverture would be deported to France soon after the arrival of the expedition. The period that followed his 1802 abduction, termed the War of Independence (1802–1803), saw the mass desertion of plantations by the self-liberated, who had been made wage laborers by the French colonial administration and Louverture's organization. Marronage and the organizational practices therein had become "a movement of popular resistance," involving "farmers and warriors" alike.[79]

As resistance among the self-liberated spread to civilians and non-civilians, the *affranchi* Haitian revolutionary generals who arrived with the French and who fought for the French (*gens de couleurs* Pétion and Boyer, most notably) switched allegiances, as did the *affranchi* and captive generals who had fought with Louverture and joined the French following his deportation. (Consider for instance, the *affranchi* Christophe and the former captive Dessalines.) Each did so upon learning of France's plan to exterminate all adult-age African and African-descended persons once restoring slavery and the colony to French control.[80] The self-liberated never ceased fighting the French and when the creole vanguard of the Revolution proposed uniting their efforts, African leaders in the South of Saint Domingue that agreed (Goman, Gilles Bénech, Nicolas Régnier, among others) avoided the generals' liquidation of their northern peers. These were African leaders who were assassinated because they refused to serve under generals they regarded as fair-weathered. The eliminated leaders include Halaou, Petit-Noël Prieur, Sans Souci, Macaïa, Sylla, and others.[81] Dessalines would declare Saint Domingue independent on January 1, 1804, and rename the colony *Ayiti* in honor of the island's Indigenous peoples.[82] *Ginens* would Africanize the name in honor of themselves and popularize the nation as *Ayiti Ginen*.[83]

GINEN

The term *Ginen* is inextricable from this history of resistance. It names a resistant people and their decolonial consciousness and broadly denotes the revolutionists who are sidelined in classic Caribbean writing of the Revolution. The latter generally showcases and/or conceives the Revolution as directed and determined by *affranchi* revolutionists, persons who in this book are termed creoles—a title that, firstly, signals the Caribbean origin of many; secondly, denotes the particularities of an existence determined by mastery of and identification with French colonial culture; and thirdly, references the reading practices of the influential Caribbean writers studied here, who perceive the Haitian revolutionist as a simulacrum of colonial power alone. *Ginen* lies outside these conceptions. It names the African and Africanized peoples who emerged in solidarity with one another in pre-revolutionary Saint Domingue and the Haitian descendants of these peoples in nineteenth- and twentieth-century Haiti. Given that "almost the entire population of Haiti—more than 90 percent—descends directly from [*bossales*]," the term *Ginen* makes plain how African the first non-Indigenous Haitians were.[84] It also brings to light how the collectivist culture *bossales* created in Saint Domingue countered slave-making with *Ginen*-making, a purposeful acculturation into resistant African-ness. This transformation will be detailed momentarily and is understandable with attention to *bossale* epistemology, which functioned as a collectivist faith-based knowledge practice according to Casimir and Mocombe. Mocombe refers to *bossale* epistemology as "the Vodou Ethic and the spirit of communism," which he defines as an "alternative . . . system and [form of] social integration [led by] *oungan yo, manbó yo, gangan yo,* and *granmoun yo,* [(vodou priests, vodou priestesses, and elders) that] seek[s] to constitute and recursively (re)organize and reproduce [the *bossale* majority's] African Kreyol and Vodou practical-consciousness . . . via its Vodou ideology *(konesans)*; modes of productions, i.e., subsistence agriculture, husbandry, and komes; and ideological apparatuses."[85] Casimir does not name *bossale* epistemology, but the features he attributes to it (namely "the counter plantation system") accord with Mocombe's definition.[86] *Bossale* thought is maintained today through Haitian Vodou, a religion that is rightly understood as "Africa reblended."[87] In this faith, *Ginen* is knowable firstly as a place and an embodied consciousness.[88]

Ginen names an ancestral point of origin being *Lafrik Ginen* (Guinea Africa), the home *lòt bò dlo* (across the water); but it also names a sacred realm *anba dlo* (beneath the water), where the spirits of the Vodou pantheon *(lwa)* reside and are born.[89] This *Ginen* also houses the spirits of the ancestors and the newly deceased, who in entering *Ginen* fulfill their captive forebears' longing to re-cross the water and return home.[90] As an embodied consciousness, *Ginen* functions as "a state of mind," one "that anchors Haitian Vodou to Africa, the life force, the energy on which the spirits live," notes visual artist and Haitian Vodou initiate Sokari Ekine.[91] This conception of *Ginen* is why the decision to be a practitioner of Vodou is relayed in Kreyòl as "'*sèvi Ginen*' or '*Ginen yo,*'" which as Black studies scholar Claudine Michel explains "roughly translates as I serve the spirits, the *Lwa* from Guinea, Africa's good deities."[92]

Anthropologist and popular Haitian musician Mimerose Beaubrun explains that when *Ginen* is used as a direct reference for *lwa*, it distinguishes between *lwa* who are inherited and who make reasonable care-based demands on a supplicant in return for aid, versus *lwa* who are not inherited and *achte* (brought) via initiation. The purchased spirit will claim the life of someone close to the supplicant and/or large monetary sums for the assistance provided. The enormous demands this *lwa* makes show that it is not *Ginen*.[93] This usage of *Ginen* reveals how the term exists as a cultural barometer for acceptable ethical conduct that Haitians view as deriving from Africa directly, that is, from "Africa's good deities," to borrow again from Michel.[94] The implication here is that the capitalist component of buying a *lwa* derives from cultural traditions that are not natal to the Africans who became Haitians, which accounts for the purchased spirit's alien (non-culturally conforming) self-interestedness. *Ginen*, as an embodied consciousness, references then the decision to follow the path of the spirits, the path back to *Lafrik Ginen*, the home *lòt bò dlo*, where one is guided to embrace "African-derived principles," which include a "holistic conception of life, human-centered orientation, centrality of the community, honor and respect for elders, beneficence, forbearance, forgiveness, and a sense of justice."[95] These "principles" ultimately help one conceive of existence through the consciousness of the spirits. It is in this respect that *Ginen* is a consciousness that is embodied: it is an ethos guided by African ancestry (one inherits one's *lwa*) as well as ancestors; and within the context of revolutionary Saint Domingue, these ancestors are real, adopted and fictive—the direct result of the *bossale*'s insistence that she alone determines herself, which, in turn, is the direct outcome of her epistemic originality.

GINEN-MAKING

This originality is evident in the *bossale*'s collectivist knowledge practices. Casimir writes that the captive African "extracted a form of knowing that liberated her, making it possible to construct a universe where she could realize herself as she envisioned. This knowledge began with solidarity with her companions in misfortune."[96] These "companions" included creole captives and a "small number of free people of color," explains Eddins. Both Eddins's and Fouchard's research on marronage personalizes the drive for new knowledge as derivative of the captives' self-possession.[97] Their studies show how *bossales* created "knowledge that [could] surpass the conditions of survival," to borrow from Casimir, because of their faith in themselves.[98] This faith was collectivizing and occurred largely because marronage and Vodou solidified their commitment to ensuring the natural freedom of Africans and their descendants. Where Eddins and Fouchard stress how marronage achieved this by fostering pride in African-ness or African origin, Casimir emphasizes the importance of the *"lwa of Ginen"* to the emergent collective's sense of self.[99] He writes that real or fictive memories of their loved ones and cultures flourishing without them in Africa emboldened captives, granting them the license to reimagine their relations in the past and present.[100] These new relations replicated the novel kinship ties that were made through marronage, which recreated associations around a shared pride in oneself. An ancestor one knew negligibly, perhaps only by name or profession, served the same purpose and united one captive to another, especially if the imagined common ancestor had a similar appellation, occupation, or characteristics. The point is not that the ancestor is real, or that the kinship created through marronage completely replaced blood ties but that the effort was made to create them; for in creating them, captives ensured that they would no longer be "mismatched," to quote Trouillot.[101] The conflicts colonists sought to forge and augment by "mismatch[ing]" Africans on plantations who were from enemy cultural groups, who spoke different languages, or who would otherwise never know each other, lessened in significance; as did the effects of the anti-African harassment African-born captives faced from the freed populace and creole captives, since the new relations they created solidified their will to live and live in the community of others on their terms.[102]

Slave-making, the "intense torture" by which captives were violently acculturated into French colonial society as enslaved subjects of France, could not continue in Saint Domingue in this context.[103] Slave-making could not continue since the individuals designated as slaves universally began to see themselves as captive Africans and thus as free peoples notwithstanding if they were Caribbean born and enslaved at birth. Because *bossales* took a re-membered Africa as the conceptual point for thinking and being in the colony—that is, an Africa reconstituted through pride and a spiritualism guided by nostalgia and fantasy—they instituted *Ginen*-making: they outfitted captives and their allies among the freed with the critical capacity to be "in a universe governed by the principle of slavery" and not be overdetermined by this "principle."[104] Specifically, they gave them the imaginative means to not exist as a people dispossessed of their own ideas. In this context, African-ness became emblematic of "the freedom to imagine what you wish" for existence.[105] I therefore argue that African-ness is not adherence to the customs of one's Congo or Arada ancestors, though as a Haitian these customs might be passed down to you; nor is African-ness about genetics or physiognomy. African-ness, here, means adherence to a way of thinking and being that radicalizes one against the colonial project, which makes Africa less a continental home because of ancestry, and more of an imaginary for radical decolonial action and thought. Modern Haitians like Jacques Junior Baril, Haiti's 2016 high commissioner to South Africa, implicitly understand Africa thusly. They can reason Haiti's inclusion in the African Union as given because the Africa that Haitians received from their captive ancestors provided them with the conceptual ground to envision and realize *Ayiti Ginen*: this imagined Africa, quite literally, mapped the path beyond French colonial rule.[106]

A New World

This path was forged by *bossales* whose cartographic genius made *Ginens*, past and present, Africans by design. Their prowess as thinkers, liberators, and builders of worlds is featured here to underscore the planetary shift in thought and being that occurred in Saint Domingue before, during, and after the Revolution among *Ginen* peoples. This shift parallels the alteration in Western European thought and conduct that occurred after Columbus's 1492 voyage, which changed how Western Europeans conceived of their world and the world at large.[107] Columbus's voyage also inaugurated Western Europe's birth as the West, which is not a "place," to borrow from Glissant, but a "project."[108] It exists as a civilizational projection of Western European colonial aspirations made real through extractive warmongering. I write Haiti as a counter abolitionist project. It exists as a civilizational projection of the decolonial aspirations of captive peoples made real through their speculative genius and epistemological refusal of the West as the locus of knowledge and the human's true form of being. "Haiti," as Chelsea Stieber writes, exists as "a critique, its very existence [is] a reminder of the limits and possibilities" of the Enlightenment, "of the meaning of liberty, civilization, and the West."[109] I extend Stieber's reading and invite readers to see Haiti's existence as a critique and a refusal. A Haiti understood as a critique and a refusal makes plain the revolutionary conduct of the African and Africanized rebels of Saint Domingue. These persons not only changed their world, but they also changed how captive peoples and the racially minoritized of the globe conceived of their worlds and the earth at large. They made real the actuality that other spatial territories are discoverable and readily within reach.

Ginens successfully expanded their planetary orbit. In having done so, they illustrate how "freedom relies on human imagination and the ability to put it into practice" as Armando García argues.[110] Their remapping of their world is a testament to their practical application of their decolonial imagination. I define a decolonial imagination as a disobedient and curious skepticism that thinks outside of and opposed to colonial knowledge systems; and I treat the Revolution as a "struggle not just against, but also more importantly *for*—for the possibility of an otherwise"—to showcase how this imagination materialized in Saint Domingue and Haiti.[111] Walsh writes that "uprisings, rebellions, and movements [are] not just political. They [are] also conceptual, epistemic, and existence based. They introduce the possibilities of an 'otherwise' into the social conscience of at least some sectors of society.... This 'Otherwise' is of perspectives and frameworks not based in market capitalism, consumerism, western rationality, or the exploitation of nature, but rather in relationality, in a living 'with.'"[112] I conceive of the Revolution as a cerebral happening to capture how *bossale* and creole captives chose to forge a life on their terms by "living 'with'" each other. I follow Walsh and decolonial feminist María Lugones and engage resistance as a collectivist "response" versus reaction. This means that I foreground the "thoughtful, often complex, devious, insightful response to the ... intricacies of" colonial power put forth by captives when discussing *Ginen* knowledge practices.[113]

These practices promoted solidarity, and they not only introduced an otherwise—"perspectives and frameworks not based in ... western rationality"—but they also invited persons to "imagine otherwise."

Avery Gordon, following Patricia J. Williams, writes that the assertion "imagine otherwise" "is a folk theoretical statement." [114] This "statement" permits dissident speculation, the kind that says, "we need to know where we live in order to imagine living elsewhere. We need to imagine living elsewhere before we can live there."[115] *Ginens* knew Saint Domingue. They deployed Africa as an imaginary to conceive it differently and they used this conception to seize and re-map the colony as *Ayiti Ginen*. I use the term "otherwise" to denote the act of introducing a possibility, what Tiffany Lethabo King, Jenell Navarro, and Andrea Smith denote as "something or anything else; something to the contrary."[116] I also use the term to denote the imaginative license needed to pursue this possibility, as both iterations of "otherwise" were key to *Ginens'* propagative refusal.

Refusal is understood here as propagative to capture *Ginens'* expansive sense of the possible. My engagement with *Ginens'* vast sense of what is feasible builds on the critical thought of Black studies scholar Keguro Macharia, who, in thinking with Mariame Kaba, Elizabeth Povinelli, Audre Lorde, Samuel Delaney, and Ruth Wilson Gilmore, understands refusal as a "proliferation and intensification."[117] Refusal, for Macharia, entails not only saying "not this" to the "harmful and unhumaning practices and institutions" of oppressive power, but he argues it involves saying "more that"—more to the fugitive futures that exist furtively within the white colonial order.[118] I show how *bossales* and their allies refused to accept the cultural supremacy of the French and chose instead to say "more that" to themselves. They put themselves first and said "yes" to the limitless possibilities of what life can be; "yes" to being unprepared, unschooled, and hapless on the journey to uncharted life paths; and "yes" to their capacity to be inventors of thought and forgers of new worlds. This "yes" fueled their knowledge practices with genius and originality, the kind that could *and did* render colonial knowledge nonsensical. The popular Haitian idiom *tout moun se moun men tout moun pas menm* (all people are people, but all people are not the same) demonstrates this as it shows thinking that refuses the colonial difference and its logic of racialization. The *tout moun se moun* idiom was authored in the colonial past as a reparative communal accord, but today it is most often voiced in interpersonal conflict. Imagine that a friend shares that they were devastated by a callous remark received from an intimate, a person who knows the malicious nature of their words because of their knowledge of the other's life. To ease their pain and embolden their diminished sense of self, they are told, *tout moun se moun men tout moun pas menm*. This dictum acknowledges their hurt and the needlessness of the disrespect experienced while prompting them to recognize that humans are not a monolith. The respect given to others, the care expected from others, will not always be reciprocated; and because humans are diverse and nuanced all that can be done when navigating a life predicated on relations with others is to maintain a firm sense of self, which is to say: know yourself for yourself and the malevolent speech and action of others cannot determine who you are in the present and future. What is to be made of the defiant affirmation of self evident in this saying, but that the people who conceived it were creative and confident in their difference? These are persons you want on your side in conflict, the kind whose genius nourished the mental fortitude needed to live with *and* resist inexplicable violence, whose *genius made life bearable*.

Casimir imparts that *bossales* conceived this maxim; and from its contemporary meanings it is clear that they invented *tout moun se moun men tout moun pas menm* to make sense of the gratuitous emotional and bodily harm they experienced at the hands of their enslavers.[119] French colonists denied them and their descendants the dignity of unsullied human relations, a life where a birth can just be a birth and not a means for the colony's continuation. Captives had to create thought that could help them live a corrupted life without becoming corrupted themselves. They had to pursue knowledge practices that allowed them to remain Africans as opposed to slaves. Madiou asks, "Though the African was enslaved, did he ever stop being free," when writing of Saint Domingue on the eve of the Revolution. This query gets to my point as it acknowledges *bossales*'s creative capacity to remain who they are notwithstanding their enslavement.[120]

When removed from the intricacies of interpersonal discord and rooted in its place of origin among the *bossales* of Saint Domingue, the *tout moun se moun* adage affirms the importance of existing outside of the colonizer's dictates. It promotes the practical necessity of remaining unbothered by the opinions of others notwithstanding their power to harm, while deepening self-awareness and self-love. Casimir writes that the "corollary of [the *tout moun se moun* saying] is ... sovereignty—namely that a sovereign people is one that is responsible only to itself."[121] He perceives a legislative accord when assessing the saying, and he is thinking with decolonial thought against colonial legalisms. I think with the scholarship of feminists of color like bell hooks, Cherríe Moraga, Chela Sandoval, and María Lugones, and perceive a maxim that could also serve as a reparative communal accord; their writings on love and affective political action references the repair to self and others that is needed to see, and thereafter declare oneself, "a sovereign people." Each discusses the political necessity of instrumentalizing self-reflection and love of self in a colonial context where love of sameness (i.e., whiteness, white maleness, and Western-ness) produces totalizing harm to the colonized and/or racially marginalized.[122] The *tout moun se moun* maxim shows *Ginen* recognition of the political necessity of self-love and criticality; for if "Africans [managed to always remain] free," as Madiou notes, it is because they had to create critical thought that could elicit *and* sustain love for themselves as they were, enchained and proudly African.[123] They had to create thought that refused the colonial difference and, in refusing this difference, could reimagine the terms of human belonging outside of colonial power.

Decolonial theorist Walter Mignolo writes that "the colonial difference operates by converting differences into values and establishing a hierarchy of human beings ontologically and epistemically. Ontologically, it is assumed that there are inferior human beings. Epistemically, it is assumed that inferior human beings are irrational and aesthetically deficient."[124] Rather than diminish their reclamation of self as persons who are not slaves with opposition, via an us-versus-them framework that allows "the colonial difference" to maintain its epistemological bearings, captives refused it altogether. They chose instead to create a new epistemological standard for their existence. This standard not only invalidated the very idea of "inferior beings," but it debunked a value-laden articulation of differences, which is evident in the *tout moun se moun* maxim. The saying articulates the human as genre (we are persons, yes; but we can express our personhood in many ways) and exemplifies how captives reasoned beyond the West. They thought the colonial impossible (humanity as more than white and Western) into the decolonial possible (humanity as African and as Black). I read the Haitian Revolution as the decolonial possible and argue that the Revolution was always intrinsically achievable and thus spectrally present in Saint Domingue because captives refused the idea that knowledge has but one cultural source (Western Europe) and chose, as a result of this refusal, to think outside of a culture that could hold such a conviction. They "'travel[ed]' . . . against the grain" of power, to borrow from Lugones, forging collective thought and behaviors that were not only resistant but richly speculative since both harnessed the power to imagine and thereafter seize a world of their own making.[125]

A New World Unseen

The critical intervention this book makes in literary studies of the Revolution is to foreground the new world that is Haiti and its impact on art and criticism about the Revolution. I underscore the distinct novelty of Haiti and its peoples' planetary existence and argue that it is because of the obscured yet still present manifestation of *Ginen* thought and action in the foundational works studied here that they continue to expand the decolonial horizons of scholars and artists of the Revolution. In this regard, understanding how the Revolution occurred and how *Ayiti Ginen* came to be discloses how texts that maintain a colonial understanding of Haiti and Haitians manage to still offer valuable articulations of decolonial thought and action. I argue that the enduring value of the classic works studied here lies with their use of Haiti to resist US imperialism and think beyond a world defined by the colonial project.

I recognize that the menacing nature of US imperialism in the Caribbean of the nineteenth century onward occasioned a discovery of Haiti's revolutionary past for Caribbean artists and thinkers writing in the twentieth century that has positively shaped Caribbean cultural thought. I treat two temporal periods I term revolutionary Haiti and post-revolutionary Haiti to index the importance of US imperialism to Caribbean classics of the Revolution. The Revolution's duration and the collective sovereignties of a succession of Haitian revolutionary generals turned political leaders of early Haiti are treated here as revolutionary Haiti (1791–1825).¹²⁶ I restrict the period termed revolutionary Haiti to Boyer's signing of the 1825 indemnity to France, since the economic decline and political instability it occasioned directly accounts for the predatory intrusion of the United States in Haiti in the early twentieth century.¹²⁷ I consign post-revolutionary Haiti to the time of and after the first US occupation of Haiti (1915–1934).

Prior to this occupation, the United States established its fictitious right to intervene in Caribbean and Latin American affairs in the nineteenth century via the Monroe Doctrine (1823) and then the Roosevelt Corollary (1904). It would appropriate Puerto Rico (1898) and then occupy Cuba (1906–1909), Haiti, and the Dominican Republic (1916–1924) at the start of the twentieth century. Caribbean writers positioned outside of Haiti were particularly drawn to Haiti at this time because its past revolutionary glory materialized again via its Cacos Resistance (1915–1917) to the first US occupation. The actions of the Cacos, and the discovery of Haiti's Africanist folk culture by Caribbean and US artists and intellectuals in the same moment, placed the nation at the forefront of Caribbean cultural thought.¹²⁸ Haiti would remain at the fore of the Caribbean cultural imaginary because of James's *The Black Jacobins*.

James composed his 1938 history as Cuba, Haiti, and the Dominican Republic were first occupied by the United States. His book would be republished twenty-five years later in 1963. In this moment, Caribbean writers from all linguistic regions were encouraged to see themselves as "Jacobs" for having a history of resistance: in other words, they were encouraged to see their Caribbean-ness through the lens of Haitian Revolutionary action, which made Haiti key to how many writers of Caribbean origin positively made sense of their history, their present, and their future.¹²⁹ Haiti became an ideation as much as a place for Caribbean writers, which accounts for why most of the classic Caribbean authors studied here minimize and look past Haitian history in the period of 1825 to 1915. They choose instead to make sense of Haiti and the Revolution from the historical particularities of the twentieth century, since they are not interested in Haiti directly, not its people and history. What interests them is the Haitian experience of resisting and persisting through colonialism and imperialism on Haitian terms, as that experience can teach them about their own potential to similarly resist and persist on terms they define for themselves.

The Guadeloupean writer Maryse Condé captures this interest and its entanglement with US imperialism best when stating, "The major writers of the French Antilles . . . were to appropriate [Haitian revolutionary] heroes into their theater and [were] to enrich their writings with ideas from Haitian intellectuals. . . . Suddenly, with the end of the Duvalier years, . . . the stuff of myths crumbles. . . . The tragedy of the boat people replaces the tragedy of King Christophe, and the distress of today's Haiti thrusts itself on our imagination."[130] As some twentieth-century literatures of Haiti were authored to affirm the Caribbean's sense of itself, indeed, as some drew from Haitian criticism, others in the French (and outside of the French-speaking) Caribbean became overwhelmingly desolate, catastrophic, and piteous in substance. This changed occurred because of writers' attention to the destructive effects of US imperialism in Haiti. This new focus explains Condé's references to the US-backed dictator, François Duvalier (1957–1971) and to the crisis of "boat people," a happening sparked and sustained by US imperial policies in the nation.[131] Caribbean literature about Haiti began to focus on the damning effects of US imperialism in Haiti because the writers of these works recognized that their own homelands were not immune to the destruction Haiti faced (and continues to face). The change in focus from "the tragedy of King Christophe" to the "tragedy of the boat people" attests to their own concerns about US imperialism and their fears as well as doubts about overcoming it. For if Haiti, the place where "negritude rose for the first time and stated that it believed in its humanity," could become trapped in the crosshairs of US imperial violence after defeating a colonial power, then so can they who have not bested such a foe.[132]

The fear of US imperialism produces writing about Haiti wrought with projections that show how the very act of writing about Haiti and its Revolution, in particular, produces fiction—whether the writer sets out to write fiction or not. The works produced are literary in nature, in large part, because "the subject of the dream is the dreamer," to borrow from Toni Morrison.[133] Caribbean classics of the Revolution are the product of the author's dreams and fears of freedom and are therefore imbued with the real emotions of political angst and contestation, which makes them grounded in real-life events and in the writer's imagining of these events. I therefore make no distinction between the historical study that is *The Black Jacobins* and the drama that is *Monsieur Toussaint,* because both are a product of these writers' decolonial imagination; and as such, they are key iterations of the Caribbean writer's use of Haiti as a means to search for and declare an investment in "an otherwise," in "perspectives and frameworks not based in ... western rationality ... but rather in [a] relationality," that can envision and realize Caribbean liberation.[134]

UNSEEN

Lest the reader take critique for misapprehension, this book celebrates and knows that James's commitment to an otherwise future for the Caribbean not only inaugurated a Caribbean tradition of imagining liberation through Haiti, but it galvanized African and Caribbean peoples fighting for decolonization. *Chapô ba James, you moved readers closer to envisioning an otherwise.*[135] It equally celebrates and knows that Carpentier's theory of the marvelous and his novella *The Kingdom of This World* are firmly of the Caribbean tradition James began, since it inculcated in Caribbean and Latin American peoples a sense of their own cultural significance and potentialities beyond the West. *Chapô ba Carpentier, you moved readers closer to envisioning an otherwise.* It celebrates and knows also that Césaire and Glissant also write from this tradition: the former added to his already extensive anticolonial oeuvre with *The Tragedy of King Christophe* and did so to help colonized peoples make sense of the process of decolonization; and the latter wrote *Monsieur Toussaint* to deconstruct the material absence of liberation in the Caribbean so as to outfit anticolonial dissidents with the tools to demand more and to see the sociopolitical problems that exist in the colonized Caribbean. *Chapô ba Césaire and Glissant, you moved readers closer to envisioning an otherwise.* Each wrote literatures of the Revolution that strove to politicize or radicalize their readers; and they did so by using the Revolution as a medium for developing decolonial thought. This thought could celebrate and speak to the lived experiences of colonial subordination while endeavoring to imagine existence beyond colonial power. Their texts are classics rightfully and are widely studied in Caribbean studies, Black studies, postcolonial studies, and Haitian studies because they created anticolonial work that took their positionality as the colonized as a point of enunciation, by which to speak and think alongside the revolutionary actions of peoples who were more besieged by colonial power than they were (being captives), but succeeded in their fight against it. I admire their efforts and extend a critique of their works because I recognize how they are partisans in the task of making the world anew through thought and art that is resistant and relational like *Ginen* revolutionists. I do not obfuscate or discredit the monumental work each has done in this capacity. I sit with these thinkers and demand more of them, as they demanded more of their audiences; and I do so for their future readers so that they continue to try, as each did, to think beyond the world as colony, as the West.

The world had to be more than the West for James, Carpentier, Césaire, and Glissant, because the political urgencies of their moments asked them to resist US imperial actions in the Caribbean *and* the paradigmatic actions of Western European colonial powers. The latter's ongoing importance to the former is why this book reads influential literatures of the Revolution within the genealogical framework of decolonial thought, which locates the origins of the colonial project at the onset of the late Middle Ages. Like Yomaira C. Figueroa-Vásquez in *Decolonizing Diasporas: Radical Mappings of Afro-Atlantic Literature*, I "tak[e] the fifteenth century's imperial/colonial project into account as a foundational violence" to not only "make the ideological and structural reach of colonialism and coloniality visible," but to illuminate Haiti's powerful disruption of this project's racially violent temporality for being.[136] James, Carpentier, Césaire, and Glissant wrote with cognizance of this disruption and with earnest hope for a second Haitian Revolution for the colonized worldwide. The pressing issue this book has with their works is that each produced literature of the Revolution that sides with *les damnés de la terre* and yet forgets them because of the Eurocentric frameworks they use to make sense of the Revolution. James chose the Enlightenment and the French Revolution; Carpentier, Columbus and the marvelous; Césaire and Glissant (by proxy), French revolutionary republicanism, to orient their Haitian Revolutionist texts. Their distinct colonial referents animate their revolutionary fictions and histories' imaginative pursuit of a decolonial future, a terrain unknown. The importance of these referents to their narration of the Revolution ultimately positioned their pursuit of a decolonial future toward the West, a terrain known, as the latter offers an intellectual cartography of thought that solely maps the colony and the road to nowhere for anticolonial writers and thinkers. They pursued this dead end even as they authored their Haitian Revolutionist texts because they know that "the maps of spring always have to be redrawn again, in undared forms."[137] Put otherwise, in colonial modernity, *Ginen* revolutionists are knowable only as the vanquished and thus the damned to be forgotten. In the achievable decolonial future that these writers know is within grasp, these revolutionaries and their descendants are not damned; but what they are escapes these thinkers because they want to know Haitians through the knowable, that is, through ideations derived from colonial power that cannot grasp Haitians as *Ginens* and thus as inventors of thought and originators of worlds.

Víctor Figueroa's decolonial reading of Caribbean classics in *Prophetic Visions of the Past: Pan-Caribbean Representations of the Haitian Revolution* underscores the originality of Haitian Revolutionary action. Where Figueroa's reading argues that a pan-Caribbean telling of the Revolution attests to its importance to the growth and critical interrogation of the modern/colonial world system, I stress the novelty of *Ginen* thought and action to critique how Caribbean writers reproduce colonial ways of knowing Haiti and Haitians that leave Haiti unseen as *Ayiti Ginen* and Haitians as *Ginens*. "Unseen" is used in this book to index how each of the influential authors studied here writes around and without *Ginen* Haitians; and as such, each minimizes or altogether excises the enormity of their political power from the story of the Revolution and independent Haiti thereafter. Where James writes as if Toussaint Louverture's *Ginen* cultural context could not possibly have inspired his radicalization, Césaire and Carpentier write as if the Revolution must be reimagined without Haiti's first revolutionist-statesmen, a position predicated on the absolutism of their imagined power. This position casually invents constituents who are conceived as casualties of power alone; and Glissant is so concerned with engaging other Caribbean writings of the Revolution that Haiti and Haitians are materially there but immaterial to his project. These authorial choices evidence a problem of thought rather than politics and disclose a colonial inheritance predicated on a "forgetfulness of the damned."[138] Maldonado-Torres writes that this "forgetfulness . . . is part of the veritable sickness of the West, a sickness that could be likened to a state of amnesia that leads to murder, destruction, and epistemic will to power—with good conscience. The opposition to modernity/racism has to address this amnesia and the invisibility of the damned."[139] I understand that the call to write the Revolution is an act of "opposition to modernity/racism."[140] I also understand that writing the Revolution without knowing Haiti or Haitians within the cultural framework of the majority preserves the epistemic racism of colonial knowledge practices. This racism of thought renders invisible and/or trivializes the non-Euro-centered; and, in the context of this book, I argue this results in a discursive blindness to *Ginens* and *Ayiti Ginen* in Caribbean classics of the Haitian Revolution.

"Unseen" illuminates then how writers of canonical Haitian Revolutionary literatures write *Ginen* revolutionists' radical seizure of self-autonomy in sameness, as though Western ideas and Western figures of resistance can be simply mapped on to Haitian ideas and Haitian agents of resistance. A query worth asking is: why is the subjected, ever-laboring peasant a constant presence in Caribbean writing of the Revolution that chronicles post-independence Haiti? Why is the creole revolutionist at the helm of the Revolution when this figure constantly aspires to the West? What kind of break with the past could this colonial mimic truly offer his people when he can only be imagined as a Hamlet or a Black Spartacus, persons who are cultural distillations of the Western Europeans enslaving his people?[141] "Unseen" points readers to how coloniality frustrates earnest efforts to think beyond the colony. Coloniality, which references the "long-standing patterns of power that emerged as a result of colonialism [and that continue to] define culture, labor, intersubjective relations, and knowledge well beyond the strict limits of colonial administrations," explains the colonial knowledge practices that account for the persistent need to reduce Haiti and Haitians to the asymmetry of the powerful and powerless present in classic Caribbean writing of the Revolution.[142] This tendency takes the social categories of conquest, or what Lisa Lowe terms the "colonial divisions of humanity" (manifest here as the divide between conquerors and the vanquished), as absolute; and it takes the condition of subjection as the essence of Haitian being versus recognizing it as an imposition of colonial power.[143] Post-independence Haiti is thus oligarchic alone (determined by political elites, persons imagined as being just like colonizers who conquer), and Haitians (the majority in particular) are vanquished colonial subjects, mere "bodies . . . to which [things] happen."[144] "Unseen" ultimately serves as a way to denote an unwillingness to want to know Haiti and Haitians on the majority's terms and it illuminates the Caribbean writer's desire to preserve an idea of the Revolution that accords with the Western world *as it is* and not within the planetary sphere of *Ginens*, for whom the world was made new and continues to be remake-able as new.

READING FOR THE UNSEEN

This book insists that writers of the Revolution and the scholars who study their works should want to know Haiti as *Ayiti Ginen* and Haitians as *Ginens*, since not doing so is destructive to Caribbean efforts to think liberation into being. I make this argument because of the immense space Haiti holds in Caribbean imaginings of freedom and revolution. To make sense of Haiti, the Revolution, and Haitians through reasoning that maps the colony as it denounces colonialism's continuation in the Caribbean is hugely problematic because reasoning of this kind will only bear a denigrated Haiti and victimized Haitians. Both a demeaned Haiti and debased Haitians will, in turn, yield stunted visions of the Caribbean's futures. Simply put, both yield a resigned Caribbean, one imagined as forever fixed in the mire of imperial or colonial rule because how Haiti and Haitians are pictured in Caribbean writing of the Revolution is directly tied to how (or if at all) decolonial futures are presented as possible for the Caribbean. The existence of *Ayiti Ginen* and of art and criticism inspired by *Ginen* revolutionary action help to galvanize conviction in the possibilities of these futures; and because of this, reading for *Ginens* in foundational Caribbean literature of the Revolution is a way to work around the writer's own misdirection toward these futures.

The reading practice I use to reveal the obscured yet still vibrant presence of *Ginens* in the literatures studied engages Caribbean classics from the position of disobedience that inspired the writer's turn to the Revolution in the first place. Disobedience here references the writer's commitment to "undoing" the colonial project with their Haitian Revolutionist literatures. It is an idea borrowed from McKittrick's work on the methods and methodologies of Black study, where she thinks alongside Wynter to critique how "discipline" is a function of "empire" in the academy.[145] McKittrick's scholarship furnishes much of the language for how I read for *Ginens* because it captures a key aspect of *Ginen* cultural praxis that I privilege: Black existence as a critical resistance, one that involves, as McKittrick writes, a "kind of analytical maneuvering ... that dwells on and thinks about the questioning and overturning of normative systems of knowledge."[146] Reading for the anticolonial disobedience that drew writers of Caribbean classics to the Revolution requires recognizing, firstly, that "the history of blackness provides the conditions to learn and live and love our world differently."[147] Secondly, it requires recognizing that writers of influential Haitian Revolutionist literatures themselves know this about "the history of blackness." They write the Revolution because they know that Black people "know."[148] To quote McKittrick, "we know more than the abjectness that is projected upon us.... We know. We know ourselves."[149] This recognition of knowing is a radical starting point that fixes their texts, however confused they can be, in a *Ginen* matrix for being. Indeed, the absence of this knowing in texts about the Revolution, or that draw on its signification, reproduces colonial notions of Black existence as the inability to know. This is evident in works like the film *Black Panther: Wakanda Forever*, which uses Haiti and its Revolution to signal radical Blackness but articulates this radicalness from a position of Black knowing that must be hidden (in Wakanda) and thus segregated from a wider world in which the idea of Black people as persons who know is not available. This is a bad faith articulation of Black knowing since it leaves unchallenged how colonial knowledge produces and sustains the idea that Black people cannot know—that is, they do not have ways of knowing, or the ability to know outside of "the abjectness that is projected onto [them]."[150]

How do the writers studied show their knowledge of Black knowing? The readings offered are animated by this question and implicitly or explicitly stress learning (James/Glissant), criticality (Carpentier), and refusal (Césaire/Pontecorvo) for the more acclaimed texts and a dogged pursuit of an otherwise existence (Danticat) in less studied Caribbean literatures of the Revolution. The presence of these specific modes of expressing that Black people know shows the way each writer mirrors, in their narrative's execution, the cultural practice of *Ginens*. Recall that this praxis includes reflection, refusal, and forging ahead and is, at heart, a critical thinking against oppressive power. In practice, the signs of the writers' expression of their knowledge that Black people know themselves and have ways of knowing the world outside of colonial modernity places *Ginens* in the realm of the unthought within Caribbean classics: they are the sense that makes a narrative presentation of liberation comprehensible.

In the opening chapter on James and Glissant, the presence of *Ginens* manifests in James's fixation with documenting Louverture's literacy. James knows that Black people survive and resist the "assigned places" they have been given in the West by searching for and acquiring knowledge; he simply gets lost when he attributes this pursuit of knowledge to Louverture alone.[151] *Ginens* are present in James's intention to showcase Black knowing and foreground the captive masses' contribution to their liberation through their knowing. They are the unthought he thinks with and past to write his imagining of Haitian Revolutionary history. Likewise, for Glissant, who submits Louverture to misreadings by his revolutionary peers, they are the unthought that reside in what is missed and lost in conveyance. They are the integral part thought past by creole revolutionists and the writers who write about these revolutionists alone when depicting the Revolution. Carpentier, too, knows that Black people know, and as discussed in Chapter 2, he opens his narrative of the Revolution meticulously detailing a captive in thought. *Ginens* are obviously present here but they are also present in his theory of Caribbean and Latin American exception, the marvelous real, where they are less visible to scholars and readers of Carpentier. They are the verb through which Carpentier theorizes the marvelous, the presence that is thought by Carpentier but unthought by his readers. Césaire refuses the world as the West and his insistence that the world ought to be more exposes the *Ginen* process of resistant inquiry that lies at the heart of his work discussed in Chapter 3. Reading for *Ginens* ultimately requires a reading practice that is knowledge oriented and thus equipped with the tools to make the reader curious about how stories of the Revolution are told. It requires a practice that encourages the reader to feel the need to discover whether these stories of Haitian resistance know that Black people know.

With and Against the Canon

The choice to closely read the Caribbean classics studied here reflects how their anticolonial politics are the result of their awareness of Black knowing; and it reflects their status as foundational in Caribbean studies, Black studies, postcolonial studies, and Haitian studies. Of interest then is interrogating why these literatures of the Revolution occupy the immense space they do and what that has meant for each field's understanding of Haiti, Haitians, and the story of the Revolution. Equally important is Haitian studies' use of each field's distinct approach in its engagement with Haiti/Haitians. Both the Revolution and Haiti serve "as a symbolic place of encounter" in Caribbean studies, offering the conceptual ground to confront "contemporary problems" of race, gender, and imperialism (among others) in the Caribbean.[152] In this context, Haiti functions as "mirror, warning, and inspiration."[153] In Black studies, both signify the vibrant presence of the Black Radical Tradition, a politics of liberation political scientist Cedric Robinson defines as an ever-evolving "collective consciousness informed by the historical struggles for liberation and motivated by the shared sense of obligation to preserve the collective being."[154] This political commitment has made the Revolution and Haiti key to the field's efforts to reimagine the human outside of whiteness and counter racial capitalism through abolitionism, Pan-Africanism, and the celebration of self-affirming African cultural retentions.[155] Postcolonial studies, as literary critic Doris L. Garraway notes, has largely absented the Revolution and Haiti from its intellectual concerns.[156] An exception to this elision is Srinivas Aravamudan's book

Tropicopolitans: Colonialism and Agency, 1688–1804, and Philip Kaisary's book *The Haitian Revolution in the Literary Imagination*. The Anglophone bias of the field occasioned Francophone postcolonial studies, a specialization that examines and critiques the knowledges the Revolution and Haiti are thought to produce. This field also resists how both the Revolution and Haiti can exist in Caribbean studies and Black studies as free-floating signifiers of thought.[157]

Notwithstanding the different approaches to the Revolution and Haiti, Caribbean studies, Black studies, and postcolonial studies have produced book-length treatments of twentieth-century Haitian Revolutionist art by Caribbean authors writing outside of Haiti that privilege the work of James, Carpentier, Césaire, and Glissant, especially. What comes to mind is Kaisary's aforementioned *The Haitian Revolution in the Literary Imagination* (2014, postcolonial studies), Figueroa's *Prophetic Visions of the Past* (2015, Caribbean studies), and Jeremy Matthew Glick's *The Black Radical Tragic: Performance, Aesthetics, and the Unfinished Haitian Revolution* (2016, Black studies).[158] These monographs show that the study of influential Caribbean literatures of the Revolution is often limited to the meanings derived from the works themselves. The radical or conservative aesthetics the Revolution elicits is a point of interest (Kaisary); how Haiti functions as a conceptual hub for thinking Pan-Caribbean unity and decolonial politics is another (Figueroa); and last, the laboratory of political thinking, Black theatrical productions enacted by thinking with the Revolution is also a key concern (Glick). The question unasked in these literatures and rarely asked in their respective fields is: Why these writers and their texts of the Revolution? I address this untreated why and foreground the canonical status of James, Carpentier, Césaire, and Glissant to show how their institutionalized acclaim obscures the way their Haitian Revolutionist writings unwittingly uphold the white colonial order at the expense of Haitians and Haiti. In their conceptions, both signify the vanquished or, more generously, the vanquished miming the colonizer (with respect to the creole revolutionist turned political leader), and each remains as conceived by the slavery apologists and enslavers of the West, who have never had anything kind to say about Haiti and Haitians since their advent. I show, however, how the African and Africanized Haitian revolutionists and Haiti *itself* invalidates the very knowledge system that bore this conception of Haitians/Haiti and other colonized peoples and lands as vanquished.

I build on Kaisary, Figueroa, and Glick's studies of the Revolution and add that scholarship about the Revolution must become critical of which artists and thinkers are most often called to shape academic understanding of the monumental events of 1791. The aim here is not to cast out these recognized thinkers as antiquated and irredeemably prejudiced; but the intervention put forth is to showcase that when scholars do the work of scholarship, they do not need to throw their interlocutors away if the writers studied fail to meet their ethical standards. They need, however, to understand why these writers are here. In this sense, this book is an urgent contribution to the growing field of Haitian studies. It invites scholars of the field to consider what Haitian studies would and could be if voices external to Haiti were not central to how the field engages the Revolution, Haiti, and Haitians. The question asked of Haitian studies is, What if scholars of the field led with Haitian thought as it engaged the plethora of work that exists about Haiti? Relatedly, what if the culture and its ideas of being were integral to the study of the nation and its peoples? This book seeks to move Haitian studies beyond writing about Haiti to sitting with Haiti, and poses that consideration of the why—why particular writers are here, at the forefront of how scholars think about the Revolution and Caribbean liberation—is key to new advances in the study of Haiti, the Haitian Revolution, and Caribbean anticolonial thought.

REPUBLICANISM AND THE CANON

Advancing the study of Haiti, the Haitian Revolution, and Caribbean anticolonial thought (produced in relation to the former two, Haiti and the Revolution) demands reassessing the general understanding of the Revolution as a triumphant narrative of overcoming; or as a cautionary tale of anticolonial failure, as these readings hinge on a simplistic assessment of the Revolution as *only* a fight against the French. Rather than these interpretations, I encourage readers to avail themselves to the discords, competing ideologies, and clashing philosophies of being that made the Revolution a fight against *an idea of existence* that says the world can only be like the French or something French adjacent (Western). This conception of the Revolution makes the new world building initiative of *Ginens* discernible. It also helps readers to see that how they know the Revolution, and how James, Carpentier, Césaire, and Glissant know the Revolution, as well as the scholars who study their works, has been shaped by the political commitment of some Haitians "to cast the nation within the dominant norms of civilization and humanism."[159] And it also has been shaped by the political commitment of "foreign powers" to demean and marginalize a *Ginen* refusal of the world as the West.[160] The latter is detailed in Daut's and A. James Arnold's respective scholarship on the sensationalist depiction of violence in art and criticism of the Revolution composed with attention to eighteenth-century race science (Daut) and nineteenth-century Romanticism (Arnold).[161] The political intrigues that emerged in Haiti immediately after the Revolution account for the former. A central position held in this book is that knowledge of the Revolution must be tied to Haitian thought of the Revolution; and, in this sense, critical and artistic work of the Revolution must not only use Haitian sources, as so many of the writers studied here do, but they must also avail themselves of the cultural knowledge and the cultural ways of seeing and being that shape how these particular sources came to be. This involves being cognizant of what could be said and thus authored in a particular moment and what could not be. In other words, it requires attention to the "silences" (Trouillot), "disavowals" (Sibylle Fischer), and "racial tropics" (Daut), mediating how the Revolution was imagined and authored not only outside of Haiti but in Haiti as well.[162]

Attention to the Revolution's authoring in early Haiti, in particular, requires consideration of Haitian republicanism and this politics's anti-Dessalinean ethos, which I read as an anti-*Ginen* compulsion. Newly independent Haiti was guided by *Ginen* thought at its onset through Dessalines, who assumed power as the new polity's Governor General following the formal declaration of Haitian independence in 1804. Dessalines would name himself emperor in 1805 and issue a new constitution meant to unify a divided populace. In this constitution, he equalizes all Haitians by naming them as Black and attempts with this naming to secure the populace's tenuous relations through the *Ginen* imperative that *"tout moun se moun,* every person is a person."[163] This proved to be difficult. *Affranchis'* class history of freedom acquired by blood or service had inculcated a Eurocentrism that set many at odds with the self-liberated, whose history of freedom seized without permission and Africanist culture radicalized them against the colonial project and its Eurocentrism. *Affranchis* with republican politics, in particular, like the future president of the South, Pétion, and his presidential successor Boyer, were not only in conflict with the self-liberated but they were also in disagreement with fellow generals in the Revolution—specifically, those who did not share their republican politics like Dessalines.[164] Republican antagonisms with the self-liberated and the generals closest to them occasioned Leslie Manigat's assertion that the majority of *affranchi* were not "partisans of the creation of a black nation-state," as persons who saw themselves as French and who tried to act the part of a French republican.[165] A significant number of French-identified *affranchi* left Haiti soon after independence, but some remained and maintained their republican politics while assuming important positions in Haiti's first political elite.[166] This furthered the discord at the heart of the new nation because these *affranchi* became Haitian reluctantly. France rejected them, writes Casimir and Mary Claypool; they did not reject France.[167] Despite France's rejection, the republican contingent who would guide Haiti with Dessalines and his supporters—the same contingent who would orchestrate Dessalines's assassination in the name of republicanism on October 17, 1806, and who, after the civil war period ended that followed his murder (1807–1820), would go on to govern a united Haiti—still conceived of the Haitian Revolution as an extension of the French Revolution.[168]

Republican understanding of the Revolution as akin to the French Revolution did not dissipate their staunch opposition to slavery or white supremacy; nor did it prevent them from becoming proudly Haitian and defenders of Haiti in time but it did make them poor stewards of the Haiti that stood before them at the nation's onset—African and staunchly anti-Western.[169] The *Ginen* Haiti republicans were to lead was not within the universality of the Enlightenment that they held dear; and its people were not who Western theorists of political liberalism conceived of when formulating rights discourse, being the property of those with rights. The republicans prized rights discourse and had not thought that through, nor could they have because of their cultural identification with the West, which was, for them, the epitome of civilization.[170] Dessalines, who was notoriously weary of "the temptations of civilization, which for him meant a new, more subtle servitude," did think through the limits of republicanism.[171] He sought to lead *Ayiti Ginen*, which is why Grégory Pierrot rightly regards his political philosophy as an "attempt at lighting a beacon beyond the confines of white Western thought."[172] I add that he and his supporters in the elite did this to strive for "the possibility of an otherwise" existence alongside *Ginens*.[173] In that vein, Dessalines and his allies not only "challenged the putative universalism of the Enlightenment," but they also felt that "humanity was guaranteed through [a collective's] own act of self-liberation."[174] This entailed "wresting [liberation] from those who purported to grant it by defining it through their own words, acts and terms," which is a distinctly *Ginen* idea.[175]

The hatred Dessalines's anticolonial governance prompted from his republican peers is understood here as not simply a hatred of Dessalines and the tyranny he supposedly represented—as was the charge levied against him by republicans for his stance against rights discourse. Rather, it was a hatred of governing Haiti *en Ginen*—beyond and outside the West.[176] This hatred of Haiti as *Ginen* results in *Ginens* themselves emerging as the unthought (or better yet, the refused to be thought) in this moment of Haitian Revolutionary history. Where they were the unprocessed point of inquiry that furnished writers of Caribbean classics with the means to express their awareness of Black knowing in the twentieth century. In the nineteenth, they are the deliberately thought past by republicans and future partisans of their idea of the Revolution. In other words, they are the shunned thought that contextualizes why Dessalines's marginalization in the Revolution and in the immediate years after its conclusion indexes a moment in Haitian Revolutionary history where the Revolution's radicalism becomes unfathomable and unmooring for the Euro-centered *and* their antagonists with anticolonial politics. The *Ginen* demand that Haiti be new and a world of its own is not merely unseen then. More profoundly, it is lost altogether because of its voicing in Dessalines's political thought, which has been successfully demeaned and silenced by republican revisionism *and* "North Atlantic scholarship of the Revolution." The latter, writes Stieber, "shroud[s]" the "post-1804 context" of Dessalines's anticolonial governance, republican counter-Haitian Revolutionary politics, and civil war discord "because of what . . . 1804 [is desired] to be: a radical, liberal universal revolution."[177] This is a colonial desire, as it is guided by thinking that conceives of existence as universally Western. Though misguided, this reasoning was placated by the republican rebellion against Dessalines, which republicans discursively relayed as "the true Haitian Revolution."[178]

The republican rebellion helped popularize an image of the Revolution removed from *Ginen* peoples when silencing what Stieber describes as the "Dessalinean critique of [the] Western Episteme," and this book argues is better termed as *Ginen* cultural praxis.[179] This image not only centered French thought and action in the Revolution but it stripped Haitians of the possibility of creating something new politically: Haiti was to be just like the First Republic of France (1792–1804), a bastion of political liberalism and universal equality—no more and no less. Thinkers and artists outside of Haiti latched on to this false idea of the Revolution with ease, and with that same ease the writers studied here fail to realize that Dessalines's politics were far more aligned with their own anticolonial politics than the republicans' ideals. Because this was inconceivable to them, each treats Dessalines and his anticolonial governance reductively, if at all, when post-independence Haiti is depicted. Yet without nuanced attention to Dessalines, the political horizon of newly independent Haiti (1804–1807) and its *Ginen* culture is absented from the reader's purview, and what is left in the Haiti after this (in the civil war period and beyond) is a reformist colonial-inspired republican effort. This Haiti gives rise to art and criticism that blatantly or indirectly judges Haiti and Haitians harshly for failing to live up to the Revolution's republican promise (Césaire and Carpentier); or it invites work that lauds the Revolution as the pinnacle of French revolutionary radicalization in the Caribbean (James). Furthermore, it bears texts that are a product of both engagements being embedded within a discourse that inadvertently substantiates the republican essence of the

Revolution (Glissant).[180] I address the republican subtext of classic Caribbean engagements with early Haiti as a colonial reading practice that reduces *Ginens* to that which must be unthought, and by proxy, cannot be seen. I also treat this subtext as a reading practice that disproportionally privileges *and* overly maligns creole revolutionists in narratives of the Revolution.

The effort undertaken here to showcase *Ginen* people and culture in classic Caribbean writing of the Revolution necessitates writing creole revolutionists anew. Notwithstanding the existence of Vastey, Dessalines, and Christophe, most creole revolutionists did not have the desire or aptitude to invent decolonizing thought.[181] Yet even as creole revolutionists were unimaginative, I am weary of the whitewashing present in the creole framing of the Revolution, which elicits both Walcott's static figuration of Christophe and Dessalines as "slave kings" in his essay, "What the Twilight Says," and Toussaint Louverture's figuration as a Black Spartacus or figure of enlightenment in Caribbean art and thought.[182] Each depiction (un)wittingly conceives these revolutionaries as persons who uncritically adopted white colonial attitudes and thoughtlessly absorbed Western European culture. Each is redemptive in essence, meant to redeem the culture of white supremacy in the early colonial moment and in this longer colonial present. For if Christophe and Dessalines acted just as abhorrently as white slaveholding colonists to their own people, how bad was slavery really? How bad were slavers? If Louverture found value in Western European culture or at the very least acted in a manner that suggested he did, how bad could white supremacy, the bedrock of modern Western European culture, really have been in the revolutionary moment? Colonialists and their slavery supporting sympathizers are shielded through the discursive minimization of captives and the vilification of creole Haitian revolutionists. They are also shielded via the praise of creole Haitian revolutionists who embody white supremacists in essence, being a Spartacus and enlightened. I do not write the creole generals as if they were white; nor do I write Saint Domingue's captive populace as if they were vanquished slaves. The Haitian Revolution and early post-revolutionary Haiti are not stories authored by colonial power. Their principal agents cannot be indistinguishable replicas of colonizers and their heroes; and nor can they be constructs of colonial thought. I choose to show how both *Ginen* captives and the more known creole generals exist beyond the limits of the colonial world; I show how they reside in the messiness of forcibly becoming Haitian and thus *Ginen* by association.

Book Overview

This book opens counterintuitively with a reading of Louverture and the dead conversations concerning Caribbean revolution and white colonial power he indexes. I begin with Louverture because coming to know Haitians as *Ginen*, and coming thereafter to discern the constructive and conscriptive power of their decolonial thought and action in the revolutionary moment and in early Haiti, requires clearing away the immense conceptual ground creole revolutionists are granted in the Caribbean cultural imaginary. This requires deconstructing the praise and vilification heaped upon creole revolutionists who are too readily figured as agents of white colonial power by Caribbean writers and thinkers; they were not that, however problematic they were. It also requires understanding how Louverture, in particular, was culturally *Ginen* and not a man apart, removed from and immune to the collective power of *Ginen* captives.

Chapter 1, "Dead Conversations," studies James's *The Black Jacobins*, the Jamaican anthropologist David Scott's reading of James's history *Conscripts of Modernity: The Tragedy of Colonial Enlightenment*, and Glissant's play *Monsieur Toussaint*. I build from Laurie Lambert's literary study of women in the Grenadian Revolution, and I assess how the Haitian Revolution has been recounted in Caribbean cultural production through a masculinist tradition of writing Caribbean resistance.[183] Lambert shows how this tradition consistently writes unruly revolutionary subjects out of consequence. I draw from her work to address how this tradition is epistemically colonial since its misogyny not only writes exemplary Black men of the Haitian Revolution as white men because of their unprecedented successes in war, but it also writes out *Ginen* women and men from the story of the Revolution given their lack of exception in the colonial moment. *Ginens* cannot be easily likened to persons afforded gender in colonial modernity and thus cannot signify as white men or white women. Louverture, the unseen *Ginen*, seemingly can signify as a person in colonial modernity (and thus as a white human who is male), and he can do so because of his enlightenment according to James. I turn to Charles Forsdick, Srinivas Aravamudan, Paul B. Miller, Nick Nesbitt, Deborah Jensen, and Marlene Daut's respective literary scholarship on the Enlightenment and Louverture to reconceive Louverture beyond his common figuration as a subject of enlightenment.[184] I argue that characterizations of Louverture as a figure of enlightenment traffic in the gendered colonial politics of the human, which signify the human as white and preferably male. These characterizations subsist by not only making Louverture synonymous with the Revolution but by also actively abstracting Louverture from his culture, the *Ginen* people that made him, and from his lived experience of anti-Black racialization. The conversations concerning Caribbean liberation Louverture indexes are consequently dead conversations. They are designed to reify the cultural and racial supremacy of Western Europe and, in turn, conceptually obfuscate the *Ginen* cultural refusal to recognize Western Europe and Western Europeans as supreme.

The second chapter, "Seen/Unseen," addresses how Carpentier reads *Ginen* cultural thought as decolonizing. Where Chapter 1 sat with creole Haitian revolutionists, this chapter turns to *Ginen* revolutionists and immerses readers in their cultural praxis of resistant self-authorship. I primarily read Carpentier's novella *The Kingdom of This World* and theory of *lo real maravilloso* (the marvelous real) to convey their praxis of freedom, but also treat his novels *The Lost Steps* and *The Harp and the Shadow*. I regard these writings as Carpentier's corpus of Haitian Revolutionary texts and the reading I offer turns on Carpentier's efforts to connect 1804 to 1492 via *The Kingdom of This World* and the novella's prologue. The prologue is where Carpentier first articulates his theory of the marvelous. This theory provides the discursive basis for the Revolution's new world building nature and his critique of race in *The Kingdom of This World*. I show how Carpentier's attention to the racialization of existence post-Columbus occasions his novel reading of *Ginen* Haitian revolutionists as new world builders due to their innovative faith-based thought practices.

Carpentier's interest in Columbus and race invites comparison with Wynter's extensive writings on Columbus, knowledge production, and race. I bring the two in conversation to critically assess Haiti's presence and absence in Caribbean engagements with the encounter, racialization, and Eurocentric knowledge practices. Haiti's presence in these engagements explains Carpentier's interest in the Revolution and the anticolonial nature of his Haitian corpus, which contends with the ongoing political project of white colonial rule in the past and present. His Haitian texts, however, are profoundly troubling for how they collectively elide the living presence of liberated Haiti. They absent what Black thought and Black life can *and did* produce in our biosphere: a new world. The diminution of the new world that the Revolution made occurs largely because the Haitian Revolution is racistly presented as an ambitious, though largely ineffective, potentiality in Carpentier's principal Haitian text (*The Kingdom of This World*). Carpentier writes as if *Ginen* revolutionists, their predecessors, and their descendants did not create lasting material and ontological conditions for a distinct decolonial world. Accordingly, where I show that newly independent Haiti was governed by a decolonial ethics of the plain human, Carpentier depicts post-revolutionary Haiti as a neocolonial banana republic of Black leaders existing in white face. He writes the nation unseen and is helpful in establishing how the turn to and subsequent rejection of Haiti in the work of both Carpentier and Wynter reveals how untenable Haiti's decisive claim to Black humanity remains. It is untenable precisely because it requires the abolition of the West—that is, the complete rejection of a world imagined and imaged in Western Europe's white colonial schema.

Chapter 3, "Not This!," considers the problem of time in Haitian Revolutionist art, that is, how the colonized and racially marginalized are to journey beyond the time of the colony in the postcolonial moment. It places *The Tragedy of King Christophe* (primarily) and *A Tempest* (secondarily), two dramas by Césaire, in conversation with Pontecorvo's film, *Queimada!* and picks up where the second chapter leaves off with attention to the new world-building nature of *Ginen* revolutionary action. I read Césaire's plays and Pontecorvo's film because of their attention to the orienting nature of revolutionary Haiti for radical anticolonial action; Césaire, in particular, has an extensive Haitian Revolutionist oeuvre that treats this. I focus mainly on *The Tragedy of King Christophe* because it is less driven by his investment in the myth of Haitian republicanism. This myth overdetermines Césaire's Haitian corpus and has resulted in writing that leaves Haiti and the Revolution unseen as *Ginen* political feats. Still, Césaire's *The Tragedy of King Christophe* and *A Tempest* are generative because they showcase Haiti's pivotal disruption of the Columbian narrative of discovery as well as its attending colonial orientation of time as progressive and as progressively white.

Césaire's dramas call for a new temporality for existence in the postcolonial present. This call accords with Pontecorvo's critique of progressive time in *Queimada!*. The film treats progressive time as a technology of power that serves the colonial project's civilizing mission. I bring Casimir's writings to bear on Césaire's Haitian Revolutionist work and contextualize Césaire's plays with attention to his political career and essays "Culture and Colonization" and "Letter to Maurice Thorez," and I read the film alongside Neelam Srivastava's work on anticolonialism and Italian colonialism.[185] I use Césaire's essays and the critical studies of Casimir and Srivastava to show how both Pontecorvo and Césaire's art of the Revolution heighten scholarly recognition of the functional necessity of a Haiti that is liberated but politically and economically compromised. Together, Césaire and Pontecorvo's imaginings of Haiti and the Haitian Revolution reveal that Haiti's importance for anticolonial thought and agitation lies in how the nation shows that there is a time beyond the colony and its ordering of existence as progressively *and* naturally white, as well as culturally Western European. I bring both Pontecorvo and Césaire in dialogue because this realization makes them compatriots of *Ginen* revolutionists. The inventive thoughts of *Ginen* rebels offer the discursive ground to chart a new way to exist in time and implicitly lie at the heart of both artists' Haitian Revolutionary art. Here *Ginen* Haitians are in absence but vibrantly felt via the intellectual and creative moves of Césaire and Pontecorvo, who are inspired by their praxis of freedom notwithstanding that both convey this inspiration through Haitian revolutionaries who are creole revolutionists.

The closing chapter, "Défilez!" offers a reading of Haitian Revolutionary history that genders the story of the Revolution. I analyze Danticat's short stories "Nineteen Thirty Seven" and "A Wall of Rising Fire," and I draw from Colin Dayan and Jana Evans Braziel's literary work on the female Haitian revolutionist Défilée to unpack the nuances of Danticat's feminist approach to the Revolution.[186] This approach provides the discursive ground to extol the merits of ongoing revolutionary striving, as I do in this chapter, despite the losses in persons and the seeming nonexistence of sociopolitical advances. I tie the work of anticolonial criticism to the decolonial resistance of Haitians in Haiti as documented in Danticat's stories, and I do so to expand the bounds of this criticism so that it not only includes *Ginen* cultural difference but it also resists thinking the Revolution with Haiti and Haitians unseen.

I invite readers to see both by immersing them in the Vodou imaginary that shapes the Revolution's presentation in Danticat's short stories. This imaginary contextualizes Danticat's writing as distinctly *Ginen* as it centers Haitians and Haiti in her treatment of the Revolution. I read Danticat's concerted rewriting of the Revolution through female figures as a deliberate way to spotlight the struggle for an alternative lived existence that was waged by the Revolution's *Ginen* peoples. I argue that once unveiled, the women within the revolutionary record point to the distinct non-republican and anticolonial future that the Revolution was to engender for Haiti, and that the Revolution must be continued to occasion in the present. For the women in Danticat's stories, this future is rooted in the firm conviction that the time to come can—*and must*—reside in a locality of one's own imagining.

This chapter talks back to contemporary Caribbean writing of the Revolution by unearthing the *Ginen* women and men for whom Haitian decolonial striving *is* the only option for a human existence. I end with Danticat because her stories show her cognizance of how her peers have imagined Haiti and the Revolution. Equally important is her location in the diaspora: she writes in English, for an English reading audience primarily, and has produced Haitian Revolutionary writing born of having experienced one's culture and its resistant sensibilities through the reproachful appreciation of her US audience and similarly imperiled Caribbean writers. Yet she depicts the visionary nature of the Revolution and writes imparting the importance of thinking with the decolonial sensibility of *Ginen* revolutionists. To end with her is to leave readers immersed in *Ayiti Ginen* and a knowing of Haitians as *Ginens*.

Each chapter of this book, save the introduction and conclusion, opens with an excerpt from an homage to Haitian revolutionaries. This is a deliberate honoring—one meant to celebrate the persons who made Haiti *Ayiti Ginen* because they thought to say no. They reflected and decided to refuse the colony as existence and encouraged awareness of how like "hope," no "is a discipline," to borrow from prison abolitionist Mariame Kaba.[187] No is propagative and a practice of self-directed thought. It furnishes conviction in otherwise ways of being and relating in the world and says, "this self-denigration I am asked to internalize and embody as a Black person, a colonized person and/or a racially marginalized person, is not for me." When scholars and enthusiasts of the Revolution read canonized Haitian Revolutionist literature with new eyes and come to know Haiti, Haitians, revolution, and liberation differently, as I insist, what they see is that each is driven and sustained by the power of no. And each is met with immense reactionary violence trying, with all of its might, to turn that no into a yes—yes to my inferiority, yes to my colonization, yes to white power. But it is the no that should stay with us because *Ginens* have shown us that little else is needed to create the lives we want, the world we want, outside of the collective processing and harnessing of our nos.

CHAPTER 1

Dead Conversations

> ... the return [to Africa] occurs when slavery and domination disappear. That's why I said that Columbus leaves, but I'm the one who returns.
>
> —Édouard Glissant

> Nou pap bliye.
>
> —Haitixchange User

I search for Toussaint Louverture in Caribbean cultural production and find Christopher Columbus, an icon who has yet to take leave of the Americas, no less Haiti. Columbus was banished from Haiti in 1986: his statue "removed from its pedestal and dumped... into the sea" by a group of people the cultural anthropologist Michel-Rolph Trouillot describes as "the most miserable people of Haiti's capital."[1] The destitute people of Port-au-Prince took to the streets to celebrate the momentous fall of Jean-Claude Duvalier's fifteen-year dictatorship, jubilantly desecrating every monument of despotic power. Columbus returned to Haiti in 2014. On May 13 of that year, the American explorer Barry Clifford claimed to have uncovered the remains of "the Santa Maria," the flagship vessel of Columbus's fleet near the city of Cap-Haitian. Clifford would go on to widely publicize his finding despite not having the legal authority to work in Haiti.[2] Columbus's curious emergence in 1986 Haiti and in 2014 Haiti was striking. On the one hand, there was the unsettling nature of the Columbian imprint of Clifford's disregard for Haitian sovereignty—who but an heir to Columbus would act with such gross entitlement? On the other, there was the eeriness of Columbus's return to Haiti just six months before Duvalier's death in the nation. Although he lived in exile in France for twenty-five years after his 1986 ousting, Duvalier returned to Haiti in 2011 to begin his brief residence in the country. He departed in death in October of 2014, dying in the city whose most marginalized inhabitants jubilantly celebrated his expulsion by tossing Columbus's statue into the sea. Columbus's ousting and curious return tie Haiti's notorious twentieth-century experience of tyrannical governance—first father, François "Papa Doc" Duvalier (1957–1971), and then son, Jean-Claude "Baby Doc" Duvalier (1971–1986)—to his 1492 arrival in the Caribbean. His (dis)appearances also bear the colonial hallmarks of despotism in Haiti, with dictator-colonialists and a discoverer-colonialist claiming Haiti as a fiefdom for their individual wants alone. And yet, what was striking was not simply the Columbian currents of the Duvaliers' governance or those innate in Clifford's pursuit of a needless relic. Rather, what resonated was the haunting potency of Columbus's continued relevance to Haiti, the territorial space he declared a "marvel" for its extractive potential.[3]

The persistency of Columbus's presence in Haiti links decades of pre-Haitian Revolutionary resistance in Saint Domingue, Haiti's famed thirteen-year revolution (1791–1804), and the two-hundred-plus year-long counter-revolt against liberated Haiti waged by white colonial powers. These linkages are deeply unsettling since they name the vibrancy of the counter revolutionary presence in Haiti via its natal and foreign minions. Still, the disconcerting significances of Columbus in twentieth- and twenty-first century Haiti ought not to eclipse how the Columbian subtext of the Duvaliers' governance, in particular, illuminates the Haitian Revolution's greatest lesson for writers and scholars of the Revolution: the dissident perceptual power of the absented. The "most miserable people" of Port-au-Prince are the city and nation's castoffs, persons more readily looked past than acknowledged. The absence of consideration that attends the lives of the socially and politically abandoned perhaps shaped their own awareness of how there could be no colonialist despot—no Baby Doc or Papa Doc—without Columbus, the signifier of white colonial despotism the world over. I lead with their perceptual power when reading the Trinidadian historian and Marxist theorist C. L. R. James's formative history of the Haitian Revolution,

The Black Jacobins: Toussaint L'Ouverture and the San Domingo Revolution, the Jamaican anthropologist David Scott's reading of James's history, *Conscripts of Modernity: The Tragedy of Colonial Enlightenment*, and the Martinican writer and philosopher Édouard Glissant's play, *Monsieur Toussaint*.

I read these works from the *Ginen* (African Haitian) cultural ground the dispossessed urbanites of 1986 Port-au-Prince share with their revolutionist ancestors. Of import to this book is the way this ground is absented in classic Caribbean literature of the Revolution along with the *Ginen* (African and Africanized) revolutionists who created it. I show how both are removed from how Caribbean writers think the Revolution and its figures; and my analysis works around this elision by re-centering Haiti and Haitians in the literatures of the Revolution authored by James, Glissant, Alejo Carpentier, and Aimé Césaire, which are read from the African sensibility of *Ginen* Haitians. The latter refuses the universality of French culture and the cultures of other Western European colonial powers and chooses instead to be guided by the particularities of *Ginen* history and *Ginen* ideas for being. I argue that recognizing the *Ginen* insistence for difference outside of the West exposes how influential *Ginen* thought and action are to canonical Caribbean writing of the Revolution. To that end, this book does not simply critique seminal writing for thinking the Revolution without *Ginens*, but it also details how *Ginen* Haitians are still present even as they are unseen by the writers studied here. "Unseen" is used throughout to primarily index the author's projections of who Haitians are, what the Haitian Revolution is, and what the nature of a regional Caribbean revolution should be. Secondarily, it denotes the absenting of Haitian difference, which is manifest in the desire to write the Haitian revolutionist as aspiring to the West when revolting. This is the subject of this chapter, which reassesses the stories of the Revolution that have been distilled through the beloved Haitian revolutionist Toussaint Louverture. The intent here is to challenge how this exemplary general has been conceived in classic Caribbean writing of the Revolution. Of concern is the pervasive manner in which Louverture is written as a non-*Ginen* because of a masculinist tradition of writing Caribbean resistance. In this tradition, Columbus never "leaves," no matter how radical the anticolonial writing.

Glissant's anticolonial writing and his musings are radical and undeniably so. Although what follows is a critique of his thinking (as relayed in the epigraph), his play about the Revolution is the only Haitian Revolutionist text in this chapter that creates space to rethink why Louverture is authored in the unproductive, anticolonial manner popularized in Caribbean arts and letters. This chapter's opening epigraph is drawn from the 2008 documentary, *Édouard Glissant: One World in Relation* and its discussion of "multiplicity."[4] It reads, "the return [to Africa] occurs when slavery and domination disappear. That's why I said that Columbus leaves, but I'm the one who returns."[5] Glissant is not talking about Haiti or the Revolution in the documentary. He is focused on Columbus and leaving the West he represents behind, but in his effort to "leave" Columbus he does invoke Haiti and the Revolution in absence, since *Ginen* revolutionists did exactly that: they left Columbus behind when liberating themselves.[6] How they did that is outlined in the introduction and will be discussed again momentarily. Of import here is how a masculinist tradition of writing Caribbean resistance annuls Glissant's radical intent, since it aligns his thought with Columbus when his intentions lie with *Ginens* (or resistant Black peoples more broadly). Literary scholar Laurie Lambert cites James as the originator of this tradition. She notes the regional importance of *The Black Jacobins*, which told the story of the Haitian Revolution through Louverture's life, and James's equally influential essay, "From Toussaint L'Overture to Fidel Castro," published in the 1963 edition of *The Black Jacobins*. This essay tied revolutionary striving to Caribbean regional identity and further established a tradition of writing Louverture as the Revolution. It also provided the foundation for a genealogy of Caribbean discursive resistance that would cement revolutionary activity solely to men of the Caribbean. Lambert writes "the genealogy that James lays out [in the essay] is not only distinctly Caribbean," with influential figures from the French-, English-, and Spanish-speaking Caribbean, "but [it is] exclusively masculine-identified in its gender politics."[7] Indeed, each of the dissident regional figures that are presented as consequential "to the timeline of cultural and political resistance in the region is a Caribbean man."[8]

The problem with a masculinist tradition of writing Caribbean resistance is implicitly articulated in the Jamaican philosopher Sylvia Wynter's discussion of gender in colonial modernity. She states, "from the very origin of the modern world, of the Western world system, there were never simply men and women."[9] There were "whites who see themselves as true men, true women, while their Others, the untrue men/women, were now labeled as indio/indias (Indians) and as negros/Negras."[10] Wynter's incisive articulation of the newness of the modern articulation of the human as white alone underscores how gender expression in colonial ontology is tied to physiognomy and what physiognomy articulates about one's human-ness: womanhood, for instance, exists as the purview of "true women," that is, women who are anatomically female and phenotypically white.[11] In this context where Black peoples are unknowable as men and women and also considered ontologically unable to perform manhood or womanhood (a gender presentation reserved for whites only), a masculinist tradition of writing Caribbean resistance unwittingly serves the political function of re-inscribing an intrinsically white supremacist understanding of gender (whites as true men) and of the human (the human as phenotypically white and culturally Western European). Furthermore, it produces thought that aligns one with the colonizer; so even as Glissant's anticolonial politics are sound—indeed, even though he speaks not of men but of Columbus in the abstract—men (i.e., the "whites who see themselves as true men") are still centrally present in his philosophy of liberation.[12]

Glissant follows his contention about Columbus with an explanation: "I don't mean myself, I meant that they return not only free but having gained something. What have they gained? Multiplicity. Compared to the unity of the slave driver's will; we have the multiplicity of the anti-slavery will. That is what we've gained, and that is the real return."[13] "Multiplicity" denotes a coalition of resistant communal resolve grounded in an "anti-slavery will": disparate persons of the African diaspora come together because of a shared investment in eradicating anti-Black racialization and the Western political project of white colonial power on which this racialization is predicated.[14] In this respect, "multiplicity" is a conceptual offshoot of Glissant's earlier political declaration in the 1989 essay collection *Caribbean Discourse: Selected Essays*, where he argued that "the West is not in the West. It is a project, not a place."[15] Glissant re-signifies "the West" in *Caribbean*

Discourse as a concept rather than a geographic place in order to make it clear that the West is *one* form of existence among others, and it is therefore possible to offer a new paradigm of human existence that is invested in leaving behind the political project of the West. Glissant situates this new paradigm in the diasporic notion of "return," which he articulates as a radical homecoming predicated on a restructuring of wills, desires, and perspectives.[16] This restructuring would institute "multiplicity" as the controlling paradigm of human existence, a formulation which entails "know[ing] ourselves as part and as crowd," to quote Glissant in *Poetics of Relation*.[17] A collectivist figuration is opposed to the singularity of the Columbus descendant, the slave driver, and the slave driver's white and white-identified progeny. The latter is the controlling paradigm for Glissant's long colonial present and this longer colonial present. Henceforward the "real return" is to return to what is possible, to the world as it could be, to the world made in the image of the absented who manifest "the anti-slavery will" and who accordingly constitute themselves in the unified heterogeneity of "multiplicity" (where "one is part and crowd") versus the homogenizing partitioning of singularity (where the "part [*is*] the crowd").

Glissant does not simply speak of return but *imagines* with and further than colonial knowledge systems. He thinks in excess of the West. In his radical imagining, Africa becomes a new horizon for existence: "it is a project, not a place," to use his language.[18] As a project, a reconceptualized Africa annuls a Western understanding of return, which has always entailed the violent seizure of a peopled place for new peoples. Glissant's return suggests the possibility of an otherwise existence not rooted in genocidal theft and displacement; a position he arrives at by countering two Western expressions of an "ideal subjectivity," the "*ego conquiro*" and the "*ego cogito*."[19] Drawing from the philosopher Enrique Dussel, decolonial theorist Nelson Maldonado-Torres writes, "The certainty of the self as a conqueror, of its tasks and missions, preceded [René] Descartes's certainty about the self as a thinking substance (*res cogitans*) and provided a way to interpret [this self]."[20] To articulate the new paradigm for human existence that return requires ("multiplicity), Glissant displaces the "*ego conquiro*" as Columbus "leaves." He dethrones the singular thinking subject, "*ego cogito*," for a subject constituted as "part and crowd"—his "they." The latter speculative effort disavows the centrality of his singularity to underscore the importance of the collective when he states: "That's why I said that Columbus leaves, but I'm the one who returns. *I don't mean myself*, I meant that *they* return not only free but having gained something. What have *they* gained? Multiplicity."[21] The originality of Glissant's musings here cannot be denied. His trajectory of thought unmasks, however, the conceptual snare implemented by the individualist singularity of white colonial knowledge systems: the latter fixes thought on a male subject. In the future moment of liberation that Glissant theorizes, the masculine remains as *the* structuring conceptual proxy for radical Black liberation: as the liberation to come passes solely through men—Columbus, Glissant, and a "they" that is ungendered but causally must be men too—*even as* Columbus "leaves."

Ginen revolutionists also reimagined Africa as a horizon for being. It ceased to be a home or place of ancestry and became instead a stratagem for envisioning the end of Saint Domingue and the advent of a new world, *Ayiti Ginen* (Africa Haiti). Where a stratagem is diffusive in nature, spreading ideas outward, a project is a projectile, missile-like in conceptual focus and direction. One idea will take precedence over others and one person can become representative of that idea. This is not so with a stratagem, especially the one devised by *Ginen* captives. No one person or gender authored it, no singular subject took precedence over the collective in the inventive process that went into making them a people. Indeed, no effort was made to think with and beyond the epistemological dictates of the West, which is to say where "Columbus leaves" for Glissant he is nonexistent for *Ginens*. He was expelled from their purview and cerebrally tossed in the sea well before the idea of *Ayiti Ginen* came into being. In other words, *Ginen* thought gives teeth to Glissantian thought. It resists working within a knowledge system that demands Black people "ask for permission to be."[22] Glissant is still asking for permission, notwithstanding the radical nature of his thinking. In this respect, the *Ginen* refusal to ask permission illuminates the instructive shortcoming of his philosophy of liberation. This shortcoming is evident in its analytical orientation, which is guided by a masculinist perspective that does not question the vantage it is asked to adopt when thinking with and in excess of the West. Furthermore, it illuminates the failings of a masculinist tradition of writing Caribbean resistance, which is evident in the latter's operative genuflection. It exposes the acquiescence to the West built into assessments of the Caribbean past and present when a masculinist perspective is the dominant lens. This lens is reformist and fixes attention on persons who can be easily positioned as iconic in the manner that Columbus is iconic being similar to, *and* the other, of Columbus. It accordingly reifies whoever can signify anticolonial resistance *and* the ongoing efficacy of the white colonial order.

Louverture has become this person within scholastic and creative studies of the Haitian Revolution, which makes the search for him in Caribbean arts and letters a near impossibility, since what authors his iconicity is a masculinity that is colonial and white in essence. Indeed, to find Louverture is to face a corpus of thought that absents others like *Ginen* revolutionists, who cannot signify as human being denied gender expression in colonial modernity, and finding a select few, like Louverture, who are imagined as being able to express their humanity normatively within colonial modernity, i.e., as the "whites who see themselves as true men."[23] The work undertaken here makes friction against a masculinist tradition of writing Caribbean resistance and heeds the *Ginen* cultural call to remember Haitian revolutionists by their radical deeds and not their significations, hence the second epigraph's imperative, *Nou pap bliye*.[24] This declarative is from an homage authored for Haitian revolutionists, and yet not one of the popular Caribbean-born revolutionists is named, specifically Louverture, Dessalines, Christophe, and Alexandre Pétion (among others). Instead, the homage invokes revolutionaries routinely absented from Caribbean cultural thought, opening with the Black and Indigenous dissidents who existed in Spanish-ruled Santo Domingo prior to the Revolution and concluding by naming the Revolution's long-overlooked female generals. In not remembering Louverture, in particular, the homage asks scholars to consider what it is about Louverture that merits forgetting. What is it about how he is canonized in Caribbean letters, in particular, that invites denying him ancestral remembrance?

In addressing this query, I trace the vestiges of Louverture's *Ginen* person through the communities of resistance consequential to his success. I show how Louverture the *Ginen* troubles the masculinist rendering of Louverture first offered by James, redeployed by Scott, and also partially reimagined by Glissant. This Louverture of Caribbean cultural thought is an enlightened person, described as a reasonable, literate, liberal democratic subject. Yet despite these glowing characteristics, he is also presented as tragically flawed and unable to bring fundamental change to the Caribbean precisely because of his enlightenment. James, most strongly, argues that his enlightenment prevented him from reconciling anticolonial action with republican ideals. Of specific interest is how this ideological framing of Louverture functions to sustain a particular representation of Caribbean anticolonial possibility that invariably sustains coloniality. Indeed, renderings of Louverture as a subject of enlightenment traffic in the gendered colonial politics of the human, and these ideations necessarily subsist by not only making Louverture synonymous with the Revolution but also by actively whitening him and rendering him complicit with white supremacy past and present. His complicity, in turn, facilitates the Revolution's discursive trivialization, prompting the question: was the Haitian Revolution really necessary? If the conceit that opens this chapter regarding Columbus and his damning significations in Haiti and the Americas is clear, the masculinist whitening of Louverture (and thus the Revolution) foregrounds the conceptually dead (that is, un-generative) dictates of whiteness and the associated cultural supremacy of Western Europe within critical mediations on Caribbean liberation. Cast in colonial fashion as acting like white men of the Enlightenment, Louverture is constituted by the spectral fixity of Columbus and the supremacist colonial project he names in the Americas. He is unseen, in this respect, and the conversations concerning Caribbean liberation that he, as the icon of the Revolution, indexes are consequently dead conversations. They are designed to reify the cultural and racial supremacy of Western Europe and, in turn, conceptually obfuscate the *Ginen* revolutionary refusal to recognize Western Europe and Western Europeans as supreme.

Collectivism Unseen

Louverture is not there. Look hard at canonical Caribbean writings of the Revolution and you will find an archive denuded of the radical pulse of united wills that Louverture, himself, was beholden to. What comes to mind is Louverture in 1797: with Maximilien de Robespierre fallen and revolutionary France under the guidance of the Directory, Louverture (then General in chief of the French Republican army in Saint Domingue) faces an uncertain political horizon. The Directory is increasingly at the mercy of pro-slavery lobbyists. Aware of this, Louverture pens a letter admonishing France for entertaining slavery's return to the colony. Of interest here is who he outlines as leading the revolutionary charge in Saint Domingue. He writes,

> Do they [pro-slavery lobbyists] think that men who have been able to enjoy the blessing of liberty will calmly see it snatched away? They supported their chains only so long as they did not know any condition of life more happy than that of slavery. But to-day when they have left it, if they had a thousand lives they would sacrifice them all rather than be forced into slavery again. But no, the same hand which has broken our chains will not enslave us anew.[25]

He continues more forcefully, stating, "But if, to re-establish slavery in San Domingo, this was done, then I declare to you it would be to attempt the impossible: we have known how to face dangers to obtain our liberty. We shall know how to brave death to maintain. . . . This, Citizens Directors, is the morale of the people of San Domingo, *these are the principles that they transmit to you by me*."[26] "They" compel him. The captives who constituted Louverture's army, who freed themselves within two years of the Revolution's 1791 onset, and who forced the French into a state of desperation that occasioned Léger-Félicité Sonthonox's belated 1793 declaration of emancipation, made *him* an instrument of their will.[27]

In the years leading to the Revolution, a substantial number of Saint Domingue's northern captives had been radicalized against slavery and French colonial rule. Freedom, for these mostly Africa-born persons (or *bossales*), no longer meant absconding from the plantation but, as Trouillot notes, it now "meant *koupe tèt boulé kay*."[28] This call to freedom, "Cut off heads, burn down houses," is most commonly associated with Boukman Dutty and then Jean Jacques Dessalines, but it emerged among them first.[29] Its longevity in the revolutionary moment is a testament to how increasingly militant captives were in their resistance against slavery and it is also a testament to the culture of resistance they had created. Both Trouillot and sociologist Jean Casimir understand the culture of captives in the North as the South and West of Saint Domingue as Africanist like this book, which uses the appellation *Ginen* to make the culture's African essence plain to readers. Each regards this *Ginen* culture as one "born in struggle"; born, explains Trouillot, because "it was fighting."[30] Historian Sudhir Hazareesingh does not describe captive culture in Saint Domingue as African but he contends that the fighting ethos this culture produced bore "a fully-fledged revolutionary culture" in the North especially.[31] This fighting ethos grew exponentially when captives began to listen to the colonial discourse of the day (republicanism).[32] It grew more when they saw colonists win skirmishes with guns since they reasoned that they could do better with guns; indeed, many had already done so in Africa.[33] It deepened when they practiced Vodou and spoke Kreyòl, which inculcated "dissension against the upper classes."[34] And when they leaned into Makandalism, a *Ginen* politic of self-determination, their resolve to continue to fight hardened and dovetailed with their growing realization that total autonomy, of self and nation, was the only way to secure their liberation.[35]

Makandalism was especially important given that it made pointed use of the creative tools captives had readily at their disposal to dogmatize their resistance, specifically, their wits, faith, and language. The politic's resourcefulness encouraged them to think for themselves and envision a future beyond the colony, as expressed in the movement's ultimate goal which was to "destroy white settler dominance and . . . achieve black emancipation."[36] Though the maroon and Vodou priest who created this 1740s movement, François Makandal, was executed in 1758, Makandalism succeeded as a politic insofar as it "create[d] a common consciousness among black slaves."[37] This consciousness encouraged more and more captives to envision freedom as a fight versus a flight. It also made them eager to create and join organizations that would champion "freedom for all people."[38]

Louverture's coalition became that organization in 1793.[39] Trouillot writes that he "abandoned the position of the leaders of the rebel slaves in order to defend a basic interest of the slave class: freedom for all people," gaining him mass support.[40] For as long as Louverture's organization "defend[ed this] basic interest," for as long as it resisted dependency on France and any imperial nation, Trouillot states that the people were with him, furthering his political and military influence.[41] It did not matter that the formerly captive "masses hadn't been enjoying the lands controlled by Toussaint's organization" following the 1793 emancipation order.[42] It did not matter that "in the North, as in the South, they'd been working like mules so the leaders could run free."[43] Trouillot explains, "the freedom they'd acquired in 1793–94 was getting more deeply rooted each day, and there wasn't a soul who could take it away from them anymore."[44] Their determination to be free created a matrix of power that Louverture would depend on as evinced in his 1797 letter to the Directory. It leverages the threat of their collective power precisely because the formerly captive populace had changed the political dynamics of the colony and forced every other class to acquiesce to its political will. Even the Directory was constrained. It wants to rein in the Revolution, scale back its radicalisms and depose Louverture (hence the acerbity of his letter); but the newly liberated would not give them the political latitude to do so. Their matrix of power forced the Directory to parlay with Louverture, and their power made him the figurehead of the Revolution. It is his own recognition of that which should shape his figuration in art and criticism of the Revolution. Because when he forgot their power, when he thought his alone sufficed and began to increasingly act outside of their collective interests, pursuing economic policies that reinforced dependency on foreign markets and sanctioned the return of plantation industry, he lost; they did not. He was deported and imprisoned; they won the Revolution and secured Haitian independence.

Louverture understood his ties to his revolutionary peers and knew the power of their collective efforts in 1797 and the years prior. Yet as James's own discussion of Louverture's letter shows, many needlessly harp on his "personal ambition" to divest him from the communal fight for "freedom for all people," and from collectivism on the whole. What is the purpose of this divestment? It is comprehensible only as a scholarly effort to write Louverture white and in so doing diminish the harm that was slavery; that is anti-Blackness and that is white fidelity to white supremacy then and now. James writes, "Superficial people have read [Louverture's] career in terms of personal ambition. This letter is their answer. Personal ambition he had. But he accomplished what he did because, superbly gifted, he incarnated the determination of his people never, never to be slaves again."[45] James is correct to maintain that Louverture's "personal ambition" did not negate his commitment to the abolition of slavery; nor did it diminish his concern for the community of people he was aligned with—despite his paternalism and classism—since both affected him as a Black man. Yet in recent years much has been made of the successes of Louverture's political machinations and economic maneuvers with contemporary biographers of the general suggesting that these successes, as opposed to his collectivist investment in Black liberation, were the chief impetus for his revolutionary efforts.

Louverture biographer Madison Smartt Bell writes in his 2009 book that "Toussaint had a large material investment in the colonial status quo," an assertion that likely prompted his most recent biographer, Hazareesingh, to write in his 2020 biography, that "contrary to later rumours, [Louverture] did not at this time accumulate a huge fortune or own large properties," when living as a free man before the Revolution.[46] To be clear, Hazareesingh is not directly responding to Bell but he *is* responding to a body of scholarship in line with which Bell is writing. This is the scholarship of slavery apologists, who authored "rumours" about Louverture's massive wealth before the Revolution and leveraged his accumulation of capital and properties over the course of the Revolution as evidence of how he is just like the planters he opposes and was steadfastly against in slavery. Historian Gabriel Debien discusses these rumors and argues that the claim that Louverture had 648,000 francs in 1789, money that could secure a large plantation, was propagandist.[47] Historian Stewart King notes, in turn, that this wealth was at odds with the lifestyles within reach of most manumitted captives such as Louverture.[48] Hazareesingh has to distinguish between Louverture's middle-class life before the Revolution and his wealthy life during, to signal to readers his awareness of the bad faith rumors circulating in his lifetime, which sought to discredit his commitment to the abolition of slavery and legitimate white people's financial and cultural investment in Black enslavement. Yet when Bell says that Louverture has a "material investment in the colonial status quo," he is repeating the same rumors in good faith, and furthering the way the uncritical repetition of these rumors as scholastic truths, has made a body of white supremacist disparagement canon.[49] How they are canon is evident in the advent of revisionist twenty-first-century biographies about Louverture which function as conservative apologia for imperialism.

Bell's biography is one example; historian Philippe Girard's 2016 biography *Toussaint Louverture: A Revolutionary Life* is another. Where Bell writes that Louverture was "in with *grand blancs* [affluent merchants and planters]," Girard writes that he wanted to become one.[50] He states that Louverture "was no black nationalist" as his foremost aspiration was to be a "Frenchman" and "become a 'big white' [i.e., *grand blanc*] in his turn."[51] Girard writes as if the desire to be French was tied to an abstract depoliticized idea of French-ness versus the politicized state of unmolested freedom that being French appeared to offer free and captive Black peoples. To secure one's status as a "Frenchman" is to secure an un-dominated lived existence: the end goal is not to be French but to exist securely in freedom. What's more, becoming a "Frenchman" does not make one a blind acolyte of France.[52] Trouillot writes, "it's true that [Louverture] called himself a 'child of France,' but he was a child born out of wedlock. He was born in slavery, he'd fought against France. . . . The *nouveaux libres* [the self-liberated] owed nothing to France and Louverture owed nothing to France."[53] Girard ignores that Louverture had a life outside of France and French colonial culture. He ignores that his aspiration to be a "child of France" was shaped by a cultural foundation that made him resistantly French, if French at all.[54] Bell ignores this as well when suggesting that Louverture took part in a royalist conspiracy at the Revolution's onset spearheaded by *grand blancs*, who secretly fomented the Revolution's early happenings to prevent destitute whites from seizing power.[55] Louverture biographers Charles Forsdick and Christian Høgsbjerg write that Bell builds on the work of "earlier [Louverture] biographers such as Ralph Korngold" to resurrect the baseless "allegations levelled at Toussaint during his own lifetime," which claimed that he was prodded to rebel by royalists' planters and his own self-interest.[56] Bell goes so far as to suggest that Louverture allied with *grand blancs* because his "economic interests made him [their] natural partner," an assertion that would have readers believe that Louverture had no aspirations beyond France; worse, that he would do anything to be like an affluent Frenchman.[57] Both Girard and Bell think the Revolution through their vantage and not that of the persons who enacted it. This vantage is hubristically white. It pretends that there exists a body of mutual relations that lessened the irreconcilable life experiences separating Black and mixed-race peoples from white peoples in the colonial moment. It pretends that Black actions are legible through the quotidian actions of white men in colonial modernity; and it pretends that the biographies themselves are not steeped in "white rage," in the anti-Black racialisms that shaped US cultural production in the United States during Barack Obama's presidential ascent.[58] A brief biographic sketch of Louverture's life not only underscores the distinct life experiences white peoples and Africans as well as their descendants had in the colonial moment, but it also shows how absenting this difference effectively expunges in narratives of Louverture and the Revolution, more broadly, how culturally *Ginen* the general was.

Louverture was born in Saint Domingue in the early 1740s and bore the name François-Dominique Toussaint Bréda for the plantation of his enslavement. He was freed in the early 1770's after a stint as a runaway, became an owner of a captive man in 1776, and he worked as a salaried coachman for the overseer who freed him (Bayon de Libertat) after he manumitted the man he owned.[59] When the Revolution began in August of 1791, Louverture secured the safety of Bayon de Libertat and his family while working behind the scenes of the revolutionary struggle. He was present at the ceremony of *Bwa Kayïman*, in dialogue with the Revolution's first leaders (Boukman, Jean François, and George Biassou) and began working as an advisor to Biassou in October of 1791.

He would command five hundred soldiers by mid-1792 and assume the name Toussaint Louverture on August 25, 1793, with the rise of his military successes.[60] The little known of Louverture's early life, outlined here, was touched by the predatory dictates of white existence; his movement from captive, runaway, master, salaried employee to revolutionary, attests to the deferential ties free and captive had to have with white individuals for survival (Bayon de Libertat). And yet in the midst of this compulsory dependence, Louverture forged bountiful ties with captive and free Black peoples.

He married twice, first to the free Cécile when he was eighteen and then to Suzanne Simon-Baptist, a captive laundress who remained his wife for the duration of his life.⁶¹ From these marriages, he maintained a "sprawling family network that allowed him to cope with slavery [and that] much later . . . would form the backbone of his revolutionary regime."⁶² This vast family network included immediate and extended family, who with him ascended classes as he ascended classes: he left no one behind. Hazareesingh writes that he chose to remain on the plantation of de Libertat and be "formally listed as a slave [in order] to use his influence to promote and protect them" all.⁶³ If Louverture thought to care and protect his large family, it was a testament of his faiths (he was a devout Catholic and practitioner of Vodou) and his cultures. Louverture was Alladan because of his parents and *Ginen* because of his socio-political surrounding.⁶⁴ He spoke the Fon language of Allada and remained in close contact with other Alladans and closely related African peoples because of the collectivist orientation of his ancestral culture.⁶⁵ He carried this culture forward in his life practices, working (like his father) as an herbalist before the Revolution; like his contemporaries, he spoke Kreyòl and was radicalized toward Black collectivity and the political project of Black freedom by the *Ginen* culture that bore Kreyòl and Makandalism, the dominant political ideology of the northern captive population.⁶⁶ Louverture was a teen when Makandal was publicly executed and very much aware of the movement's politics and its impact on the free and captive peoples of the north. He would routinely borrow Makandal's famous line, "après Bon Dieu, c'est Makandal" and rephrase it by "replacing 'Makandal' with other names" in his speeches to speak directly to the people in the *Ginen* cultural terms they shared.⁶⁷ "His extended family," "his Alladan culture, . . . his creole and *bossale* [Africa-born] brethren, and . . . the men and women who shared his Catholic faith," were not ancillary to his personal ambitions.⁶⁸ These communities of care created the network of relations for the wealth that scholars conceive as negatively coloring Louverture's dedication to Black freedom.

Scholarly accounts of the general too often absent these communities and their importance to Louverture because they overly privilege his personal ambition. Attention to these communities is critical to augmenting how scholars and artists understand him. Furthermore, it is critical to debunking how poor a lens personal ambition is for understanding Louverture's commitment to Black liberation. This framing not only necessitates that scholars read Louverture in the same fashion as the colonists and colonialists who wrote slavery apologia, but it favors racist fantasies of Black avarice and villainy to discount the complexities of Black communal relations, which are forged by the omnipresence of white supremacist violence and the surety of Black suffering and death. The radicalization of Louverture's contemporary, the *affranchi* Jean Louis Vastey, who was King Henry Christophe's famed secretary and a renowned nineteenth-century antislavery as well as anticolonial essayist, is relevant here. Literary scholar Marlene L. Daut discusses his life when detailing "the relationship of color prejudice to black death" in *Baron de Vastey and the Origins of Black Atlantic Humanism*. She shows how this "relationship . . . ultimately caused [the] son of a former slave owner, Vastey, to join the side of Dessalines's *armée indigène*, [a move which] illustrates a fundamental clash between one's economic interests in slavery and a personal belief in the rights of all people to live with dignity."[69] She continues and writes, "This clash would ultimately convince [Julien] Raimond, [André] Rigaud, and Vastey, all from slave-owning families of color, to turn their backs on their properties and join the Revolution."[70] Raimond and Rigaud did not join the fight for independence; their idea of the Haitian Revolution was republican and French, which meant that they sided with the French at the Revolution's end. Still, as Daut notes, their dedication to their idea of the Revolution, which prized liberalism and equality, complicated how they lived their lives as wealthy slave-owning free men of color. The challenges they faced were not theirs alone: free peoples of African descent and manumitted Africans who held antislavery politics secured their livelihoods with financial decisions that tried to reconcile the irreconcilable, support of Black political freedom while profiting from Black economic subjection. And where some, like Raimond, Rigaud, and Vastey, had to navigate the ethics of generational wealth built on Black subjugation, others like Louverture had to navigate the ethics of building wealth off of reforming and not dismantling the colonial system. The financial decisions they made to sustain their affluence or attain affluence does not lessen their monstrosity, but they do attest to the evil of those who designed, sustained, and endorsed the colonial project.

Louverture made terrible decisions; the ghastliest were in line with the ordinary demands of colonial modernity. He issued edict after edict from 1798 onward trying to force the self-liberated back to plantation labor to sustain the existing economic structure of Saint Domingue, and before that he owned a human being, however briefly.[71] The personal financial decisions Louverture made before the Revolution and the socioeconomic decisions he made during it do not show a blind pursuit of wealth that made him just like white colonists. They show a too simplistic acceptance, on his part, of what life was and what life could be. They expose, in other words, an absence of imagination, not mimicry of whiteness. Indeed, Louverture could not have built the vast community of relations he had if he wholeheartedly aspired to be like a "big white."[72] He would have abandoned his family and relations at every opportune moment. He did not do that. He picked and chose between abhorrent means of upward mobility proffered by the French and fellow Western European colonizers; which is to say, his navigation of a societal design meant to corrupt communality and promote the single-minded individualism—that reasoned the colonial encounter, Black and Indigenous servitude, and colonialism into being—shows an ongoing (and at times tepid) refusal of the colonizing culture of the French and the West, more broadly. For, if it is true that Louverture was Dessalines's former manager (who was leased to him from his son-in-law, who owned Dessalines), then the very fact that Dessalines chose to fight alongside him speaks volumes to how distinctly non-Western (indeed non-white) Louverture pursued his "personal ambitions."[73]

Bell, Girard, and likeminded scholars, past and present, absent Black communality, care, and Black self-love in their portraits of Louverture. They ignore how Black survival depends on non-compulsory care-based relations, the very relations that are the bedrock of Caribbean anticolonial thought in the eighteenth century onward. One need only recall regional cultural and political sayings like *"tout moun se moun"* (*Ginen* Haiti), "I and I" (Rastafari Jamaica) and "forward ever, backward never" (revolutionary Grenada). With respect to Louverture in particular, they write him as white to absent his life as a *Ginen* person from their readers' purview, a move that furthers scholarly efforts to unsee how Louverture was not only fighting for Black people due to his personal conviction, but doing so because he recognized their collective determination to be free with or without him.

Louverture draws his remarkable 1797 letter to a close clarifying where he will stand when his sistren and brethren take up arms against the French, should the Directory heed pro-slavery lobbyists and attempt to reinstate slavery in Saint Domingue. He writes,

> My own you know. It is sufficient to renew, my hand in yours, the oath that I have made, to cease to live before gratitude dies in my heart, before I cease to be faithful to France and to my duty, before the god of liberty is profaned and sullied by the liberticides, before they can snatch from my hands that sword, those arms, which France confided to me for the defence of its rights and those of humanity, for the triumph of liberty and equal.[74]

In true *Ginen* and Caribbean collectivist fashion, Louverture will also join them. That he is forcibly removed from the revolutionary scene in 1802 means little as the fight continued without him, attesting to how prescient he was about the actions of the self-liberated women and men of Saint Domingue. Their singular will for freedom was evident to General Charles Leclerc, the French general who deported Louverture and who spearheaded Napoléon Bonaparte's 1802 expedition to retake Saint Domingue and reinstitute slavery. Writing to Bonaparte, he declares: "It is not enough to have taken away Toussaint, there are 2,000 leaders to be taken away."[75] And yet these "2,000 leaders" are largely absent from the literature treated here, even as "the records are there."

The Black Jacobins

James pronounces, "The records are there," when speaking of the absented *Ginen* revolutionists who are present in the historical archives of the Haitian Revolution but who were nonetheless omitted from *The Black Jacobins*.[76] He offered this admission in the last book talks of three that he gave at the Institute of the Black World's Summer Research Symposium in 1971. This final lecture, "How I Would Rewrite *The Black Jacobins*," reveals a James eager to engender revolutionary striving and anticolonial dissidence among the disaffected present at his talk—the academic, activist, or intrigued listener in the crowd who were all experiencing the lived effects of a heavily policed and defanged Black power movement in the United States and the uneven successes of anticolonial movements in the Caribbean, Africa, and Asia. Ever the anticolonial Marxist, he invites his audience to see how they can transform their world when professing that were he to rewrite *The Black Jacobins* he would do so articulating what the text in its present form as a tribute to Louverture, the icon, cannot convey: "all insurrections which attack constituted authority . . . come from *below*."[77]

James relays this point when paraphrasing Pamphile de Lacroix, a French soldier who noted the mass base spearheading the Revolution when serving in Saint Domingue during Bonaparte's re-enslavement expedition. The expedition arrived in the colony in February 1802 and launched soon thereafter the War of Independence in July (1802–1803), the last siege of the revolutionary struggle. James states, "I will read again from Pamphile de Lacroix: No one observed [but he did] that in the new insurrection of San Domingo, it was not the avowed chiefs who gave the signal for revolt but obscure creatures."[78] Of these "obscure creatures" and their instrumentality to history proper, James acknowledges their erasure from the annals of history and his complicity in their effacement when documenting the Haitian Revolution. He states,

> The burning of Moscow by the Russians (you know that story, *War and Peace* by Tolstoy), how Napoleon carried his army there and fought, but the Russian army retreated before him and the population wouldn't join him. They burnt Moscow and that fills the histories of the time. I say they were anticipated and excelled by the blacks and mulattoes of the island of San Domingo. And then comes something which was shameful. The records are there. I should have put it all in. I didn't. I mean, if I were writing this book today, I would have page after page of that. And I say the records are there, I had read them, but . . .[79]

The shame James feels is not his alone. When he states what Lacroix perceived—"No one observed [but [de Lacroix] did] that in the new insurrection of San Domingo, it was not the avowed chiefs who gave the signal for revolt but obscure creatures"—he offers an intriguing aside reminding his contemporary audience of their mutual willingness to look past the "obscured creatures" in their moment. He states: "(They were not only in San Domingo obscure. They were obscure in Watts, they were obscure in Detroit, they were obscure creatures in Newark, they were obscure creatures in San Francisco, they were obscure creatures in Cleveland, they were obscure creatures in Harlem.) . . . Is that clear?"[80] This would not be "clear" to James's audience. For like James in 1938 and like readers of this monograph today, most have long been conditioned to unsee the legitimacy of Black dissidence, no less the agency of Black peoples. James wants them to recognize the validity of Black protestations no matter the form, be they led by the obscure or the respected. And this is where his lectures depart from his famed history: he prioritizes those readily absented and reorients revolutionary striving so that they take precedence over the Louvertures of a revolutionary moment.

The Black Jacobins is not easily laid to rest, however. It did not just write Louverture as the Revolution, but it wrote Black history and positively expressed Black humanity. James was not immediately aware of the importance of this aspect of his work. In the first of his *The Black Jacobins* lectures, "How I Wrote *The Black Jacobins*," he writes that the book was written so "that people should think about the African revolution and get their minds right about what was bound to happen in Africa."[81] Yet in the second lecture, "*The Black Jacobins* and Black Reconstruction: A Comparative Analysis," he reveals that an underlying impetus for the text was:

> to demonstrate that we [Black peoples] had a history, and in that history there were men who were fully able to stand comparison with great men of that period. That was my aim. I wasn't so conscious of it when I was writing, but now when I reread that passage [from *The Black Jacobins*—"By a phenomenon often observed, the individual leadership responsible for this unique achievement was almost entirely the work of a single man—Toussaint L'Overture. Beauchamp in the *Biographie Universalle* calls Toussaint L'Overture one of the most remarkable men of a period rich in remarkable men.—], I see that was my aim.[82]

Because this was his intention, James unconsciously wrote Black history as Black men's history. The story of the Revolution necessarily became the story of Louverture because James set out to prove Black male worth above and beyond the fact that Black history exists.

He states in his second lecture that "I set out to prove it. Dr. Du Bois didn't," and references W. E. B. Dubois's refusal to prove the human and historical worth of Black men (and women) in his foreword to *Black Reconstruction*.[83] Dubois wrote knowing that ordinary Black people had history and made history. He did not offer "facts" about how "the Negro was [not] a distinctly inferior creation," James acknowledges that he did just that in *The Black Jacobins*, an admission that is not simply about Dubois's ready acceptance of Black people's agency but it is also about how easily Dubois could see that Black men too are active agents of history.[84] If James needed to prove what Dubois knew, it is because his colonial context made it difficult for him to see as clearly as Dubois since it denied him a masculinity that Dubois's colonial context never questioned. Black men are supermen in the US colonial imaginary, virile and predatory in their masculine essence.[85] In the English colonial imaginary, Black men are beasts before men and removed from masculinity. The Victorian discourse that governed English imperial thought during James's youth held that "black masculinity [was] the real essence of blackness [and] black men more so than women [were considered] closest to the savagery of Africa."[86] Literary scholar Belinda Edmondson discusses the profound influence of Victorian thought on renowned male Anglophone Caribbean writers like James, as well as V. S. Naipaul, George Lamming, and Derek Walcott in her study of migrant women's fiction, *Making Men: Gender, Literary Authority, and Women's Writing in Caribbean Narrative*.[87] She writes that each of these acclaimed writers held deeply rooted "Victorian sensibilities" and produced "oppositional discourse to Britain [that was] marked by a utilization of a specifically English vision of what constitutes intellectual production."[88] Victorian thought not only "speculat[ed] on whether men could be 'made' out of black West Indian men," but it deemed "intellectual labor [to be] the realm of 'real' men, 'gentlemen,' middle-class / upper-class Englishmen."[89] This yielded anticolonial literature from the likes of James (and others) that sought to prove the manliness and thus worth of Black men.[90]

The Black Jacobins was born from this impulse: it writes back to the Victorian thought that questioned James's manhood because of his race and that likewise disparaged Louverture. Victorian historian

James Anthony Froude, for instance, needlessly invokes Louverture in his 1888 travelogue, *The English in the West Indies, or the Bow of Ulysses*, writing "there has been . . . no hero [in the West Indies] unless philonegro enthusiasm can make one of Toussaint."[91] This statement says less about Louverture and more about how fearful Froude was of retributive Black resistance, writing as he was in the wake of the 1865 Morant Bay Rebellion in Jamaica.[92] James approached Louverture and the history of the Revolution through the burdensome weight of Victorian ideas of masculinity and writing. He accordingly wrote the Revolution using Louverture as a platform to articulate a desired masculine sense of self, miming how Victorian writers used Black men to articulate their supremacist masculinity. Froude's anti-Black reading of Louverture is one example: it distills that when racist white men think about Louverture (and the Haitian Revolution, in turn), they all too often think about their racism and its "bothersome" side effects—the loss of white power and the rise of justified Black resistance (e.g., 1865 Morant Bay Rebellion in Jamaica). Conversely, when Black Caribbean men, such as James, think about Louverture, they think about their marginalization among white men and the enforced racialized abjection of their people. Both are figuring Louverture for their particular ends and using him to validate an idea of human worth and historical consequence that ultimately remains the purview of white Eurocentric men. Louverture, in this respect, is unseen. He is absented like the *Ginen* revolutionists he overshadows because his Blackness is unable to denote his humanity.

The white supremacist logic that necessitates reasoning Louverture through an idea of the human that is white and male would suggest that he mimed white men when carrying out his revolutionary deeds. Yet Louverture was no mimic of white Western European men. Among the Napoléons and Thomas Jeffersons of the Age of Revolution, Louverture's greatness is distinct quite simply because his is not predicated on self-aggrandizing warmongering and white supremacist violence. Louverture's greatness—in truth, the greatness of all Haitian revolutionaries, known and unknown—lies in a refusal of the Western European cultural practice of seizing foreign lands and enslaving foreign peoples for personal power. It lies in the refusal to regard some people as human and others as not. James knows this and yet he still writes Louverture white in *The Black Jacobins*, that is, along the limited gender and human lines outlined by Wynter. Recall that she states, "from the very origin of the modern world, of the Western world system, there were never simply men and women"; there were "whites who see themselves as true men, true women, while their Others, the untrue men/women, were now labeled as indio/indias (Indians) and as negros/Negras."[93] The James who wrote *The Black Jacobins* takes readers along a narrative path that does not question this logic; and still, this James remains useful to defend against Bell, Girard, and other prejudicial readings of Louverture's "personal ambition."[94]

James's intent was to disobey the white colonial order and inspire others to do so as well. His rebellious intent accounts for why he wanted readers of the history to "think about the African revolution and get their minds right about what was bound to happen in Africa."[95] This ask, "to think about," is important, since it situates readers within a discursive context shaped by an "analytical maneuvering" that Black studies scholar Katherine McKittrick argues is specific to the lived realities of Black histories of being, which "dwell on and think about the questioning and overturning of normative systems of knowledge."[96] In this respect, *The Black Jacobins* radically departs from racist engagements with the general because it is expressive of Black knowing: James knows that Black peoples know what is best for them. He understands that they "know more than the abjectness that is projected upon [them]. . . . [They] know. [They] know [them]selves."[97] Because this is clear to him, he recognizes how attention to Louverture's "personal ambition" is one way to write him as not having the ability to think, to know, and to be on terms emergent from his own personhood and experience of existence.[98] He knows that this reading is epistemically violent and telling of an a priori dismissal of Louverture's humanity, which is to say, he knows that these readings are racialized to make a preferred way of being in the world appear as *the only way of being in the world*.

James wrote *The Black Jacobins* because he wanted more than the world as the West and though he tells the story of the Revolution as the story of Louverture, it is a tale whose radical significances remain vibrant because *Ginens* are present in absence: they are the unthought that makes Louverture legible as a collective symbol of Black liberation.

James acknowledges in his 1963 book about cricket, *Beyond the Boundary*, that "the last stones ... of a pyramid," which constituted his political thinking, included the "Matthew Bondman[s] and the ... Arthur Jones" of the Caribbean, Black cricketers whose poverty placed them at the margins of respectable Trinidadian society.[99] James's recognition of the importance of these persons to his thought invites consideration of "a key aspect of his political thought," writes Black studies scholar Minkah Makalani, "specifically, the possibility he saw in art and, equally important, the place of Africa in his thinking."[100] Makalani's reading of *Beyond the Boundary* details how Africa figured prominently for James despite his Eurocentrism.[101] It helps situate the Louverture of *The Black Jacobins* as a still forming ideation for James, one that is telling of his latent interest in how the Caribbean folk transformed Western European traditions into something new and distinctly Caribbean because of their African "lifeworlds."[102] Makalani writes,

> central to [the] practice [of making that which is foreign new and natal] is how art taps into and expands on a popular consciousness—the virtuoso's ability to shape national consciousness and convey popular desires. The cricket of a Bondman, a John, or a Sobers thus subverts the very social hierarchies attendant to coloniality. These artists—the ne'er-do-well, the African Maroons who originated the Caribbean nation—have pioneered into the regions Caesar never knew: coloniality as the very condition of possibility for modernity.[103]

This is the still forming idea that lies at the heart of *The Black Jacobins* and is why Louverture's literacy, which will be discussed momentarily, gets so much attention in the history. For James of *The Black Jacobins* as the James of *Beyond the Boundary*, the Caribbean artist—like the Caribbean intellectual—resists by knowing and revamping the traditions granted to them. That they do this, is because ordinary Black peoples are artists of thought: the "analytical maneuverings" needed to thrive within the anti-Black strictures shaping their lives have given them the creative means to invent and transform inherited schools of thought.

James knew this when writing *The Black Jacobins*, but he lost the plot when attributing the artistry that is the Black popular pursuit of knowledge and the transformation of Western traditions to Louverture alone. Indeed, he lost the plot when attributing Louverture's quest for knowledge as a search for Western knowledge only. *Ginens* are present in James's intention to showcase that Black people not only know themselves, but they are also artists of thought since their knowledge of self and what the world could be fuels Black liberation efforts, past and present. *Ginens*, in other words, are the unthought he thinks with and past, to write his imagining of Haitian Revolutionary history. Every hagiographic praise of Louverture reading names *Ginens*. Every sentence detailing and bemoaning how Louverture's enlightenment was his downfall names *Ginens* because they make James's enthusiastic treatment of Louverture's literacy knowable as a collective practice of Black resistance. They give his depiction of Louverture meaning and relevance beyond Western traditions, beyond the colony. The critique that follows keeps that relevance in mind while deconstructing James's youthful characterization of Louverture as an enlightened French Europhile. This characterization is worth discussing and critiquing because it continues to shape how scholars and artists conceive Louverture, notwithstanding James's own revision and notwithstanding how this characterization has deleteriously affected conceptions of the Revolution and Caribbean anticolonial liberation.

Louverture, the Man

To write Louverture as an enlightened figure, James absents Louverture's *Ginen* cultural life and prioritizes his individual person instead, which he stresses is exceptional. He frames Louverture's decision to join the Revolution at forty-five years of age as telling of his scholastic pedigree and emphasizes his singularity, when writing, "like so many men of better education than the rank and file, he lacked their boldness at the moment of action and waited to see how things would go" before joining the Revolution.[104] Louverture did not "lack their boldness"; he lacked their free-ness to act without consideration of a white benefactor (i.e., his former master, Bayon de Libertat). Rather than consider this, James chooses to cast the time it takes Louverture to openly act in the Revolution through the bias of his own scholastic pretensions.

He assumes that education results in a reticence to act and uses this assumption to encourage his readers to imagine that a great distance separates Louverture from lesser educated captives. He augments this distance when writing that Louverture "had exceptional opportunities, and both in mind and body was far beyond the average slave. Slavery dulls the intellect and degrades the character of the slave. There was nothing of that dullness or degradation in Toussaint."[105] James insists that his readers know Louverture as exceptional and writes Louverture to prove what he need not: Louverture's human worth, historical consequence, and his own, in turn.

The sweeping sentimentality of the aforementioned quote and the quote that follows underscores how James was writing himself as he was writing Louverture. He notes,

> Out of the chaos in San Domingo that existed then and for years to follow, he would lay the foundations of a Negro State that lasts to this day. From the moment he joined the revolution he was a leader, and moved without serious rivalry to the first rank. We have clearly stated the vast impersonal forces at work in the crisis of San Domingo. But men make history, and Toussaint made the history that he made because he was the man he was.[106]

Louverture makes history because he is a man exceptionally; he makes Black history *history*. James does not write this, but he certainly implies this because of the awe with which he writes his imagined Louverture into being. Like him, this Louverture is a reader and a man destined for greatness because he is a reader. He writes, "He had read Caesar's Commentaries, which had given him some idea of politics and the military art and the connection between them. Having read and re-read the long volume by the Abbé Raynal, on the East and West Indies [*Philosophical and Political History of the Establishment and Commerce of the Europeans in the Two Indies*], he had a thorough grounding in the economics and politics, not only of San Domingo, but of all the great empires of Europe which were engaged in colonial expansion and trade."[107] Did Louverture not read the fear of white colonists in the 1740s when Makandalism took root in the North? Did he not read the boldness of the free and captive beholden to Makandalism and gain awareness of the potentiality of

Black power politics? Surely the atmospheric change in the North that inspired more and more captives to fight versus take flight was read also; as were the songs, proverbs, and Vodou chants that deepened the resistant revolve of his community. Louverture read many cultural texts, most that were more *Ginen* in essence then Western. Yet James prioritizes the latter to show how Louverture epitomizes and exceeds the cultural standards of the West. He therefore writes him as coming into revolutionary consciousness by repeatedly reading Raynal's declaration that "'a courageous chief only is wanted. Where is he?,'" to underscore his radicalization by way of Westernization, a move that also distills how Louverture is a man's man—of the English West and the West, more broadly, being Caribbean.[108]

Literacy establishes Louverture's manliness and has cemented his ubiquitous association with the Enlightenment in literary studies of the Revolution. Charles Forsdick writes, "Details of the then Toussaint Breda's education, acquisition of Latin and exposure to the (in this context, neatly prophetic) writings of l'Abbe Raynal have been repeated so often that they have achieved the status of orthodoxy, providing a teleological explanation of the ex-slave's rise to prominence."[109] Daut terms this "orthodoxy" the "Enlightenment literacy narrative of the Haitian Revolution," since it "helped spread the idea that Louverture was inspired to rebellion through his Enlightenment education."[110] Raynal's text was popular among Leftists of the French Revolution since it radically prophesied the rise of a "Black Spartacus." Louverture is commonly read as having responded to Guillaume-Thomas [l'Abbe] Raynal's call in light of a 1799 French news story covering his appreciation of the text and his own superb mediatic abilities.[111] Deborah Jenson writes, "whether through personal inclination or purely strategic navigation of discursive identities [Louverture] drew heavily on Enlightenment and sentimentalist tones and values" to offensively and defensively enable the very idea of Haitian independence; for Jenson, he was the ultimate spin doctor and would have likely weaponized a story like the narrative of him having read Raynal to his benefit.[112] Srinivas Aravamudan writes, in turn, that "if Toussaint never really read the Black Spartacus passage, Haitian historiography would have needed to invent an equivalent incident," since it "both confirm[s] and undermine[s] established truths" while illuminating "a world turned upside down" in *Tropicopolitans: Colonialism and Agency, 1688–1804*.[113] James's depiction of Louverture reading Raynal's text has been instrumental to figuring the general as radicalized because of his Enlightenment education; however, his reading of Raynal, Diderot, and the Encyclopedists also serves as an imagined point of commonality between James and Louverture.[114]

If James's "tone reaches the highest panegyrical levels when Toussaint's literacy is discussed," as Paul B. Miller notes, it is because James is writing him as a gentleman, more aptly as an Englishman.[115] Edmondson writes that in nineteenth-century English intellectual discourse "intellectual labor is [executed by] 'gentlemen,' [who by definition are "real men" being] middle-class/upper-class Englishmen. For nonwhite, non-English men [to be men capable of governing themselves and independent polities they] must state their case as gentlemen, which means they must, in essence be 'made' into Englishmen." To be made into an Englishman requires outperforming "predetermined" ideas of Black manhood held by Victorian thinkers, who conceded that Black men had the potential to be men should they strive to be scholars.[116] Yet, as Edmondson writes, Victorian thinkers thought they were too "lazy and docile" to stay the course and become scholars.[117] James's Louverture is neither lazy nor docile. He is a man of thought and action, and his reading materials exemplify this. They show a man destined to live free and to lead others toward a free existence because of his commitment to thinking with Western Europe's great thinkers.

As a man who is like an Englishman, Louverture is great because he is enlightened and he is enlightened, in turn, because he reads and reads well. James thus figures him as having the intellectual capacity to recognize the importance of the French Revolution, which, for James, broke with imperialist conventions of the West. He writes Louverture's admiration of the French Revolution as unyielding, citing his assertion that the French revolutionary struggle has "enlightened Europeans" who now "love and we[ep] over" Blacks.[118] This admiration is the result of Louverture's manliness, of having improved himself through his reading of Enlightenment thinkers. However, this improvement comes at a cost since it occasions Louverture's tragic flaw as interpreted by James since it results in an Aristotelian "hamartia," a "total miscalculation of the constituent events" of the Haitian Revolutionary moment.[119] James writes, "If he was convinced that San Domingo would decay without the benefits of the French connection, he was equally certain that slavery could never be restored. Between these two certainties, he, in whom penetrating vision and prompt decision had become second nature, became the embodiment of vacillation."[120] Louverture is a tragic figure precisely because his vacillations are tied to his Westernization, which prompted his radicalization but limited how far he could act against France. James thus writes that his "failure was the failure of enlightenment."[121] Literary critic Kara M. Rabbitt argues that James's use of classic Aristotelian drama's attention to the rise and fall of a hero creates the conditions in which readers are "made to feel . . . the inevitability of [Louverture's errors], . . . [specifically] their tragic nature."[122] This "inevitability" and James's deliberate relation of Louverture to the tragic heroes "Prometheus, Hamlet, Lear, Phèdre, [and] Ahab," mythologizes Louverture, granting the general the universal salience of the aforementioned tragic subjects.[123] He exceeds the Englishman, in this respect, and is man, an exemplar by which to read the human experience. James carries Louverture to new heights of exception through his characterization of him as a tragic figure of enlightenment: he is not only a cut above the rest in the revolutionary struggle, but he is singular among the greatest of Western European men mythologized in tragic drama.

James's emphasis on Louverture's uncommon educational pedigree, his saccharine praise of his literacy, and his concerted effort to make Louverture a tragic hero, underscores how much he projects on to Louverture his own positionality as an educated Black man living under colonial domination. Implicit in his characterization of Louverture as a man who is like an Englishman yet exceeds Englishman-ness being an exemplar of man is the latent presence of the educated Black colonial man. This post-enlightenment masculine figure is resigned to know little of his Black past and present cultural realities and yet is well versed in Western Europe's contemporary happenings and its past events. He is a figure James knows well and that he admits in his second 1971 lecture on *The Black Jacobins* he unconsciously had in mind when seeking to prove the existence of Black history. Yet little about this figure evokes Louverture or the *Ginen* peoples who supported him. Louverture was not in competitive dialogue with a framework for being in which he is only a "distinctly inferior creation," to quote James in his second lecture.[124] The figure James superimposes on him *is*, however.

Accordingly, while James's Louverture is clearly remarkable and intelligent, so much of his intelligence and exception is proffered as necessarily indebted to knowledge of Western European economic practices and intellectual traditions. It is as if Louverture asked for permission to be and thus sought the tutelage of France. It is as if he had no sense of self outside of France or the West. It is as if he were not *Ginen*. Louverture of *Ayiti Ginen* is absented from the reader's purview, even as the genius that prompted Louverture to manipulate Enlightenment thought for his political gain also prompted him to manipulate Vodou and Makandalism for his political benefit, which is to say, the mythos that he created about himself relied on many cultural texts, not just those provided by France and other Western European countries. Absent from James's figuration is the Louverture who aligned himself with specific *lwa* (their colors and customs) when speaking publicly. Missing too is how this association assisted his efforts to fabricate the supernatural abilities so many in his moment ascribed to him.[125] Trouillot writes that "Even while he was crushing Vodou, . . . the rumor ran through Saint Domingue that Toussaint was a *makandal*. That is, he was everywhere at once."[126] This rumor existed because Louverture used "religion (both Christian *and* Vodou) to disguise [his] political power as a magical power, a special power that supernatural forces (either God or the spirits) gave the uncle so he could run the country."[127] Notwithstanding how Catholic Louverture professed to be, he "unquestionably hijacked Vodou's subversive capacities for his own political ends" writes Mariana F. Past; and because he did so, Louverture as "a *makandal*" is known readily in Haiti, serving as the inspiration for François Duvalier's draconian political theater and that of others.[128] Yet for James these cultural aspects of Louverture are negligible as is the pre-revolutionary influence of Makandalism on Louverture's political thought; and "the records are there" just as the records of the "2,000 leaders" James writes out of his history of the Revolution.[129]

James refused to acknowledge the aspects of Louverture that are identifiably Haitian since these are the attributes of a "distinctly inferior creation." He sought to prove Louverture's worth and his own and curated a Louverture so solitary in his excellence, so exceptionally brilliant that he unwittingly availed his remarkable work to the abstracting impulse of white colonial logic, which centers whiteness and white masculinity only. Accordingly, for some readers of *The Black Jacobins*, Louverture is not merely a champion of Black freedom; he is the emblem of white entrepreneurship. Ben Horowitz, a prominent venture capitalist, implies the latter as he has cited *The Black Jacobins* as his favorite book on leadership.[130] He has done so "without any self-consciousness about James's Marxism," as historian Alyssa Goldstein Sepinwall notes, or awareness of his Black radical politics.[131] According to Horowitz, "Louverture is a model for CEOs, who should learn about the Haitian general's exemplary leadership skills by reading James's classic study."[132] This interpretation is hardly James's point; but it is an idea that can be gleamed from his work however un-nuanced it is, because of James's masculinist presentation of Louverture as great *like* the great white men of his moment. What is alarming about the misappropriation of *The Black Jacobins* is not the existence of such a gross reduction, but how nuanced reflections on the text and Louverture's portrayal can still manage to fix Louverture and the Revolution he names into the narrow parameters of the white colonial imagination. Louverture, the dispirited neocolonial puppet, becomes the figuration disseminated by Jamaican anthropologist David Scott in his engagement with James in *Conscripts of Modernity: The Tragedy of Colonial Enlightenment*, a text that is worth discussing for how it implicitly invites readers to view Louverture in Bell and Girardian fashion, as beholden to his personal ambitions.

Dead Conversations

Conscripts of Modernity is written with the Caribbean in mind, specifically the state of the region following the turbulent anticolonial movements of the twentieth century. The text is haunted by the specter of the Grenadian Revolution (1979–1983), which occasions Scott's disenchantment with anticolonial revolutionary politics. According to Scott, the radical intellectual leadership of the Grenadian struggle failed to follow through with its populist approach to governance. It turned, instead, to a vanguardist method and proved as willing to turn to violence to suppress dissent as the prior Grenadian administration, Eric Gairy's dictatorship. In an interview with the Jamaican cultural theorist Stuart Hall, Scott underscores the importance of these events, stating, "The 1970s was my generation's short decade of hope and expectation and longing. . . . The 1980s brings this lurching to a close with the assassination of Walter Rodney in January 1980; the defeat of Michael Manley in October of the same year; and the implosion of the Grenada Revolution in 1983."[133] He continues, stating "I am old enough to have believed in the 1970s, but I am also young enough to be skeptical of the mythology of the narrative of emancipation and to be able to cast an impassive eye on its rhetorical structure. This is the generational vantage from which I come at *Conscripts of Modernity*."[134] When Scott reads *The Black Jacobins* in *Conscripts of Modernity*, he does so to critique how Caribbean studies and postcolonial studies scholars misinterpret a present charged, in his estimation, with the failure of anticolonial revolution versus the success of anticolonial overcoming.[135]

Scott maintains that a longing for anticolonial overcoming or total revolution (an interpretive mode he terms "romance") ought to give way to the realization that political life is not a stable environment of truth and principle, but it is an ambiguous and ever wavering place of unexpected happenings (a mode he terms "tragedy").[136] A discursive transition from romance to tragedy will presumably help scholars see modern power as constructive and modern political life as defined by tragic reversals and contingency, versus a mounting progression toward anticolonial triumph. Scholarship should therefore assess how the formerly colonized are made, like Louverture, into conscripts of modernity: persons whose personal choices and revolutionary actions are enabled by Western modernity and shaped, in turn, by the constructive influence of white colonial power. The latter sets the terms and conditions for how all action is undertaken and conceived. Accordingly, just as Louverture bartered liberation for freedom, when choosing to "secure the economic (necessity) over the risk of the political (freedom)" through the autocratic preservation of plantation industry, Scott argues so too have many twentieth-century Caribbean states' people. They have ensured that Caribbean peoples experience independence as a new kind of political enchainment in the wake of the regional anticolonial movements of the twentieth century.

Scott is uncritical of the portrait James authors of Louverture. He even furthers Louverture's exception by suggesting that he is the exemplar for twentieth-century Caribbean leadership and somehow the sole arbitrator of Haiti's economic and political future, having secured "necessity over . . . freedom." To support his argument, he uses the "seven new paragraphs" James adds to the 1963 edition of *The Black Jacobins* that detail Louverture's "tragic flaw," and he also draws from George Steiner's literary articulation of tragedy in *The Death of Tragedy*.[137] Tragedy is the highest art form for Steiner and one driven by persons of noble bearing. Because it is darkly aristocratic in substance, he argues that it is incompatible with the democratic leanings that guide the modern moment. Steiner has "mistaken the representation for reality, the map for the territory," to borrow from Wynter, as the democratic aspirations that guide modernity are not the same as the actual colonial realities of modernity.[138] Notwithstanding this, Steiner posits that tragedy cannot take root in modern drama, particularly one emergent in a staunchly liberal democratic moment, because it posits no resolution to injustice. Steiner's understanding of "tragedy underscores the hopelessness of our attempts to remake the world."[139] This reading cannot be divested from how justice has been implemented and thought as "just us" since 1492, for white Western Europeans and North Americans alone. Scholars should be wary of colonial interpretations of tragedy as they readily obfuscate the human agency at play ensuring that there can be no successful "attempts to remake the world." These interpretations overly illuminate the sense that human agency is insignificant to the contingencies created by politics and thus the partisan pursuits of human beings. Another life has always been possible, and tragedy has been too conveniently used to obscure this truth.

Scott writes without awareness of this possibility in *Conscripts of Modernity*. Heeding an articulation of tragedy that is beholden to one culture's localized vision of existence, indeed which takes this vision as universal, Scott articulates a tragic ethos for the long colonial present based solely on the persons at the helm of postcolonial inequity—the "brown middle class," the very persons Louverture, with his vacillations, seemingly exemplifies.[140] By positing a particular (in the modern ruling and intellectual Caribbean class) for a whole (the modern Caribbean experience and its disparate persons, more broadly), Scott seizes onto James's figuration of Hamlet as an embodiment of "'a new type of human being'" in the modern intellectual.[141] This is a modern subject for whom "thought *is* his conception of action" and for whom ". . . the demands of social responsibility, on the one hand, and the individual commitment to freedom of thought, on the other . . . is at once poignantly conscious and unmasterable."[142] Seemingly paralyzed by thought and historical circumstance, Scott interprets James as creating in Louverture a Hamlet-like figure.[143] As the "first and greatest of the West Indians" and thus the archetype of the modern Caribbean man of letters, Louverture, for Scott, bequeathed to all Caribbean subjects of similar intellectual and political ilk a tragic inheritance, and by proxy he gifted to the poorly educated or uneducated a legacy of eternal insignificance. Upon reading Scott's devastating indictment of Louverture and Caribbean anticolonial revolution, one cannot help but ask, "why should [Scott] adopt the restricted view that Toussaint's (the intellectual's) tragedy remains the fundamental story of our time" to quote literary scholar Chris Bongie?[144]

Scott's reading warrants the additional query: does not unprovoked deference to James's figuration of Louverture as Hamlet-like continue the undue valorization of the great men (read white men) of Western culture? Bongie writes, "we find a lingering 'romantic' attachment to the idea of 'great man'" in Scott's book.[145] One could take this attachment as a desire to further James's articulation of Louverture as an educated Black colonial man akin to the great white man of history. This furtherance grounds Scott's deployment of tragedy in a masculinist tradition of writing Caribbean resistance that is diametrically opposed to a *Ginen* reading of Louverture as constituted and imperiled by the captive collective. It also absents from thought the speculative investment in thinking with similarly situated others beyond the white colonial order that *Ginen* peoples harnessed to wield the immense political power they had during and after the Revolution. There is no decolonial praxis here that can hold space for *Ginen* resistance. There is no consideration of the efforts of *Ginen* women and men against white colonial power; and there is no possibility of a decolonial understanding of tragedy.

Tragedy does not have to serve as the literary-philosophical attendant of white colonial rule. Athenian tragedy's origins lie in subjection: it was used as a tool of political suppression against Athenian women and their mourning practices. And yet it nonetheless gave voice to the displaced and un-see-able Athenian women (and barbarian others) who were banned from existing freely in the polis, as both are obsessively present in tragedies via the chorus. They are visible and yet dismissible as peripheral to the plot when read by modern readers fixed on characters of exceptional standing.[146] When grounded in its historical specificity, a gendered understanding of tragedy is particularly adept at calling to critical awareness the presence of absented persons and epistemologies that challenge the one-sided exchange of epistemic influence through which one culture wholly conscripts another. Tragedy, in this respect, does not have to be used as an obfuscating instrument of modern colonial power; it can signify beyond the colony.

Scholars of the Caribbean, Black studies, and postcolonial studies should be suspicious of literary paradigms that function as universal templates, applicable to all and yet concerned with a tiny proportion of a select few. The questions scholars need ask of the long colonial present must not simply concern the constructive nature of modern power as that draws them only to the Louvertures of the anticolonial record; *but* they ought to also examine how in spite of the positive influence of modern power there still existed (and still exist) persons emblematic of "other futures, of projects not realized and ideas rarely remembered," to borrow from Sibylle Fischer.[147] In both James's and Scott's works the captives of Saint Domingue are bit players, inconsequentially vital to the efforts of Louverture. And yet they, for a lack of "enlightenment," never wavered in their efforts for total liberation, nor did other island-born members of the Revolution's vanguard. Bongie astutely contends that Scott "erase[s] from consideration a range of other, perhaps equally flawed, responses to the 'tragedy of colonial enlightenment'—be it those of less Hamletian leaders, such as Dessalines . . . or the 'colonial bureaucrats' whose very existence is inseparable from 'marginal disputes,' scribes like [Jean Louis] Vastey," secretary of Haitian Revolutionary general turned King of northern Haiti, Henry Christophe.[148] With respect to the captives themselves, Rabbitt is the first to draw critical attention to how James's dramatic figuration of Louverture upstages the masses he, as a Marxist, privileges in principle. She writes: "His figuring of Toussaint into a tragic archetype, important for his development of the morals to be learned from the 'story,' precludes an in depth analysis of the 'lesser figures'—the vital 'chorus'—who surrounded and defined him."[149] The "story" James wishes to convey, and Scott by proxy, about anticolonial possibility is made universal through his diminution of the "chorus" just as the story of the West and North would not be possible without the diminution of the global south. This was not James's intention and yet Scott writes as if it is, denuding the text of its radical impulse and Louverture of his long-standing revolutionary consequence: indeed, what good is remembering Louverture if he has bequeathed to Caribbean peoples the very leaders working hand in hand with Western European powers and North American imperialists to undermine equity and freedom in the region? What good is remembering Louverture and the Revolution he names if he is little more than a figure whose vacillations bolster Western Europe's imperial ascendancy, that is, if the salient questions and answers he prompts about the long colonial present are structured to speak to Western Europe's narrative of imperial self?

What is un-generative about postcolonial query and scholarship in Caribbean studies is not the romantic longing for an anticolonial overcoming long deferred, but the persistent need to center Western European cultural thought and its paradigms for being when assessing or imagining the prospect of anticolonial revolution in this present. *Ginens* thought their own epistemology into being by refusing to cede thought to the French and other Western European colonizers. They knew that they could think for themselves. Surely scholars can imagine them thusly and also think thusly. The centrality of Western European cultural praxis to not only the sociopolitical efforts of Caribbean leaders but to Caribbean thinkers of the anticolonial and later (post)colonial present has produced dead conversations: discussions mitigated by and bound to the conceptually dead (i.e., un-generative or anti-speculative) dictates of a masculinist idea of the great man of historical worth, for whom few among the racialized peoples in the Americas can embody or seek to emblematize. As "sovereign peoples" with their own ideas of existence, their horizon for being has not exclusively entailed mimicking the Western colonial project (its leaders and ideals) but seeking its decisive end.[150] Yes, leaders have proven ineffective, but does that necessitate calling for the end of all speculative academic engagements with anticolonial overcoming, or worse yet, implicit cynicism concerning the very possibility of popular attempts at anticolonial revolution? Anticolonial movements, like the antislavery struggles of the past, have their ebbs and their flows: they do not end because changes in law and human conduct lessen the burden of anti-Black violence or amplify the power of the white colonial order. They end when liberation is at long last achieved, which is to say, what appears as an end is likely an ebb toward the movement to come. Furthermore, political leaders are poor representatives of this reality because their horizon is the now of their influence and dominance; the narrowness of their political vision tethers them to a reformist engagement with the present, since prevailing notions of influence and dominance often have a Western European antecedent. Louverture's life exemplifies this. By contrast, anticolonial overcoming is the project of the absented for whom the ever-present future is the now. In this respect, their demands for change in the present are charged with the potentiality of a distinct lived existence evident in past struggles like the Haitian Revolution. When Louverture is figured in masculinist fashion by Scott, both the vast speculative reach of the Haitian Revolution and Louverture's own life are constricted by a discursive whiteness that cannot render his personal struggle for autonomy legible nor that of the Black liberation struggle (in his moment and today), which is scripted by the colonizing logic of Western cultural thought as having no foreseeable future. This, to reiterate, was not James's intention, but it is Scott's, who misappropriates James's articulation of Louverture (an educated Black colonial man akin to the great white man of history) to establish his own Louverture, a figure cobbled by the constructiveness of white colonial power and made the tragic Black figurehead of the indomitability of the white supremacist West.

To extend the query first asked at the onset of this chapter, where is Louverture in the Caribbean cultural imaginary? The only answer is that he is quite simply not there. By way of conclusion, I end with a reading of Glissant's play, *Monsieur Toussaint*, a drama which addresses the sterile ideas produced about Louverture in Caribbean cultural thought. In the preface to the play's first edition, Glissant acknowledges the importance of James's reading of the Revolution to his work.[151] Glissant also cites the significance of Aimé Césaire's 1961 book, *Toussaint Louverture: The French Revolution and the Colonial Problem*, a text that he finds is "imbued with a tragic sense of [Louverture's] revolutionary destiny."[152] In Césaire's history of the Revolution, he reflectively addresses what he considers as Louverture's rewriting of French colonial republicanism and treats, in turn, the possible political state of existence this reconceptualization might have provided Haiti. In this respect, James and Césaire produce very similar portrayals of Louverture grounded in an enlightened French liberal democratic sensibility, the former offering a narrative of masculinist overcoming and tragic flaw and the latter providing a narrative of heroic sacrifice for the future of Haiti; no matter that Louverture, himself, insists that he was taken by force from Saint Domingue.[153] Both James and Césaire situate Louverture as great because he was as excellent, if not better, at French political and intellectual praxis than the French. Each, accordingly, uses Louverture to offer a masculinist iteration of Caribbean resistance predicated on Louverture's easy signification as a great Black man of historic consequence because of his intellectual and cultural proximity to a republicanism that denotes the racial singularity afforded to whiteness.

Glissant complicates these related iterations of Louverture with this play, inviting consideration of the Caribbean cultural imaginary's static investment in one idea of Louverture. And while the play, itself, falls short of writing *Ginens* into presence since the Haitians depicted index a conversation about the Caribbean's discursive relation to white colonial power, versus revealing a distinctly Haitian cultural self; it does show how the canonized idea of Louverture occludes perception of the abolitionist demand of the Haitian Revolution, which was to remake the world outside of the West. Furthermore, the play invites recognition of how classic Caribbean engagements with the Revolution are mediations on Black knowledge or what I have discussed as Black knowing. Specifically, foundational writings studied in this book "dwell on and think about the questioning and overturning of normative systems of knowledge."[154] They take part in an "analytical maneuvering" that is specific to the lived realities of Black histories of being. Because this is their basis, they either over-valorize Western epistemology, under-treat African thought, or simply contrast the two. Glissant showcases the former two (over-valorization and under-appreciation) in his drama. He is helpful in showing how classic Caribbean writing of the Revolution treats knowledge as cultural and thus critical to anticolonial literatures about Haiti's famed revolt.

The play is set in the confines of the cold prison cell that housed Louverture following his deportation to France in 1802. It offers a portrait of a man coming into his opacity or awareness of himself as other. In other words, it shows how Louverture exists as a colonial subject perpetually in translation because of his fidelity to Western ideas of being, ideas that pose as universal. Glissant stresses the colonized's need for difference from the West in *Caribbean Discourse*, writing: "We demand the right to obscurity. Through which our anxiety to have a full existence becomes part of the universal drama of cultural transformation: the creativity of marginalized peoples who today confront the ideal of transparent universality, imposed by the West, with secretive and multiple manifestations of Diversity."[155] "Transparent universality" references the West's long-standing practice of presenting Western colonial culture and its system of knowledge as the culture of all peoples. As such, the transparent universal is a technology of colonial power that claims to know all the world's peoples without actually engaging these peoples. It allows colonizers to talk to themselves since it condemns "communities" of the colonized "to painless oblivion."[156] Colonizers can secure this "oblivion" because the word (the creation of ideas and thought as well as the expression of both) is theirs alone being universal. In the play, Louverture has fallen for the lie that is the West's transparent universal. He must learn to harness a word that speaks to his existence, which requires taking active part in "the drama of creolization."[157] The latter references the aforementioned "drama of cultural transformation," which, for Glissant, is achieved through a people's creative use of the word. He advocates in *Caribbean Discourse* for the "possibility of the Caribbean creating a word that is its own," and he suggests that it is through their seizure of expression and knowledge production that they can engender a word that speaks to their ideas for being, which, in turn, will be liberating.[158] Readers of the drama are made to witness Louverture's journey toward opacity, which Glissant outlines via the competing cultural and ideological interests animating the Revolution. These interests account for the drama's atemporal movement and for how the dead are presented as in constant communication with the living. They continually haunt and torment Louverture for his revolutionary deeds and situate the divide between the enlightened and nonenlightened subjects that ground Caribbean discourse of the Revolution. Accordingly, that which elevates Louverture to the status of icon within Caribbean cultural thought, authored outside of Haiti, is the very thing that draws the rancor of other revolutionary actors.

One such actor, the deceased African rebel leader of historic fact, Macaïa, sarcastically implores Louverture on one occasion to escape from his prison of enlightenment and republicanism. Glissant writes in Macaïa's voice, "Grab the keys. Grab them! You who opened the pathways. But who with all your grand words has been little more than a traitor. Nothing more than a traitor, I tell you! Coachman in the plantation house, look at him, he dozed in the shade of the verandahs. So, from the very start, he longed for his prison. It was waiting for him!"[159] Later, he states offhandedly in a less hostile manner yet with equal disgust: "I tell you, this man has the soul of a republican. He thinks of tomorrow."[160] Macaïa's scornful attention to Louverture's "words" specifically, his republican rhetoric, and his attention to the privileged pre-revolutionary position Louverture held on the plantation as a coachman, immediately directs the viewer to the class and ideological tensions that shape how Louverture has been conceived by Caribbean writers. Imbued with a "republican soul" that shapes what Louverture terms as his "universal faith" in liberal democracy, Louverture is positioned in dramatic relief against the non-republican sensibility of Macaïa and the other dead persons in the play as the two embody opposing cultural epistemologies.

Macaïa is referred to in the play as a "man of the forest," a man who Louverture seeks to move beyond. Louverture sweepingly states, "Forget the forest, the hatred! They mean nothing but sterility. Let us fortify our positions; let us clear the space around us. But let us also get scholars, engineers involved. Knowledge is universal."¹⁶¹ What the Louverture of Glissant's imagining seems to desire is that all persons stand as carbon copies of each other, abstract equals seeking progress through the rejection of an Afro-Caribbean epistemological sensibility. He states at one point "there is no Legba, no Ogoun. There is science and knowledge now," dismissing the Vodou spirits he names.¹⁶² Macaïa responds to his rigid investment in Western notions of being by accepting and owning his difference, "I am a man of the forest. So that means I am anarchistic and sterile. Ah! The time in which I dwell is not the time that takes you forward!"¹⁶³ The differing ideas each holds of existence is telling of Glissant's attempts to point his audience to two differing ideas of how to exist in time. These opposing ideas not only drove Caribbean conceptions of the Haitian Revolutionary struggle (i.e., James and Césaire) but the region's long history of antislavery and anticolonial struggle in the Caribbean. While "[Louverture] thinks of tomorrow," believing that "some day men will know one another, they will weep for the same sorrows" as they make monetary gains through the clearing of space for industry, Macaïa demands attention to the now.¹⁶⁴ He cries out in response to Louverture's enlightened longings, "But today! Today, today, today."¹⁶⁵ Louverture's republican vision is reformist, grounded as it is in an abstract flattening out of difference (evidenced in his use of "men"). Accordingly, he conceives of change in idealistic terms that need not actualize real sociopolitical and socioeconomic transformation based on equity and the disparities that Black peoples have had to experience. Macaïa's insistence, in contrast, on "today" puts forth a decolonial vision invested in an abolitionist engagement with the present. He demands both an improved present and future lived reality.

The enduring demands of a today still shaped by the colonial excess of the past, which Macaïa discloses, call for a revised rendering of how Caribbean writers of the Revolution prefer to imagine Louverture. Glissant thus subjects Louverture to instances of (mis)translation and re-readings from fellow revolutionaries, some of whom are ghosts and others who are projections of spatially distant revolutionary insurgents fighting for Saint Domingue's liberation as Louverture sits in his cell. One instance involves Moyse, a beloved general in the revolutionary moment who was Louverture's adopted nephew. He would be executed by Louverture during the Revolution because of his solidarity with *Ginen* peoples.¹⁶⁶ Moyse iterates his difference from and yet likeness to Louverture and outlines the parameters of the Louverture idealized in canonical Caribbean writing of the Revolution. He states, "I seek the people. You say, 'the people,' I say, 'the disadvantaged.' You say, 'the people,' with your republican high-mindedness; I see only those who weed, cut, and bundle sugarcane. In sackcloth, sweating, their heads turning giddy under the sun. The Republic designated us general and governor. Why, why? There was a beguiling mirror in our officer's gold braid, we got lost in it."¹⁶⁷ Glissant suggests that the iconic Louverture did in fact "get lost in" his "officer's gold braid." Later in the play, Napoléon's chief interrogator dresses down Louverture, stripping him of his regalia as the dead recite the formal pronouncement that made him governor general of Saint-Domingue. It is only after he is symbolically ousted from his role as general in the French Republic and forcibly dressed as the peasant/captive of Saint Domingue that Louverture comes into awareness of his own opacity. It is only then that he understands that he exists in translative mediation, always and already subject to colonial domination. He states to his prison guard: "I write the word 'Toussaint,' Macaïa spells out 'traitor.' I write the word 'discipline,' and Moyse without even a glance at the page shouts 'tyranny.' I write 'prosperity;' Dessalines backs away, he thinks in his heart 'weakness.' No, I do not know how to write."¹⁶⁸

These instances of (mis)translation and re-readings point to a subject facing his lack of transparency. Louverture is not understandable by all and cannot be since he sought to exist within a cultural frame for being that cannot give expression or legitimacy to Macaïa's reasoning or defiance, nor can it express or legitimate Moyse's or Dessalines's. And yet, he wanted persons who sought to exist outside of the universal, who sought to resist its transparency, to see the validity of his inclusive position. By inclusive, I reference Glissant's assertion about "the West['s] secretive and multiple manifestations of Diversity," which, for him, reinforces the singularity and thus purported universality of the West.¹⁶⁹ The West presents diversity and inclusion as assimilation into its culture, as opposed to understanding diversity as "ways of moving and being in the world, and in the word," as Glissant desires, asserts Jonathan B. Monroe.¹⁷⁰

Louverture's republican notion of inclusion is telling of his rendering as a colonized subject who performs a particular kind of writing and reading derived from the popularized ideals of the Enlightenment. This kind of person cannot conceive of cross-cultural relations because there is only one culture worth relating to. He cannot conceive of a relation that takes part in "the drama of creolization" and thus cannot understand human experience through the medium of many cultures and epistemologies.[171] Because a person like this is invested in a transparency he cannot have, he is emblematic of the Black subject's identification with his colonizer, and in the case of Louverture, in particular, this Black subject of French colonial power will never possess the means with which to write himself anew. His self-awareness is mediated through a West that gives him language and philosophies for freedom, but denies him the imaginative autonomy to implement freedom, damning him and his constituents to an uncreative and deferential colonial existence.

Through his deconstructive treatment of the iconic Louverture, popularized by James and Césaire, Glissant proposes ideas that became a central tenet of his Antillean project of cultural and political decolonization: specifically, the task of re-making "the word" to reflect the Caribbean experience and the Black struggle for anticolonial liberation that fundamentally shapes it. He writes in *Caribbean Discourse*, "Our aim is to forge for ourselves . . . a form of expression through which we would consciously face our ambiguities and fix ourselves in the uncertain possibilities of the word made ours."[172] This defiant insistence on the need for Caribbean, and more broadly Black, self-expression is echoed in the documentary, *Édouard Glissant: One World in Relation*. In it, Glissant vocalizes the importance of Columbus's departure for the Black diaspora's liberation, as it is with this departure that a new self-articulated paradigm for being ("multiplicity") is achievable. Glissant never stopped believing in or thinking about Black liberation, much like James, who pursues the prospect of Black liberation with his Haitian Revolutionary work. Yet James never quite resists a hagiographic telling of Louverture's revolutionary deeds in *The Black Jacobins* or his lectures. Louverture remains in both texts an iconic man apart—that is, not a man made by the absented *Ginen* women and men of the Revolution, but the face and governing head of their endeavors.

Recall James's statement concerning Louverture's "personal ambition" in *The Black Jacobins*, "Superficial people have read [Louverture's] career in terms of personal ambition. This letter is their answer. Personal ambition he had. But he accomplished what he did because, superbly gifted, he incarnated the determination of his people never, never to be slaves again."[173] The formerly captive women and men of Saint Domingue are "incarnated" in Louverture, an avatar of their will, notwithstanding Louverture's own insistence that he serves them. Louverture's singular distinction is also echoed in James's lectures via his myopic devaluation of the future emperor of independent Haiti, Dessalines. James states, "Toussaint didn't hurl himself [against the French] because he was a highly civilized creature, and Dessalines hurled himself because he was a 'barbarian.' Dessalines did not have the restraints that Toussaint had, but it was those restraints and the knowledge that helped Toussaint to build the state and the army which Dessalines was able to use."[174] Say what one will of Dessalines, but "barbarian" is far from apropos. This belittling moniker does not describe him but implicitly supports a republican talking point (which originated in Haiti) and a white supremacist talking point (which originated outside of Haiti) about the general's bloodthirsty quest for vengeance.[175] These talking points taint the Revolution with the lie that vengeance is wrong and that vengeance alone and not liberation is the heart of Black revolutionary action. Ultimately, the denigration of Dessalines furthers Louverture's exemplarity, allowing him to emerge again in iconic fashion as a man apart in *The Black Jacobins*, where Louverture is of the Revolution but greater, of the known and unknown soldiers in arms, but not.

Yet even as James cannot resist lionizing Louverture, his shame regarding the absented and their deliberate excision from his history of the Haitian Revolution so as to better prioritize Louverture's impressive life is not his alone and I will not write as if it were. Privileging those seemingly most like the dominant so as to come to see the consequence of Black thought, Black culture, and Black peoples, is the rite of passage of Black scholars and artists writing generatively about Black peoples. What is remarkable about James and *The Black Jacobins*, when read with attention to James's lectures on the book, is the sheer brilliance of his ability to critically reflect and acknowledge he got it wrong. This brilliance extends beyond my discussion of his lectures and history. Raj Chetty's reading of the 1967 play version of *The Black Jacobins* reveals a James who reimagines the history of the Revolution without Louverture and his tragic leadership in favor of the comedic stewardship of Moyse and the masses; this shift, argues Chetty, enables "James['s] trenchant critique of postcolonial African and Caribbean leadership's failure to usher in the postcolonial futures that anticolonialism had imagined;" and it shows how "James . . . retains hope" for these futures via his belief in the coming "emergence of the masses into political and social control."[176] This hope is built into *The Black Jacobins*, which "approaches [the Haitian Revolution] from a profoundly contemporaneous standpoint . . . of anticipated radical change" writes Natalie Melas.[177] James never stops anticipating this change; and his genius shines precisely because he is willing to envision beyond the colony again and again.

The iconic Louverture of Caribbean cultural thought that James made integral to thinking both about the Haitian Revolution and anticolonial liberation, however, remains a problem: this Louverture cannot give rise to the "possibility of the Caribbean creating a word that is its own" through its letters and politics.[178] He not only upholds the Western epistemological framework grounding colonial inequity, but he is lauded precisely because he does so. He is unseen, in this respect, a figure more Western then *Ginen* in mind and being. This leaves scholars of the Caribbean, Haiti, Black studies, and postcolonial studies with one question: if Louverture only speaks to an epistemological framework that sharply contrasts the distinct possibilities for decolonial change that existed in the Haitian Revolutionary moment, then how can any expect to read in him, and in the Haitian Revolution he represents, the liberatory possibilities desired in the revolutionary past and in this long colonial present?

CHAPTER 2

Seen/Unseen

> Depi ane 1492 jis 1791 te rive . . . kè yo tap boule, kè yo tap mande Jistis. Ou kwè nou deja bliye yo?
>
> —Haitixchange User

Who are the Haitian revolutionists guiding scholastic understanding of anticolonial thought and Caribbean liberation? *Ou kwè nou deja bliye yo?* (Can it be that we have already forgotten them?) Who among the Revolution's long cast of heroic figures are the intellectual anchors of scholars of the Haitian Revolution from Caribbean studies, Black studies, postcolonial studies, and Haitian studies? If Louverture, which one? The Louverture imagined by the Trinidadian C. L. R. James, the Jamaican David Scott reading James, or the Martinican Édouard Glissant as discussed in Chapter 1? If Henry Christophe, the Christophe of the Saint Lucian poet-playwright Derek Walcott, in his 1948 play *Henri Christophe: A Chronicle in Seven Scenes*, or the Christophe of the Cuban writer Alejo Carpentier, in his 1949 novella *The Kingdom of This World*? Truth be told, I claim no Louverture or Christophe as imagined by the foundational Caribbean writers studied here. The Louverture who suffered from Hamlet-like vacillations of thought is unrecognizable to me, as is the Louverture who identified with France so much that he could be iconized as the harbinger of the impossibility of anticolonial overcoming. The Christophe whose "orchestrates [and military] uniforms . . . were all the product of a slavery as abominable as" French enslavement is also unfathomable.[1] Equally unbelievable is Walcott's portrayal of Christophe as a Jacobean despot in *Henri Christophe*, a portrayal that is perhaps telling of youthful folly (he wrote the play when a teen). However, there exists the Jean Jacques Dessalines of his drama *The Haitian Earth* (written when middle aged). Víctor Figueroa asserts that Walcott's "Dessalines will not allow . . . inclusion any more than Napoleon."[2] Surely it cannot be that contemporary *Ginens* descended from revolutionists who mimicked colonizers alone. No, the bulk of our ancestors fought for an *otherwise*, for "perspectives and frameworks not based in . . . western rationality . . . but rather in [a] relationality," that could envision their liberation.[3] How then can Hamlet illuminate Louverture? How can the fictional characters of the very people who enslaved *Ginen* captives serve as equivalent comparative replicas for reading Christophe's or Dessalines's post-revolutionary conduct, or that of any revolutionary for that matter?

Louverture, Dessalines, Christophe, and others fighting in Saint Domingue from 1791 to 1804 and in post-independence Haiti thereafter (1804–1825) did not act as white Western Europeans, white North Americans or white, mixed-race, or Black hemispheric Americans acting in whiteness then or now. Writing them as if they did not recognize the humanity of Africans and their descendants and simply brutalized others for personal gain like white colonizers requires a sleight of hand that obscures the wholesale criminality of those who designed and sustained the colonial project. Again, it is worth re-asking: scholars who read foundational Haitian Revolutionary writing composed outside of Haiti, *which revolutionists steward our thinking about anticolonial thought and Caribbean liberation*? If the work of the aforementioned disciplinary fields is rooted in the freedom-seeking project that is hemispheric American anticolonial activism and contestation by the region's demonized peoples, then the task before scholars is to both unpack which historic figures guide scholastic thinking about the Revolution and how it is that they have been memorialized in regional arts and letters as *the* couriers of our critical thought. The latter endeavor was pursued in the previous chapter. Of interest here is attending to the decolonial thought practices of *Ginen* captives and detailing its influence in classic Caribbean literatures of the Revolution.

My intent is to bring the absented *Ginen* Haitian revolutionary into our field of vision when engaging canonical Haitian Revolutionist writing. In this book, the absented primarily references *bossale* (African-born) Haitian revolutionists and Africanized creole (Caribbean-born) revolutionists overshadowed by the creole generals of the Revolution. It secondly references the coalitions and decolonial paths not so readily subsumable within the procolonial iterations of being, which have ensconced Louverture, Christophe, and Dessalines in a colonial white maleness that cannot make sense of their revolutionary actions during and after the Revolution. I refuse to obscure the singularity of Louverture's, Christophe's, or Dessalines's lived Blackness or the magnitude of Alexandre Pétion and Jean Louis Vastey's marginalization as mixed-race peoples of African descent. I will not minimize the racial particularities of the struggle for liberation in slavery and in post-independence (geopolitically ostracized) Haiti by writing any of these persons as just like or comparable to white colonizers. I also refuse their too gigantic presence in Haitian Revolutionary narratology and will not remember them alone no matter if this work chooses to remember them anew. There are others to see and embrace as stewards of our critical imaginings. *Onè e respè, Papa Dessalines, Papa Toussaint, Papa Christophe, Papa Pétion, Papa Vastey e tout gro ero independans yo. . . . Nou pap bliye.*[4]

The homage from which the opening epigraph of this chapter is drawn, and which inspired the quoted benediction to the most recognizable figures of Haiti's revolution (outside of Haiti), directs scholars to the varied many who should guide our thinking.[5] Offered to commemorate the Revolution's beginning stages (August 14 to August 21, 1791), the homage affords the struggle a long gestation period as it names Taino chieftains as revolutionary ancestors of consequence. In broadening the Revolution beyond its accepted timeline, it invokes revolutionaries whose "hearts burned for justice" (*kè yo tap boule . . . tap mande Jistis*) and whose hearts necessarily burned for Native lives and Black lives collectively. There are no white lives symbolically invoked, and thus no Haitian revolutionary who could be remembered as white is named. The homage sees others and affords the focused intentionality on absented persons and coalitions in the revolutionary moment to pursue the decolonial thought illuminating new kinds of critical stewards in the Haitian Revolutionary work of Alejo Carpentier.

Carpentier is perhaps a curious point of departure for such an effort. He was a white Cuban whose anticolonial novella of the Revolution, *The Kingdom of This World*, relied on racist and antiracist sentiment to issue its critique of the colonial project. Lizabeth Paravisini-Gebert observes that he was "not unwilling to fetishize aspects of" Vodou or draw inspiration from sensationalist writing about Haiti for his own work (e.g., William Seabrook's *The Magic Island* [1929]).[6] He was also quite willing to corroborate the racist lie that nineteenth-century Haiti was a failing (if not a failed) state by his narrative's end. The very presence of this untruth in the novella "reveals his uncritical stance toward prevailing Euro-American biases about contemporary Haitian people and culture," as Ali Tal-mason asserts; it also reveals his willingness to place *all* the blame of Haiti's post-revolutionary difficulties on Haitians alone and ignore the machinations of white imperialist nations.[7] Carpentier's reading does not consider these external factors and is wrong-headed as a result. This is discussed further at the chapter's conclusion and at the start of Chapter 3. The novella is full of racialist ambivalences, which Katerina Gonzalez Seligmann reconciles by considering Carpentier's "alignments." She writes that "Carpentier's alignment as a Swiss-born immigrant to the Caribbean [he moved to Cuba when an infant], who by the time of [*The Kingdom of This World*] had also lived extensively in France, erupts into" the text, shaping its attachments to "a European perspective."[8] The narrative "is also structured by his conscious alignment as a radical antiracist committed to overturning European social, intellectual, and aesthetic hegemony in the Americas."[9] I build from Paravisini-Gebert, Tal-mason, and Seligmann and add that the messy racialisms present in *The Kingdom of This World* can be explained by the conditional whiteness of white Cubans in 1940s Cuba.

Carpentier composed the novella in a moment when *all* Cubans were made to accept the racist subjection of the United States. Following the conclusion of the Spanish-American War in 1898, the resultant declaration of Cuban independence from Spain in 1902, and the institutionalization of the United States–authored Platt Amendment in Cuba (which outlined US political control over the Cuban economy), the United States became newly independent Cuba's neocolonial steward. This was a colonial guardianship which subsequently marked Cuba as a racialized nonwhite space, notwithstanding the nation's similar colonial history of rule by racist Western European descended whites.[10] This racialization of Cuba as geopolitically nonwhite occasioned a conditional relation to whiteness for white Cubans, which can account for a positive anticolonial identification with the hemispheric Americas as a home on par with Western Europe and North America. This particular sentiment naturalizes the desire to find kinship with revolutionary Haiti, for example, who bested Western Europeans despite the engrained fear of Black rebellion so key to an identification with whiteness and its supremacist requirements. However, the conditionality of whiteness for white Cubans can also account for a latent (yet foundational) anti-Blackness with respect to the region's Black peoples. Both elements of the lived conditionality of Cuban whiteness inform Carpentier's Haitian work in varying degrees; indeed, the anticolonial preoccupations of Carpentier's famed theory of *lo real maravilloso* (hereafter, the marvelous real), which prefaces *The Kingdom of This World*, evidences the former, and the undeniable racist depiction of independent Haiti, the latter.[11]

I sit with Carpentier, as I sat with James and Glissant, because their engagements with the Revolution or Haiti proper bore foundational modes of anticolonial philosophy that have shaped anticolonial thought and criticism in the fields of Caribbean studies, Black studies, postcolonial studies, and Haitian studies. I read their Haitian Revolutionist writings as decolonial in substance because of their commitment to reclaiming difference, that is, to authoring their cultures and the Caribbean removed from the West's colonial order. This reclamation of difference is read as undertaken to help all Caribbean peoples chart in thought what *Ginen* Haitians did in mind, body, and collective being: a path beyond the white colonial order. *The Kingdom of This World* journeys toward this path. It is forward thinking in its celebratory focus on captive revolutionaries as opposed to the Revolution's famous Caribbean-born generals. It also stands apart from the classic Haitian Revolutionary literature produced by prominent Caribbean writers in the twentieth century because it stresses that the success of the Revolution resides in the fact that captive revolutionaries thought beyond the world as it was. The novella shows how they thought instead toward the world as it could be, without having read any piece of white cultural production. In this respect *alone*, the novella is worthy of the immense readerly attention it has garnered, as new stewards of thought within the Revolution emerge here and *only here* when Carpentier rightly recognizes how *Ginen* captives thought their world anew.

This chapter opens showcasing Carpentier's delineation of *Ginen* cultural thought in *The Kingdom of This World*, moves to Carpentier's famed theory of the marvelous real, and touches briefly on his later novels, *The Lost Steps* (1953), and *The Harp and the Shadow: The Beatification of Christopher Columbus: A Novel* (1979). I regard these texts and the essays, "On the Marvelous Real in America" (1967) and "The Baroque and the Marvelous Real" (1975), as Carpentier's Haitian writings because they continue a line of inquiry first formulated in *The Kingdom of This World* concerning the possibilities of rebuilding the world. I build from this interest and address how Carpentier's pointed attention to the innovative thinking of revolutionists who were not in leadership roles establishes *Ginen* captives as new world builders. My analysis foregrounds Carpentier's insistence that his readers understand how ordinary African and Africanized revolutionaries acted with arms *and* with self-fashioned as well as self-originating genius to contest a colonial criterion of being, which narrated their existence as a slave's existence alone. I detail Carpentier's concerted efforts to depict *Ginen* decolonial thought and *Ginen* spirituality as resistantly innovative to showcase the creative power needed to refuse this criterion and to think toward something distinct. Of interest here is how Carpentier's investment in detailing the epistemological innovations of *Ginen* revolutionists shapes his critique of the colonial project's racialization of existence, which has made some people incontestably human and others dubiously human. This critique accounts for his interest in the way *Ginen* captives augmented how the human could be known to include them; and it occasioned the anticolonial radicalism of his theory of the marvelous, which builds on the inventive daring of *Ginen* cultural praxis (as exemplified by captive revolutionists) to galvanize artists and thinkers to create work reflective of their cultures and their desires for existence.

Carpentier's theory of the marvelous is an anticolonial call to wonder, where the thing and/or happening that stands as marvelous signifies astonishing artistic and political possibilities for a present. The theory was authored as an "antidote to existing and exhausted forms of expression," writes Lois Parkinson Zamora and Wendy B. Faris, which explains why its theoretical imperative is political.[12] The political nature of this imperative was not evident to Carpentier's peers. Nicholas Micheal Kramer writes that Carpentier "came under fire from a number of Latin American intellectuals for his lack of political commitment."[13] Seligmann notes, in turn, the ease with which Carpentier's work was embraced by literary magazines in Cuba with diametrically opposed politics, which likely furthered the prevailing opinion that Carpentier did not hold serious political commitments.[14] The marvelous suggests otherwise as it tasks artists and thinkers to approach the hemispheric Americas with Black Atlantic faith so as to see and perceive the extraordinary in the ordinary. I think alongside Annaliese Hoehling and regard the theory as "challeng[ing] the reader to recognize . . . the limits of epistemological perspective[s] to organize reality," and I build from Hoehling to stress how Carpentier invites readers to recognize their "capacity to escape those limits."[15] In other words, I see Carpentier as asking readers to be curious with his theory. My analysis shows how the marvelous encourages artists and nonartists to politicize their curiousness, as the theory tasks both with the aptitude to critically assess and radically reconsider the imperial strictures of our planetary existence.

Carpenter's theory of the marvelous is inspired, firstly, by Black epistemologies of being, which is to say, it is driven by Carpentier's recognition of how Black peoples in the Americas have similar and divergent African lifeworlds that have given them their own ways of knowing the world. These ways exist outside of "the abjectness that is projected onto [them]" by technologies of colonial power and are powerful tools of decolonial analysis as a result.[16] The theory is inspired, secondly, by Columbus. It draws heavily from Columbus's discursive deployment of the marvelous in his letters and journals in order to challenge his imperial articulation of existence. Because this theory prefaces *The Kingdom of This World*, it also ties the new world making and world breaking feat that was the Haitian Revolution to the new world making and equally world breaking feat that was Columbus's voyages to the Americas.

Where Columbus's faith-inspired intellect has been seen as key to his 1492 voyage, Carpentier points to the faith-inspired genius of captive Saint Dominguans for the Revolution's success in *The Kingdom of This World*. Eminent Jamaican writer and philosopher Sylvia Wynter has extensively shown that the colonial order governing the Western hemisphere could not come into being without a concerted move on the part of Western European laymen, like Columbus, to push past the epistemological dictates of the Scholastic order.[17] The Scholastic epistemological system governed knowledge production in fifteenth-century Western Europe and held that the hemisphere containing Haiti could not exist. Likewise, it is my contention that Carpentier recognizes (and helps his readers to grasp) that the decolonial world that Haiti inaugurates, names, and makes tangible as a discoverable world within reach of all racialized peoples could not come into being without a concerted effort on the part of *Ginen* Haitians to think and act themselves free. Carpentier, in this respect, is allied in thought with Wynter. I bring them in conversation to foreground the unique way *Ginen* revolutionists exceeded Columbus in their appropriation of Saint Domingue and their transformation of it into Haiti. I therefore write with and against Carpentier whose Haitian corpus, while anticolonial because of its fight against the colonial project's continuation, is profoundly troubling for its elision of the living presence of post-independence Haiti. This elision effectively obscures what *Ginen* thought and life can *and* did produce in our biosphere: a new world.

The diminution of the new world that the Revolution made occurs largely because the Haitian Revolution is presented as an ambitious, though largely ineffective, potentiality in Carpentier's principal Haitian text (*The Kingdom of This World*). Carpentier writes as if *Ginen* revolutionists, their predecessors, and their descendants did not create lasting material and ontological conditions for a distinct world. Accordingly, where my analysis sees (and shows) liberated Haiti as governed by a decolonial ethics of the plain person, evinced in the Haitian saying, *tout moun se moun*, Carpentier sees (and depicts) post-revolutionary Haiti as a neocolonial banana republic of Black leaders existing in white face.[18]

Of interest here is how the turn to and subsequent rejection of Haiti in the work of both Carpentier and Wynter reveals how untenable Haiti's decisive claim to Black humanity remains when this claim requires (as *Ginen* Haitian revolutionaries demanded) the total demise of the West—that is, the complete rejection of a world imagined and imaged in Western Europe's cultural schema.

Where Carpentier attempts to account for the radical break in being Haiti presented to the colonial world in his early Haitian work (*The Kingdom of This World* and his theory of the marvelous real), Wynter cannot acknowledge Haiti as such. She chooses instead to focus the regional project of re-ontologizing existence on the undeniably vital global anticolonial movements of the 1950s and 1960s and the civil rights movement in the United States. This is in addition to tying this effort to radically transform being to the still critically important intellectual contributions of the famed Martinican thinkers Frantz Fanon and Aimé Césaire.[19] Wynter reads both as thinkers who push the West toward actualizing its own radical dictates.[20] The Revolution and Haiti prove unable to do this re-ontologizing work for Wynter, who argues that *Ginen* peoples' most daring epistemological strivings are too firmly anchored within a Vodouzian worldview to be politically effective.[21] Just as the local culture of the West must be set aside, Wynter argues that this worldview must also be moved beyond. Letting both go, for Wynter, secures the potential of a future "redrawn again, in undared forms."[22]

Like Wynter, I find that a future existence must be remapped. Yet where Wynter cannot see the efforts of Haiti's *Ginen* people (in the revolutionary moment or in the twentieth century) in facilitating this re-mapping because of a devotion to Vodou knowledge systems, I show that their efforts have been pivotal in fostering a move beyond the local culture of the West. The distinct epistemological frame for being that Vodou provided in the revolutionary moment, and that it continues to afford today, demands rejecting the West, which is not a "place," to quote Glissant, but a "project."[23] This rejection entails pushing past its proscribed dictates for existence and moving toward a distinct decolonized reality. Proposing this does not necessitate minimizing the importance of the global anticolonial movements of the twentieth century, the civil rights movement in the United States, or Fanon's and Césaire's instrumental writings to scholarly understanding of the disparate ways human beings are made to unequally exist in the world. But it does mean recognizing and thereafter establishing as fact the long-existent genealogy of new world building intrinsic to the Black decolonial politics critically constituting anticolonial thought and action in this hemisphere. Establishing this as fact requires critical attention to the *Ginen* Haitian Revolutionary challenge to the West's ordering of existence and its culturally specific iteration of the human.

Wynter's generative philosophical writings invite scholars to be critically aware of this challenge even as she minimizes its importance in light of a corrective exposition of past new world building efforts. Her articulation of Fanon's sociogenic challenge to our governing biocentric epistemological model for being ("besides ... ontogeny there stands sociogeny") is issued as a corrective for what came before.[24] Fanon's challenge operates like Columbus's and Copernicus's intellectual stand against the Scholastic order, where a change to the prevailing epistemological system for all thought occurs, but this challenge is still constituted by the past knowledge system. As such, this new world building still carries the prejudicial inefficacies of the prior epistemological system forth in the present, via repurposed categories for existence, which damn othered human beings—hence Wynter's articulation of the partial victory of 1492 with respect to Columbus's and Copernicus's distinct challenges. This partial victory is discussed in relation to Carpentier, revolutionary Haiti, and Wynter's concept of the "demonic" later in this chapter. What bears underscoring now is that the Scholastic (pre-imperial) West, the Christian (imperial) Humanist West and the biocentric (still imperial present day) Humanist West, to use Wynter's terms, cannot divest from extractive hierarchical forms of political communality. Notwithstanding Columbus's, Copernicus's, or Fanon's challenge to Western knowledge systems, the West has yet to create a new way of knowing that engenders a political community with an ethics of freedom that actively works against the oppressive cultural systems it favors (like racialization, capitalism, or imperialism, among others). It has been unable to create a decolonial system of thought because of its deep investment in supremacy, which is the air in the West as anti-Blackness is the weather, to borrow from Christina Sharpe.[25] To sit with the Haitian Revolution and with Haiti is to resist settling for corrective reforms to a Western trajectory for existence. It is to demand instead the continued abolition of the West, which began most prominently but not exclusively with the Haitian Revolution.

What follows is not a critique of Wynter's critical writings concerning Columbus and the human. It is a "yes" and "but also," a "yes" and "please consider"; in other words, this reading is a critical extension of Wynter that refuses the scholarly language of departure which does not serve the Black freedom strivings that constitute her work and this project. Wynter's innovative scholarship on Columbus and Blackness provides the critical praxis needed here to account for the anti-Blackness that marks Haiti's disappearance in Carpentier's later Haitian works, and the prejudicial treatment afforded to the nation and Revolution in writings of fellow Caribbean and Latin Americans invested in working toward a decolonial future. I am cognizant of the fact that using Wynter to make sense of Carpentier's Haitian Revolutionary project overlays this analysis with the weight of Wynter's disavowal of Haiti's monumentality to the decolonial project of making the world new.

Cultural Thought as (De)Colonial Praxis

Carpentier's investment in this project is why his Haitian writings begin with *The Kingdom of This World*, a novella that invites Cubans to creatively think and act against their colonial subjection. This invitation is extended to facilitate a key demand Carpentier directs towards his Cuban readers—be new. He, specifically, asks Cubans to want to be new kinds of humans with the narrative. This ask is directly tied to the colonial circumstances Cuba faced in Carpentier's moment. When Carpentier published *The Kingdom of This World* in 1949, Cuba had experienced forty-seven years of independence and four hundred and fifty-seven years of colonial subjugation. This prolonged experience of colonial subjection did not end with independence from Spain in 1902. Immediately after securing independence, Cuba became the neocolonial subject of the United States.[26] The colonial order flourished in independent Cuba, and it did so not simply because Cuba was nominally self-governing, but because Carpentier's Cuba was rabidly anti-Black. Literary critic Roberto González Echevarría writes that "when Carpentier began to write [in the 1920s] ... intellectuals were preoccupied with [the nation's political status, the European avant-garde, and the Afro-Cuban movement, three issues that had] at least one common denominator: the problem of assimilating a large and impoverished Black population, the backbone of the labor in sugar industry, into the mainstream of political, social, and cultural life."[27] Black Cubans were a "problem" population for Cuba's white and white-identifying governing elite because they were Black *and* other. The virulent anti-Black racism that constrained their economic, political, and social prospects, from the colonial period to independence, created the context where a distinct West African cultural identity could be maintained.[28] This identity threatened the modern, US–approximate republic that elite Cubans strove to create, as it too closely associated the entire nation with Blackness.[29] US intervention, however, had already cemented this association with Blackness. The racial anxiety that gripped Cuba's white and white-identified governing class concerning its Black populace at the start of Carpentier's literary career is not simply an outcome of the nation's slaveholding past, but it attests to how very much the governing class desperately tried to retain a cultural whiteness that the United States called into question. The overwhelming concern with "assimilating a large and impoverished black population" cannot be divested from the realization that Cuba was being treated, on the whole, as if each and every one of its citizens was Black and thus fit for racist oversight.[30]

Carpentier began writing in the 1920s when assimilating Black Cubans was a key concern because of Cuba's neocolonial condition. He composed *The Kingdom of This World* in the 1940s when conformity prevailed over assimilation, and foreign Black immigrants were eagerly cast off because they did not fit the Cuba the ruling bourgeoisie had in mind. From 1898 until 1933 "two hundred thousand to as many as six hundred thousand" Haitian laborers had migrated to Cuba to supply US sugar companies with cheap labor.[31] Of the Haitian migrants that chose to remain in Cuba "approximately thirty-eight thousand" were deported in a repatriation process that began in 1933 and ended in 1939.[32] The deportation occurred in part because influential members of the Cuban elite "fear[ed] ... a 'disproportionate' increase in the black population" would forestall Cuban modernization.[33] Cultural studies scholar Yanique Hume writes, "the Haitian cane-cutter [became and remained well into the revolutionary period] synonymous with an image of the savage slave past ... thwarting Cuba's vision of a modern republic."[34] Haitian migrants, like Black Cubans, were an othered, marginalized population because they also possessed a distinct cultural identity that was regarded as "primitive" in orientation and innately rebellious because of their revolutionary history.[35] The number of Haitian migrants would add to an already culturally distinct Black population and was imagined as sufficient enough to further regress a purportedly backward demographic toward barbarity and, worse yet, radicalize them against whites. The addition of Haitian migrants to the natal Black population accordingly rekindled white Cuban fear of "black rebellion similar to that of 1912 in Cuba and 1790 in Haiti," instances where Black people rose to counter white supremacy.[36]

The increasing angst concerning Black peoples in neocolonial Cuba underscores how the nation's colonial condition was intricately bound to the relative absence of Black autonomy in the nation and in colonial as well as postcolonial spaces in Carpentier's moment. The absence of this autonomy disproportionately affected Haitian migrants in Cuba. Haitian migrants were marginalized in Carpentier's homeland because they were Black within a nation-state clinging to a self-determination it could only exercise through anti-Blackness. Furthermore, Haitians were subjugated because they were symbolically representative of Black power politics and Black defiance, which threatened both the US imperial project and the Cuban nationalist project, as the latter not only agreed to neocolonial subjugation under the United States but did so to revive a sugar industry predicated on Black exploitation.[37] The precarious lived existence of Haitian migrants in Cuba serves as the necessary context to recognize Carpentier's project as foregrounding how the colonial order's deep commitment to racialization and anti-Blackness gave rise to and sustained coloniality in independent Caribbean and Latin American nation-states.[38] This commitment also explains why Cuba's cultural acceptance of white supremacy legitimated its colonial subjugation under the United States, since it allows race—and the colonial project—to exist unthought, as natural facts of existence.

The Kingdom of This World insists on thinking each through. It addresses race and the colonial project in the early moment of the encounter and in Carpentier's own contemporary Caribbean to create space for an otherwise, for thinking that can envision beyond the rationalities of the West. His efforts to show how *Ginen* revolutionaries are distinctly human on their own terms (via how they are thinking beings) are a way to showcase, first, that resistant thinking against the West is possible. Secondly, it discloses how thinking is cultural not racial. It is shaped by a culture's specific ontology, which is to say, if Haiti has a *Ginen* culture that gives it a different way of knowing, then Carpentier reasons that Cuba (and the entire Americas) must also have a distinct cultural framework through which it can express its own decolonial knowledge. Thirdly, the way revolutionists articulated their idea of the human outside of whiteness helps to assuage Carpentier's own anxieties about his humanity, tied as it was to a whiteness that sustains the colonial project. The novella treats these issues implicitly via its broader plot, which concerns the day-to-day exploits of a nondescript captive Black creole (Ti-Noël) and his lascivious white and French-born enslaver (M. Lenormand de Mézy).

GINEN DECOLONIAL THOUGHT

The Kingdom of This World begins in the mid-1700s, before the maroon, rebel, and *oungan* (Vodou priest) François Makandal's siege of poison, his death, and simultaneous resurrection in 1758.[39] Makandal's rebellion is treated at length in the novella and sets the stage for Carpentier's portrayal of the Haitian Revolution, which is largely rendered through the Vodou ceremony at *Bwa Kayïman* that provided the logistical groundwork for the 1791 revolution. The novella ends in the early 1800s with the fall of King Henry Christophe's reign and the unification of Haiti under President Jean Pierre Boyer. Although *The Kingdom of This World* is framed by revolts that precede and follow the Haitian Revolution (Makandal's rebellion and the uprising against King Christophe, respectively), the 1791–1804 revolution is its principal subject. Carpentier's recounting of this historic insurgency is largely divested of the famed leaders through which the Revolution is often told. Louverture, Dessalines, and Pétion are dealt with minimally, if at all. Carpentier does provide extensive attention to the former revolutionary general turned king, Christophe. Christophe's heroic revolutionary personage is not of significance to the narrative; his reign and the cycle of tyranny it unleashed are, however. With the intent to write the Revolution without its most heralded figures, the novella is centered on Ti-Noël, through whom Carpentier presents the *Ginen* captive's experience of revolutionary events. Ti-Noël's intellect critically constitutes this experience and serves as a "kind of mental counterpoint" to Western thought.[40] The opening chapter details this "counterpoint," as it chronicles Ti-Noël's deliberations concerning his servitude.

Set in the colony's capital (Cap Français or Le Cap), the chapter depicts Ti-Noël accompanying M. Lenormand de Mézy from the city's port to a barbershop, and finally onward toward de Mézy's plantation, as the latter runs errands. At every point along de Mézy's route, Ti-Noël is silently attentive. He is cognizant of his surroundings and the discursive parameters of his enslavement, which have reduced him to a "body of flesh to which [things] happened."[41] He counters this reduction with his own narrative of the self. Key to this narrative are the heads of calves, wax figures, and painted figureheads, as it is through them that Ti-Noël shows his cognizance of the biocentrism of slavery and white colonial rule. Put otherwise, he knows that both systems of oppression are biology centered as Sylvia Wynter argues.[42] They not only reduce the captive to a body without agency (or a "flesh to which [things] happened") but also divest the captive of human essence since they are "flesh" alone.[43] Ti-Noël understands the nature of his subjection and knows that, for the colonist, he is the nadir of the human, if human at all, since he is enfleshed in a body that is Black and made to labor as a captive being Black.[44] He tracks the heads he sees along his journey to ridicule colonists and their way of thinking.

Carpentier writes that Ti-Noël "gazes at the four wax heads" present in the barbershop and the other heads nearby while de Mézy waits to be shaved. Ti-Noël, conveys Carpentier, notes the "amazing coincidence" that is the juxtaposition of the "four wax heads" and the "calves' heads" in the "tripe-shop next door."[45] He is pleased to "think that alongside the pale calves' heads, heads of white men were served on the same tablecloth."[46] Surely Carpentier does not intend for readers to perceive Ti-Noël as questionably human; the latent reference to cannibalism, via the pleasure he takes from imagining "white men's heads" on a "tablecloth," implies this should readers reason from the onto-epistemic standards of colonial modernity. Rather than reason with the colonial rationalities that they are most familiar with, Carpentier invites readers to perceive Ti-Noël as human on his own terms. When Ti-Noël goes on to take note of a copper engraving of a "French admiral or ambassador being received by a Negro" at the neighboring bookshop, he "boldly inquires" of the bookseller, "What kind of people are those?" He then proceeds to affirmatively reflect on the majesty of Africa after receiving the reply, "That is the king of your country."[47] The two pages that follow are devoted to Ti-Noël's comparative meditations on great African kingdoms (the "Popo . . . [the] Arada . . . the Nagos, and the Fulah"), and they are also devoted to African distinction in battle and governance.[48] Both mediations attest to white Western European mediocrity in war and monarchial rule, both show the thinking that bore *Ayiti Ginen* into being. They showcase, in other words, the rich cultural life of captives and Carpentier's characterization of Ti-Noël as critically resistant because of his culture.

Ti-Noël's African culture has made him unconvinced of the purported superiority of the whites of Saint Domingue or elsewhere; and his skepticism about white colonial power is why I read the novella as conversant with *Ginen* cultural praxis. This praxis refuses to reason within the colonial framework of the West and leads with skepticism—*Sa blan dit?* (What did the white say?)—when making sense of Western ways of knowing and being. Because Carpentier characterizes Ti-Noël as resistant in mind and being, he avails his narrative to the lived materiality of the African and Africanized captive's experience of enslavement and colonialism; or what I see as the *Ginen* ethical imperative that is *tout moun se moun* (all persons are persons). In the narrative, this imperative is expressed as a reflective practice, modeled by Ti-Noël. This critical practice takes as its departure point an imagined and/lost place of being (Africa); and yet is guided by a future space of free Black being (*Ayiti Ginen*). Put differently, this imperative permeates the narrative with a collective initiative to "imagine otherwise," a remark Avery Gordon describes as a "folk theoretical statement" that nurtures understanding of one's present and future place of existence. She writes, "We need to know where we live in order to imagine living elsewhere. We need to imagine living elsewhere before we can live there."⁴⁹ Ti-Noël can conceive of where to go—toward Africa and beyond the colony—because he knows Saint Domingue and his place there. He can also conceive of where to go because of Makandal and his stories. Carpentier writes, "Although Ti-Noël had little learning, he had been instructed in these truths [concerning African governance] by the deep wisdom of Macandal" and therefore knew that African kings were "true kings, and not those sovereigns wigged in false hair."⁵⁰ Carpentier continues, writing:

> In Africa [Ti-Noël muses] the king was warrior, hunter, judge, and priest; his precious seed distended hundreds of bellies with a mighty strain of heroes. In France, in Spain, the king sent his generals to fight in his stead; he was incompetent to decide legal problems, he allowed himself to be scolded by any trumpery friar. And when it came to a question of virility, the best he could do was engender some puling prince who ... bore the name of as harmless and silly a fish as the dolphin.⁵¹

The reading Ti-Noël offers of noble African conduct versus Western European regal bearing reveals his superior personal sensibility. It also attests to his self-conception as one who is unconvinced of his purported inferiority or that of the captives in the Caribbean and Africans in Africa. In fact, his reasoning implicitly questions the very efficacy of de Mézy's qualification to dominate him. If a Western sovereign's rule can be reduced to superficial vanity (as signaled by "wig[s]" of "false hair") and dismissed as fundamentally wrongheaded because of this superficiality, then the slaveholding colonist who awaits a shave, wears a fashionable wig (like de Mézy), and mimics his sovereign's vanity is an unsuitable overlord of the captive.⁵²

The clear defiance in this way of reasoning attests to Ti-Noël's cognizance of contemporary Western cultural mores and his rejection of its white supremacist framework.⁵³ This framework legitimates and makes knowable the bookseller's and de Mézy's grasp of geospatial knowledge (Africa as country versus continent), appropriate royal comportment ("generals" who fight in a king's "stead"), and proper master/slave colonial conduct (whites as the purported natural rulers of Black people).⁵⁴ Makandal's tales, however, make other kinds of knowledge knowable *and* other ways of knowing perceivable. For readers of the novella, the stories show how Ti-Noël and his captives peers had long thought beyond the dictates of the colonial world because they positioned themselves elsewhere—in the present past of Africa embodied in "the *lwa* [ancestral spirits] of *Ginen*."[55] Jean Casimir writes that the *lwa*—spirits who recalled the great African monarchs and ordinary African peoples—helped captives preserve "memories of real and fictive loved ones as well as cultures thriving without them."[56] For Ti-Noël and other captives in the narrative, Makandal's stories help to legitimate the possibility of a new temporality for the present.

This temporality exists side by side with the colonial present and affords captives the means to think against it. Accordingly, when de Mézy emerges from the barbershop "with heavily powdered cheeks," Ti-Noël is struck by his incompetence. He observes how de Mézy's "face now bore a startling resemblance to the four dull wax faces that stood in a row along the counter, *smiling stupidly*."[57] Ti-Noël knows that he is seen as a servile being, meant to exist in silent obeisance, and he plays his part well, as de Mézy is completely unaware of Ti-Noël's defiant self-awareness. Ti-Noël's thoughts, however, reveal that he knows that he is not a slave or meant to exist as such. Indeed, that Carpentier writes Ti-Noël's self-awareness with attention to the various heads he encounters positions readers to discern the latent and ongoing wrangling with a human's sense of being that necessarily constituted the captive person's lived experience, and that necessarily spurred his or her efforts to hold on to and/or create a distinct cultural ontology. It is this dissident cultural frame for existence that shapes the decolonial nuances I attribute to Ti-Noël's likening of a calf skull to de Mézy's "bald head."

Carpentier writes that after leaving the barbershop, de Mézy buys "a calf's head in the tripe-shop" and hands the head over to Ti-Noël, who then "clasped that white, chill skull under his arm, thinking how much it probably resembled the bald head of his master beneath his wig."[58] By associating de Mézy's "bald head" with the "white, chill [calf] skull" he is made to carry, Ti-Noël naturalizes de Mézy's incompetence, fastening it to his person. In doing this, Ti-Noël decisively counters the terms and conditions of his own biological dehumanization with his distinct ontological framework. If in de Mézy's cultural frame for existence the captive can be known only as dubiously human and in need of lordship because s/he is Black and afforded a biology meant to labor and serve because s/he is Black, then in the *Ginen* cultural framework tied to Ti-Noël, the colonist and the Western European is marked as vapid and vain and is thus knowable as stupidly human, unfit to rule themselves, least of all Africans and their descendants. de Mézy does not just hand a "calf's head" to Ti-Noël; readers are encouraged to understand that he gives him a symbolic presentation of the end of his own time—in other words, the demise of de Mézy's rule over Ti-Noël and white rule of Saint Domingue. de Mézy cannot discern what he has done because he does not possess the cultural ontology that could reason this future moment of African liberation and Black rule as a viable option for being. He is too entrenched in the colonial moment, whereas Ti-Noël is grounded in the decolonial possibilities of what the past present of Africa reveals is attainable in the future present of Saint Domingue.

The novella's first chapter ends underscoring how captives are resistant because of the Africa they preserve within themselves. Carpentier writes that as Ti-Noël and de Mézy travel back to the plantation, de Mézy "whistle[s] a fife march" in remembrance of his past "days as a petty officer" and "Ti-Noël, in a kind of mental counterpoint, silently hum[s] a chanty that was very popular among the harbor coopers."[59] This "chanty" "heap[ed] ignominy on the King of England," who Ti-Noël "had little esteem for."[60] Ti-Noël reveals that the wives of both the King of England and the King of Spain "tinted their cheeks with oxblood and buried fœtuses in a convent whose cellars were filled with skeletons"; these skeletons, he reasons, "had been rejected by the true heaven, which wanted nothing to do with those who died ignoring the true gods."[61] Like the aforementioned comparative reading Ti-Noël offers of African royal bearing and Western European stately conduct, his concluding thoughts reveal a dissident cultural sensibility that refuses to accept the validity and singularity of Western Europe's norms for existence. Carpentier gives Ti-Noël language that vilifies Christianity in the sordid manner commonly used to condemn Vodou and other non-Christian spiritual practices in Western Europe and its colonial cultures in the Western hemisphere precisely for this reason. Of value here is how this vilification expresses the vibrancy of the captives' dissident African culture. This culture's roots in an Africa that is out of reach yet still alive in the lifeworld of captives explains why a Western European cultural object (a shanty) can become emblematic of African thought and African resistance. Africa, as their logos, is the lens through which captives reason, and because it licenses the pleasure Ti-Noël derives from thinking against planters, Western Europe, and slavery, African culture (imagined and real) is the chief way Carpentier brings Ti-Noël's positionality as a *Ginen*—a person who knows himself outside the West—into thought for readers.

This positionality is not discernible within colonial modernity, which refuses to see or heed any cultural life that objects to its articulation of the world. Readers of *The Kingdom of This World* are nonetheless still invited to see the dissident cultural life of Saint Domingue's captive population; and when faced with the inference that Ti-Noël is cannibalistic for his thoughts about calves' heads and the heads of white planters, they are invited to resist how this inference positions Ti-Noël as thoughtless. Michel-Rolph Trouillot asserts that the colonial trope of the African and the African-descended person's proclivity for cannibalism has long served to convince white peoples and the white identified "that enslaved Africans and their descendants could not envision freedom—let alone formulate strategies for gaining and securing such freedom."[62] The popular colonial idea of innate Black thoughtlessness with respect to liberation (in truth, with respect to all things) was, as Trouillot argues, not "based . . . on empirical evidence as on an ontology, an implicit organization of the world and its inhabitants."[63] It was not based on any understanding of Black peoples and their lifeworlds, nor was it based on an understanding of existence that Africans or Africanized captives, as Carpentier shows with Ti-Noël, adhered to. This racist trope, however, plays into readers' perceptual whiteness and the epistemic racism of colonial ways of reading Black peoples. Most in the hemispheric Americas have been instructed to accept the discursive vilification of Black peoples and to take part in excusing, ignoring, and/or trivializing the barbaric violence that was enslavement and the ongoing reality of anti-Black prejudice. Most of Carpentier's readers understand that this kind of malicious anti-Blackness is an acceptable and normal aspect of existence, which for Carpentier is a problem because it ensures that the exploitative nature of a world built on slavery, genocide, ecocide, and colonialism can remain uncontested in thought, and continue to make perfect sense in collective practice.

The colonial trope of cannibal that frames Ti-Noël's decolonial musings could very well abstract the narrative ground of this opening chapter, namely its focus on *Ginen* dissension and this dissension's roots in the *Black* lived experience of enslavement and colonialism. This ground remains at the fore of readers' engagement because Carpentier insists that they experience the opening chapter through the ingenuity of a captive person. Readers therefore enter the novella open to seeing how captives regarded existence as legitimately within their purview and thus as rightly guided by a way of being that regarded them as persons alongside other kinds of persons. In this respect, Carpentier primes them to understand how *Ginen* revolutionists prompted generals at the helm of the Revolution to declare and politically administer the decolonial fiat, "Enslaved? . . . Let us leave this description for the French; they have conquered but are no longer free."[64]

MOUN

Jean Jacques Dessalines spoke these words aloud when publicly proclaiming Haiti's independence on January 1, 1804. With this utterance, he, and his fellow writers of the Haitian Declaration of Independence, addressed the question of who Haitians are as a people. The answer they provided firmly negated the too-ready response offered by French colonists and the colonial West, which defined them as nominally human laborers. The revisionist and contrarian interpretation of "enslaved" they offered clarifies how Carpentier came to chronicle the Haitian Revolution with attention to the captive revolutionary's wrangling with her biological denigration. Furthermore, their decolonial interpretation of "enslaved" captures what drew Carpentier to the Revolution: the *Ginen* revolutionist-in-the-making's deliberate, self-initiated reconceptualization of herself into a new kind of human among other kinds of human.

Dessalines's aforementioned rhetorical query borrows from the *Ginen* peoples of Saint Domingue, who referred to each other as *moun* (plain person) in deliberate contradistinction to French colonial discourse. In a 2018 lecture commemorating the Battle of Vertières, the last major military contest Haitian revolutionaries waged against the French, Casimir addressed how Haitian revolutionaries came to know themselves *for themselves*—that is, in a way that was distinct from how they were perceived by French colonists. He states,

> To circumvent deadly aggressions from the plantation management, [the free and enslaved] had to be knowledgeable of the plantation management, they had to be knowledgeable of the peers' characteristics and, at the same time, to be aware of the enemy's eventual moves. By synchronizing this dual exigency, they generated themselves and the others as *moun* or plain people. The struggle to overcome destitution brought into being the *Tout moun se moun (All people are people)*, as the central value of life in society.[65]

To consciously decide to be a "plain people" is to deliberately resolve to upend the epistemological validity of white supremacy and white colonial power, both of which rest on the exceptionality, and hence unplainness, of white peoples. Moreover, this decision to be "plain" is to resolve to exist otherwise, beyond the rationalities that reasoned and enforced white supremacy and the colonial project.

Dessalines's rhetorical query must be understood as oriented by the captive masses' radical appropriation of "plainness" and their repudiation of the logic that designated them as "slaves." The latter designation carried with it a grammar for being intended to make legible what constitutes human status (whites who conquer) and what barred one from consideration as human (the enslaved who cannot have ever conquered being non-white). For Dessalines and his fellow writers of the Declaration, Haiti's existence logically signified beyond Saint Domingue, a place formed by reasoning Black peoples as natural slaves. The French then cannot be free in a world in which Haiti now exists because their freedom is still bound to a world view in which it is reasonable to conceive white conquerors and white enslavers as the one and only true humans. The decolonial logic of Dessalines and fellow writers of the Declaration ultimately wed a proclamation of sovereign being to a seizure of human being. The issuance of Haitian Independence bore, in this sense, the ceremonial markings of a new narrative of the human;

as the Blackness of some human beings (such as newly formed Haitians) could change how the human has been known, articulated, and conceived in the West.

The maxim *tout moun se moun* is often followed in Haitian Kreyòl by the saying, *men tout moun pa menm* (but all persons are not the same). This qualification posits the human as genre and further showcases how *Ginen* captives resolved to think outside of French colonial culture and the West. Their collective efforts to think outside of the West exposes how the struggle against slavery and French colonial rule in Saint Domingue required freedom from the lived conditions of enslavement *and* from a widespread system of thought that maintained that Africans and their descendants could only exist in the world as property. This onto-epistemic struggle is as consequential to the narration of the Haitian Revolution as the diplomatic savvy of Louverture or the military genius of Dessalines. This little-discussed aspect of the revolutionary struggle carved out a new way of being human that did not denigrate Africans, their Black descendants in the Americas, the Black cultures these descendants created, or the latter's collective experience of enslavement. It also established how readily the human and the world can be thought anew. Carpentier wants his readers to value Black existence and he wants them to understand that they can be like *Ginen* revolutionists and think a new world into being, as finding commonality with these revolutionists will help them in their own fight against the colonial order. His distillations of Ti-Noël's contemplations at the novella's onset are politically motivated, in this respect. They serve as a way to acknowledge the validity and decolonial importance of Black thinking on existence; and they show how novel thinking is new world making. Indeed, the sense-making practices of *Ginen* revolutionaries shifted their world and the very foundations of a larger world that had cast them as mere property amongst property; their radical means of reasoning was Columbian in scope and, for Carpentier, distinctly marvelous.

Demonic Ground

The Kingdom of This World opens with an epigraph from Spanish playwright Lope de Vega's seventeenth century drama, *The Discovery of the*

New World by Christopher Columbus, which is intended to convey the historical reach of the Revolution. It ties Columbus's 1492 voyage to Haiti's long revolutionary history to stress that the finding *and* founding of a new world can be achieved in the post–Haitian Revolutionary present. This achievement is possible if a decisive shift in epistemology occurs on an individual and collective scale. Together, both the epigraph and the prologue, which outlines Carpentier's theory of the marvelous, make plain Carpentier's investment in leveraging *Ginen* cultural praxis to grapple with the racialization of existence post-Columbus. Both also serve as a way to stress to his readers that the Columbian project of race can be upended. Indeed, in bringing 1492 in conversation with 1804, Carpentier emphatically suggests that revolutionary Haiti's lasting contribution to all hemispheric Americans lays not only in the Revolution's success, *but* in the realization that the new world can be made new again with faith and unconventional epistemological praxis. de Vega's play helps Carpentier make this point by facilitating two important ends: on the one hand, the drama lends credence to the new world making properties of the Haitian Revolution as it lionizes Columbus for his remarkable Christian faith and intellect and, as such, makes much of how Columbus thought the world anew with faith—a feat Carpentier argues Haitian revolutionaries likewise did in Saint Domingue. On the other hand, it also makes plain that only Spaniards can be classified as human while effacing the Western European–born anti-Blackness that made this classification articulable and implementable in the West via Native subjugation.

De Vega's lines in the epigraph to the novella's opening section transport readers of his drama to Columbus's consciousness via his personified imagination. Within this imagination, the audience is availed of a remarkable happening: "The Devil's" appeal to join a judicial proceeding officiated by "Providence," concerning Columbus's right to take the West for "The Christian Religion" from "Idolatry," "The Devil's" minion. Carpentier excerpts the moment where "The Devil," once admitted into the tribunal, introduces himself as "the King of the West" and implores "Providence" to reconsider "sending Columbus/To renew [his] evil deeds."[66] In the text cited by Carpentier, "The Devil" concludes his request by posing the rhetorical question: "Know you not that long since/I rule there?"⁶⁷ This provocative question frames Carpentier's Haitian Revolutionary novella with the spiritually inspired counter reasoning that Columbus employed to negate the Scholastic epistemological order, which governed geographic knowledge in his day and which created new kinds of human beings in the Eastern and Western hemispheres.

Scholasticism and its "arbitrary model of divine creation" held "the earth of the Western Hemisphere [as having] to be entirely submerged under water" because it was "outside the Christian God's providential grace."⁶⁸ The devil was accordingly thought to have ruled the West because the region's providential banishment rendered it uninhabitable. Immediately prior to the epigraphic scene in de Vega's play, Columbus systematically thinks through Scholasticism's understanding of geography and declares, "But heaven inspires me to a contrary belief; it tells me that there ought to be people there and that our pole has antipodes."⁶⁹ Wynter writes that Columbus's "heaven inspired" realizations re-conceptualized "the earth in apocalyptic millenarian terms: given the imminent Second Coming of Christ, the urgent need for all 'idolaters' to be converted, and the divine purpose of creating the earth for the salvation of souls, it followed not only that all seas had to be navigable but that all areas had to be homogeneously habitable."⁷⁰ Columbus's millenarian re-conceptualization of the earth as "navigable" and "homogeneously habitable" is significant to Carpentier's treatment of the Haitian Revolution because "his religiously inspired counterchain of reasoning ... made possible a veridical image of the earth" (knowledge of the earth's surface through empirical reflection), which, in turn, made new humans of Western Europeans.⁷¹

Columbus's inspired millenarianism helped solidify veridical knowledge as the basis for critical inquiry in Western Europe, as knowledge production would now operate under "self-correcting findings" as opposed to the divine dictates of the Scholastic order.⁷² In this respect, Columbus created a "root expansion in thought" whose "self-correcting" (veridical) basis, would prove capable of delegitimizing the feudal hierarchies which had consigned the vast majority of Western Europeans to their social stations—stations that were providence ordained under Scholasticism.⁷³ If, as Wynter writes, label and image served as a boundary marker of uninhabitability, and therefore predetermined, that [certain] lands should be represented as necessarily submerged, in its "natural place" as the heavier element of earth, under the lighter (and by implication, more spiritually redeemed) element of water. Analogically, [then] the fallen realm of the terrestrial, of the human, was necessarily represented as being ontologically subordinated to the spiritually perfected realm of the celestial, the divine: [these] representations . . . were, at the level of the feudal social structure, correlated with the empirical subordination of the peasantry and other non-noble categories to the nobility, and of the lay intelligentsia (men like Columbus), to the spiritually redeemed and therefore cognitively empowered mainstream academics, the clergy.[74]

de Vega's presentation of Columbus in spiritually inspired thought is intended to show how the human of Western European origin is no longer "ontologically subordinated to the spiritually perfected realm of the celestial, the divine." He is free to think and imagine as he desires.[75] More importantly, "non-noble[s]," like Columbus, can now be perceived as just as equally "spiritually redeemed and therefore cognitively empowered" as "mainstream academics, the clergy." Europe's socially damned are free now to be seen as thinkers and thus are theoretically the equals of Europe's privileged classes. Indeed, de Vega's play takes this newfound equality one step further and declares that "all Spanish" are "noble."[76] The nobility of "all Spaniards" reveals the extent to which Columbus's intellectual intervention was popularly received in the century immediately following his 1492 arrival in the Bahamas as having made all Western Europeans similarly human. His faith-inspired voyage arguably engendered a gradual democratization of human standing in Western Europe that, for Carpentier, would occur in far greater totality and radicality centuries later in revolutionary Haiti.

Carpentier's decision to bring de Vega in conversation with the Haitian Revolution calls much needed attention to how far-reaching in scope the thought practices of *Ginen* revolutionaries were with respect to equality when compared to Columbus and his peers. This is evident by the fact that de Vega's play begins with the sociopolitical act that launched the Haitian Revolution, the slave trade. The play dramatizes the Spanish crown's expulsion of the last ruling Moors from its territory, which set in motion the rise of Spain as a colonizing Christian state whose economic power was largely derived from slave labor. Slavery came into prominence on the Iberian Peninsula with the seizure of the latifundias from the Moors. Wynter writes that following Portugal's successful finding of a "sea route around [what had been conceived under Scholasticism as the] nonnavigable Cape Bojador on the bulge of West Africa" in roughly 1441, the Portuguese established the Western European trade in Africans.[77] For the Portuguese, and later the Spanish, Africa became "above all else, a source of slaves, of labor power to work on the latifundia—the large estates recaptured from the Moors, who, in 1492, after some eight centuries, had finally been driven from the Iberian Peninsula."[78] De Vega does not treat the fact of African enslavement in the scenes devoted to the Spanish military campaign against the Moors, nor does he treat the fact of Native enslavement at any juncture in his telling of the story of Columbus. His account of Columbus's spiritually inspired intellectualism completely obscures how the democratization of social standing in Western Europe emerged directly from the devaluation of non-Western European life.[79]

De Vega's nobility-based understanding of the human exposes the inherently exploitative basis of the human Columbus bore into being. Wynter importantly denotes this rendering of the human as "Man" to signify how this Columbian human has standardized the human as necessarily white and culturally Western European.[80] Wynter stresses in her essays that because Columbus's arrival in the Caribbean confirmed his conviction that all lands are habitable, it soon came to be recognized in Western Europe that all lands and all peoples could be rationally perceived as governed by the same empirical rules for existence. This realization laid the foundation for a new (counter-Scholastic) epistemological system (Christian Humanism), which took the conceptual uniformity of the land and earth as indication of the human's uniformity.[81] All humans could *and* would be perceivable and know-able through the cultural and gender specificity of the kind of humans who radically changed geographic and planetary knowledge in Western Europe: that is, de Vega's "nobles," "the Christian, heterosexual, aristocratic men" of Western Europe.[82] Revolutionary Haiti cannot articulate the human in this precise manner because its experience of white supremacist capitalism (via genocide, colonialism, and chattel servitude) demands a less exploitive conceptualization (Haiti's *moun*), one in which the human does not demand a class of others justly reduced to laboring beings.

Haiti's distinct articulation of the human is what drew Carpentier to the nation and its histories of resistance. Of import to Carpentier is how the new kind of humans that run-of-the-mill *Ginen* revolutionists created acted demonically, that is, from a "vantage point outside of the space-time orientation" of the West.[83] Wynter describes the demonic as the onto-epistemological position of impossibility that exists within "our present mode[s] of being/feeling/knowing."[84] It names sites that are disruptive to the colonial order since they are "both a form of life and of possible critical interventions" that oppose "the dominant cultural logic" of the West.[85] Haiti's origin story locates it in and yet outside of the West. Its existence on the outside of the West is why it is demonic, and its demonic relation to the West is why the nation, for Carpentier, is *the* measure by which to make sense of how the Columbian figuration of the human (Wynter's "Man") damned both specific kinds of peoples and specific geographic spaces.

In the immediate wake of Columbus's 1492 arrival in the Caribbean, outmoded geographic categories of the temperate and torrid (preserved from Scholasticism) would now be mapped onto human beings, making them into racialized others under the new epistemological models. These models include Christian humanism and later the secular biocentric humanism that Wynter argues determines our moment. This mapping of the old epistemological frame onto the new frames governing human beings naturalized a division of existence into geographic zones of the human, once thought to be guided by Christ (Scholasticism's temperate area of Europe now home of the human), and zones peopled by racialized others, the idolaters once thought to be ruled by the Devil (Scholasticism's torrid zone of Africa and of the Americas, now home of the nominally human). Carpentier's framing epigraph lays bare how a perceptual mode for being, embodied in de Vega's "nobles" and Wynter's theorization of "Man," bore the discursive purchase that would position Haiti as heretically grounded. When viewed from the vantage of colonial powers and their technicians of thought (clergy, explorers, scholars, and laymen), Haiti is a place suited to colonization and slavery because the Devil rules there. The closing question of the epigraph—"Know you not that long since / I [the devil] rule there"?—brings to the fore of Carpentier's novella the too easily obscured racial consequences of Columbus's counter-reasoning; his reasoning ultimately helped to create the fixed geospatial bounds outlining who is human in a world now veridically navigated.[86] And yet this closing query urges readers to push past the gross limits of a geospatially and imperially raced human, who is phenotypically white and culturally Western European, as it also discloses the productive impossibility that is Haiti. This Haiti-specific impossibility signals an opening toward something new and decolonial in orientation.

Carpentier's reorientation of revolutionary Haiti in spatial relation to early Western European cartographic knowledge invites readers to recognize how Haiti serves as a meaningful site of decolonial thought making for persons living outside of the nation. Haiti shows how captive and colonized Black peoples embraced the demonic to their unique end, that is, to delegitimize by themselves and for themselves the empiricisms of Western Europe's racist knowledge systems. In this respect, the "Devil's" institutionalized rule in the Americas (and in Haiti in particular) is generative for anticolonial action and decolonial praxis since it renders that which is deemed impossible in Western European knowledge systems (namely, Black emancipation and self-governance) *possible*. Black self-directed liberation is not only achievable; it is advisable because it can chart a new course for existence. Accordingly, if Columbus's voyages changed the world as it was known and navigated by all peoples, creating the imperial bloc that is the West and providing Western Europeans with the opportunity to become new kinds of human beings (de Vega's "nobles" and Wynter's "Man"), then Carpentier's reading of the Revolution with attention to the thought practices of *Ginen* revolutionaries discloses how Haiti's unprecedented disruption to this colonial world's expression of self signals a change in how this world can be known and navigated. *Ginen* revolutionaries' cerebrally willed creation of new humans in their image and on their novel terms necessarily expands thought, propelling a new direction for humanity on the whole; as the human cannot simply be analogously white, supremacist, and Western European: the human must now exist plainly (*moun*), in nonsupremacist fashion and in varied cultural and phenotypic form.

The varied articulations of the human that exist in the many spaces and places of the world underscores literary critic Katherine McKittrick's point about geography's dynamism. Geography is the product of creative action, which prompts her to write that it "is not . . . secure and unwavering; we produce space, we produce its meanings, and we work very hard to make geography what it is."[87] Understanding geography as a product of creative action is key to recognizing the concerted efforts Black peoples have made to root themselves and re-make themselves in spaces they have come to call their own. *Ginens* and their captive and free compatriots in the Americas made spaces and places new with their distinct ontologies; *Ginens*, in particular, did so as a result of their plain (*moun*) iteration of human existence. Carpentier drew inspiration from this iteration to create his theory of the marvelous real, which uses Black spiritual thought to showcase how new worlds can be built within the world.

THE *GINEN* MARVELOUS

Carpentier's theory of the marvelous approaches existence as a multiverse to show how the Western colonial world is just one world among the others in existence. It is a faith-based expression of lived wonder and unprecedented potentiality principally concerned with Caribbean and Latin American existence. This anticolonial theory was occasioned by Carpentier's 1943 visit to Haiti and broadly denotes a real and, at times, historically verifiable Caribbean and Latin American occurrence that appears so fantastic and inconceivable by Western ontological standards that it defies reason (as defined by the West). Because of its defiance of Western reason, the marvelous happening is perceivable only because of the viewer's Black Atlantic spiritual conviction. Vodou is therefore key to Carpentier's theory. It is significant because of its importance to the revolutionary struggle. It is also significant because Vodou underscores, firstly, the defiant power that resides in distinct cultural realities; and it shows, secondly, how steadfast conviction in Black Atlantic spiritual practices can be as generative for the dispossessed as the ardent millenarian Christianity that Columbus turned to when creating the world anew for white Western Europeans and their descendants. In other words, Black Atlantic spirituality can engender radically new epistemological practices, paradigms, and ways of being. The *Ginen moun* who became revolutionaries declared *tout moun se moun* (all people are people), and the revolutionary vanguard following them declared, "Enslaved? . . . Let us leave this description for the French; they have conquered but are no longer free" while officially resignifying their world as new. Carpentier, in turn, has his prototypic revolutionary chant a prayer to the *lwa* Ogoun Faï—"Santiago / Can't you see I am the son of war?"[88] This prayer mirrors the new world-building effect of *Ginen* cultural thought, and it shows how captives were able to cognitively map their way to liberated Haiti in the first place.

This aforementioned prayer to Ogoun Faï closes a chapter titled "Santiago de Cuba," which fictionalizes the white flight from Saint Domingue to neighboring hemispheric American cities that occurred throughout the Haitian Revolution with attention to M. de Mézy's move to the Cuban city of Santiago de Cuba. In focusing exclusively on the flight of white émigrés, the chapter minimizes the accompanying (compelled and voluntary) movement of Black peoples that also took place during the Revolution. This movement is far more consequential because it gave rise to the Black majority (white identified) nation that Cuba was in Carpentier's moment and that Cuba remains today. The collapse of Saint Domingue's sugar industry gave Cuban planters the opportunity to "emulate the magnificent wealth and power of the Saint Domingue planter class."[89] Historian Ada Ferrer writes that ambitious Cuban planters "ramped up [sugar] production, purchasing more and more land and mills and enslaved laborers to fill the world demand for sugar" that Saint Domingue previously satiated.[90] As a result of this fervent activity, a "society with slaves [became in a short span] a slave society."[91] The city of Santiago de Cuba, and much of eastern Cuba where sugar and coffee cultivation dominated industry, was soon governed by the political and economic desires of Cuba's planter class and, consequentially, increasingly peopled with captive Black laborers. Émigrés, like de Mézy, who chose this city as their port of entry did so because it was the closest to Saint Domingue; and while Cuban planters remained apprehensive of their steady arrival, fearing the free and captive Black people who disembarked with them, the revolution did not arrive. Ferrer writes, "curiously, the place closest to Haiti, with the largest concentration of French people of color, slave and free, appears to have produced no slave conspiracy or rebellion, even though it, too, was witnessing a boom in slavery as a result of the Haitian Revolution."[92] Still, even as Cuban planters, colonial officials, and enterprising white émigrés managed "to contain Haiti" as they replicated Saint Domingue, Ti-Noël's prayer suggests that a revolution was nonetheless produced in colonial Cuba as it was in Saint Domingue.[93] Ti-Noël's direct address to the city of Santiago intimates how Carpentier viewed the Haitian Revolution as uncontainable even with Cuban colonial efforts, as the chapter's last word is unyielding Black resistance—"Santiago / Can't you see I am the son of war?"[94]

This defiant final word points to captive resistance in Cuba among its natal captive population, which occurred because of the colony's ever-increasing commitment to slavery and plantation industry. It also references the established idea that Black Saint Dominguan *and* Black Cuban participation in the Haitian Revolutionary struggle required little more than the attempt to think toward freedom. For Carpentier, a break with colonial ontology had to happen for the Revolution to occur, which Ti-Noël's prayer shows. In the scene in question, a destitute de Mézy attends mass in search of Christian salvation while Ti-Noël, present because of his enslavement, seeks a salvation all his own. The aforementioned chant to Ogou Faï was originally "an old song that [Ti-Noël] learned from Macandal"; the song is offered as a prayer because the Cuban Cathedral's "Voodoo warmth" led Ti-Noël to reason, "St. James is Ogoun Faï," the *lwa* "under whose spell Bouckman's followers had risen."[95] Ti-Noël is an early member of Boukman Dutty's army and served as a delegate at the famed *Bwa Kayïman* assembly that laid the strategic ground for the Revolution's opening sieges.[96] Ti-Noël participates in the attack on de Mézy's plantation when the rebellion commences and is forcibly removed from the struggle once captured by colonial authorities. He is sentenced to death soon after and subsequently "saved" by de Mézy for re-enslavement in Santiago, Cuba.[97] He remains a devout "follower" of Boukman without ever inciting an antislavery rebellion or conspiracy, even while held captive in Santiago, because he consciously chooses to envision his own humanity. He reasons that "St. James is Ogoun Faï" and attempts to conceive beyond the pale of a colonial world in which his captivity is normalized through Judeo-Christian teachings. Accordingly, if the Catholic saint, "St. James," is too complicit with a colonial order deeply committed to slavery and white supremacy then the estimation that "St. James is Ogoun Faï" divests the saint from this collusion; it repurposes him as a *Ginen* deity who can readily see (and help embolden others to see) that a colonial order, predicated on Black enchainment, is unjust and should be resisted. In this respect, "St. James is Ogoun Faï" is an affirmation of a way of being fundamentally opposed to the Eurocentric and white supremacist worldview that bore chattel slavery and made anti-Blackness an acceptable norm within the Americas.

Carpentier's decision to depict Ti-Noël's conscious alteration of Christian iconography with Vodou cosmology demonstrates a concerted effort to read *and* represent *Ginen* Haitian Revolutionary resistance as momentous precisely because average, plain people (here *Ginen* captives) thought and acted their liberation into existence. Their onto-epistemological practices—their myths and spiritual beliefs—made the possibility of a new kind of existence real. They were, in other words, conceptually marvelous and decolonial in orientation. This is especially so because these knowledge practices provided the cognitive ground for the armed component of the revolutionary war, which Carpentier's theory stresses. If, as Carpentier writes, "the sense of the marvelous [firstly] presupposes . . . faith," the faith evident in contemporary Haiti—which he describes in the prologue when noting, "the magical portents in the red roads of the Central Plateau" and "the drums of the Voodoo gods Petro and Rada"—underscores how Vodou created a mappable cultural reality for Haiti's revolutionaries.[98] This unique reality, specific to the people of Haiti, reveals how Vodou reshaped the geography of Saint Domingue with objects and sounds that could inspire captives to think that another world is not only possible *but* achievable. This kind of faith ultimately shows how Haiti articulates existence as a multiverse—multiple worlds in the world—since the nation denotes an idea of the marvelous that is culturally rooted and geographically creative for Haitian existence. It also shows why Carpentier reads Haiti's existence as refuting what Columbus's marvelous normalizes: Christian imperialism's homogenization of knowledge and existence as knowable through the West alone.

THE COLUMBIAN MARVELOUS

Christian imperialism denies speculation about the nature of existence and produces a notion of the marvelous in line with its thinking. The medieval marvelous does the opposite and accords with Carpentier's *Ginen* inspired idea of the marvelous because of its emphasis on rumination. The writings of early Western European travelers like Marco Polo and Sir John Mandeville outline the medieval marvelous, which seeks to "inspire ... wondering speculation" about the nature of the world as it is.[99] Its emphasis on speculative awe accounts for the query Carpentier poses with part one's epigraph; specifically, its closing question, "Know you not that long since / I [the devil] rule there?"[100] Literary historian Stephen Greenblatt, drawing from historian Jacques Le Goff, writes that "the medieval sense of the marvelous ... expressed perceptions of nature [that were] potentially or actually inimical to the transcendental being and providential authority of the Christian God and His servant the Church."[101] The marvelous "stood for all that could not be securely held, all that resisted appropriation" about existence on the whole.[102] In other words, in medieval travelogues, the marvelous referred to alien forms of nature that invoked curious astonishment about existence because it confounded the mind's eye. If the medieval marvelous was rooted in that which cannot be knowable and articulable, the Columbian marvelous was grounded in the Christian state's political usurpation of the apocalyptic millenarian fervor that said the Lord made the earth for humankind (*propter nos*) and was thus knowable. Christian imperialism used this new understanding of the human's capacity to know the world to produce knowledge practices whose "rhetorical task [was] to bring together commodity conversion and spiritual conversion."[103] These practices made all things perceivable as new. The perceivable newness of things wedded the expansion in veridic knowledge to the simultaneous demonization of African and

Indigenous peoples in the Eastern and Western hemispheres. Africans and Natives not only exist in spaces that could now be conceived as sites of idolatry, but they, being idolaters, could now ensure the salvation of Christians by being forcibly made Christian via enslavement. Put differently, their lives could be bartered to free their souls (once deceased) and the lives of living Christians, who could materially create their promised land in the kingdom of this world.

Columbus's detailed depiction of the Indigenous in his letter to Santángel shows how he reasoned their enslavement as beneficial to his salvation and that of all faithful servants of the Spanish crown. His depiction frames the Indigenous as ignorant of trade and as like Africans. He writes that the Indigenous "have no iron or steel or weapons, nor are they fitted to use them. This is not because they are not well built and of handsome stature, but because they are very marvellously timorous."[104] The marvelous, in this context, is a descriptor of the marketable worth of things (commodified as valuable or not). It helps Columbus mount a case for the Indigenous as thingifiable—as natural commodities that could be valuable to Spain. The Indigenous "are very marvellously timorous" precisely because they do not know about a civilized and thus developed life, not having iron, steel, or weapons of war. The inference here is that they are harmless and not a threat; and when Columbus goes on to state that they are "savages," he names them thusly because of their ignorance of trade. He writes that the Indigenous acted "like savages" because they took part in barter without understanding the value of things, giving "what they had" for "broken hoops of wine barrels."[105] Columbus wants his readers to understand that the Indigenous should be knowable as commodities because they do not understand trade and because their way of life suggests they could not possibly understand trade. When he goes on to state that they accepted the "thousand good things" he gave them without thought, he finalizes his rendering of them as commodifiable things by inferring that they are idolaters and thus like Africans.[106]

Prior to his 1492 voyage to the Caribbean, Columbus visited "the trading fort built by the Portuguese at El Mina on the west coast of Africa in or around 1482" to engage in the African slave trade.[107] Upon setting sail for the Indies, Leo Wiener writes that "Columbus carried [hawk's] bells specifically for the purpose of trading with the Indians, no doubt, because voyagers to Africa had found them acceptable to the Negroes."[108] Wiener understands the peoples of Africa to be "Negroes" because the trade in Africans begun by the Europeans of the Iberian Peninsula re-conceptualized all Africans and their descendants the world over as Blacks or Negroes. Wynter writes, "Through the institution of the latifundium [a large estate manned by enslaved peoples] ... the black entered the Western architecture of signs conjoined as fact and fiction—black slave. He was black (*negro*) because he was naturally a slave (*esclavo*); he was a slave (*esclavo*) because he was naturally black. To be Negro was to be a slave."[109] Weiner does not question the African's signification as a natural slave (Negro) and nor does he question how this signification invites thinking of Natives as natural slaves, but he is aware of how Columbus sought to relate to Indigenous peoples as he related to African peoples. Weiner writes, "at every meeting, [Columbus] distributed these [bells] to the Indians, who were crazy for them and ready to give much gold for the hawk's bells."[110] The "thousand good things" that Columbus mentions in his letter to Santángel surely must be these bells. If these bells are accepted as gifts by Indigenous peoples, then the Indigenous, themselves, are asserting their innate desire for subjection. In other words, they have established by their own accord their likeness to peoples who were deemed justly enslave-able, and they must now be saved from themselves.

Columbus could reason enslavement as just because he was a sponsored agent of a "Christian State [Spain], whose raison d'etre is power in the world," and he could reason servitude as just because he was an ardent practitioner of "the Christian faith, which denies the world."[111] Because of these identities, he adhered to the illogical rationalism, prevailing in Iberian Europe, that "exalted" Christianity's power "to *convert* opposite (in terms of color) to its own faith, to its own white/Christian identity."[112] This reasoning furthered the legitimacy of the latifundium, which as Wynter writes, was the "institution" through which the African became a slave and was re-ontologized as a Negro.[113] The latifundium added to the fantastical way Europeans of the Iberian Peninsula made sense of Africans. Before entering "the Western architecture of signs conjoined as fact and fiction—black slave," Africans previously denoted the devil.[114] As followers of Islam, Africans within the Moorish empire signified the inverse of the Western European (Christian and white) and were persons to be feared "because of [their] religion."[115] With the latifundium's naturalization of Africans as Black and as slaves because they are Black, enslavement presented a way to cast out the devil literally and figuratively—that is, the Black Moor who poses a threat to Christianity. Even as Christian theologians in Columbus's moment affirmed "that there was nothing in the Law of Christ which stated that the liberty of the soul must be paid for by the servitude of body," enslavement as salvation prevailed because of the steadfast belief in Christianity's power to convert.[116] This logic guides Columbus's presentation of the Indigenous in his letter; his reasoning mirrors the "justification" offered by "the Christian nations of Spain and Portugal" for the enslavement of Africans, which "couched [the merits of bondage] in terms of exchange [where] the 'native' gave his material labor in exchange for his spiritual freedom."[117] This exchange prompted Columbus to bring "hawk's bells" for a people he is unsure exists. He believed that these new peoples could be saved from eternal damnation by becoming like him, Christian and white; and he was prepared to convert them to his cultural likeness by force.[118]

Western Europe's religiously oriented anti-Blackness provided the ideological framework that would determine how Native peoples were to be perceived as a collective. Like Africans, they were to be saved in the name of Christ through servitude. The "root expansion in thought" that can be rightly attributed to Columbus must be discussed in full recognition of how it is deeply imbricated in an imperial logic of Christian anti-Black Islamophobia, which bore anti-Native bigotry in the Americas.[119] This logic made all Europeans nobles, to borrow from de Vega, and made vanquishing the African and Native a divine right.[120] Greenblatt writes that when Columbus details how he takes possession of the Indies for the Spanish crown in his letter to Santángel and his other writings, he pairs "marvelously" with "bestowed" and discloses how the act of possession allowed him "to make an absolute gift" to his Christian god.[121] He asserts thereafter that Columbus "seeks earthly gain in order to serve a divine purpose; the Indians must lose everything in order to receive everything; the innocent natives will give away their gold for trash, but they will receive a treasure far more precious than gold; the wicked natives (the 'cannibals') will be enslaved in order to be freed from their own bestiality."[122] If Native peoples in the Caribbean are "marvellously timorous," they are so because Columbus sees them as ideal mediums through which to serve his god and because of that their conversion through enslavement justifies Columbus's apocalyptic millenarian conviction that the Indies was a promised land. It was a place where faithful Christians could adequately establish their knowledge of the earth while aggrandizing their existence in the kingdom of this world. Carpentier's novella, however, begs the question: what of the captive (the Black and Native), what of their kingdom in this world?

THE MARVELOUS AS ANTICOLONIAL PRAXIS

Carpentier's theory of the marvelous real addresses this question. It thinks with *Ginen* revolutionists in its insistence on a plural understanding of peoples and their worlds. This insistence is what politicizes his theory. It occasions his attempt to spur hemispheric Americans to become resistant in their thinking, art, and politics, on the one hand, and proudly Caribbean and Latin American, on the other. Carpentier's politicizing effort is evident in his discussion of Haiti's famed La Citadelle (the Citadelle, hereafter) and Vodou, which appear in the prologue to *The Kingdom of This World* and in his expanded essays on the marvelous.[123] Commissioned by Dessalines and built by the Haitian Revolutionary general and later king, Christophe, the Citadelle was originally erected following Haitian independence in 1804 to protect the northern coast from the threat of a French reinvasion. For Carpentier, it served a far more important function; it attested to the distinctiveness of the Americas in comparison to Western Europe. He stresses that the fortress is "without architectonic antecedents [and] portended only in Piranesi's *Imaginary Prisons*."[124] In other words, it is conceivable only through the imaginative unreality of Western Europe's fantastical arts, be they the unusual engravings of Giovanni Batista Piranesi or surrealist fiction.[125] The Citadelle underscored how Caribbean and Latin American realities were ripe with wondrous actualities that Western European artists and thinkers could only realize as real via fictive art. The specific uniqueness of the Americas becomes readily identifiable with attention to the Citadelle (for instance) because it exists wholly in the real. More than that, it is grounded in the history and culture of a new kind of people (Haitians), who have forged their own distinct cultural realities against unprecedented odds.

Accordingly, the turn to Haiti's most potent cultural realism, Vodou, in the prologue establishes how distinct cultural invention promotes politically effective realities. Carpentier writes, "I tread[ed] earth where thousands of men eager for liberty believed in Macandal's lycanthropic powers, to the point that their collective faith produced a miracle the day of his execution."[126] *Ginen* captives engendered a "collective faith" in rebellion notwithstanding violent reprisals (e.g., Makandal's execution); in remaining steadfastly resistant, they show why faith is important to Carpentier's theory of the "marvelous real." Faith provides the gumption needed to unabashedly avail oneself to the rapture of possibility and the actuality of a human initiated miracle (consider Makandal's death defying survival of his execution in the novella).[127] Carpentier therefore writes that the marvelous is "perceived with peculiar intensity due to an exaltation of the spirit which elevates it to a kind of 'limit state.'"[128] This "limit state" points to how the intense devotion that Vodou fosters engenders not only a belief in the otherworldly and its transformative effects in the present; but such faith encourages awareness of the transformative power of individuals to themselves shape the world as they see fit. In this respect, *Ginen* cultural praxis made real, for Carpentier, how inspired radical thought can engender a preferred lived reality.

Caribbean and Latin American people have largely been unable to actualize their preferred existence. For Carpentier, their inability to do so is telling of the controlling and corrosive influence of white colonial domination (or the Columbian project for being), which makes it so that all thinking and all imaginings must conform to the epistemological and ontological standards of the West. If, however, Western Europeans were ill equipped to imagine a structure like the Citadelle because their own cultural realities normalized the racial enslavement that the Citadelle was built to stand against, then, for Carpentier, their culturally specific and racially proscribed modes of thought for art, politics, and existence on the whole would be equally unable to contend with a hemisphere whose entire topography and peoples were shaped by enslavement and resistance to enslavement. Carpentier therefore argues that in much the same way that the Spanish archetype of imperial politics, Hernán Cortez, could not describe the Americas—"As I do not know what to call these things, I cannot express them"—the French surrealist and heir to Cortez's Columbian inspired imperial project, André Masson, would prove equally unable to depict the region's vegetation.[129] He remarks, "observe that when André Masson tried to draw the jungle of Martinique . . . the marvelous truth of the matter devoured the painter, leaving him just short of impotent when faced with the blank paper. It had to be an American painter—Wilfredo Lam—who taught us the magic of tropical vegetation."[130] The marvelous as a theoretical construct is purposely anticolonial in orientation precisely because it is intended to inculcate within Caribbean and Latin American thinkers, artists, and laymen a firm sense of cultural self-worth and distinction from Western Europe. This self-worth and singularity are intended to spur them toward accepting the fact of their racialization as persons born on demonic ground. Accepting this fact grants the imaginative license to rethink how they relate to each other; they could refuse, in other words, to be racist. It specifically means resisting their internalization of anti-Blackness, which, in turn, for Carpentier, will help them to become curious about their region and creative in their resistance against the West.

The absence of this curiosity is why Carpentier introduces his readers to Haiti, a nation that is not readily associated with "the Latin American world that the author wants his theory [of the marvelous] to apply to [given that this world] is defined to a greater degree by indigenous and European peoples," writes Kramer.[131] Kramer finds it "striking that [Carpentier] chooses to highlight that his inspiration for a theory of the marvelous real . . . occurred in Haiti, a [Francophone] nation dominated by people who trace their ancestry to Africa."[132] But it is not just Haiti that inspires the theory, it is the Black peoples of the Americas and their cultural works. In addition to a Haitian Revolutionary edifice (the Citadelle), a pre-revolutionary rebellion (Makandal's campaign), and Haitian Vodou, the prologue also notes that the Black peoples of Cuba and Venezuela have produced marvelous cultural productions, consider "the dances of Cuban Santeria" and "the prodigious African version of the Corpus festival" found in "San Francisco de Yare, Venezuela."[133] To find it "striking" that Carpentier is inspired by Haiti is to miss the political imperative guiding Carpentier's theory: people can remake their worlds anew. Haitians (as well as other Black peoples in the Americas) have created art, edifices, and philosophies that have the capacity to chart a new course for their worlds. This capacity is not readily noted in art, criticism, or politics in the Americas (among the prominent and powerful) because of an ingrained regional bias against Black peoples and Black cultural production, which Carpentier challenges (to a degree). Yet, for him, it is Black peoples' capacity to chart a new course for the world (via their cultures) that is desperately needed to successfully resist the West. Ultimately, readers must know about Haiti and other Black cultures in the Americas so that they can become curious about their world and the worlds around them. This curiosity nurtures skepticism of Western norms of being, which Carpentier wants. He wants his readers to question the applicability of Western conventions to their art and their polities; and he also wants them to learn more about their homegrown innovations, many of which are shaped by Black peoples. These wants require thinking with Haiti because it shows how the world can exist *propter nos*: for the new humans existing on demonic ground.

Haiti Unseen

Despite wanting his readers to think with Haiti and see the importance of Black thought and action to the Americas, Carpentier writes against his noteworthy presentation of Black hemispheric American culture as politically and culturally transformative by *The Kingdom of this World*'s end. The chapters in parts three and four of the novella depict the newly emancipated as nominally free. King Henry Christophe's reintroduction of forced labor to construct the Citadelle and palace Sans-Souci is treated at length.[134] The institution of obligatory farming that follows the collapse of Christophe's northern kingdom and that prompts the country's reunification into a republic is noted as well.[135] The entire post-revolutionary Haitian experience is reduced to an "endless return of chains, [a] rebirth of shackles, [and a] proliferation of suffering."[136]

This reduction has provoked criticism of Carpentier's work, causing literary critic Philip Kaisary to persuasively argue that Carpentier's pessimistic portrayal of the Revolution's hereafter "undermines the unprecedented historic actuality of the transformational actions taken by enslaved blacks in Saint Domingue."[137] Carpentier merits the criticism he has received regarding his presentation of post-revolutionary Haiti, as it is far too reductive. I have argued that Carpentier's gauche rendering of newly independent Haiti ought to be read with attention to the stateless Haitian migrants suffering in Cuba as he composed *The Kingdom of This World*; however, I also recognize that this reading cannot account for Carpentier's conflation of Black post-revolutionary Haitian leadership with white colonial rule.[138] The analysis offered here is less interested in his diminution of the Revolution and its captive agents and more concerned with how his racist portrait of liberated Haiti subsumes the new world space that is 1804 Haiti into the old-world colonial order that Haiti's existence upends and delegitimizes.[139]

Carpentier subsumes new world Haiti into the colonial world order through his portrait of King Christophe. Carpentier writes Christophe as having acted *just like* the French in Saint Domingue. In other words, he writes him as being the same, if not similar to a white slave-holding colonist. He writes,

> [Ti-Noël] began to think that the chamber-music orchestrates of Sans Souci, [and] the splendor of the uniforms . . . were all the product of a slavery as abominable as what he had known on the plantation of M. Lenormand de Mézy. Even worse, for there was a limitless affront in being beaten by a Negro as black as oneself; as thick-lipped and wooly-headed, as flat-nosed, as low born. . . . Besides, in other days, the colonists—except when they had lost their heads—had been careful not to kill their slaves, for dead slaves were money out of their pockets.[140]

In what world did a slaveholding colonist, least of which one from Saint Domingue, a colony that was notorious for its brutality, care enough for the captive so as to not rashly commit murder? Laurent Dubois addresses the colony's genocidal violence toward captives when writing, "of the half-million slaves in Saint Domingue on the eve of the revolt of 1791, about 330,000 had been born and raised in Africa. Most of them were quite recent arrivals; more than 40,000 had stepped off the slave ships just the previous year."[141] *Bossales* (the Africa-born captives) accounted for a large amount of the population of captive people in Saint Domingue precisely because murder of captives was the norm. I find it troubling that Carpentier ignores this given how well researched the novella is; Echevarría and Paravisini-Gebert detail the extensive primary historical documents and fictional texts he uses to write his narrative in their engagements with the novella.[142] And Carpentier, himself, stresses the historical veracity of his depiction of the Revolution, colonial Saint Domingue, and Haiti.[143] History aside, the lie that is the colonist's reluctance to harm captives is all the more disquieting because Carpentier has a Black character voice this untruth racistly. Consider Ti-Noël's needless miming of racist thought with respect to Black physical features and Black peoples in governance (specifically, the idea that Black rulers are innately given to dictatorial excess and extravagance)

Carpentier ends his novella casting Haiti as a failed state because of post-independence leadership; in presenting Haiti in this manner, he wittingly or unwittingly redeems white peoples at the expense of Haitians and Black Cubans. He makes the Columbian project of white supremacist exploitation a broad human failing and not the particular failing of a specific human collective: white Western Europeans and white hemispheric Americans. As a result, he effaces the overwhelming criminality of white peoples so that he can put forth the position that Black people also enslaved other Black humans and as such make the implicit case that we are all (Black peoples and white peoples) equally at fault for maintaining the colonial order when Black peoples are not. Black post-revolutionary leaders did not wed the institution of chattel slavery to one people among the world's population. Black leaders of newly independent Haiti did not thereafter profit off of this servitude *or* the institutionalized un-human-ing of Black peoples via egregious self-serving scholarship and judicial edicts. No. The tyranny of Black leaders in early Haiti is the tyranny of the catch up—of the racially marginalized feeling as though they have to be like white Western Europe and achieve civilized status in the ways that "civilized" white peoples achieved their own purported civility: through violent theft of land, of life, and of labor and through the equally violent hoarding of resources.[144]

Carpentier's refusal to distinguish between the vulturine behaviors of white Western Europeans from the despotism of Black leaders in early Haiti betrays his investment in whiteness; for what is the work of this depiction of liberated Haiti if not that of redeeming whiteness? What other purpose can it serve? In choosing to minimize the criminality of white colonial action in Haiti, Carpentier grants white peoples in the region a racial innocence that is nonexistent. Worse yet, this innocence effectively elides what the Revolution and liberated Haiti jointly articulates: the necessity of ending the West, its white supremacist knowledge systems, and its extortive hierarchical cultural systems. The *Ginen* revolutionists of *Ayiti Ginen* understood this and acted accordingly. Carpentier chose to maintain his racial innocence and ignored their sagacity. Because of this, he does not simply present post-revolutionary Haiti as a locus for ongoing colonial predation spearheaded by Black leaders; but he openly invites his readers to question the *fact* of Haitian liberation.

The majority of revolutionaries—the *Ginen* who interests Carpentier and the non-republican creole generals of the vanguard—*together* created lasting material and ontological conditions for a distinct decolonial world in Haiti. At the heart of the nation's intra-social relations is a decolonial ethic that Kreyòl, the language of the nation, maintains and disseminates. The Haitian idiom *tout moun se moun* (all people are people) exemplifies this and underscores what Carpentier cannot see: the foundational conditions for a world continually rendering its decolonial communality into perpetuity. If a communal consciousness of a decolonial self existed in colonial Saint Domingue, among the plain *Ginen* or captive and freed peoples (*moun*) who would constitute the revolutionary armies, surely this consciousness was maintained in liberated Haiti. Casimir states,

> reciprocal assistance that oppressed people weaved in their community and private lives eroded inter-ethnic divisions and negated modern racial stratification. Toussaint could write *From the first Black to the first White* embracing all shades of color in the population; Dessalines could issue

article 15 of the 1805 Constitution which brought together all Haitians under the generic label of *Blacks*. The *All people are people, Tout moun se moun* became a unifying principle. New generations learned it while practicing the national language, away from their scant use of French.[145]

How Haitians have chosen to articulate their existence, that is, how they speak this decolonial sensibility in insisting on the personhood of every person via idioms like *tout moun se moun* in colonial Saint Domingue and independent Haiti, reveals that the world they created when making Haiti is not a mini replica of Saint Domingue, with Black rulers acting as white colonists. Their world is distinct. Yes, it is a fragile world. It is subject to the colonial mindset of Haiti's oligarchy and the anti-Black attacks of white geopolitical polities burgeoning with citizens ever ready to assert white power via the force of their pens, their arms, and their supremacist iteration of Christ. But even with that, Haiti remains a new and distinct world.[146]

Haiti, the new world, is unseen by Carpentier; and because it is unseen the epistemic importance of Black peoples and Black cultures to his decades-long engagement with hemispheric liberation is also unseen by readers of his Haitian corpus. This engagement with hemispheric liberation is evident in the latter two narratives in his Haitian oeuvre, *The Lost Steps* and *The Harp and the Shadow*. Both build on Carpentier's turn to the Haitian Revolution to think toward (and help call into being) a decolonized American hemisphere as they return (in fictional form) to the theoretical premises of the marvelous real without its constitutive element: Black thought, Black cultural production, and Black peoples. *The Lost Steps* chronicles an unhappily married white composer and musicologist's return to his Latin American homeland from an extensive yet unfulfilling sojourn in New York City. His journey home (without his white US-born Southern wife) fosters a rediscovery of the region's innate geographic wondrousness and cultural distinction from Western Europe and North America. The composer's awareness of the singularity of Latin America was suppressed within him because of a prior overvalorization and identification with the Western European heritage of his father, a musician who immigrated to Latin America. This narrative motif of past Europhilia is largely conveyed through the unnamed composer's nostalgic passion for Beethoven's Ninth Symphony. The composer is cognizant that the wondrous land and culture of the Americas (the Andes primarily) is his rightful heritage, but he cannot fully immerse himself in this birthright as he will not exist in a world outside of the West despite his misgivings about it. He refuses to relinquish his whiteness and exist as a non-Western European and a non-white North American to be at home in his native region. This aversion occurs notwithstanding his love for an Indigenous woman (Rosario) who serves as his cultural informant and anchor to the region.

Although the composer is at peace in the Andean village in which he lives, he leaves the village and Rosario behind and returns to New York to secure writing instruments for compositional work that has little cultural value in his new Andean home. It is not that the villagers do not appreciate music, but the composer is hesitant to make a life with an Indigenous woman and is very taken with the cachet of bringing "primitive" musical sounds to a white civilized audience. Mid divorce, he returns to the Andes at the novel's end when faced with the superficiality of New York (despite the critical acclaim he receives for his Andean-style composition). Rosario and the village, however, are nowhere to be found: the composer's steps are ultimately lost as his journey to the Americas, from the novel's onset and end, retraces a path to nowhere. His journey is already mapped out, completed by Columbus centuries earlier, whose route established racialized categories of cultural being that—when adhered to (as in the case of the composer)—negate all efforts for a life outside of the West.

As with *The Lost Steps*, Columbus returns as a focal figure in Carpentier's last Haitian text, *The Harp and the Shadow*. The narrative recounts two stories: The first opens and closes the text and chronicles the quest to canonize Columbus by Pope Pius VII, and the second depicts a dying Columbus confessing, to himself alone, all his misdeeds in the Caribbean. Columbus returns as a spirit at the narrative's end to witness the papal beatification proceedings, which block his canonization. Upon seeing this, a dejected Columbus vanishes, returning to the cadre of "Invisible One[s]" (wandering spirits) who become "one with the transparent ether."[147] Where the marvelous real is present in Carpentier's attention to the unique topography of Latin America and the propensity of hemispheric American artists to adhere to Western cultural standards when creating art in *The Lost Steps*, in *The Harp and the Shadow*, the marvelous real is seen in both Carpentier's attention to the geography of the Americas and in his depiction of Columbus's spiritual ascendancy into the collective of "invisibles."[148] Carpentier's use of "invisibles" calls to mind Black Atlantic spiritual traditions of ancestral veneration where deceased ancestors become part of an unseeable collective watching over all. His decision to make Columbus an "Invisible One" is both an act of reclamation and release. In other words, he embraces Columbus (his importance to the region as it stands now) so as to move beyond Columbus and the colonial order he inaugurates.

Yet this still begs the question: where is the agency of the hemispheric American people? Where, indeed, are the Black peoples and Indigenous peoples (among other racialized groups) for whom Columbus is hardly consequential and who have already repossessed their region through their innovative cultural practices? They are there with the Haitians laboring under the tyranny of Christophe as Carpentier describes in *The Kingdom of this World*. They remain, in other words, the vanquished and exist geospatially determined as the inferior others who made Europeans "noble" (following de Vega). Because they must know themselves through Columbus, via his fictional story or by retracing his steps, they cannot reimagine themselves through the *Ginen* revolutionist, the everyday Black hemispheric American or any other resistant person within their cultural context. Their art and politics must be aspirational as a result, and indicative of how they are culturally Western European. Moreover, their personhood exists derivatively. It must accord with how the West defines the human, no matter that the vast majority of hemispheric Americans cannot embody the human in this limited sense.

The cost of the *Ginen* revolutionary's or the everyday Black hemispheric American's absence in Carpentier's Haitian writings is great, as their erasure maintains the West's homogenization of the human as white and culturally Western European. Their erasure also obscures how the thoughts and cultures of Black peoples shape Carpentier's delineation of the marvelous in the Haitian texts that come after *The Kingdom of this World*. Furthermore, the absence of the *Ginen* revolutionist or the everyday Black hemispheric American in Carpentier's Haitian writings invites skepticism about decolonizing our worlds and this skepticism diminishes the political impact of Carpentier's Haitian corpus. This oeuvre is worth discussing alongside other Caribbean literature of the Haitian Revolution precisely because of its political origins in refuting the colonial order via the marvelous and the story of Haiti's Revolution. I privilege this origin when reading Carpentier's Haitian corpus. And I choose to lean into the speculative breadth of his work, notwithstanding his negation of the new world that is Haiti, because Carpentier invites thinking otherwise. The political origins of his Haitian writings imbue his literatures with the *Ginen* will to think the world anew, which was necessary in Carpentier's moment and which remains necessary today. To read Carpentier's Haitian writings is to be reminded of this necessity, and of the identifications that make us like Carpentier himself, obedient and disobedient subjects of the West.

CHAPTER 3

Not This!

> A century is over and there is another world to invent.
> —Aimé Césaire

> August 14–August 21. Sèt jou . . .
> —Haitixchange User

> "Not this" makes a difference even if it does not immediately produce a propositional otherwise.
> —Elizabeth Povinelli

A new world was created by Haitian revolutionaries in 1804 and there remains still "another world to invent."[1] The pressing question is whether the latter actuality invalidates the veracity of the former. Is it paradoxical to write in support of the decolonial world *Ginen* captives made, as done in the previous chapter, given that Haiti today stands occupied—its sovereignty crippled under the weight of a one-hundred-year-long occupation by the United States, the North Atlantic Treaty Organization, the International Monetary Fund, and the World Bank? Am I propagating a political fiction when sitting with *bossales* (the Africa-born) and their Africanized descendants? Am I propagating this fiction when stressing the importance of their lives and their world to Haiti's rich histories, when Haiti's many friends and foes are both united in their view of the nation's post-revolutionary disequilibrium? Both are unwilling to see the resistant nature of these histories and as a result cannot name Haiti's long occupation as consequential to its political difficulties.

The Martinican writer, philosopher, and politician Aimé Césaire is a sincere friend of Haiti. His literature about the nation affirms the Revolution and Haiti's importance to Black liberation. They include the recently recovered play ......*And the Dogs Were Silent* (1943), a similarly titled poem, *And the Dogs Were Silent* (1946), his book *Toussaint Louverture: The French Revolution and the Colonial Problem* (1960), and play *The Tragedy of King Christophe* (1963). Yet, he offers the following when in conversation with the Guadeloupean writer Maryse Condé in 2004. He states,

> The Haitians didn't even buy their liberty, they fought for it. They conquered their freedom not only for themselves but for all of us. We should be grateful for that. But ever since, apart from that episode, they have never known a reasonable organization that ensures a certain equilibrium. . . . They conquered their freedom but the society did not change as deeply as they had hoped. There . . . was the intermediate class who replaced the Whites and unfortunately retained a lot of the bad old habits, and did not play the role expected of it, and Haiti is searching for its equilibrium. It still hasn't found it.[2]

Césaire rightly acknowledges that Haiti exists in the patrimony of all Caribbean peoples: the Haitian fight for freedom was a Caribbean fight for freedom. He forgets, however, the nature of that struggle. Haitians paid to safeguard "their liberty" even as they had successfully fought to secure their freedom, paying a whopping twenty-one-billion-dollar indemnity to France for the loss of human "properties."[3] The decision to offer this payment after the Revolution's end was a republican political initiative born in a divided Haiti.[4] The inheritance Caribbean peoples have gained from Haiti must include more than a story of antislavery and anticolonial overcoming. It must include cognizance of the Revolution as it was, and Haiti as it came into being: the latter was a struggle of conflicting interests and the former the product of an independence forcefully appropriated.

Jean Casimir, Eglantine Colon, and Michelle Koerner write that "the creation of Haiti's state in 1804 was not a choice."[5] The genocidal excess of the French forced the persons who would constitute Haiti's first oligarchy "to declare the colony independent," as did the captive majority's steadfast conviction that another world was possible.[6] Haiti's first political elite emerged from a beleaguered position of utter powerlessness before the French and a majority that refused to exist as chattel. Its compromised position is masked to enthusiasts of the Revolution because its members were acclaimed creole revolutionists who were mostly *affranchise*—in other words, Black and/or mixed-race persons who were manumitted before 1791 and ranged from impoverished to largely middle-class individuals; this emancipated group also included freed Africans. Influential and/or moneyed mainly mixed-race persons who were born free, whose families were often generationally free, and who more readily owned large numbers of captives were also within this class of free peoples (*gens de couleurs*).

The leaders of Haiti's first elite were overwhelmingly former *gens de couleur* from rich slave-owning families and their recruits, which included persons emancipated before 1791 and prominent Black officers from the *armée indigène* (Haitian Revolutionary army) who might have been freed after 1791.[7] The republican politics of a contingent within this class profoundly shaped its leadership and aligned the class in thought with the French. Their politics prompted Michel-Rolph Trouillot to write, "on the left hand, a revolution; on the right hand, a coup," when describing early Haitian history, as these were Haitian revolutionists who governed in opposition to the Haitian Revolution.[8] Their pursuit of counter-Haitian revolutionary politics, evident in their use of colonial labor codes and their political liberalism when at the helm of Haiti, emerged from their Eurocentric values, which clashed with the African values of *Ginen* peoples. Because of the cultural and ideological differences between the *Ginen* mass and the oligarchic class, "between 1803 and 1806" many *gens de couleur* who would have been included in Haiti's first elite sold "their property and [fled] abroad," and those that stayed harbored "doubts about the viability of national independence."[9]

Haitians did not enter the annals of history as a united people with all of its revolutionists in happy accord. The Caribbean's Haitian inheritance ignores this and is predicated on an expectation of unity, first; on a willed forgetting of a complicated history that makes unity difficult, second; and, third, on an ignorance of the Revolution's most radical agents—*Ginen* captives. They have been made immaterial to the story of the Revolution and to early Haiti because "the role expected of" leadership was never deemed theirs to fill.[10] So immaterial are they that they have been cast out of prominence in Haiti's post-independence political intrigues, which results in a Revolution reimagined as having been failed by leaders who were never powerful enough to steward the Haiti they desired to bring into being. The misreading of the Revolution and early Haiti results in a damning criticism of both, which wittingly or unwittingly condemns Haiti to an inborn instability. This instability is plausible as a reading only through the total negation of the persistent fight against colonial power undertaken by Haiti's discounted majority. Haiti's friends should know better. The road to freedom in Saint Domingue was not paved by leaders but by armed and unarmed people working in consort with one another, promoting and removing leaders at will. Historian Carolyn E. Fick writes of southern Saint Domingue, "there was no single or exceptional leader to direct and coordinate opposition to the French army during the early stages of the struggle. Rather, individuals serving in various capacities, both civil and military, had taken the initiative of organizing themselves clandestinely . . . to build a network of resistance."[11] This "network" was not visibly present in the North of Saint Domingue because of the emergence of "exceptional leader[s]" like Toussaint Louverture, Henry Christophe or Jean Jacques Dessalines.[12] But even there, *Ginen* captives acted autonomously to secure the lives they wanted to lead notwithstanding the well-known authority of creole revolutionary leaders who if they survived to see Haiti became oligarchs themselves.[13]

If Alejo Carpentier's novella of the Revolution, *The Kingdom of This World*, remains a favorite it is precisely because the narrative privileges the agency of Saint Domingue's captives as opposed to the more famous creole generals. The preceding chapter discloses Carpentier's attention to *Ginen* revolutionists and the marvelous thought practices they engendered to both wage the revolutionary struggle and to secure a new world via liberated Haiti. Carpentier's affinity for the Revolution is obvious, but, like Césaire, he critiques the nation that the Revolution bore. Where Césaire issues his critique without prejudice, Carpentier offers a racist reading of post-revolutionary Haiti's early years. This reading concludes the narrative and rests heavily on the ills of early Haitian leadership.

The Kingdom of This World ends with 1825 Haiti in ecological ruin: a devastating hurricane ends the main character's (Ti-Noël) life and destroys the Northern plain. Prior to this, the closing chapters are primarily devoted to the revolutionary general-turned-king, Henry Christophe, and his tyrannical rule. Passing, yet pointed, reference is also afforded to the equally tyrannical governance of the former revolutionary general and later president Jean-Pierre Boyer's liberal democratic regime, as he assumes power after Christophe's suicide in 1820. The novella depicts them through the way they governed: in Western European style with lavish courts and corvée labor (Christophe) or republican austerity and corvée labor (Boyer).[14] The narrative's ending in ecological ruin is telling, given that nature in the novella is routinely depicted as both acting against and signifying the ready injustices of the human world to underscore Haiti's marvelous reality.[15] What should readers make of the narrative's final moment of ecological devastation *except* that this catastrophe portends the socio-political and economic disintegration Haiti will experience in the years thereafter, due to the dictatorial excesses of its leaders? The political divisiveness of the early post-revolutionary moment cannot simply be a product of a homegrown tyranny as Carpentier suggests. French colonial rule ends in Haiti in 1804, but Western imperialism does not. Carpentier ignores this and he ends his narrative accordingly, without reference to the harassment that post-independence Haiti faced from France's armed and naval forces, the political embargo that France levied against Haiti, and the lengths that the early Haitian states went to, to navigate hostilities from major white geopolitical powers.[16] The indemnity Boyer unwisely agrees to pay France is also passed over in silence. Worse yet, there is no recognition of the fact that the anti-Black bigotry that encouraged the republican political leaders of post-independence Haiti to discount the decolonial vision of the *Ginen* populace is the very same prejudicial logic that engendered Carpentier's own racist condemnation of Haiti's post-revolutionary leadership.

Haiti's early leaders (excluding Dessalines) deserve extensive critique for their colonized political visions. However, their paucity of imagination does not surpass the constitutive effects of white imperial power. Casimir writes that Haiti's "ruling minority can only secure its prevalence thanks to the flagrant and decisive interventions of foreign powers, whether the expeditions of Leclerc's army in 1802, the interventions of the US Marines in 1915, or the troops of the United Nations after the fall of the Berlin Wall. Left to itself, the ruling minority would gradually be engulfed by those it wishes to exploit," namely, the nation's *Ginen* majority.[17] To critique Haitian leadership alone is to take the posture of dominance as actual dominance. To quote Césaire in conversation with Condé, it is to assume that the retention "of . . . bad old habits" is Haiti's chief problem and not the power that normalized and sustained the "old habits" themselves."[18] Carpentier's concluding chapters are ultimately unsatisfying because they leave Haiti unseen: they divorce the geopolitics of white supremacy and imperialism from Haiti's post-revolutionary reality and further obfuscate its relevance to the nation's twentieth-century experience of economic devastation and political unrest. Notwithstanding, it is this unrest that Carpentier reads into nineteenth-century Haiti via his ending; and it is this unrest that the United States would cite to justify both occupying Haiti in 1915 and seizing the nation's national treasury to better manage Haiti's manufactured debts.[19]

Both Carpentier and Césaire critique post-revolutionary Haiti without attention to its histories. How should readers process a critique, however distinct, that necessarily leaves the nation and its people unseen? Both make Haiti an exception to the Caribbean experience of imperialism and both have authored literatures that inculcates blindness to white imperial machinations in the nation.[20] What should readers of their Haitian works make of their unwillingness to name white imperialists as the principal architects of Haiti's post-independence difficulties, rather than the Haitian leaders they so readily criticize? I open with the common ground Haiti's friends share with the nation's foes to pinpoint a problem of thought not politics. Carpentier and Césaire possess impeccable anticolonial politics. Césaire especially so because of his unwavering support of Black liberation. My analysis does not contest their significance to the Caribbean's rich tradition of discursive resistance, nor does it contest Césaire's relevance to Black decolonial politics. Césaire matters and should continue to matter. I think that he gets Haiti wrong even as he rightly recognizes Haiti's significance to anticolonialism in the past and present. He gets Haiti wrong because of his commitment to a republican reading of the Revolution, which fixes his attention on Saint Domingue's *affranchi* and the oligarchy that emerged from it in post-independence Haiti. This fixation muddies Césaire's sharp thinking on Black liberation and it does so because republicanism offers a cartography of thought that solely maps the colony. Césaire's intended destination in his literatures of Haiti is a world beyond the colony. His desire for this world is why I value his writings, and it is why I maintain that the issue here is not politics but reasoning that misdirects the politics. My argument acknowledges that two things can be right with respect to Césaire: he is the artist you want to think alongside when affirming the inventiveness of Black existence in the Americas; he is not the artist you want to conceive Haiti as *Ayiti Ginen*. Still, I focus here on Césaire's dramas, *The Tragedy of King Christophe: A Play* and *A Tempest* (1969), which I discuss alongside the Italian filmmaker Gillo Pontecorvo's film, *Queimada!* (*Burn!*; 1969), because they showcase Césaire's attention to the orienting nature of Haiti (as idea) for radical anticolonial action. Put otherwise, these plays trouble the republican agenda of his Haitian Revolutionary corpus because of their fixation on time.

Césaire writes Haiti as the compass directing feasible anticolonial praxis in the twentieth-century Caribbean in *The Tragedy of King Christophe* and *A Tempest*. The plays index Haiti's pivotal disruption of the colonial project's white supremacist narrative of being. The difficulties Haiti has faced since the Revolution calls the importance of this disruption into question. I read his dramas to invite attention to the problem that post-independence Haiti poses for Caribbean anticolonial thought produced with attention to the Revolution. Revolutionary Haiti (1791–1825) is a muse in the Caribbean cultural imaginary, post-revolutionary Haiti (1915 onward), warning. Each time period engenders distinct imaginings of Haiti and each imagining yields a Haiti unseen, obscured by the writer's refusal to face the scale of white imperial power in the nation. This refusal is understandable because of what it says about the possibility of decolonial liberation for the Caribbean; still, not facing it incurs the defeatism and disenchantment that courses through the classic Haitian Revolutionist literatures studied in this book. I find that it is both too easy to blame Haiti's political elite and too easy to ignore white imperial power. Rather than accept what is easy, I juxtapose readings of Haitian Revolutionary striving that lead with state power (*The Tragedy of King Christophe* and *A Tempest*) versus that of the sovereignty of the dispossessed (*Queimada!*) to highlight the difficulties of artistically staging and imagining a life beyond the colony. *Queimada!*, as Philip Kaisary argues, showcases the sovereignty of the dispossessed because it "communicates a powerful condemnation of colonial and neocolonial interference and insists upon the cause of liberation as an ethical imperative for the dispossessed."[21]

In reading Césaire's plays and Pontecorvo's film, I place the symbolic tension between revolutionary and post-revolutionary Haiti in the Caribbean cultural imaginary in conversation with the equally evident pattern in Caribbean arts and letters of discussing revolutionary Haiti alongside the colonial encounter. I do so to firmly situate Haitian Revolutionary striving in the origin story of the Americas. Carpentier's Haitian oeuvre is one literary instance of a Caribbean reading of the Haitian Revolution with attention to the encounter, and George Lamming's *The Pleasures of Exile* (1960) is another.[22] Césaire's offering is less evident since the "literary revolution that [the Haitian Revolution] engendered for Césaire," to borrow from E. Anthony Hurley, is not as explicitly tied to the colonial encounter.[23] The thematic substance of his Haitian works is "the praise of Haiti as the place where *negritude* stood up for the first time," and they engage the nation and its revolutionary history to firmly situate resistance against Western Europe, the United States, and colonized home-grown leaders as key to Caribbean art and politics.[24] While *The Tragedy of King Christophe* is a drama invested in examining the residual effects of colonialism in post-independence Haiti, Césaire's last play, *A Tempest*, writes the resistance of the colonized into the very fabric of the colonial encounter through the characters of Ariel and Caliban, and in this respect, he returns to the animating interests of his previous work focusing on Haiti.

The continuing salience of resistant efforts to Césaire's writing underscores how Caribbean dissension to the hemispheric Americas' socio-political colonization by Western Europeans and their hemispheric American descendants often begins with a turn to Haiti and moves to considerations of the encounter. Césaire's move from Haiti to the colonial encounter is of particular interest here because it indexes how the problem of post-revolutionary Haiti for Caribbean writers and thinkers is less a problem with Haiti, the postcolonial nation state, and more a problem with the available paths for existence that newly liberated colonies are afforded within the governing colonial world order. Attention to the colonial encounter and the narrative of discovery produces the necessary context to discern that the central issue of the Caribbean cultural imaginary of Haiti—the apparent disharmony between, on the one hand, the vast socio-political possibilities evidenced in revolutionary Haiti, and on the other, the seeming dead end state of the conflict-ridden post-revolutionary nation—is understanding how former slave colonies are *made to* function as particular kinds of nations in today's world. Understood thusly, these distinct ideational polarities (revolutionary Haiti versus post-revolutionary Haiti) potently illuminate the functional necessity of Black geopolitical failing for the colonial order of white Western European and North American rule.

I bring Pontecorvo in conversation with Césaire's treatment of revolutionary Haiti and the colonial encounter, firstly, because Pontecorvo's film helps to situate Césaire's Haitian writings as *Ginen* in their critical refusal of the colony as existence despite their republican (anti-*Ginen*) point of origin; and secondly, because Pontecorvo's interest in progressive time as a construct of the colonial project's civilizing mission heightens scholarly recognition of the functional necessity of Black geopolitical failing. Pontecorvo was an Italian Jew who came of age under Benito Mussolini's fascist regime (1922–1943). He became a Communist upon leaving Italy for France in light of anti-Semitism and took part in the resistance efforts against Mussolini that occasioned the Italian civil war (1943–1945), removing Mussolini from power. His film *Queimada!* is aligned with his personal history of resistance; it tells the story of a slave revolution orchestrated by England in a Portuguese colony subsisting through sugar cane cultivation. Once independent from Portugal, the nation-state of Queimada faces an anticolonial rebellion in light of ongoing colonial predation from self-interested white and white-identified creole leaders and from a multinational company, backed by England, eager to exploit the country's sugar production. Pontecorvo's attention to time, race, and coloniality in the film is of specific interest here because it highlights the way Black polities and Black peoples are made to move progressively in stasis, in and across epochs, following the colonial encounter. In other words, the film showcases how Black polities and peoples are made to move along an evolutionary timeline for being whose end goal is modeling the imperialist behavior of Western capitalist civilizations, no matter how opposed this end result is to the radical aims and intentions of Black antislavery and anticolonial movements. In *Queimada!* this compulsory evolutionary movement pivots on Haiti's powerful disruption of this administered pro-colonial temporality, and as such the film's provocative invocation of Haiti readily complements Césaire's long critical engagement with Haiti as the starting point for a new way to exist in time.

Accordingly, where depictions of overly present or extensively absented revolutionary figures drove the readings offered of James's history and Carpentier's novella in Chapters 1 and 2 of this book, Césaire's and Pontecorvo's invocation of revolutionary Haiti through obscure *and* untaken socio-political paths constitutes the decolonial ground treaded in this chapter. What is decolonial here is how Haiti serves as the compass for not only what to do, the task of seizing a world of one's own imagining, but for the doing: Haiti specifically emblematizes the effort and will needed to achieve a decolonized existence, the very thing that is deemed impossible within the colonial strictures of our world. Together, Césaire and Pontecorvo reveal that Haiti's importance for anticolonial thought and agitation lies in the fact that Haiti illustrates there is a time beyond the colony and its ordering of existence as progressively *and* naturally white as well as culturally Western European. I read both as affording the discursive context to reconstitute the narrative of discovery so that it relays a finding of regional self, of a people's self-worth and self-potential as exemplified by decisive acts like the Haitian Revolution. In this way, Césaire and Pontecorvo have created art pieces in line with the decolonial thought practices of *Ginen* Haitian revolutionaries, which are addressed in discussions of their decolonial philosophy for being. I build on this book's earlier analyses of *Ginen* cultural thought to show how this philosophy offers the discursive ground to chart a new way to exist in time.

The momentousness of this new existence in time is crystalized in the second epigraph's invocation of "Sèt Jou" (seven days); the seven days in question recalled by "Sèt Jou"—"August 14 – August 21"—open the ancestral homage to the Revolution provided in the appendix and reference both the day the ceremony at *Bwa Kayïman* occurred (August 14) and the day captive peoples launched the first coordinated attacks against white colonists in 1791 Saint Domingue (August 22).[25] Opening the ancestral homage with these specific dates and moving thereafter to commemorate revolutionaries grounds the revolutionary struggle in the deep heartfelt appreciation of self (of one's desire to live with autonomy and agency) that bore the revolutionary struggle and carried it forward. I pair this loving remembrance of the defiant self-love that spurred "August 14–August 21" and that ensured the Revolution's success with the decolonial imperative that anthropologist Elizabeth Povinelli outlines in the third epigraph, "'Not this' makes a difference even if it does not immediately produce a propositional otherwise."[26] I pair both to give voice to what obscure paths illuminate: the refusal of the colony and its modus operandi (slavery, colonialism, coloniality, capitalism, and white supremacy) is *enough*. Haiti's existence is enough *as it is* in the twentieth century (conflict ridden and impoverished) and *as it is* today (conflict ridden and impoverished). The nation need not be *and should not* be a replica of modern colonial powerhouses to signify that anticolonial and oppositional anti-Black agitation is worthwhile and decolonial change is possible. It need only proclaim and signify (*as it does*) "not this."

Thinking Haiti as "not this" is a guiding anticolonial concept in Césaire's and Pontecorvo's art pieces. This enthusing idea does not, however, produce a time of decolonial difference in their pieces: the Black subjects of their works remain constrained by anti-Blackness and colonial power. And yet both Césaire and Pontecorvo stage the viability of this decolonial time to come and the importance of having the example of Haiti to recognize that this time is within reach. I draw from Césaire's and Pontecorvo's willingness to think Haiti as a worthwhile refusal of the colonial project to argue that Haiti occasions engagement with the colonial encounter precisely because it legitimizes uncharted thought and action. If the time of the colony is mapped out and absolute, if it adheres to the white supremacist dictates of the colonial world order alone and necessarily impels colonies and former colonies along a socio-political path that requires that they model the colonial practices of Western capitalist civilizations, then I name Haiti's disruption of that time as *enough*. I posit that it is better to be unmoored in time than fixed in the toxic temporality of this long colonial present.

1944 Haiti

Césaire's interest in time and Haiti serves his efforts to interrogate colonialism and its present continuities in Martinique and the Caribbean. Haiti, he argues, is the "first . . . in modern time to have posed . . . in all its social, economic, and racial complexity, the great problem that the twentieth century has exhausted itself trying to solve: the colonial problem."[27] The care with which Césaire pursues Haiti's attention to this problem in *The Tragedy of King Christophe* demonstrates both his interest in learning from and thinking with revolutionary Haiti, as well as his investment in the pressing saliency of "not this" as an anticolonial ideology and practice. I am most interested in how this insistence on "not this" situates the centrality of Césaire's political life to his career long engagement with the history of the Revolution and with Haiti's first efforts at state building in the play.[28] The tribulations he faced attempting to move beyond the colony as the mayor of Martinique resonate with the difficulties the revolutionary general-turned-king, Henry Christophe, also faced in *The Tragedy of King Christophe*. I turn to Césaire's recollection of his 1944 visit to Haiti to establish the complex nuances of his characterization of King Christophe; the histories surrounding this visit illuminate how Césaire's efforts to guide his people along an unforged course toward a decolonial present was guided, in part, by the Haiti he imagined (a nation made by republicanism) and the Haiti he encountered in 1944 (one impoverished and at odds with itself).[29]

Nineteen years before Césaire composed *The Tragedy of King Christophe*, he would visit Haiti at the age of 31, arriving in May of 1944 a "poet," as literary scholar Colin Dayan notes, "and return[ing] home [in December] a politician."³⁰ At the behest of French surrealist Andre Breton and Breton's friend Pierre Mabille (the French cultural attaché in Haiti), Césaire would spend seven formative months in the nation as a cultural ambassador of France. He would give a series of lectures on Mallarmé, Lautréamont, Baudelaire, and Rimbaud, present his famed treatise on poetic knowledge ("Poetry and Knowledge"), and begin a play about the Revolution that was lost until recently, ...*And the Dogs Were Silent*.³¹ He would do this all while Haiti stood on the brink of its second major upheaval, the Revolution of 1946. The latter marked the collapse of the tenuous unity of 1804 between Haiti's oligarchy and rural majority. This collapse was caused by the ongoing imperial presence of the United States in Haiti following the first US occupation of the nation (1915–1934).

The 1915 US occupation of Haiti was launched on the pretext of restoring order to the nation after several coup d'états, but it was more significantly a counter-Haitian Revolutionary event that established the imperial presence of the United States in Haiti at the expense of the rural majority's sovereign power. According to Casimir, Colon, and Koerner, "The power of the state, put in place by the United States, became the prime weapon for the destruction of the power in the state—that is, the minimal degree of sovereignty the habitants [rural majority] still held on to."³² Haiti's majority had long disrupted the Haitian oligarchy's efforts to wield political power for personal gain alone through their refusal of plantation industry and their willingness to collectively resist. Casimir and Claypool write that "once [Christophe's kingdom] disappeared, the state and the political class were incapable of forcing the working population to remain regimented in large scale plantation agriculture."³³ As a result, "a tacit arrangement of non-interference" existed between the oligarchy (constituted mostly by the freed before 1791) and the former captives (persons who were freed after 1791), allowing both to forge separate but parallel lives in Haiti.³⁴ Of these distinct lives, Haitian historian Thomas Madiou writes that they had "nothing in common but their love of national independence ... the inhabitants of the towns, composed of blacks and men of color, have received knowledge given to them from the first instincts of European civilization. [The] black laborers, grew up under the imprint of African customs long practiced, and still practiced today, in our countryside."[35] The successful resistance efforts of "black laborers" in the nineteenth and early twentieth centuries would preserve the decolonizing impulse of their revolutionary ancestors, create a distinct *Ginen* culture in Haiti (rooted in "African customs") and counter the oligarchy's cultural grounding in the Eurocentricism of French colonial culture.

The successes of the *Ginen* masses would begin to diminish with the advent of the modern (post-1915) oligarchy, composed of members of the Black middle class created by the first US occupation of Haiti, the traditional post-independence elite from the largely Black vanguard of the revolutionary army and the contingent of persons freed before 1791 (largely mixed-race planters/merchants). The new oligarchy leveraged the US army to maintain "military control over the rural population."[36] This action permanently changed the class composition of Haiti's political leaders, which included members from the rural *Ginen* majority prior to the US invasion; and it increased the oligarchy's wealth, effectively tying wealth accumulation to the political cession of power to the United States in national affairs.[37] The Revolution of 1946 was a direct result of this cession: the events of this resistance effort were fueled by the colorist appointment of state officials. Then-Haitian president Élie Lescot continued to abide by US imperial policy in Haiti (notwithstanding the occupation's termination twelve years prior) and for the first time in Haiti's history "the distribution of power had become explicitly colorist," with lighter skinned Haitians solely in governance.[38]

At the moment of Césaire's 1944 visit, an imperial power had successfully leveraged the greed of Haiti's oligarchy and tipped the balance of power in Haiti, undoing the structural anticolonial, anti-racist, and anti-classist changes the *Ginen* captives of Saint Domingue implemented via the revolutionary army. These changes are evidenced in the non-colorist governmental bodies of early state formations and in the vibrant political representation of rural people in Haitian politics before 1915. And yet "in his first public speech [upon] returning to Martinique," Alex Gil notes that Césaire "bemoan[ed] in particular the way the 'mulatto capitalists'—a reference to Élie Lescot's regime—have replaced the white plantation owners in their exercise of power over the Black agrarian masses."[39] Furthermore, when he recollected his stay in Haiti in a 2004 interview, his focus remained on persons like these "capitalists." He states in the interview, "In Haiti, I saw above all what should not be done! A country that had supposedly conquered its liberty, that had conquered independence, and what I saw was more miserable than Martinique, a French colony! The intellectuals intellectualized, they wrote poems, they took positions on this or that issue, but with no connection to the people themselves. It was tragic, and it could have also happened to us Martinicans."[40] Césaire is right. The "Haitian intellectual elite" of the nineteenth century "gave itself a civilizing mission [with respect to the masses] based on the assumed savagery of Africans and the idea that France was a benevolent benefactor who had pulled them out of [Africa]."[41] Because of this mission, this elite and its progeny in the twentieth century were not disposed to thinking favorably about Haiti's *Ginen* folk majority, since two-thirds of their revolutionist ancestors were born in Africa.[42] "Intellectualiz[ing]" is an apt description of their preoccupations as it underscores how abstracted *Ginens* and their world were from their purview.[43]

Still, Cesaire's condemnation is also misguided. The Revolution has nothing to do with the Haitian intellectual's disregard for the people, yet he speaks as if the Revolution should have resolved the differences that exist between Haiti's peoples. He implies this even as he painstakingly demonstrates in his 1960 history of the Revolution, *Toussaint Louverture*, how "conflict and negotiation occurred repeatedly between and within all three populations [of Saint Domingue] (white, Black, and *gens de couleur*)."[44] The question is why? Why is Césaire surprised by the colonialist behavior of "'mulatto capitalists'" in 1944? Why is he just as surprised by the colonialist behavior of Haitian intellectuals in his 2004 recollection? And why does his surprise hinge on an understanding of the Revolution as having implicitly failed, given the disharmony between Haiti's peoples? The answer lies with the republican standard Césaire holds the Revolution to and Haitians, as the Revolution's agents. In Césaire's mind, this standard places Haiti as of but removed from the Caribbean, and as like France, but distinct from France. In other words, Haiti is place and principle.

As both, Haiti "conquered its liberty [and] had conquered independence," which is to say, to come into being it enacted revolutionary republicanism, making it like revolutionary France as it established itself as Haitian and thus Caribbean.[45] Césaire's remarks imply this because of their republican framing of the Revolution. French revolutionary republicanism prized universal rights, the equality of all peoples, popular sovereignty, and the colonial right to conquest.[46] The French revolutionary moment (1789–1799) transitions relatively seamlessly into the Napoleonic age (1799–1815) because both the liberal ideas of the former and imperial ideas of the latter are shaped by a Western political tradition in which the "ideal" self is both the *ego conquiro* (the self who conquers) and the *ego cogito* (the self who thinks).[47] The philosopher-politician (Robespierre) and the philosopher-conqueror (Columbus) are two sides of the same coin, which Césaire recognized in *Discourse on Colonialism* (1950). The imperial undercurrent of republicanism explains then Césaire's use of "conquered," "liberty" and "independence";[48] and it explains why his speech in Martinique following his 1944 stay in Haiti references Haiti's "mulatto capitalists," persons who call to mind Martinique's exploitive white settler class (*békés*). This moment crystallized how these "capitalists" have forgotten the meaning of their ancestors' conquest and are now conquering for personal gain.[49]

Haitian republicanism is also a key factor shaping how Césaire makes sense of the Revolution and Haiti.[50] Césaire drew from the nineteenth-century Haitian scholar Beaubrun Ardouin's history, *Études sur l'histoire d'Haïti*, to compose his first play.[51] Ardouin was a "faithful supporter" of the republican cause and wrote in support of the "myth of Haitian republicanism."[52] This myth was spearheaded by a small faction of Haitian revolutionaries-turned-politicians in post-independence Haiti.[53] Dissatisfied with Jean Jacques Dessalines's anticolonial governance (1804–1806), which they regarded as an assault on the rights of man, republican revolutionists assassinated Dessalines and launched a period of civil war in Haiti that ended when Henry Christophe, the revolutionary-turned-monarch of Northern Haiti, committed suicide (1807–1820). During the revolt and after, when Haiti was unified under republican rule following Christophe's death, republicans discursively recast the Revolution as oriented by liberalism and rights discourse. Their actions gave rise to "the myth" that the Revolution was waged in the republican tradition of the French Revolution.[54] Their false narrative was immensely popular outside of Haiti. Its popularity aligned with the world as it is in places external to Haiti, colonial and Western. It did not align with the non-Western and decolonial world that existed in Haiti among the majority. Césaire sees past this world despite the fact that his anticolonial politics ally him with Haiti's folk, hence his concern with the Haitian intellectual's absence of care for them. Indeed, the extent to which their world is thought past is evident in his description of the Haitian peasant in 2004.

Prior to his critique of the Haitian intellectual, Césaire states, "While I visited the countryside, I'd see the *nègres* with their spades, working like chained animals and speaking warmly to me in Creole with a wonderful accent. They didn't understand French. They were authentic and pitiful."[55] Césaire suggests that the Haitian peasant is being worked to death by the "capitalists" he references in his speech upon returning to Martinique from Haiti in 1944.[56] They are a step removed from slaves if not slaves, as the Haitian intellectual, who he references in the sentences after, contemplates existence. Césaire's recollection of the Haitian peasant's relationship to the Haitian oligarch begs the question: if French colonial power could not make the captive ancestors of *Ginen* peasants into slaves, how is it that the capitalists of 1944 Haiti could make peasants into "pitiful" laboring "animals"? The French ostensibly possessed "slaves" in Saint Domingue and yet after 1789 they "could no longer appropriate the bodies of captives, their movements, space, time, biological reproduction, private lives, free time, well-being, beliefs, and knowledge" writes Casimir.[57] Like French colonists, Haiti's post-independence leaders sought to consign the nation's *Ginen* peoples to capitalist drudgery as is detailed in the official records of "Toussaint Louverture, Jean-Pierre Boyer, or François Duvalier."[58] Despite the issuance of "rural police codes" not one "possess[ed] the power to put [them] into practice," or the ability to "gaug[e] the extent of the opposition raised by their fictive rural workers."[59] Yet Césaire claims to have seen these victims of exploitive power working as decreed, notwithstanding that their culture of resistant self-invention makes that impossible.

Moun is one apt example of this invention, as it shows how *Ginens* invented a new modality for being when declaring themselves to be plain people (*moun*), that is, persons who are opposed to the colonial idea of one's human's superiority over others. In addition to *moun*, captives and their descendants appropriated the term *habitant* and they named themselves *moun andeyo* in post-independence Haiti.[60] Haiti's peasantry worked as exploited laborers, yes, but they were not determined by said exploitation as Césaire imagines. I understand that Césaire is unnerved by the injustice that is their exploitation. I cannot accept, however, how his indignation deprives them of agency and the immense political power they, their forebears and their descendants have always had in Haiti. Césaire cannot imagine this power and because he does not it behooves scholars of his Haitian writings to see how his anticolonial thinking was compromised by his republican idea of the Revolution. Because of this idea, Césaire *thinks of* peasants; he does not *think with* peasants.[61] He stood with them in *Ayiti Ginen* (Africa Haiti) and still did not realize that he was in a new world entirely, with distinct onto-epistemic measures for being.

Césaire's inability to perceive alongside *Ginens* does not mean that he could not see that Haiti possessed "language [and] customs [not] watered down" by "European civilization."[62] He saw that clearly. In fact, in a 1971 interview with Haitian poet René Depestre, Césaire lauds Haiti's African culture when stating,

> from the moment I discovered the black North American experience, that I discovered Africa, I ended up exploring the whole of the black world, and so it was that I hit on the history of Haiti. I adore Martinique, but it is an alienated land, while Haiti stood in my mind for the heroic Caribbean, and also the African Caribbean. I connect the Caribbean with Africa; and Haiti, the most African island in the Caribbean, is at the same time a country with a remarkable history.[63]

Césaire sincerely appreciates Haiti's African culture, and his "aim" when writing his Haitian texts involved, as Gil notes, "rescu[ing] a revolution in the Caribbean that can be read as part *African . . . and . . . staging a victorious struggle for freedom against colonial France from within a French colony.*"[64] Still, because Césaire understands the nation through the influence of the First Republic of France (1792–1804), he views its distinction as cultural and not political. As a result, he perceives Haiti as having been, and always wanting to be, like the political variant of colonial France at its best, i.e., as a liberal democratic republic. The final scene of act two in the 1943 play ......*And the Dogs were Silent*, closes with "the silence of the Caribbean" and "*a ship in distress.*"[65] This "*ship invades the whole field of vision,*" and bears an "*inscription . . . reflected on the reefs: The Republic of Haiti.*"[66] No such republic existed in 1792, the moment the scene stages, and no such republic would exist until after the republican revolt against Dessalines in 1806, yet Césaire foretells this republic into being.

Césaire's investment in Haiti as a republic bore his conception of Haiti as having out done the French due to its republicanism. This sentiment, in turn, occasioned his fixed republican rendering of Louverture in his literature of Haiti. The "poetic I" of *The Notebook*, "push[ed] the boundaries of the [French] language, to shatter its traditional forms to make room for new ones, and to inflect it with the semantics and sonorities of creole" notes Gil; the narrative "I" of the history, *Toussaint Louverture,* is likewise deployed by Césaire to show how Louverture "push[ed] the boundaries" of French revolutionary republicanism so that it was more than colonial doublespeak.[67] In other words, this "I," which is also present in ......*And the Dogs were Silent* (Louverture is guided by "three golden words," *liberté, égalité, fraternité*), shows how Haitians did not just best the French, they transformed France from within France with their commitment to the egalitarianism of republicanism: they out French-ed the French of the First Republic to be Haiti, to be Africa in the Caribbean.[68] John Patrick Walsh accordingly argues against "the well-worn criticism of Césaire's vision of *négritude*," as a "nostalgic, essentialist conception of Africa" that "attempts to undo the Eurocentric hold on universal rights and cultural superiority" in his reading of *Toussaint Louverture.*[69] Césaire, he argues, reads the Haitian revolutionary "fight over the persistent discrimination of French republicanism" as not "the story of an African triumph," but as a fight "that Toussaint and future Haitians mastered."[70] In this respect, it is a specifically Haitian and Caribbean struggle. The question is: is Haiti the product of the French or of its own imaginings? Walsh does not suggest this but his correct reading of Césaire's non-essentialist approach to *négritude* in *Toussaint Louverture* gets at the heart of what I find troubling about Césaire's republican framing of the Haitian Revolution. It denies Haiti and Haitians a space to be something besides republicans with an anticolonial twist. It implicitly denies the fact of and existence of *Ayiti Ginen*. Césaire concludes *Toussaint Louverture* without this Haiti in mind and writes, "When Toussaint-Louverture came on the scene, it was to take the *Declaration of the Rights of Man* at its word; it was to show that there is no pariah race; that there is no marginal country; that there are no excepted peoples. It was to incarnate and particularize a principle; that is to say, to vivify it."[71] Haiti is place and principle. It is a place that signifies other places (Africa, France/Europe, and the Caribbean) because its histories name it as an idea enfleshed, having "conquered its liberty [and] independence" for and against what these places distinctly represent; and it is a principle, a true (as opposed to halfhearted) application of *liberté, égalité, fraternité*, having "conquered its liberty [and] independence" for all.[72]

Césaire ultimately misperceives the Revolution, and this misperception results in a Haiti unseen since its peoples are thought past. The high-minded republicanism that shapes his reading of the Revolution and Haiti obscures his otherwise piercing anticolonial vision, and because of it he invokes Martinique's colonial status to parentally shame Haiti. There are lingering traces of "you should be better, and you should know better" in the loaded comparison he draws between Martinique and Haiti when recollecting his 1944 visit to Haiti in 2004. Recall that he stresses that Haiti is an independent nation-state existing in a coloniallike "miserable[ness]" of its own accord (i.e., because of indifference to less fortunate others made to labor in chains. He writes "and what I saw was more miserable than Martinique, a French colony! .... It was tragic, and it could have also happened to us Martinicans.").[73] This critique is understandable: all anticolonialists want more from Haiti. They want it to not only signify as a "reminder that colonialism can be defeated, that the superiority of white power is myth," but to "develop into the model of . . . success."[74] Still, Césaire's shaming ignores that colonial dependency shapes both the colony of Martinique's existence in 1944 and the independent nation of Haiti's existence in the same moment.

Both the Haitian worker of 1944 and his/her contemporary, the overseas French colonial worker, labor in "chain[s]" notwithstanding the visibility of the Haitian laborer's "chain[s]."[75]

The idealist republicanism that shapes Césaire's thinking about Haiti and the Revolution has the unfortunate effect of elevating Haiti and Haitian workers above and beyond the region's collective experience of racialized labor exploitation. US imperialists and the machinations of white imperial power are less of a factor for Césaire when thinking Haiti. Because Haiti should be better, its problems are all its own. Furthermore, because it should be better, its peoples are imagined only as sufferers, as persons constituted by the natal violence enacted on to them, and the nation is defined as its oligarchy alone. In turn, this Haiti, perceived through the exploitive actions of its oligarchy, is taken to task in much the same way that the diehard republican Louverture of Césaire's history *Toussaint Louverture* and play ......*And the Dogs Were Silent* takes the French to task for not living up to its republican values, but what Césaire forgets is that the Revolution was not waged for inclusion in the West, nor was it waged to make republicanism better or to hold the French to their republican principles. It was waged to build the world beyond and outside of the French, its republicanisms, and any who would offer French republicanism as a way forward. Because he does not see this, Césaire never recognizes the error of his reading of the Revolution, unlike C. L. R. James.[76] Ultimately, Césaire could never make sense of Haiti as *Ayiti Ginen*—that is, as *Ginens* know it, notwithstanding that he is a compatriot of their new world building genius, committed as he was to Black liberation until his death in 2008.[77]

Haiti and Departmentalization

Césaire's republican critique of Haitian social relations is instructive when assessed alongside his political career as it attests to what most unnerved him while in Haiti in 1944: political independence led by those closest to Western Europe in thought did not guarantee new communal relations of affirmative Blackness. It does not ensure a safe territorial space antithetical to anti-Black racialism, nor does it beget a decolonial existence for formerly captive and/or colonized Black peoples. His decision to become a politician in Martinique upon his return to his homeland from Haiti in 1944 and his decision to dismantle the colony through colonial mechanisms like departmentalization while a politician are symptoms of this realization.

Upon returning to Martinique from Haiti, Césaire ran on the French Communist ticket for mayor of Fort-de-France and for the new French National Assembly. He was elected mayor on May 27, 1945, and would remain mayor of Fort-de-France until 2001, changing parties from communist to progressive in the eleventh year of his tenure. While acting as mayor, he would also serve as a deputy in France's National Assembly until 1956 and return to that post in 1958, remaining the deputy until 1993. Two years after his visit to Haiti, Césaire would support the colony's transition to a department of France, which effectively took place on March 19, 1946. Literary scholar Charles Forsdick writes that he supported departmentalization because of his anticolonial politics and his commitment to French revolutionary republicanism. He explains, "the initial championing of departmentalization by Césaire is . . . part of his active denunciation of *'le fait colonial*,' but also of an allied and continued belief in the possibility of the universal application (at long last), within what was left of the *vieilles colonies* of the French Caribbean [French overseas departments], of the egalitarian principles of the French revolution."[78] By 1956, Césaire openly acknowledged that departmentalization failed Martinicans, citing the neocolonial conditions of Martinique following its change in political status.[79]

How Césaire could have supported departmentalization while so passionately penning anticolonial poetic and prose pieces before (and after) this moment that defiantly proclaimed, "Put up with me. I won't put up with you!" is an ambiguity that Caribbeanist Nick Nesbitt resolves with attention to the radical energy of the post-World War II moment. Nesbitt writes that France's "short-lived . . . left-wing government" was receptive to decolonizing French overseas holdings.[80] It not only "pushed through a number of progressive laws related to colonial government before its dissolution in May, 1946," but the laws it pursued were pointed in their aim to improve the lived conditions of the colonized.[81] They include the "Houphouët Boigny Act, which abolished forced labor in France's colonies, and the Lamine Gueye Act, which made citizens of

France's colonial subjects."[82] Three months before the government was disbanded, "Césaire, [Léopold] Bissol [Martinique], Gaston Monnerville (Guyane), and Raymond Vergès (Réunion)," succeeded in securing the law instituting departmentalization, which both Césaire and Bissol regarded as an effective way to reduce the power of the *béké* oligarchy.[83] The law would mean that the peoples of Martinique would now have legal recourse against "the arbitrariness of [*béké*] actions," which moving forward would be guided by "a more objective, egalitarian rule of law."[84] The radical energies of the moment help contextualize Césaire's involvement, which was strategic and based on alleviating the precarity Martinicans faced as well as the racist discrimination they experienced from their elite overlords. His support of the law is also understandable, however, with attention to his telling use of the word "tragic" in the aforementioned quote about the "miserable[ness]" of the political and communal conditions of 1944 Haiti.[85]

Recall that he stated, "In Haiti, I saw above all what should not be done! . . . The intellectuals intellectualized, they wrote poems, they took positions on this or that issue, but with no connection to the people themselves. It was *tragic*, and it could have also happened to us Martinicans."[86] Césaire's use of "tragic" is certainly prosaic as the word serves as a placeholder for the communal calamity that is a governing intellectual and political class removed from its nation's majority. His use of "tragic" presumably draws as well from Western imperial philosophy in light of his attention to the jarring incongruity of "conquered liberty [/] conquered independence" existing with the appearance of neo-slavery in 1944 Haiti ("working . . . like chained animals").[87] This incongruity is tragic in the classic philosophical sense (or more aptly white colonial sense), where the tragic signifies the paradoxes of modern freedom. In *The Tragic Idea*, literary scholar Vassilis Lambropoulos articulates the tragic in this colonial tradition, stating "within the framework of the antinomies of modern liberty, the tragic stands for contradiction within human autonomy, for the conflict of freedom and necessity, liberation and legislation."[88] This common articulation of the tragic is sensical only through a type of thinking engendered and legitimized by conquest, genocide, slavery, and the political project of white supremacy. In such a case, freedom is conceived as a political and lived impossibility for all when one's political and economic structure is founded on taking freedom from others, past and present.

The "contradiction" and "conflict" that shapes a classical (i.e., white colonial) articulation of the tragic is said to have first been illuminated by the French Revolution, which politically articulates tragedy's importance to the study of revolutionary struggle in Western thought. Lambropoulos therefore writes, "since the French Revolution made palpable the ethical tensions of modern freedom, the tragic has come to represent the difficulties of resolution."[89] These "ethical tensions," for Western thinkers, certainly were not the insincerity of the *Declaration of the Rights of Man and Citizen*, which was applicable to just white men of the French empire. However, for Césaire, who wrote in *Toussaint Louverture*, "at the moment of the colonial question, the French Revolution had started to come up against itself . . . to split," *these* "tensions" were decidedly race-based and telling of the selective application of the rights outlined in the *Declaration*.[90] These "tensions," for Césaire, were less about "the conflict of freedom and necessity, liberation and legislation," and more about the unwillingness of French revolutionaries to give up white power and colonial profiteering.[91] This unwillingness prompted the reversal of the abolition of slavery in 1802 by Napoleon Bonaparte, just eight years after its abolition by the revolutionary First Republic of France, and it accounts for the "partial and subaltern" nature of the "citizenship extended to the inhabitants of the *vieilles colonies* in 1848."[92] In the years following his political disavowal of departmentalization, Césaire would offer a decidedly decolonial iteration of the "tragic" that drew from the Black Radical Tradition in public pronouncements, specifically, his 1956 speech to the First International Congress of Negro Writers and Artists ("Culture and Colonization"), and his 1956 resignation letter from the French communist party ("Letter to Maurice Thorez"). The decolonial iteration of the tragic offered in these public documents situates his damning critique of 1944 Haiti as pragmatic and Louverture-inspired. More importantly, it situates Césaire's philosophical kinship with *Ginen* captives, though he thinks the Revolution and the post-colony through the significations of Louverture alone.

Poet and Black cultural theorist Fred Moten writes in *In the Break: The Aesthetics of the Black Radical Tradition* that "the tragic in any tradition, especially the black radical tradition, is never wholly abstract. It is always in relation to quite particular and material loss."[93] The "loss" Moten has in mind emerges from his reading of Amiri Baraka's poem, "Black Dada Nihilismus," and its attention to "political homelessness," which speaks to the longing for roots and rootedness.[94] This particular absence addresses Black peoples' displacement in the Americas from an African homeland, on the one hand, and their disenchantment with a new natal setting that accepts their labor but not their person, on the other. This is a concern particular to Black identity in the hemispheric Americas and one that long governed Césaire's literary works. When speaking about why he depicts Henry Christophe as he does in *The Tragedy of King Christophe*, he states: "Christophe has been presented as a ridiculous man, a character who spent his time aping the French. This aspect, very real, has been emphasized, but I, too am a black man [*nègre*], and this black man, did not just have an ape in him. In this ape, there was also a profound thought, a real angst; I wanted to pierce through the ridicule [*grotesque*] to find the tragic."[95] That which is "tragic" about Christophe, for Césaire, rests with his lived experience of racialization and the possibilities and impossibilities this experience engendered for him. Much as Baraka, according to Moten, produced "Black Dada Nihilismus" because of his lived experience as a Black person in the United States, Césaire too approaches his characterization of his titular character in *The Tragedy of King Christophe* with nuance because of his own embodied experience of Blackness. It is this corporeal experience of Blackness and racist marginalization that literary scholar Jeremy Glick argues serves as the basis for the "Black Radical Tragic." He defines the latter as an

> expansive formal configuration, philosophical orientation, and stage-framework that understands that what Raymond Williams calls "the death of liberal tragedy" assumes an extension of democratic rights that the Black Radical Tradition knows is false. It is wide enough to balance a general preoccupation with Black transformative struggle, suffering, and insurgent sociality that connects Toussaint with [Patrice] Lumumba in a world system without playing down the particularity announced in [W. E. B.] DuBois's *Black Reconstruction*: "No matter how degraded the factory hand, he is not real estate."[96]

The analytic "Black Radical Tragic" is not used by Césaire but it does shape the decolonial registers I insist on attributing to Césaire's damning critique of 1944 Haiti.

Both "Culture and Colonization" and "Letter to Maurice Thorez" leverage the embodied racialized meanings Césaire ascribes to the tragic to express how Black peoples in colonial and neocolonial situations are denied the cultural innovation and growth that could root them in their homelands. In "Culture and Colonization," Césaire pointedly mentions the tragic, arguing that "the cultural position in colonial countries is tragic" since colonial power refuses to grant the colonized a "dialectic of *having*."[97] This "dialectic" refers to the process in which "foreign elements become mine, have passed into my being . . . because I can organize them in my universe, because I can bend them to my needs. Because they are at my disposition not me at theirs."[98] He further states, "It is precisely the operation of this dialectic that is denied to the colonized people. Foreign elements are dumped on its soil, but remain foreign. White men's things. White men's ways. Things that sit alongside the indigenous people but over which the indigenous people has no power."[99] Colonized Black peoples cannot draw from the culture of white colonizers and integrate this culture into their own, nor can their cultures thrive on their own terms when set beside white colonial culture. With a culture "condemned to remain marginal in relation to European culture," what Black peoples in colonial and neocolonial situations are made to have are "subculture[s]" that cannot "build or rebuild the world" because they are deprived of *"historical initiative."*[100] In other words, because of colonialism and its ethos of white supremacy, Black peoples are placed in a position where they cannot readily "bring valid and original solutions to all political, social, economic, or cultural problems" that they face in the "modern world."[101] Césaire therefore argues that the colonized "elite" are "placed in artificial conditions and deprived of life-giving contact with the masses and with popular culture" because of the cultural stranglehold of colonialism.[102] Elites either identify with white Western European culture or they reify their cultural traditions to the point that they are no longer dynamic and in touch with the organic cultural production of everyday peoples. Both approaches maintain colonial power and its overprivileging of white Western European culture, as it requires that elite classes distance themselves from the folk and the popular culture Black people produce. This creates the ideal conditions for elite classes to normalize the folk "work[ing] . . . like chained animals" because colonial subordination, in directing all attention to white culture, white peoples and to the power dynamics that appear to allow the colonized to replicate the political, social, and economic advantages of whiteness, thrives on maintaining and reproducing colonial hierarchies of difference.[103]

Yet even as this cultural stagnation is a central issue for Black peoples in colonial and neocolonial environments, Césaire insists in "Culture and Colonization" that they "have the courage to face squarely" this issue; and he asks that they move past the "false alternative" that is the choice between "'fidelity and backwardness, or progress and rupture.'"[104] They must trust their own knowing and recognize these spurious choices as subterfuge, as a ploy of colonial power intended to make it seem as if the viable "solutions," they engender for their "modern problems" cannot possibly succeed. Césaire understands that Black peoples are "sovereign people," to borrow from *Ginen* thought.[105] They "are parents of their own mind" (*"pep souvren granmoun tèt li"*) and, as such, they can come up with "solutions" befitting their needs for existence.[106] Indeed, because Césaire knows that Black people "know more than the abjectness that is projected upon [them]," he insists that the "solutions [found] will be valid because they are original," embodied as they will be in the Black collective's own racialized experiences of existence.[107]

Césaire returns to this topic in "Letter to Maurice Thorez," which was composed a month after "Culture and Colonization." In the letter, he writes that Black peoples must reject Western European emissaries of progress—and one could add North American—considering the rise of US imperialism in the Caribbean in the 1940s. He argues that these emissaries often believe, "that evolution as it took place in Europe is the only evolution possible, the only kind desirable, the kind the whole world must undergo; to sum up, their rarely avowed but real belief in civilization with a capital C and progress with a capital P (as evidenced by their hostility to what they disdainfully call 'cultural relativism')."[108] Césaire critiques French communists, here for their paternalist relation to Martinican communists but his rhetoric extends beyond the specificities of the reasons for his resignation from the French Communist Party. His main issue is that colonized Black peoples are denied the ability to chart their own course for existence. In the letter, he therefore asserts that his Black readers "insist" on "the right to initiative," the right to act freely (in mind, body and being) apart from Western colonial systems. With this contention, he returns to the tragic meanings he ascribes to *"historical initiative"* in "Culture and Colonization," and writes firmly within the "expansive formal configuration, philosophical orientation, and stage-framework" of "The Black Radical Tragic."[109]

With this context in mind, it is evident that elite Haitians in 1944 Haiti disclose a failed national *"initiative."*[110] Their acceptance and naturalization of colonial separatist ideas, which distinguish between better and lesser people, demonstrate in Césaire's estimation in both 1944 and 2004 how a class of Haitians created a republican-inspired political tradition where Saint Domingue could serve as the blueprint for Haiti. The choice to follow this blueprint reveals how deeply colonized Haiti's elite classes are, since they could not trust in the originality of their own cultural mores nor in their own corporeal experience of existence to invent something new; and nor were they willing to pursue the innovative ideas for existence that the folk's cultural productions would have engendered. Accordingly, the key issue Césaire has with Haiti's elite classes in 1944 is that their behaviors are not practical, which is to say: they are not embodied in their experience of being. Even if they felt culturally different from the *Ginen* masses, Césaire finds that their lived experience of Blackness (as descendants of oppressed free or captive mixed-raced/Black peoples) should have rooted them in a shared experience of resistant innovation beyond the colonial project; their republicanism, in other words, should reflect their unique experience of existence. The path beyond the colony remained imperceptible, and that it was is largely because all colonized peoples (with or without power) can "be seduced by forms of being-in-the-world that normalize violence and dehumanization."[111] They can draw from life experiences that in no way speak to the particularities of their racialized existence and fail to work toward a decolonized life. This is the failure Césaire is aghast at witnessing in Haiti and the failure that stays with him well after leaving Haiti in 1944.

Césaire's shock at seeing the nation the Revolution ostensibly bore confounded his republican vision of the Revolution. This vision is cultural as much as it is political. Literary scholar J. Michael Dash describes the differences between the French departments of the Caribbean and Haiti thusly: the former "are as different from their English-speaking and French-speaking neighbours as they are from that other country which is included under the term 'French West Indies,' Haiti. Haiti, independent since 1804, is as different as one can possibly imagine from the Overseas Departments whose relations with France go back to the seventeenth century."[112] Césaire writes as a French colonial subject and leads with France in his assessment of Haiti notwithstanding his political affinity with Haiti's Africanized peoples. His republican idea of the Revolution implicitly de-Africanized the Revolution because it foregrounds Louverture, the republican, even as Césaire (more so than C. L. R. James) acknowledges in the body of his history, *Toussaint Louverture*, the immense political influence of the captive mass. He writes the "rise of Toussaint" as the "rise of a class," and casts the Revolution along the same populist lines as Michel-Rolph Trouillot in his 1977 book on the Revolution, *Ti dife boule sou istoua Ayiti*.[113] Still, he ends this history before the advent of Haiti and fixes his reader's attention onto Louverture, who most informs Césaire's imaginings of the Revolution and Haiti. Césaire even admits to identifying with the general when stating, "there is a lot of me in this book about Toussaint Louverture."[114]

Scholars have discussed Césaire's penchant for seeing himself in Louverture from varying approaches. Focusing on Césaire's history, Forsdick discusses his interest in Louverture's anticolonial model for governance via "transnational solidarity" with France, noting Césaire's attention to how in "a residually imperial structure, such a goal of semi-independence, within a relationship of continuing dependency, comes under progressive strain."[115] This "strain," for Forsdick, exposes the "similar ambiguities [that] seem to characterize Césaire's own position on a decolonized, post-departmentalized French Caribbean."[116] Walsh situates Césaire squarely in the writing of the history, stating "Césaire's reading of the Haitian Revolution as a means to reflect on the problem of departmentalization [meant that] he look[ed] back to the past to learn from Toussaint's attempt to decolonize in order to look forward to the possibility of a future Caribbean that would include equal rights, social benefits, and political autonomy."[117] Gil focuses on the 1943 play Césaire wrote in Haiti when he was researching *Toussaint Louverture* and brings attention to how Césaire's marital woes shaped his identification with Louverture. He writes:

> Without a doubt, Césaire had come to overidentify with the character of Toussaint, which at this point was, for all intents and purposes, the Rebel of later versions [the dramatic poem, *And the Dogs Were Silent*]. The solitude he was experiencing only compounded and intensified the imprisonment and isolation of the Rebel himself—who wanted "to die here, alone." Likely around this time, and perhaps not coincidentally, Césaire also introduced the other major character of the published text: the Lover.[118]

Lastly, the anthropologist Gary Wilder acknowledges and qualifies Césaire's identification with Louverture, writing the "claim that Césaire's turn to federation was mediated by the legacy of Louverture is not to suggest that he simply imitated the Precursor. Césaire enacted a range of sometimes ambivalent identifications."[119] However discussed, Césaire's identification with Louverture is a hallmark of how scholars understand his Haitian Revolutionary work and political life. This scholarly consensus attests to how much Césaire struggled to work with and against French colonial rule to find a space for Martinicans to exist on their own terms. What bears addressing now is how this struggle has been cast as inventive when it was not.

Wilder makes this argument most explicitly and argues that Césaire's decision to support departmentalization and his ability to transition after its failure to a politics of "cooperative federalism" is telling of his efforts to try new ideas, to experiment and to innovate so as to ensure Martinique's present and future political and economic agency.[120] He argues that Césaire (and, with respect to the quote that follows, Toussaint Louverture) pursued efforts to "separate self-determination from state sovereignty" in order to establish a decentralized federation under French imperial tutelage that would work with imperialism to create improved political conditions for Antilleans.[121] Louverture became an affluent figure among his class compatriots of *affranchi* as the Revolution progressed. His identification with this class's wealth sustaining and aggrandizing economic practices produced a myopia with respect to liberation that took the plantation (and its violent industries of commerce) as central to existence. This myopia is not to be implicitly celebrated or presented as forward thinking when it was not, as it maintained the suffering of *Ginen* peoples and tied servility to their existence. To work with imperialism in this sense is to greenlight the violent degradation of *Ginen* peoples. Worst yet, it naturalizes the genocidal nature of this degradation and minimizes how murder for profit is constitutive to colonialism and imperialism. The latter two are not to be recast as benevolent when they are not; particularly since, neither have *ever*, for Black peoples, "created conditions for overcoming colonial subjection through transcontinental partnership."[122]

Wilder's reading of Césaire's identification with Louverture finds value in both Louverture and Césaire's efforts to reform colonial systems. My reading questions why reform was reasoned as a legitimate response to the colonial problem. Césaire was not in the same revolutionary moment as Louverture and need not have followed the imagined example of Louverture; which is to say, the options he had in the moment of departmentalization and later federation (while limited) did not need to be directed by those pursued by a revolutionary general, whose own options were limited. Yet Césaire chose to model Louverture to cast his fear laden thinking about the possibility of creating a new world as progressive when it was not. Césaire's thinking was fear laden because he saw in 1944 Haiti how political independence could very well atrophy cultural innovation. He chose not to advocate for independence because, firstly, departmentalization was more popular among Martinicans in the 1940s, and secondly, because of the dangers of regression, that is, of lapsing into the very worst of the colonial past (i.e., treating one's people as the colonists of yesteryear treated one's ancestors). The latter accounts for the appeal of federation post departmentalization. Césaire astutely recognized from his sojourn in Haiti that republicanism is not enough, especially if this politic is not reinvented to bring one closer to the folk and one's racialized experience of existence. He also recognized, with horror, his shortsightedness concerning republicanism in Haiti. This horror guides his Haitian literatures post 1944 and because I privilege the fear (of regression) that shaped his political maneuverings, my issue is his thinking not his politics. In other words, what concerns me is that to reason a politics of federation and departmentalization he uses Louverture and his republican actions as a cover for his own political choices. *Louverture pa dra!*[123] Césaire denudes himself of the possibility to try something beyond the pale of the colonial order by overly identifying with a Louverture he conceives as the epitome of republicanism. He does not try to think from the radical energies of his own moment or his person. The question is why does Césaire need Louverture to act, and the answer lies with Louverture's masculinist figuration, as discussed in Chapter 1. This figuration allows radical-ness without radical-ness, revolution without revolution, Haiti without Haitians. Césaire knows this (or perhaps suspects this) and turns to Christophe to think beyond the dead conversations (better yet, identifications) that are engendered by Louverture's significations in the Caribbean cultural imaginary. He turns to the general who survived the Revolution to see Haiti and who refused republicanism, Henry Christophe. Through the story of his post-independence governance as king of Northern Haiti, Césaire explores the question shaping the section that follows: how is one to fearlessly administer beyond the colony without turning to Western Europe and its culturally supremacist models for existence?

Fear and the Postcolony

Césaire began *The Tragedy of King Christophe* in 1959 at a moment when Martinique experienced a robust independence movement that likely called the Revolution and 1944 Haiti to mind. He significantly revised the play in 1970, in the wake of France's violent response to French Antillean dissension in France and in Martinique and Guadeloupe.[124] Departmentalization had failed Martinicans to such an extent that the 1950s and 1960s saw an intensification of socio-political unrest on the island and the advent of the independence movement. France's colonial response to this resistance resulted in the detainment and deportation of activists like Édouard Glissant, who resided in France, and the imprisonment as well as murder of others.[125] All of these happenings are consequential to the play's composition. I prioritize Césaire's visit to Haiti, instead of the intensification of socio-political unrest in Martinique, because it contextualizes the drama's republican subtext. I also privilege this visit because it shaped his anticolonial imaginings of life beyond the colony.

Set in the immediate aftermath of emperor Jean Jacques Dessalines's assassination in 1806, the drama absents the 1804 ascendancy and two-year rule of Dessalines to write early Haiti as always being a liberal democratic republic. Dessalines's political project was not that. It prioritized the preservation of antislavery and anticolonial politics to bolster independence and foster collectivity among Haiti's divided peoples. He ruled as an emperor to distance his polity from liberalism and the abstractions of liberal democracy, which espouses liberty for all but through its political technologies (like rights discourse) ensure that an expansive and inclusive liberty is impossible in application.[126] Marginal attention to Dessalines and his anticolonial and antislavery politics intimates a writerly desire to absent the Revolution from the political horizon of early Haiti (1804–1820) and stage the possibility of its return thereafter. In this respect, the subtext of Césaire's dramatic portrait of the play's protagonist (former revolutionary general turned king), Henry Christophe's rulership is not simply the difficulties of postcolonial statecraft but the expectations of benevolent rule that the idea of the Revolution as "radical, liberal [and] universal" invites.[127]

The absence of benevolent rulership pervades the play's opening, as the drama begins highlighting the early political divisions that destabilized early Haiti and that cast Christophe and his revolutionary compatriot (past-general and later president of Haiti) Alexandre Pétion as competing sovereigns of the country.[128] The drama then turns to the rise of Christophe's kingship in the northern part of Haiti (as Pétion rules the southwest) and focuses, for much of its entirety, on Christophe's state building efforts, exemplified by the extreme lengths he employs to complete Haiti's famed fortress, La Citadelle Laferrière. The Citadelle was initially commissioned by Emperor Dessalines to protect the northern coast of Haiti from the all too real threat of a French re-invasion following the Revolution. Recognizing the necessity of this security measure, the Christophe of historic fact would complete the fortress during his reign, erecting a massive structure that would "house a garrison of 1500 men, [and that was] capable of withstanding a siege for three years with arms and provisions stored in rooms 30–45 meters high, with walls 3 meters thick."[129] The Citadelle's vast size was equaled only by the colossal labor it took to complete it: "two hundred thousand [newly liberated] men [women and children] were pressed into constructing [the fortress]; 20,000 died" during its construction.[130] The obligatory labor Christophe used to complete the Citadelle carries much of Césaire's dramatization of the collapse of Christophe's 1807–1820 regime.

This labor, and the policy of racial uplift Césaire presents as Christophe's rationale for the fortress's construction, affords Césaire the tools with which to carefully probe postcolonial leadership's inability to conceive of sovereignty with the people as they are in the first moment of state-building (unlettered and unbothered with Western Europe). Indeed, driving Césaire's multifaceted portrait of Christophe is steady attention to how nation building in the colonial present works against the anticolonial intentions of a collectivist revolutionary and/or anticolonial struggle. Why this is the case rests squarely with a state-sponsored fixation on time in the Caribbean postcolonial present, with advancing in time or not having sufficient time to catch up to Western Europe.

Césaire's attention to the political interest in time in the independent Caribbean state occasions the complex presentation he affords Christophe's decision making, which speaks, in turn, to the anticolonial intent of his Haitian Revolutionary writings. This intent conditions Césaire's depiction of Christophe as a king pivoting toward decolonial governance, that is, rule beyond the colony, and also his portrayal of Christophe as a king whose state-building initiatives consign his people to the colonial path they resisted. Césaire accordingly complicates how his audience receives Christophe's antislavery and anticolonial political vision, as he stresses to his audience that the labor Christophe invests in the Citadelle is intended to "cancel the slave ship."[131] With the Citadelle's construction, Christophe aims to give his people a visible patrimony of Black worth they create for themselves via their own labor. He passionately exclaims: "Built by the whole people, men and women, children and elders. . . . [T]o each people its monuments! For this people forced to its knees, a monument that will set it upright!"[132] The Citadelle, for Christophe, affords former captives a new sense of their racial selves and as such it is poised to "cancel [not just] the slave ship" but the corvée labor reminiscent of slavery that he sanctioned to build the Citadelle. In this respect, Christophe is no ordinary tyrant: in leveraging corvée labor to retool his people's sense of self, he cannot be dismissed as a mere mimic of the French by Césaire's audience, nor can his actions be easily dismissed as maniacal or cruel for self-aggrandizing purposes. His actions are deeply rooted in the Black experience of racialization and therefore teeter between awareness of how Black peoples are generally perceived by white peoples and the specifically Black need for a positive articulation of Blackness. He accordingly insists that his people understand how "the crime of [their] persecutors bites at [their] heels all around [them]."[133]

When Christophe's wife, Madame Christophe, cautions him against "demand[ing] too much of men," he tellingly replies:

> All men have the same rights. That I affirm. But of our common kind, some have more responsibilities than others. There is an inequality. An equality of demands, do you understand? Who will have us believe that all men, I say all, without privilege, without special exemption, have known deportation, trafficking, slavery, collective debasement to the status of beasts . . . ! We alone . . . you understand, we alone, we blacks![134]

Christophe is a veiled republican, "all men have rights." Yet he situates the political liberalism of republicanism in a Black experience for being, which is evident in his own cognizance of the anti-Black sensibility of the larger world around him. He insists, however, that his people are equally cognizant of this sensibility. It is this insistence that casts his misguided political actions (i.e., constructing the Citadelle through corvée labor) with the decolonial insight of Saint Domingue's captive populace.

Grounding Christophe's speech is an adamant refusal of colonial power's white supremacist knowledge practices, particularly its self-serving abstractions implied here in the notion that "all peoples are the same." In this respect, Christophe's remarks are decolonial in the tradition of the *Ginen* captives of Saint Domingue because they are rooted in the realization that the course beyond the colony cannot be realized if the ideological concepts of colonial power governing how Black peoples understand themselves as persons remain unchallenged and intact. With that in mind, the refusal of the self-serving abstractions of white supremacy, embodied in the notion "all people are the same" which reifies all persons as similarly white and culturally Western European, must be understood as a move toward an uncharted decolonial path for existence. This path is necessarily one where racialization cannot adversely constrain the lived realities of select persons (here Black people). Christophe's passionate insistence on grounding his rulership in the specific realities of Black hemispheric existence serves as a powerful reminder of why Haiti remains at the forefront of anticolonial praxis and theory for Césaire. Both Haitian revolutionaries (the *Ginen* and the creole general) and post-revolutionary Haitian leaders refused to reason their humanity as their enslavers, thinking "not this" to create their world anew. Recognizing the "inequality of demands" that makes Black existence disproportionately harder than white existence, they fought to honor and make plain the particularities of their human experience.[135] And yet Césaire insists that his readers/viewers recognize that Christophe sought to forge Haiti in colonial fashion. Indeed, what one cannot escape when engaging *The Tragedy of King Christophe* is that dedication to the Black human experience did not prevent Christophe (or Pétion for that matter) from attempting to build newly independent Haiti as if it were Saint Domingue.

Saint Domingue is Christophe's point of reference for Haiti. Accordingly, much of his disdain for Haiti as it exists in his moment is the preponderance of "dust," "rubble," and "thatch" in a land once profuse with "stone" and "cement." Prior to the Citadelle's construction, Christophe laments Haiti's deteriorating state to his political advisor, Baron Vastey. Christophe states,

> . . . on the land there is nothing
> But dust, over everything
> Rubble,
> Earth and thatch, crumbling mud-wall.
> I want stone, give me stone!

And cement, bring me cement!
Everything's falling apart—oh, to set all this upright,
Upright in the face of the world, and solid!¹³⁶

The Citadelle is key to Christophe's political project of racial and national uplift because with its construction people will move from an existence predicated on "dust" and the impermanence of poorly laid plans and move instead toward a life of "concrete," with lasting examples of who they are now (free Black people) and who they can be in the future (free *civilized* Black people). This transformation will require effort however, immense amounts of drudgery. Before a crowd amassed to celebrate his impending coronation, Christophe makes this clear, declaring that he "won't have it said in the world, or whispered even, that ten years of black freedom, ten years of black negligence and irresponsibility, will suffice to squander the treasure that our martyred people amassed in a hundred years of labor and blows of the whip. Which is to say that with me, from now, you have no right to get tired."¹³⁷

Little drives Christophe's chastening of the people gathered before him but time and how others (i.e., persons outside of Haiti) have used time. Accordingly, the wasting of time, the loss of time, and the proper (labor-based) usage of time leads him to equate "ten years of black freedom" to "ten years of black negligence and irresponsibility." Christophe proposes to reclaim Black labor for Black people; as the "treasure . . . amassed" in Saint Domingue is reconceived as having served Black peoples and Black consumption no matter the lie in this reconceptualization: when the much lauded "pearl of the Antilles" (Saint Domingue) existed, Black labor and Black life were quite literally devoured for voracious colonial consumption alone. Christophe's bad faith reasoning fixes postcolonial Haiti along one path, that of the well-trodden, and forecloses the radical possibility of what the Revolution promised: a life beyond the colony. As such, it preserves Saint Domingue as an ideal economic and societal model for newly independent Haiti and because of this, his reasoning lends veracity to the colonial lies animating his speech: Black people cannot exist without paternalist oversight and Black freedom is a success only if it replicates the white supremacist conditions of the geopolitical present where oversight is rampant. Christophe accordingly concludes his tirade reminding his audience that they "have no right to get tired," leading them into yet another military contest (against Pétion) and to the Citadelle's construction.

A scene between two raft-keepers underscores, however, how very much the people and the land abhor Christophe's political vision and its preoccupation with elevating Haitians (i.e., setting them "upright") for the world outside of Haiti.[138] Césaire writes,

RAFT-KEEPER CAPTAIN: The Great Salty? It won't be long.

APPRENTICE RAFT-KEEPER: All the same, it *is* long!

RAFT-KEEPER CAPTAIN: The big truth is not in the going, but knowing which way to go.[139]

The interlude that immediately precedes this scene in *The Tragedy of King Christophe* presents the river Artibonite as the lifeblood of Haiti, carrying and thereafter imprinting the natural landscape of the country with the violent political whims and excesses of King Christophe. The scene that follows it depicts two peasants at rest, mulling over the merit of Christophe's labor-based policy of national uplift of which they (and other peasants) bear the burden as unpaid conscripted laborers of the Citadelle. These scenes tellingly afford Césaire's audience firsthand sight of peasants bemoaning their violent tethering to the land via their labor, on the one hand; and his audience discerns, on the other, how the land, marked by the political violence the Artibonite carries, desperately needs a purging and replenishing that the sea—a repository of unmarked waters—promises. Taken together, these framing dramatic moments ground the raft-keepers within a particular (and decidedly ironic) socio-political context in which their labor (like that of their peasant compatriots) is paradoxically stolen to secure their freedom, subject as it is (indeed, as nature is and all things within Northern Haiti are) to Christophe's political vision.

The raft-keeper captain's insistence that "the big truth is not in the going, but knowing which way to go," is apt in this context.[140] Christophe "know[s] the way to go," having aided in the removal of the French and in the end of slavery and colonial rule in Saint Domingue; but beyond that Césaire suggests that he does not "know where to go" as his chief state-building initiative (the Citadelle) hinges on the same political violence that spawned and sustained slavery and colonialism, namely, labor based subjection and ecocide. More than that, his fear of "everything falling apart," because Haiti is overrun with "dust" and "crumbling mud-wall," is at heart a fear of the unknown, of building Haiti up with the materials it has at its disposal at present, be it "dust," "mud-wall" or a people resistant to plantation economics and its insistence on reducing Black peoples to disposable workhands.[141] When Christophe dramatically pronounces, "the ocelot is in the bush, the prowler is at [the] door; the man-hunter lying in wait . . . and my people dance" to his wife, his care for his people's self-regard barely veils his disdain for how unprepared they are (in his mind) for the work of nation-building and its timeline of evolutionary advancement, where they build to be on par with Western Europe.[142] His dramatic declaration effectively juxtaposes the much desired need to be a master of one's own time that all formerly captive peoples have following emancipation from slavery and colonialism against the pressing sense held by their political leaders that there is not enough time for the immense work of racial and national uplift.[143]

Césaire affords Christophe the complexity of character to demonstrate the enduring importance of *Ginen* Haitian revolutionaries to anticolonial thought and praxis fixed on the lived experience of Blackness. He simultaneously insists that his audience also recognize that Christophe chose to follow the path well-traveled and furrowed by Western Europeans in the Americas with respect to state building *even as* antislavery and anticolonial liberation demands new ways of being. Césaire's complex rendering of Christophe's political actions affords his audience a careful probing of postcolonial statecraft's inability to conceive of sovereignty with the people as they are in the first moment of state-building (unlettered, poor, and unbothered with Western Europe). Indeed, driving Césaire's multifaceted portrait of Christophe is how nation building in the long colonial present works against the anticolonial intentions of a collectivist revolutionary and/or anticolonial struggle. It does so because nation building is all too often guided by a state-sponsored fixation on time, that is, advancing in time or being stagnant in time, which would mean never catching up to Western Europe. Theater studies scholar Maurya Wickstrom offers a differing interpretation. She writes that Christophe is "a character filled with the dynamism of a new time even as" the time of slavery and the colony continues to mediate his existence, prompting him to "convert [this new time] into a regime of bodily labor that is machinic and brutal."[144] She argues that Césaire presents Christophe thusly to "directly confront the problem of time . . . in a post-revolutionary, postcolonial situation," where competing coexistent ideas for being produce different temporalities and offer a plurality of times at our disposal ("what is the time that we should hear, be faithful to, in any new present?").[145] Wickstrom perceives choice where I perceive dead ends and thus a political present emblematized not by the ability to pick a time and its ontological dictates but one overdetermined by one time (that of the colony).

The colony overdetermines time for Césaire's Christophe not because he is an elitist tyrannical ruler obsessed with Black power through Black excellence, but because he is negotiating a white public as a head of state ("the ocelot is in the bush, the prowler is at [the] door; the man-hunter lying in wait.").[146] In this respect, he governs with cognizance of the dictates of a global order of white colonial power, whose temporality is fixed irrespective of his temporal shift from the revolutionary-colonial moment of time to that of the postcolonial/post-revolution moment. The colonial moment is exhaustive because it is guided by "racial time," as Michael Hanchard argues, a time of deferred catching up, of waiting, and of unpaid labor for Black peoples; and because Césaire insists that readers/viewers perceive Christophe as ever aware of this order and its racialized temporality, he denudes Christophe of the actual choice of other times even as his people insist on a contrary decolonial time (e.g., the raft-keepers).[147] The absence of a viable decolonial choice for Christophe, who is constrained by the omniscience of the white public, ensconces him in fear: fear of the unknown path and fear of the known path not pursued correctly. The parabolic exchange between the two raft-keepers is instructive in this respect, as it calls for working with and accepting one's fear of the unknown, in particular, and evokes the decolonizing initiative of "not this."

While the raft-keepers' conversation ostensibly concerns their present work-related journey along the Artibonite River to the sea ("The Great

Salty"), their discourse invokes the difficulties of politically administering beyond the colony when beholden to a white geopolitical public.[148] The political nature of the scenes framing their exchange attests to this. The conversation symbolically captures the central dilemma Caribbean political leaders, such as Césaire, faced when sitting at the helm of radically oriented Caribbean polities. This dilemma asks readers/viewers to ponder "which way," or which socio-political and socio-economic course, ought Caribbean peoples "to go" toward when decolonizing their land?[149] This decolonial query urges recognition of the viability of a path that decenters Western Europe and its colonial model for existence. Conversely, it negates demoralization ("All the same, it *is* long!").[150] Lastly, it is a query that best respects the desires of Caribbean peoples whose resistance efforts have long established their collective refusal of Western Europe's mechanisms of power (i.e., genocide, slavery, colonialism, capitalist predation and racialization).

The uncharted course toward a decolonial present that grounds the raft-keepers' parabolic discussion of the sea and that characterizes Césaire's portrait of Christophe situates the importance of this query to Césaire's Haitian writings. It also situates the centrality of cautious trepidation to Césaire's political life and to his lifelong engagement with the Revolution as well as with Haiti. In this respect, Haiti and the Revolution are potent ideations for Césaire. Both convey how postcolonial leadership is a governance preoccupied with time and the white public. This preoccupation fixes Haiti in two temporalities, however, the time of oligarchs (early Haiti) and the time of *possibility* (the Revolution). Thinking Haiti along these temporal lines absents *Ginens* and their culture of resistance from Haitian politics in early Haiti (via the excision of Dessalines). Instead, they are spectrally present through a tyrannical monarch whose Black power politics aspires to the West. The subsumed presence of *Ginens* in the play not only absents Haitian difference from the play itself (namely, the *Ginen* fight to live on one's own terms); but it also removes *Ginens* from how spectators are to understand the Revolution, Haiti and postcolonial governance (more broadly). Their absence ultimately allows Césaire to present Haitian revolutionists' radical seizure of self-autonomy in sameness, as though *all* Haitians aspired to the West when securing

Haiti. This aspiration speaks to Césaire's political preoccupations. It does not speak to Haiti; in fact, it results in a Haiti unseen.

Until When

Upon leaving Haiti in 1944, Césaire took Haiti with him throughout his political career. He did not want Martinique to become the Haiti he witnessed (socially divided and impoverished), and he did not want to act with the *Ginen* daring that made Haiti possible. And yet while his wariness of Haiti caused him to write Haiti unseen in *The Tragedy of King Christophe*, it also reinforced Césaire's recognition of how the colony cannot be the sole means of human communality, nor can it be the grounds to build a people and polity anew. A will to innovate predominates in the play as a result, leading Césaire to sit with Christophe and humanize the difficulties of building a new nation while contending with the living legacy of racialization. This will to innovate and its importance to Black revolution occasions Césaire's engagement with Haiti as an idea and it underscores why the nation is key to thinking against the colonial project. My interest in reading Césaire's play versus his other writing of the Revolution lies squarely with this engagement, as it prompts ongoing consideration of the problem that is time and being in the postcolonial present. Moreover, it offers a critique that unsettles the republican basis of Césaire's thinking on the Revolution and Haiti notwithstanding the politic's presence in the play, since the critique issued calls the entire colonial enterprise into question by confronting the limited pathways and choices the West and its antagonists (who measure existence through the West) offer (formerly) colonized peoples. There is no working with here (cooperatively or otherwise); there is the effort to think beyond. In this respect, it is when Césaire engages the Revolution and Haiti abstractly that he writes with *Ginens* and thinks alongside them against the West.

Césaire's use of the Revolution and Haiti as an ideation to think with is why I read his play beside Gillo Pontecorvo's 1969 film, *Queimada!*. Because Césaire's Haitian writing is not manifestly *Ginen*, it needs a supplement to articulate Haiti and the Revolution in *Ginen* fashion. I have chosen Pontecorvo's movie as my supplement because I am interested in how Césaire's cerebral engagement with the Revolution and Haiti invites upending how we understand civilization and progress (or movement in time). Césaire thinks against the colonial idea that is civilization and progress, which not only aligns his writing of the Revolution to a Caribbean tradition of using Haiti to reimagine the colonial encounter; but it also aligns his play with Pontecorvo's efforts to critique civilization and progress in *Queimada!*, a film Edward Said rightly regards as one of the "greatest political films ever made."[151]

Said's sentiment is aligned with my own and that of Kaisary, Charles Forsdick and Christian Høgsberg, Natalie Zemon Davis, and Joan Mellen, among others.[152] The "cool public and critical reception" *Queimada!* received upon its release, and the comparatively equal amount of criticism it has garnered from critics like, Brenda Stevenson, Alyssa Goldstein Sepinwall, Ella Shohat and Robert Stam, and Alan Stone, has helped to make *Queimada!* Pontecorvo's "most undervalued film."[153] I invite readers to think with this film and perceive how Pontecorvo strives to "imagine otherwise," and tap into the resistant philosophies of Black peoples in order to re-conceive the colonial present.[154] Pontecorvo's re-assessment of the colonial present occasions why I think *Queimada!* pairs well with Césaire's treatment of post-revolutionary Haiti, since the movie's extensive critique of civilization and progress hinges on Haiti's disruptive presence to colonial power the world over. *Queimada!* readily complements Césaire's engagement with Haiti as the starting point for a new way to exist in time, since it treats Haiti as an idea. It uses Haiti to invite deep thinking about how Black polities and peoples are made to move along an evolutionary timeline that models the imperialist behavior of Western capitalist civilizations, notwithstanding how antithetical this behavior is to Black existence, past and present.

The deep thinking the film prompts is tied to civilization's indebtedness to colonization. Césaire writes in *Discourse on Colonialism*, "no one colonizes innocently, . . . no one colonizes with impunity either . . . a nation which colonizes, . . . a civilization which justifies colonization—and therefore force—is already a sick civilization, a civilization which is morally diseased, which irresistibly, progressing from one consequence to another, one denial to another, calls for its Hitler, I mean its punishment."[155] This sentiment subtends Pontecorvo's filmography, which shows how fascist violence in Western Europe is directly tied to colonial violence in Africa and the Americas.[156] *Queimada!* critiques colonial violence and is set in the early 1800s.[157] It details the fictional Portuguese-governed island of Queimada's move from slave colony to independent nation state and lastly to a deeply indebted neocolonial nation through the story of José Delores's rise into anticolonial consciousness. Delores, played by a novice actor, Black Colombian Evaristo Márquez, is emancipated at the film's onset, scarcely surviving as a street porter. It is in this occupation that he meets the film's antagonist, the English mercenary William Walker, played by the white American actor Marlon Brando. Walker arrives to the island to foment a slave rebellion intended to give the creole colonists complete control of the island; he needs only a Black rebel leader: enter Delores. The English intend to oust the Portuguese to gain unfettered access to the island's sugar industry. The inclusion of a second Western European colonial power vying for the island drives the point that slavery and colonialism, as well as the cultural practices they engendered following their demise, are global operations that tie Western Europe to the Americas. These colonial entanglements necessitate, for Pontecorvo, Western European popular comprehension of the exploitation and destruction underwriting the lived existence of all Western Europeans *and* equally important the violence non-Westerners routinely experience as life. Delores's strikingly ethical character invites viewers to identify with his subjection and that of the island's captive Black majority, which effectively situates spectators in the violence of their collective lived existence. That Delores excels as a leader furthers their identification, as he goes on to unite the free and captive populace in the fight against the Portuguese, slavery and colonial rule on the island early in the film.

While the rebellion Delores commands gains momentum, Walker convinces influential creoles of the monetary benefits of rulership without slavery and is able to cement the revolution of the captive and free Blacks of Queimada to white creole leadership. This leadership (through Walker's direction) conveniently orchestrates a coup in the city (Delores and his army are in the countryside), kills the Portuguese governor, and declares Queimada free and independent. Delores and his men surrender their arms and agree to independence led by white creoles in 1825. Walker leaves the island after having accomplished his purpose. Ten years pass and viewers are told that the global market for sugar has increased. In this new moment of increased global demand, sugarcane workers in Queimada begin a rebellion that Delores joins and then goes on to lead, igniting a revived anticolonial military campaign against the creoles, now at the helm of Queimada's multi-racial government. This government has alienated its largely Black population with trade policies that consigned the Black majority to labor that pays little and worse yet is reminiscent of slavery. Notwithstanding the government's large army of Black, white, and mixed-race Queimadans, it turns to its main trade partner, the English-backed Royal Sugar Company, for guidance. The company re-enlists Walker, who successfully tracks Delores and his army and ends the threat with the help of the English army. The film concludes with Delores's execution and Walker's death at the hands of one of Delores's men, who, just before stabbing Walker, plays on the latter's affection for Delores by repeating the same lines Delores first utters to Walker at the film's start, "your bags, senor."[158]

The expressly neocolonial conditions of independent Queimada ties the harsh political and economic realities of the fictional nation-sate to the very conditions Césaire sought to circumvent while mayor of Martinique. Yet what expressly invites a reading of the film in relation to Césaire's musings on early Haiti in the immediate moment after independence in 1804 (*The Tragedy of King Christophe*) and in 1944/2004 is how very much the ideas of progress and civilization are leveraged against the *"historical initiative"* needed to break the hold colonialism and Western imperial cultural praxis have on Black efforts to build beyond the colony.[159] In a scene where Walker introduces himself to a select group of Queimadan creole elites and outlines their shared interests, Pontecorvo first introduces colonialism as a civilizing endeavor and articulates revolutionary Haiti as a disruptive counter to this idea. Walker states, "Well, actually England wants the same thing as you want—freedom of trade and therefore the end of all foreign domination in Latin America. But what England does not want however and what I think you yourselves do not want are these revolutions carried to their extreme consequences."[160] He continues, stating, "Men like José Delores and Toussaint Louverture are perhaps necessary to ignite a situation and then they become dangerous as in Haiti, for example. So ... uh ... gentlemen as you can see, I think our interests coincide at least for the moment. They coincide with progress and civilization and for those who believe in its importance."[161] Marlon Brando artfully delivers the performative earnestness and seriousness Walker intends to communicate to his audience. The slow conveyance of this speech accentuates the carefulness of his words and the manner in which they are curated to quell any doubts the creole elite may have concerning his presence, the interest of the English and the benefits of independence and wage labor.

Just prior to this speech, Walker opens his initial discussion with the creoles with an analogy comparing captive laborers to kept wives and wage laborers to neglectable prostitutes.[162] His point in offering this crude comparison is to make the creoles realize that independence and a transition from slavery to wage-based capitalist predation would be most beneficial to their finances. While this captures their attention, the sole nonwhite creole present at the meeting, the mulatto Teddy Sanchez (played by the white Italian actor, Renato Salvatori, in blackface) reminds his brethren of the idealistic purpose of their efforts. Sanchez draws his compatriots' attention to republican talking points of nation building as an individualizing effort, referencing the freedom to have the agency to carve out a distinct identity.[163] Borrowing from Sanchez's republican idealism, Walker begins his point invoking liberal democratic freedom in economic terms as evinced in his quick and passing reference to "freedom of trade and ... the end of all foreign domination in Latin America."[164] Walker cares little about populist ideas of freedom and independence and Pontecorvo makes this very clear with a close up of his face as Sanchez is speaking.

Walker's face is deliberately contained in the corner he occupies in the room, and this recessed positioning, coupled with the shadow cast on the left side of his face, visually accentuates the intensity of his cunning, which in turn lends greater emphasis to the machinations subtending his efforts with the creoles here. That his eyes intensely dart back and forth to gauge the room's reception to Sanchez underscores how very much Pontecorvo wants his viewers to understand that Walker's presence is steadfastly antithetical to Sanchez's idealist liberal democratic

FIGURE 1.1. Walker observing the audience's reaction to Sanchez's speech. Film still from *Queimada!*, Gillo Pontecorvo, dir., 1969

principles, let alone to the freedom efforts of the captive. When Walker speaks (in the aforementioned quote) he shrewdly marshals the white supremacist's subtext of liberal democracy's causal relation to ideas of "progress and civilization" and situates, in the process, Sanchez's inability to see the bottom line and the bigger picture of preserving white power in light of his proximity to Blackness.[165] By invoking Black vengeance in response to white violence with his reference to "revolutions carried to their extreme consequences," Walker draws on white fears of Black reprisal to undermine Sanchez and spur the other white men in the room to accept his proposal of freeing the captives, becoming independent, and working with England to maintain their racist governance of Queimada's Black population.[166] It is only after Haiti is invoked and white power called into question that the one naysayer who was unconvinced of Walker's wife/prostitute analogy is swayed toward Walker's point of view. Haiti emblematizes, for Walker and his audience, a state of being in the world that is resistant to and wholly hostile to white supremacy and its civilizational projects of slavery, colonialism, and neocolonialism; in this respect, Haiti and any freedom-seeking project like it must be negated at all costs.

The audible murmurs of agreement from the white creole men that follow Walker's strategic invocation of Haiti serve, in my estimation, as acknowledgment of Haiti's otherwise presence in the colonial world order. This presence was a well-established fact in the time period in which the film is set; and while the revolution Walker invokes is that of the assimilationist oligarch (Louverture) versus the radically anti-West *Ginen* folk, this distinction hardly mattered: Haiti, on the whole, was feared. A free but politically divided Haiti, with Christophe in the North and Pétion in the South, proved to be politically potent in the minds of colonizers like the Spanish Secretary of State and members of the Junta Central in Cuba, governing Cuba in the early 1800s. Upon having to contend with whether or not to receive emissaries from the Christophe of historic fact or Pétion, the men wrote the following in 1809,

> It is well known that the colonial system is completely opposed to the principles of liberty proclaimed in Haiti and that an imprudent and open communication between that island and ours [Cuba] could be the origin of a political upheaval, for in the end the example can be very tempting and the idea of independence is easily received in the minds of even those men who, according to some, are destined for slavery.[167]

The Haitian Revolutionary threat is clear here: to even take part in diplomatic exchanges with Haiti is to nurture antislavery resistance and Black freedom; it is to undermine the political basis of colonial rule in Cuba ("could be the origin of political upheaval"). Moreover, the composers of this document to then-governor of Cuba, the Marqués de Someruelos, implicitly acknowledge that any diplomatic relation with Haiti upends the very idea that "those men [Black men, in truth Black peoples] are destined for slavery." The murmurs of agreement that the white creole colonists of Queimada offer in support of Walker's invocation of Haiti are firmly grounded in the disquiet Haiti's oppositional presence in the colonial order caused Cuba's colonial officials and *all* white colonialists past and present. When Walker implicitly references the existence of Haiti through his comparative coupling of Delores with the Haitian revolutionary general, Toussaint Louverture, he seizes on their fears to put forth the fiction that Delores (or Louverture for that matter) could ever be controlled. Both men are positioned as "necessary to ignite a situation." The hubris of this interpretation is telling of how colonialism's white supremacist basis cannot acknowledge the agency of Black peoples.

Walker's flippant articulation of Delores's and Louverture's abilities to act for themselves (meaning, outside of white people and colonial power) invites the creoles to dismiss what they know to be true: another world *is* possible, one that can be initiated by the mere act of declaring and acting on "not this." In other words, a distinct world can be prompted by Black Queimadans' *Ginen* refusal of life as *necessarily* anti-Black and *necessarily* colonial. A path beyond the colony may be logically improbable for the creoles because the very idea is terrifyingly hostile to their worldview, but that does not mean that they themselves do not realize that this un-forged path is nevertheless thinkable *and* pursuable by determined and enthused Black peoples. Recall the disquiet of Cuban officials in 1809 who were unnerved at the very idea of entertaining Haitian emissaries on Cuban soil as their "example [could] be very tempting and [worst yet] the idea of independence is easily received in the minds of even those men."[168]

With Walker's speech, Pontecorvo makes clear to his viewers that the issue foiling a decolonized world and the radical pursuit of a new way to exist in time is white power, the fulcrum that unites the creoles' interest with that of Walker's (and England's correspondingly) and that shapes how the ideas of "progress and civilization" are articulated.[169] These particular constructs ("progress and civilization") mask how existence in Western Europe and in its past and present colonial holdings is articulated through a logic that naturalizes white supremacy and colonial profiteering. Pontecorvo's cinematic depiction of Walker's calculated manipulation of the creoles' bigoted beliefs exposes the concealment of these racist motivations and invites his audience to recognize that the very ideas of "progress and civilization" are colonial in nature and innately white supremacist, since they can so easily serve as talking points in support of limiting the agency of Black peoples. The effort to limit Black agency is evidenced in Walker's speech as these ideas follow his warning of Black vengeance and white victimization. Pontecorvo therefore goes to great pains to afford Delores an anticolonial radicalism that is clearly counter to the ideas of "progress and civilization."

These ideas are further countered later in the film when Delores begins a new anticolonial military campaign following Queimada's independence from Portugal. Martino, a rebel subordinate of Delores, is captured by Walker and discloses Delores's revolutionary program for the nation. He states, "José Delores says that if what we have in our country is civilization, civilization of white men, then we are better uncivilized because it is better to know where to go and not know how than it is to know how to go and not know where."[170] Delores's decolonial plan is purposely philosophical in nature, telling of how ways of knowing engender particular ways of living and being. Moreover, his rhetoric is decolonial in the revolutionary fashion of *Ginen* captives of Saint Domingue and Haiti's *Ginen* peasantry, since it is a program that emerges from the particularities of the Black experience of race-based subjection. This experience situates "not this" as the ideological basis of a viable anticolonial movement, which Delores expresses when proposing that "it is better to know where to go and not know how."[171] Accordingly, Black peoples committed to anticolonial agitation and change need only remain committed to dismantling existence as *it is*.

Knowledge of this possibility does not engender an otherwise existence for Queimadans, however. Immediately following the removal of the Portuguese, the creoles and Delores sit to create a government that meets all their needs. Delores soon realizes that the creoles have no intention to improve the lived existence of the newly liberated or those who had been free during slavery. In this frustrated and dissatisfied state, Walker attempts to keep him in line by stating the following, "Civilization is not a simple matter, José. You cannot learn its secrets overnight. Today, civilization belongs to the white man and you must learn to use it, without it you cannot go forward."[172] This culturally self-centered and racist rendering of existence fixes Delores and the people he leads to one way to be in existence—subservient followers of whites, those who know the one and only way to live. In this way, Delores and his people are not meant to experience time as a forward movement that suggests that life can get better; but because the formerly captive must learn from more advanced people, life must be experienced through an evolutionary stasis where time is continually reset to the point in which Delores and his people exist to emulate whites and similarly serve white interests. Delores' response to Walker, "But to go where, Ingles?," tellingly points to the confining limits of this idea

FIGURE 1.2. Delores before his execution. Film still from *Queimada!*, Gillo Pontecorvo, dir., 1969.

of civilization for the formerly captive and colonized.[173] To this question, Walker makes no reply as there is quite simply nowhere to go. This question is reiterated again near the film's conclusion and once more, spectators are made to see that there is nowhere to go (save for endless resistant violence). Uttering his final line just before his execution, Delores mockingly asks: "Ingles, remember what you said 'civilization belongs to whites.' But what civilization, until when?"[174] In leaving this poignant question unanswered, Pontecorvo compels viewers to recognize that Delores and those like him must strive for an alternative to the world as is (a world of progress and civilization) even if such an alternative means "not know[ing] how" to forge ahead. They must embrace the uncertainty of seizing and sitting with "not this" and strive, in the process, to resist the toxic paralysis of a postcolonial present frozen in the long interim of "until when."

The temporality of "until when" is one Pontecorvo invites his viewers to critique precisely because it subsists by propagating the lie that all things in existence have been discovered and all peoples situated in positions they were destined to occupy. Delores's final lines are purposefully offered with a sneer to accentuate Pontecorvo's insistence that his viewers recognize the farce that is civilization and progress for oppressed peoples. I take the nonverbal vocalization of dissension that characterizes Delores's exchange with Walker following Walker's return to the island as serving the same narrative function as the racist murmurs of the creoles once Haiti is invoked by Walker. Delores's wordless defiance intends to compel Walker to reckon with the vibrancy and truth of Black agency and with that, the malleability of the world. Delores's wordless engagement with Walker makes spectators conscious of Walker's investment in a sense of time (and an experience of time) that makes belatedness a condition of Black life. Black life, in Walker's conception of civilization, is necessarily the experience of never quite being on time for existence, incapable of catching up to the Western European world. Delores's biting question of "until when" captures how colonized Black peoples and Black polities are made to wait for a change that is due to them. Moreover, it captures how Black people must navigate beyond the temporal dictates of colonial power.

Beyond the Colony

Pontecorvo's film, *Queimada!*, and Césaire's play, *The Tragedy of King Christophe*, turn to revolutionary Haiti to present compelling questions about the persistent continuities of colonialism and the difficulties of politically administering beyond the colony. Both disclose how fighting colonial subjugation does not prepare one for the additional fight against the "false alternative" Césaire argues colonial betters put forth between "fidelity and backwardness," or "progress and rupture"; meaning "fidelity" to one's culture and decolonial vision of existence (which is regarded as "backward"), and "progress and rupture" necessitating imitation of Western Europe.[175] Both tread ground that is *Ginen* due to the questioning and deep thinking each prompts against the colonial project with their art. Thinking with them and *Ginens* occasions my decision to end with a reading of Césaire's final play, *A Tempest* (1969), an adaptation of William Shakespeare's *The Tempest*, which reimagines the colonial encounter. I conclude by bringing *A Tempest* in conversation with the readings offered of *Queimada!* and *The Tragedy of King Christophe*, to situate how the extensive attention post-revolutionary Haiti receives in Caribbean imaginings of the Haitian Revolution occurs, in large part because of the limited paths for existence that newly liberated colonies are afforded within the governing colonial world order. Indeed, attention to the colonial encounter and its discovery narrative produces the necessary context to discern the functional necessity of the colony's continuation in the Americas. The unsettling rise in neocolonialism in the independent Caribbean and Latin America showcased in *Queimada!*, and the oft noted disharmony between revolutionary Haiti and post-revolutionary Haiti in the Caribbean cultural imaginary, are symptomatic of a deferred awareness concerning how former slave colonies are *made to* function as perpetually indebted to their colonial betters by white geopolitical politics. I read *A Tempest* as building from Césaire's prior Haitian writings because it continues the conversation, *The Tragedy of King Christophe* began about the paucity of directorial choices formerly colonized polities have when independent. I find, however, that *A Tempest* is more searing in its critique of the colonial project since its criticism is not mediated through republicanism, a politic that Césaire cannot dissociate from his understanding of Haiti as well as the Revolution and that is de-radicalizing with respect to Haiti and decolonial liberation. To end with *A Tempest* is to end with a Césaire who daringly asks, if independence does not safeguard postcolonial nations from the enforced temporality of "until when," which *Queimada!* so powerfully illuminates, then why not seize the radical possibility that "not knowing how" affords? Why not journey ignorantly beyond the colony?

A Tempest ends at the moment in which Caliban (the captive native who is both Black and Indigenous) and Prospero (the white colonial usurper) are locked in a life and death struggle that the temporality of "until when" occasions. Following Caliban's declaration that he despises Prospero because he has "impos[ed] on [him] a [false] image of [himself as] underdeveloped [and] undercompetent," Prospero retorts that he also hates Caliban for Caliban's refusal to see value in his subjugation.[176] Worse yet, Prospero discloses that Caliban has "made [him] doubt [himself] for the first time."[177] Because of these reasons, Prospero decides to remain on the island, choosing not to return to Milan with his shipwrecked countrymen. Time is then said to have passed, and audience members conclude the play with a decrepit Prospero alone on the stage, vowing to "protect civilization" from "unclean nature" and offering his final cry: Caliban's name.[178] The stage directions reveal that in the far distance bits of Caliban's anticolonial song, sung earlier in the play, is heard: "FREEDOM HI-DAY! FREEDOM HI-DAY"![179] This moment calls to mind Delores's struggle against Walker and Queimada's creole leadership as it shows how the fight against colonial rule can only be imagined through an imperial presence. Prospero therefore occupies the stage and Caliban the background, an authorial choice that heightens awareness of the hierarchies brought about by the colonial encounter. These hierarchies are why Caliban's resistance functions as a reaction to Prospero's call for recognition. They occasion why Toussaint Louverture can be deemed a conscript of modernity, as outlined in Chapter 1, as one who is determined by the ideologies of colonial modernity alone. They also are why Black resistance is readily imagined as the product of white prompting alone. (Consider *Queimada!* and the popular rumor in the Haitian revolutionary moment that Louverture led the Revolution at the behest of planters loyal to the French crown.)[180] Black existence, in a colonial conception of being, is a reaction to white civilizational norms. Both Walker and Prospero's positions on civilization give rise to the subversive speech acts of their counterparts, respectively sparking Delores's renouncement of civilization and Caliban's song of freedom; these speech acts resist while concurrently affording recognition to the individuals who made subversive speech possible.

Therein lies the paralyzing condition of a temporality that confines the colonized and racially subjugated to an evolutionary experience of time as stasis: the clock continually resets to where the formerly captive first began, with an indebted existence. Each pair accordingly is made to give meaning to the other's ontological function in life—ruler and order of things (Prospero/Walker), subordinate and disruptor of the order of things (Caliban/Delores). They exist in this manner precisely because the modern moment, post 1492, has and remains governed by the narrative necessity of the victor's articulation of existence. Consequently, the play and the film are overwhelmingly conveyed through the nauseating hubris of Prospero and Walker, men who know it all and as such cannot see outside of themselves. So even as Walker is murdered by the film's end and Prospero aged with diminished powers, the worlds they created or sustained still go on to exist; but the worlds both Caliban and Delores want remain deferred in both texts. The narrative necessity of the temporality of the long colonial present, by its very constitution in conquest and by its very function through imperial hubris, cannot actualize Caliban or Delores's decolonized future. It cannot actualize Haiti either: the nation is narrated as having failed to mitigate the desire for revolution, independence, and resistant thinking among the world's colonized peoples. The only option that this toxic temporality can provide decolonial pursuits then is to subsume it within the going-nowhere-fast-get-poor-quick neocolonial nation-state that Césaire's Haiti in *A Tragedy of King Christophe* portends.

Still, there is something to be said about Césaire's and Pontecorvo's refusal to present the defeat of the colonized on stage and screen. It is as if each implores, "not this," and are aware that the temporality of "until when" is tied to the colony itself, to its manifestation in new ways in postcolonial governance. Their awareness situates their art in a horizon of thought that is decolonial in substance. This horizon politicizes their work and attests to their reluctance to belittle the myriad ways Black peoples have sought to live in the world differently. Each refuse to negate the quotidian criticality of Black freedom efforts, and each has created art aligned with the resistant deliberations of unseen *Ginens*. These are persons who are thought past by their state leaders and the chroniclers of their Revolution, but who are the grammar for the thought that inspires the leader and their chronicler. In this chapter, they are present in the oligarch's confused decolonial program (Christophe) and discoverable throughout a work in a masking presence, as in the case of Delores and his philosophies of freedom. His musings are reminiscent of the decolonial thoughts of the *Ginen* captives of Saint Domingue, but the prominence of Delores's philosophies in the film is directly tied to Delores's connection to the revolutionary general, Louverture, a figure of Haitian resistance who is more readily regarded as capable of producing revolutionary thought and action by artists of the Revolution.

The unwillingness to image defeat present in Césaire's and Pontecorvo's art ultimately speaks to how engagements with Haiti as idea are tied to what artists know to be true of the Revolution, but cannot quite communicate or at least lead with: namely, that there existed (and perhaps still exist) communities unbothered with the West. There existed peoples who envisioned and wanted more for themselves, and who inspired others to also want more. They tasked others to understand that liberation begins with the imagination. It begins with a refusal to be tied to one idea of existence and is wedded, in turn, to a desire to question the efficacies of becoming like one's oppressor in mind, body, and being. Césaire and Pontecorvo sense that it is heartening to know of these peoples since they mark a moment of what could have been. They bring an unprecedented bygone into cognizance for a new present and, in doing so, give expression to the importance of speculative thought in the political work carried out in the past and in the futures to come against the colonial order. Engaging Haiti imaginatively, as an idea, is part of this political labor. It grants artists and theorists committed to decolonial liberation the ability to avow "not this," and champion forging ahead *even as* this uncharted trajectory terrifyingly signifies "not know[ing] how" to proceed, or where to go in the journey beyond the colony.

CHAPTER 4

Défilez!

> E tout nou pa konnen ... Nou pap bliye.
> —Haitixchange User

Chapo ba, respè pou yo (big up and much respect) to all who remember those that history has forgotten, to those committed to the political work of recovering the dissension that rests with the obscured; for, if in history forgetting is political, as the cultural anthropologist Michel-Rolph Trouillot notes, then refusing history's disremembering is a political reclamation of absented dissidents, pathways, and imaginings untenable to the world that history proper archives and commemorates.[1] This refusal of history's partiality spawned the ancestral homage to Haitian revolutionaries that open each chapter in this monograph and the closing line, in particular, *e tout nou pa konnen ... Nou pap bliye.*[2] Closing the homage with this line poignantly underscores the peculiar absence of dissension in the revolutionary record as imagined by Caribbean writers of classic Haitian Revolutionist literatures. It points to the obfuscation of competing views of and/or desires for the Revolution that rest with the absented—here *Ginen* revolutionaries. These rebels are overshadowed by the overwhelming attention afforded the creole (Caribbean-born) generals who became Haiti's first statesmen in canonical Caribbean literatures of the Revolution.

Of the revolutionary ancestors noted in the homage, provided in the appendix, several are Taino, African, and creole. Not one, however, is a member of the male vanguard who spearheaded the Revolution and Haiti thereafter. The refusal to name the male icons of the Revolution counters the immense space they take up in its varied modes of narration. Toussaint Louverture, Henry Christophe, and Jean Jacques Dessalines have so shaped the landscape of fictional and theoretical representations of the Haitian Revolution outside of Haiti that each description of *Ginen* cultural praxis offered in this book somehow intersects with the individual character, action, or intention of these men—in truth, of any man within the Revolution's Caribbean-born vanguard. The homage, however, points elsewhere. If it can be said that the story of the Revolution as mediated through Louverture, Christophe, and/or Dessalines (et al.) begins in 1791 and ends in 1804, then the homage's cast of revolutionary figures calls not only the temporal span of the Revolution into question. It also calls into question the work of fixing the Revolution to its specific moment *and* to the great men of that moment. It demands that scholars ask: what revolutionary aspect, element, and/or factor is contained and/or buried by this temporal specificity and the great men of this temporality? Who and what is lost?

The homage concludes with a purposeful nod to absented revolutionaries. It brings the early colonial past in conversation with the revolutionary moment and facilitates understanding of the deleterious manner in which the Revolution has been narrated in twentieth-century Caribbean arts and letters. The narrative fixation on the period of 1791–1804 reifies the revolutionary period and encourages the dismissal of the long-term and varied dissension through which the Revolution came into being. This reification, in turn, prompts a silencing of a vast array of Haitian revolutionists to offer a rendering of the struggle fixed on its great men, a move that is both phallocentric and Eurocentric in orientation. As "figures of enlightenment" (Louverture) or as "avengers of the Americas" (Dessalines), the men of the vanguard conform to what many would prefer to know of existence: that men rule and do so in a European and North American fashion as the "enlightened" Louverture or as the "barbaric" Dessalines.[3] Both men are readable and knowable precisely because they correspond to the familiar masculinist narrative of existence authored by Western Europe being the "noble [or vengeful] savage." In this regard, they are fitting figures of the West and suitable conscripts for the ideological ends of anti-Black and anti-Native colonial rule.

The same, however, cannot be said of the revolutionaries who are absented from the Revolution by Caribbean artists and the scholars who study foundational Caribbean writing of the Revolution. That they have been minimized and/or excised within literary and critical accounts of the Revolution suggests an incompatibility with the masculinist and racialist pro-colonial narrative for existence authored by Western Europe and sustained by its North American counterparts (most notably, the United States and Canada). Yet it is precisely because they are unsuitable figures and subjects of colonial power that they serve as mediums through which to offer new ways of reading and engaging the revolutionary struggle. It is extremely significant that the last ancestor named in the homage is the female revolutionary Mar Jan (Marie-Jeanne) Lamartinère and the ancestor immediately before her is Suzette Simon Louverture. Both Mar Jan and Suzette are two of the three female revolutionaries detailed with significance in the revolutionary record. The other is Toya (Victoria) Montou. To end with the names of female revolutionaries strongly intimates an unconscious, if not conscious, desire to see the absented and in doing so acknowledge the most obscured among the Revolution's unnoted others: the women in the revolutionary record. I heed Joan Dayan's call "to consider how ... women [of the Revolution] are mentioned" in "historical narratives" of the uprising, and I extend her call by considering the implications of their absence in canonical Caribbean Haitian Revolutionist literatures.[4] I draw from Jana Evans Braziel's "historical sketch of" the revolutionary heroine" Dédée Bazile or Défilée-la-folle, and Dayan's work on the heroine, to make sense of their absence.[5] Their research facilitates my efforts to gender the Revolution's narratology with a reading of the Haiti-born and US resident Edwidge Danticat's Haitian Revolutionary stories. Danticat's short stories, "Nineteen Thirty-Seven" and "A Wall of Rising Fire," center the decolonial perspective of overlooked female revolutionaries and encourage consideration of the radical possibilities for a distinct existence that was present in the revolutionary moment and that endures today. In this respect, her work allows scholars to remember otherwise, and radically think through the counterrevolutionary impulse that shapes the Revolution's male centered narration in classic Caribbean writing of the Revolution.

Much can be said of Danticat's measured deliberation on the Haitian diaspora in her short story collection, *Krik? Krak!* (1996), least of which is her interest in the nation's revolutionary struggle. Yet if *Krik? Krak!* is recognized as a litany that names and honors Haiti's unnoted in the diaspora and at home, then its attention to Haiti's revolutionary others can be more readily discerned. The collection's composition for unnamed others who are thought past and largely unseen by persons external to Haiti is meant to intervene in a broader hemispheric American narrative that reads Haiti and Haitians through base sobriquets ("boat people" and "AIDS carriers," among others). The opening story, "Children of the Sea," for instance, chronicles two young lovers who are forced apart by a repressive military regime. The young woman finds safety in the countryside and the young man takes to the sea, joining the many "boat people" who have crossed the Atlantic from Columbus onward. In the poignant description of their love that follows, readers are presented with a minor character with an exceptionally long name, "Justin Moise André Nozius Joseph Frank Osnac Maximilien."[6] A name of this length provocatively underscores how the collection calls attention to Haitians deprived of their names in external discourses of the nation, as the forename literally names names, and is also replete with forenames held by Danticat's own family members.[7] The intimacy of relations that the name reveals affirms the immense regard Danticat has for Haitians held captive by the racist and xenophobic discourses policing their transatlantic movement, and in truth, their very existence abroad and at home in their occupied nation-state. With its opening story, *Krik? Krak!* announces Danticat's intention to clearly refute the narrative terms and conditions that make this policing possible, as her Haiti and her Haitians cannot be readily reduced to the one-dimensional appellations by which her audience has come to know the nation and its people. This introductory story, however, does more than simply add nuance to Haiti and Haitians. In its desire to name those subsumed beneath the derisive monikers given to Haitians, it also establishes who is most likely to be named when naming is a possibility: Haiti's fathers and (adult) sons.

Quite purposefully, the collection is focused on Haiti's mothers and daughters (young and old), the overlooked "kitchen poets," who have equally crossed oceans and similarly endured turmoil in Haiti.[8] Drawing from a Black Atlantic spiritual tradition in which work most commonly regarded as "women's work" (cookery and hair braiding) operates as a first step toward serving the spirits, the collection's epilogue, "Women Like Us," establishes the kitchen as the space where Danticat learned to serve "the . . . nine hundred and ninety-nine women who . . . worked their fingers to coconut rind."[9] The closing line of the epilogue, "And this is your testament to the way that these women lived and died and lived again," deliberately bookends the opening to establish Danticat's intent to honor her matrilineal relations and all women: "You remember thinking while braiding your hair that you look like your mother. Your mother who looked like your grandmother and her grandmother before her."[10] These women could not write but they certainly created and passed on the will to create. Danticat writes, "No, women like you don't write. . . . They sit in dark corners and braid their hair in new shapes and twists in order to control the stiffness, the unruliness, the rebelliousness."[11] As women constrained by the dictates of their gender, race, and class positioning (most typically poor, or lower working class, in *Krik? Krak!*), Danticat's "poets" exist in difference, in an alterity set against a human standard that is male, white (even in a Black country), and wealthy. They have had to stomach and fight against the diminution of their person, necessitating small and large acts of "unruliness, stiffness, [and] rebelliousness."[12] The stories in *Krik? Krak!* attest to this by showing the unyielding gumption needed to live as marginalized subjects in Haiti, or as the thrice-burdened Black and foreign female in the United States and the Dominican Republic. The stories also reveal that just as the "poets" exist in difference, outside an imposed human norm, they have equally struggled to differentiate themselves: working to make space for their lives and the lives of future "poets" in and beyond Haiti. They remain, in death and in life, a wellspring of defiance and are presented as "an army . . . watching over [Danticat]," granting her the tools to be a "soully gal" (a descendant who is a sister in the struggle for difference).[13] In this respect, they have provided her with the means to "talk [her] talk," "make [her words] a gun," and use their stories to write her own resistance.[14]

Danticat's literary oeuvre attests to her long-standing effort to "talk [her] talk" and march against the narratives that ensconce Haiti and Haitians in designations intended to demean their culture, individual selves, and revolutionary history.[15] Her short story collection signals the beginning of this resistant *delifez* (purposeful march). It shows the disruptions in thought that gender occasions when foregrounded in male-centered discourses. The stories, "Nineteen Thirty-Seven" and "A Wall of Rising Fire," are closely read here because Danticat's inscription of female perspectives in narratives of the Haitian Revolution deliberately re-signifies the Revolution's subjects, aims, and intentions. Her focus on gender avails readers to obscured histories that remain salient to the present precisely because they unsettle a colonial fixation on emissaries of revolution who denote resistance and yet can also be appropriated to perpetuate colonial subjugation. Of import to my analysis is the subtle but intense dialogue carried on between the two stories, which disrupts the deference afforded to Haiti's famed creole generals in canonical Caribbean literatures of the Revolution. This dialogue is facilitated by the Vodou imaginary guiding Danticat's kitchen communality and concerns revolutionary memory, on the one hand, and the narratives of existence legitimated by colonial modernity, on the other. The narratives' rich play with histories and temporalities foregrounds the violence intrinsic to the modern moment, particularly the post-1492 period. What's more, it sheds light on the manner in which a colonial imagining of existence is not only male-centered, where men rule all, but it is progress-centered, driven by the notion of "development as progress."[16]

"Nineteen Thirty-Seven" and "A Wall of Rising Fire" write against a colonial imagining of existence through Vodouzian thought, an epistemological practice that is foundational to *Ginen* culture being a key element of the freedom-seeking efforts of Saint Domingue's captive populace and Haiti's rural and urban majority. A syncretic belief system of the Americas, Vodou is an amalgamation of West African, Amerindian and European (Catholic, most predominantly) spiritual practices. It is of immense cultural significance due to the Revolution. The Revolution's success is often credited to the famed 1791 *Bwa Kayïman* ceremony said to have inspired the Revolution's early participants, and to the *lwa* (demi-gods) who are recognized as having interceded on the people's behalf. The practice itself is one of relation where one's singularity as an individual emerges from a cosmic multiplicity, from an enduring familial association with departed ancestors granted new life as divine beings. These ancestors, *lè Mò* (the dead), *lè Marasa* (twins), and *lè Mistè* ("mysteries" i.e., *lwa*), comprise the core divinities of the practice. As inherited entities, beings passed down like genetic traits from mother and father to their progeny, these ancestors are said to reside in their descendants' blood. Persons are therefore never quite "individuals" in the Western European or colonial hemispheric American sense, as they are always implicated within a broader spiritual collectivity preserved within themselves. Their blood, married with ancestral energy, creates the conditions by which they are persons who are simultaneously singular and plural, made of a particular's corporal essence and its present while concurrently shaped by their ancestors' respective pasts. These pasts are preserved in mind, body, and spirit. Therefore, when Danticat reveals that there are "nine hundred and ninety-nine women boiling in [her] blood" and that "the women in her family never [lose] touch with one another," she grounds her person and collection of stories within a Vodou imaginary. In this way, her collection is structurally *Ginen* and envelopes readers in what lies at the heart of a Vodou imaginary, mournful remembrance.

When someone entreats an ancestor for guidance or simply acknowledges their presence within them, as Danticat does, the person takes part in an act of mournful remembrance that grants the dead vitality in death and concedes the perpetuation of the past in the present. Through this act of invocation and recognition, the individual engages in a performance of grief that is fundamentally melancholic since bereavement is enacted and experienced as an enduring demonstration of remembrance, one that consciously preserves a loss (of a person or event) in the present. Whereas mourning in a Freudian sense interprets grief as a brief spell that can and must be overcome for one's self-preservation, melancholia as mourning places no temporal constraints upon grief.[17] The deceased (and thus the past existence) can remain "steadfastly alive in the present."[18] A melancholic understanding of mourning fits well within a Vodou imaginary precisely for this reason. The dead, the Freudian "lost object," never truly perish from existence within Vodou and are incorporated into one of the three sacred collectives.[19] The most honored among men and women are afforded the status of *lwa* or *marasa*. With this divine transformation, a bygone past illuminates a present, permitting, "lost pasts to step into the light of a present moment of danger."[20] The past of obscure revolutionaries can inform Haitians and Haiti today. Indeed, because Vodou privileges mournful remembrance, it allows for an "ongoing and open relationship with the past—bring[ing] its ghosts and specters, its flaring and fleeting images, into [our moment]."[21]

Vodou therefore refutes the imperative of the "new" that is central to modernization, and it helps contest colonial modernity's attack on tradition as necessarily backward and regressive. It discloses that relation to the past provides the constitution to not only resist despotic violence but create beyond a world of violence with new forms of communality. In this sense, a Vodou imaginary immerses readers in the decolonial cultural praxis of Saint Domingue's *Ginen* captives and Haiti's *Ginen* majority. This praxis prioritized solidarity above colonial power's emphasis on individualist aggrandizement. Haitian sociologist Jean Casimir therefore writes that the African captive of Saint Domingue (*bossale*) survived enslavement by "extract[ing] a form of knowing that liberated her, making it possible to construct a universe where she could realize herself as she envisioned. This knowledge began with solidarity with her companions in misfortune. Like her, they were creating knowledge that surpassed the conditions of survival and opened the doors of the prison of the chaos-order of colonialism. They initiated a new tradition, a new memory."[22] *Ginens* remade themselves through their relationships with likeminded others. Their collectivist self-invention began with the memory of the *lwa of Ginen*, which created the basis for the African captive's practice of decolonial self-authorship. Casimir argues that *bossales* could imagine their loved ones and cultures flourishing without them since they had not experienced genocide or settler colonialism. They could envisage "the *lwa of Ginen*" and the "memory that somewhere family survived, that there was a lineage and a nation that they could dream was proud, strong, and even prosperous."[23] This memory emboldened them and bore a collective rebirth that produced a cultural practice of thought and action set against colonial indoctrination. Vodou was a product of this practice and was among other behaviors that produced the counter-plantation system in early Haiti as defined by Casimir.[24]

A Vodou imaginary is key to my reading of Danticat's stories since it situates readers in the culture of critical resistance practiced by Saint Domingue's captive populace and their descendants in contemporary Haiti. It offers a way to not only bring their resistant thoughts and actions to the fore of Danticat's stories for readers outside of Haiti, but it grants a path by which to attend to the absented women of the Revolution. My attention to ignored revolutionists discloses what the absented bring to light for contemporary peoples: the ever-present and latent oppositions to the colonial project. Accordingly, of concern here is not only addressing the discursive obfuscation of women within the revolutionary record, but heeding what the obscured offer a present in dire need of an alternative means of existence—namely, the ability to envision a future of decolonial difference and the conviction needed to believe that this future can be realized.

Défilée and Boukman

"A Wall of Rising Fire" and "Nineteen Thirty-Seven" offer an alternative view of the Revolution that not only unearths the absented women of the struggle, but also illuminates the battle for existence the Revolution initiated. This contest involves the struggle for a decolonial lived existence removed from conquest, racialization, and colonialism. "A Wall of Rising Fire" openly reproduces the male focus of influential Caribbean Haitian Revolutionist writing, while asking, "How can the revolution feel so near, so eternal, yet so estranged from the postcolonial present," as Angela Naimou writes.[25] In a departure from the collection's female emphasis, male characters (Little Guy, Guy, and Boukman) drive the action of the tale and are the only subjects who invoke the Revolution's history. Despite this, the narrative works with "Nineteen Thirty-Seven" to shift scholarly and artistic attention from men alone, as "A Wall of Rising Fire" provides the contextual frame with which to question the male-centered narration of classic Caribbean writing of the Revolution. Together, both urge a critical reappraisal of the narratives for existence that the canonical Caribbean (male revolutionary) recitation supports and encourages. The exchange of ideas occurring between both short stories concerning the Revolution and colonial modernity, while lively, is largely obscured by their distinct storylines and their divergent narrative approaches to revolutionary history. I turn now to "Nineteen Thirty-Seven," which anchors the Revolution's history in female communality.

The Revolution is brought to the fore of the narrative through a character named Defile, namesake, and great-great-granddaughter of a revolutionary figure (Défilée) famous for her 1806 burial of the assassinated Dessalines. It also subtends the story through the genocide from which the tale derives its name: the 1937 Dominican massacre of Haitians, an event known in Haiti as *Kout Kouto-a* (the stabbing). Danticat uses the history of the massacre and the Haitian state's mythification of Défilée to write the Revolution alongside counterrevolutionary attacks against *Ginen* self-sovereignty, attacks led in the nineteenth century by the Haitian oligarchy, and in the twentieth by US imperialists. These attacks explain Défilée's importance to Danticat's telling of the Revolution, which is discernible with attention to Défilée's biography and mythification.

Colloquially known as Défilée-la-folle (Défilée the Madwoman), Defile's namesake, Marissainte Dédée Bazile is a woman of little-known origin. The little that can be discerned of her person is telling of the subsuming silence concealing women in the revolutionary record. Of her personal life, it is known only that she was born in Cap Français, was a captive, was said to have had a cruel enslaver, and was definitively acknowledged to be mad by all.[26] How she became mad is unclear. Some point to a sexual assault she suffered (perpetrated by her enslaver), others to the loss of several brothers and sons during one offensive of the revolutionary war, and some to the murder of her parents.[27] All acknowledge that by the time she encounters Dessalines and acts as a sutler to his army, following him throughout Haiti selling meat and (by some accounts) sex, she has long lost her sanity. This madness proves the basis for her mythic importance within Haiti, as she is widely read by the country's political and intellectual elite as the "embodiment of the ... nation: crazed and lost, but then redeemed through the body of [the nation's] savior [Dessalines]."[28]

Haiti's "savior" became so through a deliberate effort by the oligarchic state to memorialize Dessalines and subdue the political power of

Haiti's *Ginen* majority. Their power occasioned a crisis of being for the oligarchy, who sought to rule Haiti as a colony but found that they did not have constituents amenable to colonial subjection. The fiction of the nation as "crazed and lost" emerged because *Ginen* folk successfully rallied against oligarchic exploitation to the dismay of oligarchs, who "remained the product of the racialized system that created them" despite the Revolution.[29] As a class whose origins lie in Saint Domingue's populace of "free people of color and emancipated blacks," persons whose freedom serviced the colony and who were "pillars of the colonial order" as a result, the oligarchy saw little wrong with the colonial project outside of its racism, which they vehemently opposed.[30] They "had [no] intention of modifying the fate of the agricultural workers in any way" after the Revolution and viewed the *Ginen* folk's systematic exploitation by colonial norms and mechanisms as natural.[31] Casimir writes that in nascent Haiti "all progress" toward ameliorating the suffering of the majority "was the result of the subordinated classes rather than any economic projects supported by the oligarchs."[32] The folk's history of freedom seized without permission engrained a radicalization that prioritized the well-being of all, setting them at odds with the oligarchy whose class history of freedom acquired inculcated a Eurocentrism that bore the counter Haitian Revolutionary politics of the Haitian state in the nineteenth century. Unnerved by their compatriots' Africanisms and radical insistence on self-sovereignty, the oligarchy made sense of the radical reorientation of power away from their influence by miming French colonial legalisms and conduct in governance. Their political conservatism in early Haiti results in their desperate reclamation of Dessalines, a man who was reviled by his class compatriots for trying to lessen the divide between Haiti's peoples.

Like most Haitian revolutionary generals of common note, Dessalines was a part of early Haiti's political elite. Caribbean-born generals who served in the Revolution's vanguard were oligarchs by class (being free and wealthy, for the most part, before 1791) or by the accumulation of wealth and/or status from the Revolution. Dessalines, as Trouillot notes, was a millionaire by the Revolution's end with plantations in many industries that he could effectively control because of his immense political power.[33] He was an oligarch in this sense alone, and thus undeniably situated within a class that did not share his anticolonial political commitments. Indeed, he (and the revolutionists turned statesmen who sided with him in post-revolutionary Haiti) were open to the radical collectivism of the *Ginen* majority because they resisted the colonial indoctrination of their class.[34] When he assumes leadership of Haiti and reigns as Emperor Jacques I from 1804 to 1806, Dessalines's administration attempts to institutionalize the political vision of the *Ginen* majority. It mandates that Haitians try to be distinct and new. This charge is issued in the Declaration of Independence, "let us thus b[e] ourselves and for ourselves," and it is manifest in his land reform measures, which entailed confiscating property from the oligarchy to distribute to *Ginen* peoples.[35]

Dessalines institutes the *Ginen* political praxis of defiant self-reclamation in early Haiti, and he does so to give Haiti's folk population a chance to thrive on their terms. Casimir writes that the *Ginen* majority could not

> create a functional space for themselves within [early Haiti's oligarchic] government system as long as the right of conquest, the right to appropriate the property of another with impunity, remained the sacrosanct basis for private property. By seizing the lands of the country, both colonial France and the Indigenous Army [i.e., the Haitian Revolutionary army] installed their deep profession in racism—attenuated, by political necessity, through the language of color prejudice—as the backdrop for their concept of public power.[36]

Dessalines was acutely aware of the racist logic behind oligarchic land seizure following the Revolution's end. The constitutional measures he created that racialized all Haitians as Black (Article 14), coupled with his land reform measures, created the conditions where *all* of Haiti's Black constituents could secure a self-sustainable existence. In other words, he sought to legislatively annul the racializing inequity of the right to conquest.[37] Dessalines's collectivist political vision prioritized antislavery and anticolonial politics versus the colonial right to conquest to foster an independence that could end the sufferings of *Ginen* peoples and be ontologically transformative for oligarchs, who overwhelmingly did not want to reimagine themselves beyond Western Europe.[38] His assassination in 1806 by creole revolutionists-turned-republican statesmen ended these efforts, and it spawned the fiction among the oligarchy that Haiti could be constituted as Saint Domingue. From his death onward, the oligarchy sought to "impose the role of indentured laborers on" Haiti's majority to realize this fiction.[39]

Dessalines and Défilée were afterthoughts in the political machinations that followed Dessalines's murder, as a period of civil unrest took center stage and divided Haiti into two. In the north where the Black *affranchi* and revolutionist Henry Christophe reigned as monarch (1807–1820), militarized plantation industry and an agrarian policy of anticolonial care were dominant. In the south, where the mixed-race *gens de couleur* and revolutionist Alexandre Pétion ruled as president (1807–1818), a racialist approach to plantation industry was dominant.[40] Of the two, Casimir writes, "the divergences between the oligarchy of Christophe and that of Pétion with regard to popular sovereignty were limited to nearly imperceptible nuances. A state of law could not germinate in this compost without a total—and, in Haitian circumstances, impossible—assimilation of the population into their new state as people living in captivity on plantations that disposed of their labor and the fruits extracted from it."[41] Notwithstanding his efforts to "correct the harms done to the population" by ensuring the food sovereignty of former captives and respectful relations between laborers, renters, and property owners, Christophe's administration was oppressive.[42] It relied extensively on violence to ensure his militarized plantation industry was successful, which necessitated the peasant's near total "captivity."[43] Christophe's government had the military power to enforce this confinement despite folk resistance. Pétion's administration and the republicans that would follow in a united Haiti were unable to dominate the rural majority. And yet each imagined that it had the ability to bind the rural populace to servile labor.

Pétion designed an economy that formally operated "with tenant farmers [existing] in service" to the region's political elite.[44] His administration codified "parasitic" relations between the oligarchy and the *Ginen* folk through its ratification of the French colonial, "Law No. 111, Concerning the Policing of the Plantations, the Reciprocal Obligations of Property Owners and Renters, and of Cultivators" in 1807.⁴⁵ In endorsing this law, he racialized the southern *Ginen* populace as cultivators. Haitian historian and avowed republican Beaubrun Ardouin writes that cultivator was synonymous with Black person in the legal and economic codes of Haitian leaders, underscoring the uncritical continuation of anti-Black racism in Haiti.⁴⁶ Pétion could not enforce the ratification of Law No. 111, nor could his successor, Jean-Pierre Boyer, enforce his draconian agricultural code when president. Boyer, a mixed-race *gens de couleur* and republican revolutionist turned politician, became president of the south following Pétion's death in 1818 and united Christophe's northern monarchial realm with his republic in 1820 after Christophe's suicide. His agricultural code enforces the racialization of the rural population as cultivators and allows "a small fraction of Haiti's population [to] live off the majority."⁴⁷ Like the 1876 agricultural code of the republican oligarch, Guillaume Fabre Nicolas Geffrard, Boyer's was never put into practice.⁴⁸ Casimir writes, "The labor force saved the oligarchs threatened with extermination by the enemies of republican France [during the Revolution]. This increased their political power to the point that the public administration could not impose the role of indentured laborers on them any longer.... From the first days of its establishment, the republican administration was reduced to playing the role of managing the disjuncture between the property owners and the dispossessed who occupied the territory."⁴⁹ Haiti's *Ginen* folk ignored the edicts of the oligarchy and when that proved insufficient, those in the south mobilized their collective power and made Louis Jean Jacques Accau the leader of their 1844 social justice movement, which increased their political influence.

Accau was a popular *Ginen* Haitian revolutionist who rose in political prominence after Boyer's 1843 ousting. He marshaled his experience in the Revolution and his post-independence title of police lieutenant to name himself "Chief of the Demands of His Co-citizens," and lead a *Ginen* movement determined to end poverty for all Haitians.⁵⁰ His radical fervor emboldened the rural majority of the south who "followed him to conquer their rights," an act that resulted in three pivotal happenings.⁵¹ Firstly, Boyer's presidential successor, the mixed-race republican revolutionist turned politician Charles Rivière-Hérard, was overthrown; secondly, the oligarchy was forced to grant Accau a political seat among the oligarchs in central government; and in retaliation, the oligarchy, thirdly, instituted *la politique de la doublure*, a political practice where largely rural and thus *Ginen* "individuals from the population were called on to occupy certain higher-level positions."[52] The oligarchy sought to curb the political power of the *Ginen* majority with this practice, as their resistance had successfully secured their political representation in government via Accau and others who followed him.[53] Oligarchs also attempted to mitigate *Ginen* political influence via a series of public pronouncements that launched Dessalines's memorialization. Rivière-Hérard issued a speech in honor of the nation's independence in January of 1844 that leveraged Dessalines's revolutionary significance to legitimate his presidency. Rivière-Hérard "belonged to a class of citizens who saw in Dessalines nothing but a barbaric despot that they had sacrificed," writes Haitian historian Thomas Madiou.[54] His attempt "to draw on the sympathies of the people by glorifying the founder of independence" was easily discerned and dismissed as opportunistic.[55]

Rivière-Hérard's invocation of Dessalines would nonetheless inspire other opportunists in his class. Lysius Salomon, a Black oligarch, invoked Dessalines in a "petition to the provisional government of Riviere-Herard (June 22, 1843)" and again later in an October 17, 1845 speech that "blamed 'the aristocracy of color' for Dessalines's death."[56] Dessalines's Blackness was used to question mulatto leadership and to claim that Black oligarchic rule would be better for Haiti.[57] This lie granted Salomon fame as he was termed "the eater of mulattoes," notwithstanding that he served as "finance minister during *la politique de la doublure*" and acted in the interests of his class as an oligarch.[58] Literary scholar Colin Dayan writes that fifty years after Rivière-Hérard's invocation the oligarchic state would continue to summon Dessalines for its ends, and do so with the aid of Haiti's literary elite: "President Florvil Hyppolite built in France a modest monument in memory of Dessalines. Later, for the centenary celebration of the Haitian nation, which actually marked the beginning of the state cult of Dessalines, [writer] Justin Lherison composed the national anthem, the 'Dessalinienne.'"[59] Dessalines's memorialization indexes oligarchic fears of *Ginen* political power and exposed an ongoing fight over the state of Haiti—would it be colonial, an economic and political replica of Western Europe, or would it be *Ginen*, decolonial and new? Défilée's mythification was an effort to ensure the former. When the state leveraged Défilée to memorialize Dessalines in republican fashion, it sought to downplay how folk resistance overrode their authority, and because this resistance limited and forestalled their preferred colonial style of hierarchal governance, the Défilée they presented to their constituents was denuded of her individual agency and power.

State actors and intellectuals write her scripted impotence as self-sacrifice: in their memorialization of Dessalines, they disclose that Défilée briefly regained her senses and repaired a Haiti at odds with itself when she properly buried the then-emperor. Haitian historian Jean Fouchard, quoting a contemporary of Défilée, Joseph Jérémie, writes, "She enveloped the emperor's inanimate body with attention and tenderness. She slipped the head of the man who gave birth to a nation into a bag. While attempting to carry the remains of Dessalines on her womanly shoulders, one Simon de Cyrène Dauphin, another well-known lunatic, appeared at that very moment to aid the mad woman."[60] Dauphin is often excised from the burial of Dessalines to better accentuate Défilée's importance, who, as it goes, acted when no one else would. When the *Ginen* masses and those in power, drunk from the bloodshed of the war, did nothing during the attack on Dessalines—in fact, they supposedly rejoiced upon his murder—she rose above the folly of the moment and honored a man far above the degradation of his death despite her madness. She redeemed the redeemer.[61] This reading is ironic at best and cruel at worst. It not only narrates the history of early Haiti and the Revolution from a republican perspective that absents *Ginen* folk's resistance from Haitian life, but it also asks Haitians to honor Défilée through her deed, and equally pity her for the mental instability that enabled her act. The dismissal of insanity, in turn, ensures that "reason" alone is heroic here—not her. Défilée's "madness," not her action, nor the wherewithal needed to execute Dessalines's burial, shapes her memory for Haiti's oligarchy and literati. Worst yet, her mythification restores and sustains Dessalines's de-radicalized exception and effectively absents her individual power from popular anti-oligarchic action and contemporary popular consciousness.

Défilée's lunacy does not impede her personal recognition of the Revolution's importance. It does not detach her from critical and conscious thought. She *chooses* to be a sutler and aligns herself with the revolutionary fight against enslavement and French colonial rule. Joseph Jérémie, a centenarian and Défilée's aforementioned companion, attests to her commitment to the Revolution when he relates the origins of her cognomen (Défilée) in 1916 Haiti. He states, "As soon as the soldiers stopped somewhere to rest, Dédée also stopped. Abruptly, the madwoman raised the long stick [used for a crutch] held in her hand, and bravely cried out: *défilez, défilez* [march, march]. They obeyed her."[62] This is a woman whose mind, however unbalanced, is fixed on one solitary purpose—revolutionary success. "Crazed" she may be, yet she is certainly not "lost."[63] Treating her as such obscures what can be discerned from her existence: a mythic potency tied to communal preservation and decolonial difference. In this sense, Défilée's sparse biography and madness discloses not simply her devotion to the nation's "savior," but also her ability to rally and unite a collective toward an existence within terms they see and envision for themselves.[64] She embodies *Ginen* political action. What should be evident, then, is the political force Défilée quite possibly was and can be, once recalled through recollection of her own efforts.

The problem that arises is that her radical potency cannot be seen within a contemporary moment shaped by an oligarchic rendering of the past, where Défilée is no more than a madwoman. In an essay that reads "Nineteen Thirty-Seven" as Danticat's writerly attempt to cohere a collective in ruins, literary scholar Jana Evans Braziel reminds readers that Défilée is one of the better-known woman figures of the Revolution within Haiti.[65] Yet like other women of the Revolution she is still proffered as a footnote within the Revolution's history. When "named" within contemporary Haitian culture, she is often acknowledged and attested to in silence. The Haitian *rasin* band, RAM, offered homage to Dessalines in their 2008 carnival song titled "Defile," paying tribute to Dessalines in the tradition of historians and writers at home and abroad: with an eye turned to the exceptional (de-radicalized) masculine subject.[66] As they praised Dessalines and bemoaned his betrayal, they snubbed the woman through whom this honoring first took place—Défilée. Nowhere is she named within the song as a historical and revolutionary figure like Dessalines. The latter, granted the affective appellation of "papa," is honored here as founding father and as spiritual elder. Present in the duality of her namesake (*defile*), she is named in absence, seen and yet unseen. Her presence is unconsciously alluded to, and her importance intimated with each directive to *defile* (march), *balanse* (wave), *pran plezi* (let loose), *banboche* (enjoy one's self), and *layité* (see *banboche* and *pran plezi*), and within the interludes of instrumental revelry encouraging all to partake in these commands.[67] With each direction, she emerges as the collective tie that allows Haitians to carouse in honor of Dessalines. And yet, in ensuring that Dessalines is remembered, her revolutionary presence is absented as is the revolutionary significance of her call to *défilez* and seize a decolonized existence. Conscious of this, Danticat uses Défilée as a point of entry for a decolonial articulation of revolutionary history in "Nineteen Thirty-Seven."

DECOLONIZING THE STORY OF THE REVOLUTION

The decolonial nature of Danticat's writing of revolutionary history rests largely with her efforts to disclose persons and ideations of freedom absented from conventional Caribbean narrations of the Revolution. In this way, that which is decolonial here is Danticat's awareness of the "Cultural Europeanisation" of the Revolution, where a colonial (culturally Western European) iteration of freedom, liberation, and personhood subsumes the distinctly decolonial (*Ginen* Haitian) articulation of each notion.[68] Danticat details Haiti's distinct local culture and its traditions of defiant collectivism through Défilée. Her revolutionary history is used to illuminate the past and present lives of women reduced to inconsequentiality because of their gender, race, and poverty. Défilée's fictional descendant (Defile) is the centerpiece of "Nineteen Thirty-Seven," which depicts a daughter's struggle (Josephine's) with her mother's (Defile's) false imprisonment and looming death.

The circumstances that lead to Defile's incarceration involve a sick child who dies in her care. Denounced as a witch when the child dies, she is incarcerated for her "crime" and later murdered by prison guards. Years prior to this, Defile is among the few who survived *Kout Kouto-a* (the 1937 Dominican Massacre of Haitians) by leaping across Massacre River from Dominican to Haitian soil. Like her ancestor before her, Defile honors the departed demeaned with horrific death through a commemorative rite of lamentation. Without remains to bury, she returns to the river each year, inviting other female survivors, to pay homage to those who passed, most notably, the mothers and daughters lost in the carnage.

The mastermind behind Defile's loss and that of the other survivors was the Dominican dictator Rafael Leónidas Trujillo Molina. With the extermination of fifteen to seventeen thousand Haitians living in the Dominican Republic, Trujillo claimed to have avenged the innocent children lost during Dessalines's 1805 military offensive in Moca, Santo Domingo. Dessalines's military campaign allegedly seized the eastern portion of Hispaniola at the expense of the residents' lives. The latter were supposedly massacred to stop Spanish slave raiders, working with remnants of the French army stationed in Moca, from entering Haiti and abducting Haitians for re-enslavement.[69] French general Jean-Louis Ferrand had "promised Haiti's former plantation owners that they would soon be able to return to their land, once the French had reconquered the colony," and while stationed in the Dominican Republic, he "menaced the Haitian state."[70] Dessalines's attempt to protect Haiti did not result in a Haitian seizure of Moca, or the end to Ferrand's affronts; but it did create a discursive context in which to further demonize Dessalines outside of Haiti. This demonization situates Trujillo's misappropriation of Dessalines and the 1805 campaign at Moca. To conceal the Dominican state's hand in his "act of reprisal," Trujillo required that his army and corps of civilian volunteers use machetes to eradicate Haitians within the nation.[71] The massacre could then present as a popular uprising desired by the Dominican people should the genocide draw the ire of the international community.[72] Trujillo's order had an unintended effect for Haitians, however: it symbolically reenacted Dessalines's assassination by dismemberment, as the children of the "Father of Independence" were dismembered and the "sins" of the father were paid in full by Dessalines's children (i.e., Moca and Dessalines's oft criticized massacre of white colonists). Therein lies the literary foundation for Défilée's presence in "Nineteen Thirty-Seven," as she appears within the story through a rite of lamentation that recreates her burial of Dessalines on a broader scale. As the centerpiece of the narrative's mourning rite, she is no longer symbolically tied to one lost ancestor in need of proper burial, but to the thousands lost during *Kout Kouto-a* and thereafter. Through her, readers are primed to reclaim all that was lost in an enduring struggle to exist in resistant difference—as a Haitian in the Dominican Republic, a Black person in the Americas, and a woman at home and abroad.[73]

"A Wall of Rising Fire," in contrast, chronicles those lost to the seductive power of coloniality and concerns the collective and individual repercussions of the Revolution in a Haiti governed by persons covetous of white colonial power. Danticat uses Boukman's revolutionary legacy to interrogate the effects of a people's radical seizure of existence on their terms without the support of their compatriots in governance (here the oligarchy). The *Ginen* insistence that liberation constitute something more than the freedom to work is thus set against the myopic colonial imagination of French colonists and colonial bureaucrats, Haitian oligarchs, and US imperialists. Their collective understanding of Black liberation as Black toil shapes the lives of the central characters of the story, a family: Guy, Lili, and Little Guy. They are destitute, and that they are poignantly underscores the disjunction between the radical gains achieved by *Ginen* Haitians in the Revolution as well as Haiti's nineteenth century and their political disenfranchisement in the twentieth century. This latter period is shaped by the political collusion of the oligarchy and US imperialists, a collusion that results in the manufactured destitution of Haiti's majority in the twentieth century onward. The narrative addresses the orchestrated destitution of the Haitian folk via the family's struggles with chronic unemployment as well as poverty, and it shows how these issues create conflict within the family: while Lili (the wife/mother) is content with having a loving family and talented son (Little Guy), Guy (the husband/father) wants more from life. Disillusioned, he dreams of escape through a hot-air balloon owned by the wealthy proprietors of his town's sugar mill. His theft of, commandeering of, and suicide from the sugar mill's hot air balloon drive the narrative, as does Little Guy's starring role as Boukman in a school play. The extensive play with revolutionary history and early-nineteenth-century Haitian history in the story illustrates how the conflict in the family is directly tied to the continuation of plantation industry in Haiti, despite the success of the Revolution.

Danticat invites readers to understand the family's struggle in relation to the Revolution via the title of her story, which references the moment when a "wall of rising fire" engulfed the famous and prosperous Gallifet sugar plantation.[74] With this reference, Danticat calls to mind the turbulent and rage-filled nature of the Revolution's opening events. Of this moment, the pan-Africanist writer and activist C. L. R. James describes, "in a few days one-half of the famous Northern Plain was a flaming ruin. From Le Cap [the capital] the whole horizon was a wall of fire."[75] At the helm of this siege was Zamba Boukman or Boukman Dutty, a figure resurrected in the narrative through Little Guy, who is cast as the national hero in a school production of the Revolution. Boukman is credited with leading the opening rebellion in 1791. Sold to a French planter for teaching a captive to read, he was among a select class of captive persons in Saint Domingue, most often non-African born, to hold privileged positions within colonial society. Boukman was at one point a slave driver and later a coachman on the Clément plantation.[76] In preparation for the rebellion, he and two hundred other captive persons of Saint Domingue, from neighboring Northern plantations, met at a clearing (*Bwa Kayïman*) on August 14, to formulate their plans.[77] All were "upper strata slaves in whom masters [had] placed their confidence."[78] Most were drivers like Boukman, suggesting that the meeting was predominantly male. Legend indicates otherwise, however, and intimates the vibrant presence of women at the gathering.

A Vodou ceremony officiated by Boukman (an *oungan*) and a *manbò* (a Vodou priestess) was performed at the meeting. The identity of this *manbò* is largely uncertain. Some indicate that she was an old African woman, others a young mixed-race woman by the name of Cécile Fatiman, and some question her very existence.[79] The speculation that surrounds her identity pervades the entire ceremony. Scholars like historians David Geggus and Laurent Dubois and literary scholar Léon-François Hoffmann have questioned the veracity of accounts detailing the spiritual service, accounts which were first recorded in 1814 (twenty-three years following the Revolution's advent) and augmented upon each telling.[80] Others, like Dayan and historian Carolyn E. Fick, argue persuasively for its actuality despite writerly embellishments.[81] Whether or not the ceremony actually occurred is of little importance. What matters is that it is thought to have happened and that it is now mythologized within Haitian culture as the definitive ideological starting point, not only of the revolutionary struggle but of a distinct *Ginen* cultural sensibility grounded in Vodou and resistance.

Boukman marks the start of this sensibility and is closely associated with it by Haitians then and now. Zealous Protestants have routinely attempted to exorcise the spirit of Boukman from *Bwa Kayïman* in an effort to evangelize Haiti and thus "solve" its problems.[82] Socially conscious musical groups such as *Boukman Eksperyans* have appropriated his name to signal a new rock, rap and *kompa* sound rooted in Vodou rhythms. The sound is tellingly referred to as "root music" (*mizik rasin*), in light of its foundational origins in Haiti's Vodou and revolutionary traditions. The disappearance of the *manbò* from such endeavors and popular consciousness, along with the preservation of Boukman, attest to the importance of the work Danticat is doing with her collection. While she does not specifically invoke the real or fictitious Cécile Fatiman, nor the old African woman by name, her work paves the way for others to do so, underscoring the actuality that absented women revolutionaries were pivotal within the Revolution at each stage, from the beginning (Cécile Fatiman/old African woman) to its seeming end (Défilée).

Boukman died within a year of the Revolution, leaving an indelible mark on the uprising as rebel leader and *oungan*.[83] Of consequence to Danticat is that he and his fellow insurgents took the aforementioned Gallifet plantation that she alludes to in "A Wall of Rising Fire." This plantation was extremely moneyed and renowned, so much so that when describing sweetness, the colonists of Saint Domingue often stated, "as sweet as Gallifet sugar," and regarding happiness, "as happy as a Gallifet Negro."[84] The captives were not happy and would show the world the depths of their discontent when they seized this plantation, destroyed its means of production, and transformed a beacon of colonial prosperity and capitalist savvy into an antislavery and anticolonial symbol of Black resistance—"a camp for an army of slave insurgents."[85] The seizure of this plantation interrupted a booming sugar industry in the West, leading to the most severe drop in production the trade has ever seen.[86] The persistence of this commerce despite this forceful contestation is directly tied to the conditions French colonialists, Haitian oligarchs, and US imperialists placed on freedom during and after the Revolution.

When French commissioner Léger Félicité Sonthonax formally abolished slavery in the colony in 1793 in response to the mass resistance of captives in 1791, he introduced the notion of emancipation as toil through a "new" and ill-fated system of plantation wage labor. Within this system, former captives would choose a planter, return to the plantation, earn an income, and secure the wealth-generating capabilities of the colony. To no surprise, this endeavor and those like it—undertaken by French General Charles Leclerc and Haiti's own Louverture, Pétion and Christophe—never succeeded. Captives had seen the paragon of freedom, *petit blancs* (poor whites ranging from vagabonds to clerks), living in misery without occupations and land by which to survive. The freedom to work proved insufficient as a result.[87] *Ginen* captives saw through the veneer of capitalistic liberation embodied in the very idea of freedom in work and realized that no such freedom existed; if it did, it did not include the freedom to eat and live. They wanted more. Historian Jean Fouchard writes, "It was for freedom made real by possession of land that the Maroons" and their allies in captivity "had fought."[88] Both wanted the freedom to grow what labor for another could not provide: a self-sustainable debt-free existence.

Following independence, this existence seemed within reach. As president of the South and West of Haiti, Pétion parceled plantations to former insurgents in 1809 and again in 1814.[89] Christophe, as king of Northern Haiti, followed suit in 1819.[90] This helped *Ginen* peoples create the self-sustainable existence they desired to a degree. What accelerated their seizure of life on their terms was their increased political power; "the public administration" in the Haiti of Pétion and the Haiti of Christophe "could not impose the role of indentured laborers on them."[91] This was attended to earlier in the chapter, but it bears repeating, as the power of Haiti's *Ginen* people is far too often overshadowed because of the Eurocentrism that shapes how popular Caribbean writers of the Revolution and the scholars who study their works make sense of Haiti and Haitians. Their political mobilization after the

Revolution checks oligarchic predation and ensures that the draconian guidelines "prescribed by the agricultural regulations and rural police codes were impossible to enforce."[92] Indeed, because of their political power, "throughout the entire nineteenth century, property owners and the dispossessed moved closer to one another."[93] Haitians learned to live together as a people, notwithstanding the prejudice of oligarchs and their class compatriots, "and by the end of [the nineteenth century] the socioeconomic landscape offered a standard of living that was superior to that of the rest of the Caribbean. The country entered the twentieth century experimenting with forms of equilibrium [between the oligarchy and the *Ginen* mass] that were abruptly interrupted by the foreign intervention of 1915."[94]

The 1915 US Occupation of Haiti, repeated US interventions thereafter, and the colonial indoctrination of Haitian oligarchs bore the Haiti Danticat depicts in her stories—culturally rich and resistant but economically destitute and politically uncreative. As a counter Haitian Revolutionary event, the first US occupation weakened the sovereign power of Haiti's *Ginen* majority and empowered Haiti's Western-oriented oligarchy. Casimir writes, "The power of the state, put in place by the United States, became the prime weapon for the destruction of the power in the state—that is, the minimal degree of sovereignty the habitants [rural majority] still held on to."[95] The modern (post-1915) oligarchy, composed of members of the Black middle class created by the occupation, and the traditional post-independence elite, who descended from the largely Black vanguard of the revolutionary army and the contingent of those freed before 1791 (largely mixed-race planters), leveraged the US army to maintain "military control over the rural population."[96] Their use of the US army to subject the populace changed the class composition of Haiti's political leaders. The latter had included members from the rural *Ginen* majority (like Accau) prior to the US invasion. The absence of *Ginen* influence in Haiti's central administration, and the violent suppression of *Ginen* resistance in the nation, increased the oligarchy's political power and their wealth, as both were sustained by the expanding reach of US imperialism in the nation.[97] Danticat overlays her Haitian Revolutionary narrative with this history and invites her readers to understand how oligarchic subjection and US imperial predation created the destitution of Haitian peoples in the twentieth century. She calls upon readers to understand how Haitian poverty is the result of political choices, choices that she shows have forced Haiti's *Ginen* majority to choose between death and indentured servitude to survive in Haiti.

Like "Nineteen Thirty-Seven," "A Wall of Rising Fire" illustrates how impoverished *Ginen* Haitians navigate indentured labor and the will to exist on their terms. The sugar mill in "A Wall of Rising Fire" is plainly depicted as the bane of the community's existence because of its colonial operational structure. Not only are jobs passed down to adult family members already on the factory's waiting list, but the mill ensures a never-ending supply of workers by allowing the names of young children to be placed on the employment register at an early age. In this way, people can avoid the bleak circumstances facing Guy, the male protagonist of "A Wall of Rising Fire." He is unemployed for months at a time and subject to working jobs few want, such as cleaning the mill's latrines, because his parents chose not to place his name on the register and bind his existence to plantation labor. Should Guy, Lili, or the other members of the community journey to the Dominican Republic, they would work in *batey* communities, towns created by sugarcane mills, as the victims of *Kout Kouto-a* in "Nineteen Thirty-Seven." Plantation industry and indentured labor constrain the lives of everyday Haitians in Danticat's Haitian Revolutionist stories. Yet where "Nineteen Thirty-Seven" addresses the continuation of this labor through *Ginen* defiance—that is, the rebellious reclamation of persons and pasts emblematic of the ongoing struggle to exist in resistant difference—"A Wall of Rising Fire" recounts the persistence of this labor through acquiescence, specifically, the aspirational longing for colonial power.

Guy conveys this longing: he dreams of freedom, but his dream is oligarchic in nature, disclosing his emulation of colonial power. He states, "sometimes, I just want to take the big balloon and ride it up in the air. I'd like to sail off somewhere and keep floating free until I got to a really nice place with a nice plot of land where I could be something new. I'd build my own house, keep my own garden. Just *be* something new."[98] Guy's "dream," for what it is worth, is one of dominance, of "floating free" above the bulk of one's people. It is also one of discovery and implicit conquest. After all, he seeks to sail off to some uncharted land to begin anew. Where have there ever been people-less lands but in the fictitious world created with Western Europe's global ascendancy? Elizabeth DeLoughrey writes convincingly about the importance of the idea of uninhabited islands to European imperial expansion; her research prompts my query and encourages insistently asking, Where have there been lands waiting for uncontested occupation *but* in a Western European or North American imagining of existence?[99] Guy's desire for newness resurrects decidedly old colonial parameters for being (conqueror and conquered/master and slave) and runs counter to the Haitian Revolutionary efforts of his ancestors. They reasoned themselves into a *Ginen* collective and enacted their collectivism through Vodou, which allowed them to perceive the world otherwise, in communal terms applicable to their ideas of existence. Colonial power, however, prioritizes singularity and self-aggrandizing technological prowess. It is not insignificant that the first hot-air balloon took flight in the Americas on the Gallifet plantation in 1784, the very plantation on which the story is set. This history juxtaposed with Guy's "dream" discloses Danticat's reading of colonial power as prioritizing technical innovation because it furthers individual glorification at the expense of collective relations. Why else would the already famously moneyed French colonialist Marquis de Gallifet concede to have the hemisphere's first ever hot-air balloon fly on his plantation but to shore up the façade of power and wealth he wants to claim as uniquely his alone in Saint Domingue? Guy's fetishization of colonial power invites recognition of how the drive to reinstitute plantation industry in liberated Haiti was less about the security and food sovereignty of former captives or the economic solvency of the new nation and more about the individual grandeur of oligarchic leaders.

Guy's narrative shows the self-glorifying singularity of the West that creole revolutionists (save Dessalines) bought into when modeling their distinct Haitian polities after colonial power. The specifically Western drive for singularity is an un-interrogated element of the Haitian Revolutionist writings of canonical Caribbean writers that Danticat critiques. Indeed, the Haitian Revolutionist literatures of James, Aimé Césaire, and Derek Walcott distill the "Cultural Europeanisation" of the authors and their preferred subjects, creole (former *affranchi*) revolutionists turned oligarchs. Sociologist Aníbal Quijano coined the phrase "Cultural Europeanisation" and writes that "European culture became a universal cultural model" through the repressive violence of political colonization and the seductive violence of cultural colonization.[100] The latter offered "a way of participating and ... reach[ing] the same material benefits and the same power as the Europeans: viz, to conquer nature in short for 'development,'" through aspiration alone: one need only model the colonizer to achieve their political and economic standing.[101] Louverture, Pétion, and Christophe did just that: their socio-economic and socio-political schemas for the colony (Louverture) and later nation (Pétion and Christophe) were aspirational in nature, devised with Western European colonial power in mind. Casimir thus writes, excluding Dessalines, "the visible leaders of Haitian independence didn't imagine a structure for governance distinct from that of the metropole."[102] Because they chose to rule in Western colonial fashion, Haiti's famed creole revolutionists have given rise to narrations of the Revolution that write it in Western European fashion as shown by the classic Caribbean literatures studied here. The Revolution is proffered as culturally emanating from the West, a move that not only preserves the West's singularity, but it leaves uninterrogated the toxic conditions of a modernity that functions as coloniality.

Danticat writes against this myopic cultural articulation of Haitian Revolutionary history and focuses instead on the *Ginen* captives of Saint Domingue. They repudiated the idea that those who worked less arduously and yet gained more were naturally better and acted with an ethical imperative in mind: that the well-being of all should be more important than that of a few. This communal imperative lies at the heart of *Ginen* thought practices and actions they used to resist the French. It situates why Vodou demands relational awareness of persons past and present and it explains why these persons were understood to be *moun* (plain persons). They were persons who were worth fighting for because they chose to be plain irrespective of their class and color. The methods of narration concerning the Revolution diverge between the two stories, but despite their divergence, they work together to situate a *Ginen* articulation of Haitian resistance (via Vodou) that counters the too-typical story of male singularity, oligarchic leadership, and Western cultural supremacy Boukman (as a national hero) brings to bear on the Revolution. Writing Boukman as *lwa* and not as hero, Danticat repurposes his exception for the collective and invites her readers to understand the Revolution, revolutionaries, and Haitians in *Ginen* fashion.

Défilez!

Boukman is a national hero and undeniably a figure of exception. He is also a *lwa* in Haiti, among the few more widely known revolutionists (outside of the nation) who has been deified. As a *lwa*, he is much more than a hero and best understood removed from a Western understanding of heroic figures. Like humans, *lwas* are imperfect and as such heroes—remarkable individuals, who are romanticized to such a degree that they surpass their human frailty—do not exist within Vodou. The immortality of a *lwa* bears the weight of the mortality of their past existence and present lives, complicating the sanctity one well versed in Abrahamic religions may want to ascribe to a divine being. This is evident in the divine attributes and actions of Dessalines, who has also been deified as a *lwa* by *Ginen* Haitians. When Dessalines is summoned, he rides his initiate in a manner that speaks to his life and death, revealing what Dayan terms is "a double play of loss and gain."[103] He emerges with the typical fierceness that marked his human character, as he was, by all accounts, brash and abrasive. This "ferocity" is tempered by his materialization in a "piecemeal" fashion that calls attention to the nature of his passing, his assassination by dismemberment.[104] A demi-god is thus born from the remains of a "hero." Oligarchs, and the Western European culture they idealize, memorialize Dessalines and Boukman as heroes to de-radicalize them and denude them of their resistant decolonial significations. They leave people with an empty shell, "father of independence" and European-style prophets, so that these appropriated revolutionists can serve oligarchic (pro-colonial) political interests. In contrast, *Ginen* Haitians deify Dessalines and Boukman as *lwa* and not as heroes to maintain the radical decolonial meanings each represent. In this way, they can turn to these entities to embolden their own decolonial praxis in the now. Danticat draws from this ancestral practice of deification in "A Wall of Rising Fire" to write the *lwa* Boukman as the embodiment of mournful relation, an entity of a specific bygone and a cosmic multitude of absented persons and pasts unnoted.

Awareness of Boukman's mournful spiritual essence rests with that of Défilée's and the persons she inspires through her ethereal narrative presence in "Nineteen Thirty-Seven." Readers of the story are alerted to Défilée's celestial presence through her descendant's rite of lamentation. Upon witnessing her mother's (Eveline's) death at the hands of Dominican soldiers, Defile mourns her loss by making a yearly pilgrimage to the site of her mother's passing, Massacre River. By the time of her daughter Josephine's fifth birthday, Defile's once solitary act of mourning becomes a collective rite. The surviving women, clad in white, gather every All Saints Day (November 1) to honor their mothers and reaffirm the psychic bond oft-said to be present between a parent and child. Together the women preserve what was lost by creating the "flesh" to take its place.

Near the end of her life, when it is clear that the prison guards intend to murder her, Defile implores Josephine to keep the "weeping Madonna" that had been in their family for generations. As a gift to Défilée, the Madonna embodies the undying presence of the ancestors that have passed. With each tear, an ancestor and a past life is invoked and made "flesh" through the miracle of the Virgin's weeping. Defile states: "Keep the Madonna when I am gone.... When I am completely gone, maybe you will have someone to take my place. Maybe you will have a person. Maybe you will have some *flesh* to console you. But if you don't, you will always have the Madonna."[105] When Josephine is first brought to the river as a child, her mother takes her hand and places it in the water, stating: "Here is my child, Josephine. We were saved from the tomb of this river when she was still in my womb. You spared us both, her and me, from this river where I lost my mother."[106] With this utterance, Defile initiates Josephine into a sisterhood in which she is transformed into the "flesh" that *can* and *does* take her grandmother's place. She becomes the mother to the daughter that has lost her mother. As flesh, she becomes an incarnate of cosmic essence: like her mother and the other female survivors, she becomes a "daughter of the river" and is reborn as daughter and as mother. Danticat writes, "When we dipped our hands, I [Josephine] thought that the dead would reach out and haul us in, but only our own faces stared back at us, one indistinguishable from the other."[107] In this respect, the dead "kitchen poets," re-imagined here as daughter-mothers, emerge as the force that blur persons and pasts alike. Josephine is primed to personify the absented subjects and bygones that came before her, and thus live with the past forever in her present.

This communal existence is made possible by Defile's mourning rite since it grants the solace of the deceased's enduring existence to those in mourning and those, like Josephine, who are soon to be in mourning. Present in their corporal absence, the dead exist within the bodies of their descendants, who bear witness to them by acknowledging the plurality inborn within their bodily composition. Haitians need only listen to themselves, in this respect, if they are to attend to those muted by how the massacre was officially handled by the Haitian government, and to the women concealed within revolutionary history. They need only remain aware of the ancestors animating their existence, turning to the force residing in their blood.[108] This force is that of the spiritually potent "kitchen poets," the very ancestors Danticat honors in the epilogue of the collection. These ancestors are loved ones from a nearer past and they are also heroic ancestors from a more removed bygone. Danticat references both when describing Defile's death. Upon her passing, Jacqueline, who also lost her mother during the massacre, comes to Defile's house to impart the news of her death to her daughter: "your mother is dead . . . her blood calls to me from the ground."[109] That Defile's "blood calls" to Josephine is important, as it points to the manner in which Defile's blood, now married with that of her mother's and her sisters' mothers, nourishes communal relations, the bond between the "daughters," and the dead and the living. It sustains and cements the community created through Defile's act of mourning since the mother's blood is now a part of the ancestors through whom Haitians continually remember the past. Defile is thus poised to become like the Madonna herself: a revered ancestor, a *lwa*.

The *lwa* are the very embodiment of communal memory. Persons call upon the "principles of [their] patrimony" when they summon them, invoking an "ancestral progression which had successively borne [their communal] complex forward: the African tribes, the Indian allies, the thousands of individuals whose blood had nourished it and whose diverse personal genius had swelled and elaborated its manifold and various aspect."[110] In deifying select revolutionists, Haitians have given these persons the psychic power to preserve their ancestral relations and the honor of safeguarding the nation. They have also given them the ability to ensure that Haiti exists as a collective in memory, ever conscious of absented persons and bygones past, and the possibilities for difference each represent. This consciousness of an antecedent's hopes for a future is of critical importance as it can help persons re-think and re-shape a present and its future. It can re-ignite, as is the case here, revolutionary passions and help direct a beleaguered national collective toward an improved existence to come.

Keenly aware of the potentiality for a life of resistant difference the *lwa* exemplify, Danticat does what Haitians as a collective have yet to do: grant Défilée the status of *lwa* in "Ninety Thirty-Seven." Danticat turns Défilée into an Ezili, becoming one of the many manifestations of the *mystere*, who is most commonly (and rather reductively) known as the *lwa* of love. It is no coincidence that within this narrative she is aligned with the "weeping Madonna," with the Marian iconography through whom the Ezilis are identified within Vodou. Défilée's revolutionary history and Danticat's deliberate move to relate her to mothers and daughters would suggest that she is a re-imagined Dantò, a *lwa* of revolutionary origin. One of Ezili's three principal emanations (the other two being Freda and La Siren), Dantò's saintly guise is that of Our Lady of Częstochowa or the Black Madonna of Częstochowa, a saint first introduced into Haiti through Napoleon's Polish regiment.[111] Adding to her revolutionary connection, Vodou lore reveals that as a human she fought valiantly in the Revolution and gained a formidable reputation. Despite this valor, she is betrayed by her comrades who believed that she would disclose their location if captured; as result, her tongue was cut out to silence her.[112] This experience shapes her divinity in such a profound way that as a *lwa* she shields those most susceptible to silencing and victimization—women and children. In fact, she goes so far as to tell their stories in order to reinforce their pivotal, though underemphasized, social importance. She acts always as a mother, protecting her children and "mothering" remembrance of their significance for others and for themselves, should they doubt it.

Providing scholars with little in the way of the salacious details that cast Dessalines as a rogue and an avid and exceptional dancer, or the small biographic ones revealing that Boukman was a learned Jamaican, revolutionary narratology is mum on Dantò. And yet it is clear that Dantò was of significance to the *Ginen* captives of Saint Domingue. She was worth remembrance, but *why* she was is something that cannot be answered. Still, it may be suggested that in aligning her with Défilée, Danticat finds that Dantò represents the possibility of living loudly, living boisterously in resistant difference despite silencing attempts. She represents the possibility for a life of alterity without consequence that Défilée championed with her inspiring directive—*défilez*. The *lwa* Défilée-Dantò, the narrative's "Weeping Madonna," is a cosmic representation of the ever-present possibility of living otherwise, of existing openly and without repercussion. She exemplifies life outside of a now standard Western means of being, outside of a modernized existence that ensures neocolonial conformity and aspirational sameness in thought and being.

What cannot be escaped when reading "Nineteen Thirty-Seven" is the characters' alterity. Each woman imprisoned with Defile is a victim of the Anti-Superstition Campaign of 1941–1942. On the heels of the first US occupation, which set out to "modernize" Haiti by way of indentured servitude, the then-Haitian President Élie Lescot sought to ensure this "progress" continued with his ill-fated campaign against Vodou.[113] The Occupation intended to save Haiti from its persistent discord, but it was most successful in privatizing the Haitian economy for US investments. Accordingly, it "modernized" the nation through roads and railways so as to facilitate the easy dissemination of US imports and exports.[114] The history of this occupation and its temporality surfaces within the narrative through Defile's incarceration—she is held within a prison built by US Marines during the occupation and by a prison force (*Garde d'Haiti*) created by US officials. The latter was so successful in providing instruction on how to use force against the *Ginen* majority that many a *Tonton Macoute* (Duvalier's henchmen) began his career through the *Garde*. This force was also established in the Dominican Republic during the 1916–1924 US occupation of the nation (*Guardia Nacional Dominicana*). Following US departure, the chief commander of the Dominican police force was left to informally rule the country. He would do so officially in 1930, and for many years thereafter, as "Dios Trujillo."

Trujillo's Haitian extermination was like the US occupation: a move for modernization. He hoped to create a modern nation; however, the border towns of each country posed an immense problem to his modernization efforts. Their towns' remote location facilitated a biculturalism manifest in fluid linguistic, ethnic, and cultural sensibilities among the residents, and it gave would-be revolutionaries from both countries adequate cover to formulate subversive action.[115] Moreover, the town's location fostered the notion that Dominicans were not different from Haitians. For Trujillo, the modern Dominican subject was to be the stark opposite to what he imagined a Haitian to be. Dominicans were not to be African, not Spanish *and* Kreyòl-speaking, or a mélange of the two, and definitely not practitioners of Vodou. Although brutal, the massacre did succeed in incorporating the border region into the Dominican Republic. It also gave rise to feats emblematic of successful modernization—impressive roads, modern architecture, a sense of nationalism (through anti-Haitianism), and power was wielded by the state alone. It was a success, and the Dominican Republic was overwhelmingly lauded as having made something of itself precisely because of such feats. Haiti, whose violence (revolutionary and otherwise) had not been nearly as "productive," is rarely (if ever) praised for its equally violent and repressive modernization efforts.

Lescot's effort to eradicate Vodou was in line with the thinking of his day, and of today.[116] Lescot's campaign resulted in a year of religious terror via forced conversions and mob violence against accused witches, among other occurrences.[117] The victims of Lescot's crusade were most often poor women who lived unconventionally. They lived alone or spoke, like Defile, "of wings of flame," speaking with a mysticism too Vodouesque for a state and people struggling to "progress." The poverty of these women furthered their potential for victimization and is the very reason why some like Defile, and many of the "daughters of the river," made the attempt to exist in resistant difference as a Haitian in the Dominican Republic. Despite the life-threatening consequences of their choice to make a life in a country struggling like their own to "progress," Danticat suggests that it is this attempt to live in the alterity of resistant collectivism that Haiti desperately needs, as this type of communality can rebuild a nation in ruins. Through the brutality of the prison guards and the political terror relayed in "Children of the Sea," Danticat expressly reveals that Haiti is at war with itself. Its oligarchic governance is killing its youth and its women solely for power and the will to progress through achieving power. Readers are privy to a nation (an island, truly) so entrenched in a particular imagining of being, so desperate to attain its semblance, that it reproduces imperialistic violence, lashing out against any that remotely contest state efforts to "progress." The young persons of "Children of the Sea" who raised their voices against a military junta's ascendancy, and the daughters who are deemed too benighted for humane consideration, represent this contestation.

The daughters, by the narrative's end, appear as daughter-mothers in sorrow and in defiance. Nourished from the Madonna's tears, which readers are told they drink when thirsty, they refuse their alleged benightedness; and like the imprisoned women "who sat like statues in different corners of the cell . . . like angels hiding their wings," they are shunned persons whose bodies are repositories of the resistant difference that made the Revolution possible.[118] In other words, they are symbolic incarnates of an energy that is uncontainable by colonial power but wieldable by them being the cosmic progeny of Défilée-Dantò. Josephine and Jacqueline will therefore continue the fight to exist in difference. They stand together as they await Defile's flight in flame. Her corpse is to be burned and her spirit released to join that of her mothers and sisters. Josephine, reiterating the closing salutation of her mother's collective rite, states: "Let her flight be joyful . . . and mine and yours."[119] With this utterance, readers are meant to recall Defile's first flight. The narrative states that "she [leapt] from the Dominican soil into the water, and out again on the Haitian side of the river," glowing "red when she came out, blood clinging to her skin, which at that moment looked as though it were in flames."[120] Defile's emergence on the other side of the water, as a woman aflame, signifies her new existence. In that watery immersion, she is awash in ancestral energy and reborn cosmically. Indeed, readers should understand that she has gone to *Ginen* and back in the time and space compression that is the Haitian's spiritually charged blood. Like the many others who have been anointed in water by the *lwa*, Defile is primed to be recalled by her loved ones as a Défilée-Dantò and thus as a flame to inspire and embolden others.[121] Josephine's reiteration of the salutation closing her mother's rite is a clear indication then of the continuation of the "daughters,'" even with their organizer's death. It is also telling of Défilée-Dantò's ever-presence. Moreover, it is a clear indication of her deification as one who ensures remembrance of the violently marginalized and their struggle to exist otherwise. The story's closing is Danticat's nod to the continued *défilez* ("march") toward resistant alterity that her newly consecrated *lwa* championed when mortal. Danticat continues this *défilez* with her story, suggesting that this resistance must continue.

At the very end of "A Wall of Rising Fire," Danticat issues her *défilez* via the story of Guy, a man who has accepted his benightedness and sought to exist in sameness. Guy has aspired to live as a "master," an image of consequence he is denied as a poor Haitian man. It is this choice that prompts the narrative's call to arms. Turning once again to the balloon, readers see the communal costs of Guy's passion. Confessing to Lili how closely he has been watching the balloon, he discusses the apparatus in trance-like fashion. Guy states,

> I have seen the man [Young Assad] who owns it, . . . I've seen him get in it and put it in the sky and go up there like it was some kind of kite and he was the kite master. I see the men who run after it trying to figure out where it will land. Once I was there and I was one of those men who were running and I actually guessed correctly. I picked a spot in the sugarcane fields. I picked the spot from a distance and it actually landed there.[122]

Guy's speech is a chronology of self-discovery: its movement from Young Assad's ownership, his co-worker's excited pursuit, to Guy's triumph as the one who "picked" the correct landing spot, signals his new awareness of self. The speech ultimately reveals to readers and to Guy the wonder to be had with one's discovery of imperial power.

The sweeping nature of the passage shows that Guy has undergone a transformation of self that renders him (in his mind) similar to—if not wholly on par with—those who write existence into being as "masters" or as creole revolutionaries seeking to be "masters" for life. This discovery of imperial power causes a gradual shift in focus from Young

Assad (the balloon's owner and the son of the mill's proprietor) to Guy and his moment of distinction. A difference in aptitude and being is presented between Guy and the nameless men chasing the balloon. This is first evident in the specifics revealing Young Assad's exceptionality, as he pilots the balloon with the grace and skill of a "kite master." It is observable again through Guy's relative insignificance (and that of the men like him) who can do no more than trail the balloon; and lastly, it is seen through Guy's transformative moment of glory. This transformation creates the sense that Guy is undeniably distinct, not just from the men but from the man who he was before. Who is Guy in his everyday life, but a man deemed worthy of no more than cleaning latrines, a man who wants desperately to prove that he can "do other things" like his son?[123] When Guy, stunned by the accuracy of his prediction, repeats, "I picked a spot" (varying it only to state immediately thereafter "I picked *the* spot"), readers see in his speech a man in awe of himself, of his innate capabilities, and a man seeing for the very first time that he is, indeed, equal to the "kite masters" of this world. Who but a "master" in the making or one with the inborn faculty to be a "master" could determine the balloon's course, and could usurp the subject positioning of one who is already "master"? With this discovery of authorial power, Guy is positioned to act as "master." But at what cost?

When the family takes its nightly stroll to the factory grounds early in the narrative, Guy, upon seeing the balloon, "let[s] go of the hands of both his wife and the boy."[124] He is so entranced in body and mind by this symbol of freedom that he takes this decisive step from his family. In releasing their hands, he ceases to exist in collectivity. No longer conscious of his relations and without regard for their wants, he enacts the egotism of exception endemic to colonial modernity: namely, the self that knows no other and sees no other but one that is like it, a projection that is of the same mind, body and being. Fully conscious of Guy's fascination with the balloon and the growing separation between Guy and the family such an interest spawns, Lili says that "for the last few weeks she had been feeling as though Guy was lost to her each time he reached this point, twelve feet away from the balloon."[125] He is indeed lost to her, for when she later asks, "if you were to take that balloon and fly away, would you take me and the boy?"[126]

Guy's exasperated response does little to assuage her concern. His answer discloses a continued focus on the self: "first you don't want *me* to take it and now you want *me* to."[127] The "me" of Guy, however, is not Lili's focus. What matters most to her is the preservation of the family and that he includes her and Little Guy within his dreams: "I just want to know that when you dream, me and the boy, we're always in your dreams."[128] This firm assertion—of worthiness for active participation in a leading figure's hoped-for future—is one the female characters in "Nineteen Thirty-Seven" loudly utter with their *defilez*. Barred from the power to create and work alongside others who are creating a new future, they, like Lili, are unable to voice an objection that can be heard within a colonial order driven by the exceptional person. Within a social and regional setting where the extraordinary subject—who is typically male, a colonialist, and Eurocentric, regardless of race—is given precedence over all, they are silenced and absented from attentive consideration.

Guy is eager to become an exceptional person and answers Lili's earnest question in the only way he can: with an inward turn to the self. He falls asleep, completely surrendering to his unconscious and to a self that is the same.[129] He turns to one (himself) who can appreciate his dreams and bars the possibility of an alternative to his vision of a freed existence. As a result, his vision is stripped of a collective impulse and of the women on which this collectivity has so far expressed itself—Lili, Eveline, and Defile, the "daughters of the river." Rendered inconsequential and inferior, Lili's negation signals Guy's move to exception. When he succumbs to his passion and goes on to do something heroic before taking his own life—that is, fly the balloon as the men of the factory enthusiastically cheer him on, shouting, "Go! Beautiful, go!"—he becomes, however fleetingly, the self he sees in his dream: a man worthy of being (literally and figuratively) looked up to.[130] He becomes the same reborn as singular. In taking steps toward becoming "modern" and new, Danticat reveals that he, like Trujillo and Lescott, must rid himself of those whose alterity implicitly calls into question his desired existence. In so doing, he must sadly restage and reenact the colonial parameters of being set forth by the West (and enforced by the North) when assuming the posture and position of "master."

In response to this performance of exception, however, a voice of contestation lividly roars: "*a wall of fire is rising and in the ashes, I see the bones of my people. Not only those people whose dark hollow faces I see daily in the fields, but all those souls who have gone ahead to haunt my dreams. At night I relive once more the last caresses from the hand of a loving father, a valiant love, a beloved friend.*"[131] With greater intensity, it wails, "*There is so much sadness in the faces of my people. I have called on their gods, now I call on our gods. I call on our young. I call on our old. I call on our mighty and the weak. I call on everyone and anyone so that we shall all let out one piercing cry that we may either live freely or we should die.*"[132] While it is Little Guy who tearfully utters these lines over his father's bloodied body, he is not the voice Danticat wants readers to hear. His distressed utterance, described as a "man's grieving roar," is the literary flesh of the departed, offered as it is by both the boy and the *lwa* Boukman.[133] Conceived as such, this sorrowful yet furious recitation is a call to arms for the "dark hollowed faces" of the past, and for those still seen "daily in the fields." It is a call to arms for the Guys who have died for a false ideation of freedom. Notwithstanding its republican tenor ("live freely or we should die"), this is a cry for freedom that does not require the diminution of others and is one in which Guy could have lived in Défilian terms.

Written to amend the original Boukman's rhetoric to heroic standards, the Boukman of academic history in "A Wall of Rising Fire" is crafted to fit the "thick book" from which Little Guy memorizes his lines.[134] The narrator states early in the story that "It was obvious that this was a speech written by a European man, who gave to the slave revolutionary Boukman the kind of European phrasing that might have sent the real Boukman turning in his grave."[135] Constructed to relay the story of cultural sameness, colonial modernity, and the Revolution's customary narration desires of Haiti's famed uprising, these lines are a less radical rendering of Boukman's famed speech. They are a rendering stripped of the fury and fire by which Boukman initiated the *défilian* charge for revolutionary difference. In other words, they are conveyed with a restrained angst more wistful than livid in tonality, and more subdued then assertive.[136] As contrived as this reserved language is for the narrator in "A Wall of Rising Fire," Little Guy's parents are visibly stirred by it. It is so awe-inspiring that the "lightning" that erupted in Little Guy's first recitation, *"a wall of fire . . . beloved friend,"* is echoed back in the "thunder" of their applause.[137] This "lightning" and "thunder" mirrors the *"krik"* and *"krak"* of collectivity that grounds Krik? Krak! and re-creates, in this passing instance, the revolutionary collective that paved the way for Haitian independence. Lili and Guy stand in cosmic relation to Little Guy, emerging as fellow insurgents, so moved that they quite literally transcend time and place and hear the first Boukman who led the Revolution. Danticat writes, "they felt as though for a moment they had been given the rare pleasure of hearing the voice of one of the forebears of Haitian Independence in the forced baritone of their only child."[138] This voice is that of the *lwa* Boukman, cloaked though it may be beneath the "forced baritone" of Little Guy's recitation and the linguistic embellishment of a Westernized Boukman.

Little Guy is *chaj* (charged) as Haitians say, animated and fortified by surrounding spiritual energy. The text states Guy and Lili experienced "a strange feeling that they could not explain [upon hearing their son]. It left the hair on the back of their necks standing on end. It left them feeling much more love than they ever knew that they could add to their feeling for their son."[139] This curious mix of the uncanny and adoration introduces the unknown into the narrative, a bit of mysticism by which readers are afforded the fleeting manifestation of a passing *lwa*; essentially, a *lwa* who briefly possesses an individual making his or her presence known via a small gesture or an eerie hair-raising feeling. For one brief moment in time, Little Guy is Boukman in the flesh. Accordingly, when Lili states, "Long live Boukman and long live my boy" following her son's performance, she acknowledges the duality of Little Guy's performative existence and the manner in which he, like Josephine, is a divine incarnate. He is two in one—revolutionary *lwa* and boy, boy and revolutionary *lwa*. Like Josephine, he is an embodiment of a duality born of loss, born from the past and seemingly ever-present pain of unnecessary lives lost. Lili attests to the eternity of Boukman's being within the here and now, while intimating that Little Guy is also of this same perpetuity, an essence of the present that will be granted immortality through his future accession (upon death) with his ancestors. Little Guy's perpetuity, however, is also of another Défiléean cast, as he is primed to reanimate the past revolutionary fervor of Boukman in the present. After all, he is the same young man who journeys to Miami in the collection's first story, "Children of the Sea," a student-turned-activist-turned-refugee wholeheartedly committed to a new Haiti.

It is not a coincidence that Lili spoke with spiritual insight when stating "Long live Boukman and long live my boy" following her son's performance. Like Josephine, Defile, Eveline, and Jacqueline, she is also a "daughter of the river." In another story within the collection, "Between the Pool and the Gardenias," Josephine's daughter (Marie) recalls seeing nightly "old women leaning over [her] bed," and her departed mother introducing them to her, saying "'That there is Marie. . . . She now is the last one of us left,'" the "us" being the daughters who passed.[140] Danticat writes, "There was my great grandmother Eveline who was killed by Dominican soldiers at the Massacre River. My grandmother Defile who died with a bald head in prison, because God had given her wings. My godmother Lili who killed herself in old age because her husband had jumped out of a flying balloon and her grown son left her to go to Miami."[141] As a "daughter of the river," Lili is conscious of the mysticism that pervades existence. She is fully aware of the ties between mothers and daughters and is aware of the connections between the *lwa* and the people that defy the finality of death and ensure communal belonging beyond time, space, and place. This awareness of death's impermanence implicitly situates what cannot be visibly represented within Boukman's Europeanized speech: the rite of mourning central to his deification, the very one providing the basis for the daughters' ritual of lamentation.

On the eve of the Revolution, the nuns of The Order of the Daughters of Notre Dame of Cap Français claimed to have witnessed the *Bwa Kayïman* ceremony. Peering through the windows of their monastery, they offered the following account: "barebreasted Negresses belonging to the [Vodou] sect, danc[ed] to the mournful sound of the long, narrow tambourines and conch shells, and alternat[ed] with the moaning of the sacrificed creatures. In the midst of the rebels was Zamba Boukman, urging them on to the assault on the barracks and the convent, which held a good number of young girls and other colonists."[142] This testimony underscores what can and has easily been ignored within revolutionary history: the many absented women shaping and impelling the revolutionary struggle. Although led by Boukman, and perhaps also by Cécile Fatiman/old African woman, these women are key players within the ceremony. Without them and the two hundred other delegates from the Northern plantations in attendance, there would be no ceremony to speak of, as a Vodou service does not emanate from one but from a collective acting in communion. That these women come to light through a grief-laden ceremony is telling of the importance of loss and Vodou to expanding historical and theoretical approaches to the Revolution. Attention to loss unearths not only the significance of mournful relation to the revolutionary endeavor but it also discloses how this relation was an impetus for revolutionary action.

Danticat is well aware of the importance of this relation and charges the hero Boukman's speech with mournful longing. Bereavement is immediately felt when reading Little Guy's monologues, as attention is fixed on the "*sadness in the faces of [Boukman's] people*" and on the heart-wrenching demise of those who passed in suffering via the haunting "*hand of a loving father, a valiant love, a beloved friend.*" The sorrowful tone of Danticat's heroic Boukman not only mitigates the heated radicality of Boukman proper's speech, thereby cleansing him of his status as hero, but it also situates the importance of grief to the revolutionary struggle. This grief, set against a scene that reverberates with the "lightning" and "thunder" present when the original Boukman presided over the insurgent meeting at *Bwa Kayïman*—that night was, by all accounts, a stormy one—ties a culturally distinct understanding of mourning to the revolutionary moment and to the foundational mourning rite by which this instance was facilitated.[143] Grief poignantly envelopes readers in how captive insurgents likely experienced *Bwa Kayïman* and how their *Ginen* descendants have come to understand this strategic gathering. For if the account offered by The Order of the Daughters of Notre Dame of Cap Français is true, the Vodou ceremony at *Bwa Kayïman* was not merely an accord with the *lwas* to ensure revolutionary success, it was a solemn communal service for the dead. It was one that recognized the risk involved in insurrection and made plain the losses to be sustained as well as the losses already incurred for a triumphant revolutionary endeavor. In this sense, it disclosed a distinctly Haitian spiritual imaginary in which life and death, the dead and the living, are enmeshed in an intricate matrix of collective being.

The alternation between the dance and the moans of the "sacrificial creature" encourages readers to note the captive insurgent's profound consciousness of loss. Evident is a performance telling of the give and take of life and death, where life (with the dance) is set against death or imminent demise (with the "moans"). This consciousness of loss is expressed through the solemnity of the "mournful sound of the long, narrow tambourines and conch shells," which is indicative of past and present circumstances: the present and past that the original Boukman argued authorized "the god of the white man [to call upon] him to commit crimes" and which led to the haunting presence of the fictitious Boukman's "*loving father, a valiant love, a beloved friend.*"[144] Danticat's prose invites readers to note how *Ginen* insurgents' intentional immersion in loss manifests as a deep respect for those that will pass (the "creatures" and insurgents) and those that have passed (ancestors). They are encouraged to see how attentive intentional mourning manifests as a loving relationality that ensures the remembrance and thus worth of all. As result, readers can come to recognize why Haitians (in the revolutionary moment and today) insist that *tout moun se moun men tout moun pa menm* (all persons are persons, but all persons are not the same).

A Vodou imaginary illustrates how the creative philosophical norms of *Ginen* captives was grief driven and it also shows readers why Danticat conveys revolutionary history through a collectivism cemented by loss and mourning. To have Lili express a sentiment that echoes the mysticism central to Defile's collective mourning rite—"Long live Boukman and long live my boy"—not only points to the duality of being that reveals the *lwa* Boukman's presence within the narrative. It also discloses the immense importance of the absented (here the dead) to revolutionary consciousness. It forcefully discloses how the *lwa* Boukman emerges through a loving rite of lamentation that engenders his being just as Defile's begot Défilée-Dantò's. The similar cosmic origin of both *lwa* reveals Danticat's desire to disclose a parallel, though subsumed history of female revolutionary consequence.

When readers unpack Lili's sentimental words what becomes clear is that the male revolutionary dyad at the fore of her declaration (the

Boukman and Little Guy duality) is only of conceptual relevance and prominence due to its female antecedent. Readers are pushed to see more than the foundational importance of Boukman, male leadership and action to the Revolution; they are urged to note the importance of women through this antecedent's grounding in a revolutionary tradition of Vodouizan relations. Attention is fixed upon the women who thought the Revolution into being with their spirituality and acted it in their collectivity, who, like Boukman, were its harbingers, and, like Little Guy, its future purveyors. It is no coincidence that the "daughters" are tellingly described in "Nineteen Thirty-Seven" as the "embers" and "sparks" for the present and future, nor that Defile, blood-soaked from crossing the Massacre River, is described as having "wings of flame."[145] Women, Danticat stresses, are a key part of the "wall of rising fire" that *was* and that *is* the Revolution. Lili's consciousness of the *lwa* Boukman's multiplicitous energy facilitates a subtle and yet deliberate move from the masculine focus of revolutionary narratology. Readers are encouraged to see the latter's hand in the cleansing of the revolutionary past, in a Westernization that seeks to rid this history of the "barebreasted Negresses" unwilling to be fully Christianized, a Boukman of fury, and the "loving mother" to be mourned with equal passion as the "*loving father, valiant love,* [and] *beloved friend.*" With this push to see absented persons, readers are ultimately primed to see how such cleansing facilitates an assimilatory erasure of all that may contest Western imperial power; and, as result, they are primed to discern those who offer alternative ideas for existence.

"I Need Many Repetitions"

Alternative notions for existence were present among the *Ginen* captives of Saint Domingue well before the Revolution's start. In 1784, the first hot-air balloon took flight in the Americas on the Gallifet sugar plantation and upon seeing the balloon in flight, the captive peoples marshaled in attendance "could not stop talking about the 'insatiable passion' [white] men had to 'exert power over nature.'"[146] Witnessing the event as captive persons, they could not help but to see their own subjugation within this feat of technological savvy. Danticat resurrects this happening in "A Wall of Rising Fire" and underscores how Guy's response to the balloon owned by his employer (his desire to own it and wield it) is anti-*Ginen* and emblematic of the counterrevolutionary impulse present in orthodox, masculinist narrations of the Revolution by her Caribbean peers. The *Ginen* captives forced to witness the balloon's flight did not care about the technological sophistication on display before them. However, a Caribbean revolutionary record devoted to Louverture, imagined and inscribed as forever faithful to Enlightenment thought (eagerly reading Raynal's oft-cited words, "A courageous chief is only wanted. Where is he?") would suggest that the *Ginen* captives in Saint Domingue fought aspirationally, solely with the intent to wield such technology and gain the kind of influence held by European powers.[147] Christophe's reduction in Caribbean fiction of the Revolution to a body of "citadels" and "cathedrals," ruins by which to be on par with the West, is no better as this association similarly reduces the revolutionary efforts of the *Ginen* captive to emulation.

The Haitian Revolutionist writing of the Saint-Lucian poet-playwright and essayist, Derek Walcott, uses Christophe's monarchical rule to advocate for understanding the Haitian Revolution as an aspirational feat. In 1991, Walcott said the following at the International Writers Conference in Dublin: "History to me means vanity: the belief that man has belief in his destiny and I'm supposed to share, delivered from a central, focal, pivotal place. The best example is the cathedral; awe is contained in them. . . . I'm scared of the vanity of an achievement that's supposed to be in praise of God but could be about man praising God."[148] Walcott was ostensibly talking about Western Europe but present in absence was Haiti. Some forty years prior to this utterance, a younger Walcott wrote in his play, *Henri Christophe: A Chronicle in Seven Scenes*, "The violent love of self that kills the self/Cathedrals and cruelties?"[149] And twenty-one years prior to his speech in Dublin, he would write that Christophe's citadel "was a monument to egomania, more than a strategic castle; an effort to reach God's height" in the essay "What the Twilight Says."[150] There in Walcott's speech at the International Writers Conference lies what disconcerted Walcott about Haiti and a revolution cast as an oligarchic effort: the too easy acceptance of human destiny as constructed by Western Europe in its cultural vainglory. For Walcott, the Haiti born from the Revolution distilled a refusal to rethink existence through one's own "central, focal, pivotal place," a misreading that is possible only if nascent Haiti is a creolized oligarchic space and not *Ginen*.

There is little room in canonical Caribbean writing of the Revolution for Haitian Revolutionary striving that exceeds and altogether ignores the cultural paradigms of Western Europe. And yet, alternative visions clearly existed in 1784. Their existence invites recognition of the ethicality of storytelling as it pertains to Haitian resistance and Black resistance, more broadly. There are ways of telling a story that encourages what wants to be seen of the world and what wants to be remembered, a missive evident in Danticat's critique of the Revolution's masculinist narration. The enormous attention paid to the prominent male generals who became Haiti's first political leaders in classic Caribbean literature of the Revolution constraints the freedom-seeking efforts of *Ginen* Haitians and of all colonized Black peoples. It not only facilitates an assimilatory erasure of revolutionaries who challenge a Western ordering of existence, be they women or a mass of unimpressed captive spectators, but it also invites belief in their nonexistence. This belief, in turn, allows scholars and writers of the Revolution to write authoritatively in ignorance about Haiti and Haitians, without recognition of the culturally distinct *Ginen* worldview that grounds popular thought and spiritual practice in revolutionary Saint Domingue and in Haiti today. Furthermore, the erasure of *Ginen* dissension encourages scholars, writers, and thinkers to engage the Revolution as a failed endeavor and, worst yet, revolutionary striving as ineffectual, an opinion Guy also holds.

In response to Lili's joyous proclamation, "Long live my boy and long live Boukman," Guy counters tearfully with his own: "'Long live our supper' [as he] quickly bat[s] his eyelashes to keep tears from rolling down his face."[151] With this reference to "supper," attention is meant to turn from Guy's sadness and settle on an earlier lighthearted textual instance. During this instance, Little Guy prepares for his first monologue and is urged by his mother to reveal what is foremost on his mind. When in character, he decisively shouts "Freedom!" and Guy, greedily eyeing the gourds of cornmeal awaiting the family after his son's recitation, usurps the role of Boukman to "jokingly" state "supper."[152] This "supper"-specific banter, however, is no light utterance in both its first and last articulation, as the humor offered is tinged with bitterness. Guy's persistent focus on his evening meal does what Lili's declaration refuses to do: it openly questions a revolutionary endeavor that has seemingly left many in a state no different from the emaciated existence Boukman railed against. Recall that the "bones" of Boukman's speech were those of the dead *and* the living: "*a wall of fire is rising in the ashes I see the bones of my people . . . whose dark hollow faces I see daily in the fields.*" Consumed with misgivings concerning the efficacy of the revolutionary endeavor, Guy's cheerless "joke" positions a past of revolutionary glory firmly into a trying postcolonial present in order to ask: why need the heirs of the Revolution's failure remember it or its *Ginen* insurgents?

As if called forth by Guy's skepticism, the ancestral spirits of past and present "speak" to Guy in an effort to assuage his misgivings. When the family takes their nightly stroll to the sugar mill following Guy's recitation, Little Guy and his father have the following exchange,

"Can I study my lines there?" the boy said.
"You know them well enough already," Guy said.
"I need many repetitions," the boy said.[153]

Who offers the first and last lines of this conversation? Little Guy, a boy concerned solely with excelling in his role as Boukman, or the persons conjured in the *lwa* Boukman himself, he who is the very embodiment of mournful relation and thus of the past lives invoked with remembrance? The spiritual play grounding Danticat's work would suggest the latter, as would the cryptic nature of Little Guy's last line, "I need many repetitions." I cannot help but see in this line a multi-voiced statement, as it is a speech that attests to both the boy's need for performance excellence and the dead's need for a rejoinder, an adamant and matter-of-fact riposte, stressing the sustained effort needed for a successful revolutionary endeavor. The Revolution cannot be thought of as a completed occurrence. The events of 1791–1804 and all uprisings that occurred thereafter were mere rehearsals for a final production still ahead. The cool smolder of the "daughters" at the end of "Nineteen Thirty-Seven," and the furious cry of revolutionary angst offered by a boy who is at once a *lwa* at "A Wall of Rising Fire's" closing, are an affirmation of this ongoing struggle for resistant difference.

The differing and yet syntactically similar utterances of Guy ("Long live our supper") and Lili ("Long live Boukman and long live my boy") are meant to parallel the dialogic exchange between the two narratives. In turn, the dialogue is a reminder that "Nineteen Thirty-Seven" is the rejoinder to the masculinist and aspirational nature of Caribbean writing on the Revolution, which is offered and subtly debunked by "A Wall of Rising Fire." It is meant to remind readers of the absented *Ginen* women who stood in difference for a decolonial future. They stood with others for a new Haiti and for a radical revolutionary alterity of their own fashioning and imagining. That said, there is an undeniable bleakness concerning the long colonial present that pervades the texts; a bleakness that suggests the battle for a distinct decolonial existence driving the narratives has neared its closing stages. The "daughters of the river's" communality ends with the imminent death of Josephine's aforementioned daughter, Marie. Like her grandmother Defile, she is also accused of murdering a child and will face life imprisonment and certain execution.[154] Guy plunges to his death at "A Wall of Rising Fire's" end. Little Guy is abandoned by his father, and while he is infused with the revolutionary fervor for a new Haiti, he is forced into exile as a young adult and dies at sea because of his political activism. Lili, without her son, without her husband and the "daughters of the river," commits suicide as an old woman.[155] The monumentality of this extensive harm seemingly points to the ineffectuality of the Revolution and the pointlessness of revolutionary striving, which runs counter to Danticat's Haitian Revolutionist writings. Danticat does not want her readers or Haitians to lose hope in Haiti. She charges her narratives with the vibrant presence of the absented to remind all that the battle continues.

Conclusion

Ayiti Ginen+

> Pitou pitou se neg Ginen mwen ye.
>
> —Zabou

Haiti and the Revolution Unseen opened by addressing Haiti's potential inclusion in the African Union and how news of Haiti's incorporation was received by Haitians as a given. I bring this book to a close with a reading of Abderrahmane Sissako's 2014 Mauritanian French film *Timbuktu* to underscore why this inclusion remains as a given because of Haiti's radical signification as the future of Africa. I conclude with attention to this future and its embodiment in a place yet to be realized named *Ayiti Ginen+*, and I do so to capture the radical futures latent in a Haiti seen. A Black madwoman is the steward of these futures in *Timbuktu*, a film that concerns the 2012 jihadist invasion of northern Mali; (un)surprisingly this madwoman is Haitian. Also a rebel, this mad Haitian calls to mind "the mad Haitian rebel[s]" that people the Caribbean classics of the Revolution studied in this book.[1] Those rebels bear the name the Saint Lucian poet-playwright Derek Walcott granted Haitian revolutionaries in his 1958 pageant *Drums and Colours*. They were creoles, meaning they were Caribbean born, acculturated into the West, and thus the vanquished progeny of the colonial project. Zabou, "the mad Haitian rebel" of *Timbuktu*, was not that.[2] On screen, she was distinctly *Ginen*: she was an African Haitian, a Haitian whose African-ness was evident, and an African whose Haitian-ness was also evident. She spoke impeccable Kreyòl (in fact, Kettly Noël, the actor who played Zabou, was Haitian). She appeared to be a Vodou priestess (*manbò*), hummed Vodou songs (one of which led her to sing aloud "*pitou pitou se neg Ginen mwen ye*"), and she invoked Haiti's catastrophic January 12, 2010, earthquake.[3]

The rumblings of this earthquake disrupt time and space to transport Zabou to Mali. She states, "It was the twelfth of January, 2010, at 4:53 p.m. exactly, the same time as Miami. At 4:53 p.m. Port au Prince time. The earth quaked and I found myself here at exactly 9:53. Isn't that right, 9:53?"[4] She directs this question to her pet rooster, *Gonaïves*, named after a Haitian town known as the city of independence. The city of Gonaïves is where Haiti's first ruler, the revolutionary general turned emperor Jean Jacques Dessalines, signed the Haitian Declaration of Independence. Through her speech, spirituality, and experience of natural disaster, Zabou was a motley of common markers of Haiti for persons living outside of Haiti. The bulk of these markers were tied to Haiti's *Ginen* culture as I have outlined in this book (via Haiti's language and faith). Still, what made her an incarnate of the *Ginen* Haitian revolutionist I privilege in *Haiti and the Revolution Unseen* was her storyline in the film, which was resistance.

The film recounts this resistance through vignettes of everyday Malians. They are shown defiantly navigating the unreasonable exigencies of jihadists in the city of Timbuktu, who are Malian and non-Malian, Arab, Black African, and Tuaregan.[5] The people's struggles against jihadists mirrors the passive harassment a nomadic Tuaregan family faces from a lone Arab jihadist.[6] This family lives on the outskirts of the city and its patriarch, Kidane, a cattle herder, is arrested, tried, and later executed for the accidental murder of a fisherman-neighbor, Amadou, a Black Malian who intentionally killed Kidane's favorite cow. The tension between the two neighbors is old, telling of the Sahel region's complicated history of Tuaregan rule, Tuareg conflict with and enslavement of Black African ethnic peoples, and French colonialism. These tensions were heightened by the jihadist occupation, which victimized all non-jihadists regardless of race and ethnicity. Kidane becomes one of the victims of the occupation and accepts his fate (death), as do all the Malians in the film, but they do so on their own terms, taking risks to love, sing, play, and take part in commerce as they see fit. Their defiance is quiet

FIGURE 2.1. Zabou's entrance. Film still from *Timbuktu*, Abderrahmane Sissako, dir., 2014.

yet steady, and it contextualizes Zabou's presence in the film. She disrupts its backstory and exists to show how Tuareg resistance against the Malian state had come together with Islamic fundamentalism to deny all the varied peoples of Timbuktu presence outside of the religious dictates of jihadists, who were led by embittered Tuaregan dissidents.[7]

The denial of presence disproportionately affected the women of Timbuktu. Jihadists decreed that they must wear hijabs, which is not customary in the predominantly Muslim city. They decreed that they must also wear socks and gloves when outside, and they admonished women for showing their faces when in the presence of men. They demanded their absence when present. As Zabou enters the film, wordlessly negating this injunctive, her styling signifies her existence as one who lives outside of the world the jihadists wanted to usher into being.[8] The camera cultivates this signification as it moves slowly upward to give viewers ample time to take in Zabou's afro, styled in spiked tufts adorned with small red ribbons, and her bright and tattered turquoise gown, which is overlaid with black and yellow cloth. Her gown is also embellished with decorative flowers and made all the more dramatic with a train. Her red heels and the unprovoked laughter she emitted at the scene's end accentuated her eccentricity and made her an audible symbol of resistance, which underscored her presence as a *Ginen* Haitian in the film.

And yet Zabou is not perceived as a Haitian who is *Ginen*, or even as a Haitian, by the other characters in *Timbuktu*. When Zabou references the 2010 earthquake, Abdelkrim, an Arab jihadist, replies to her time-traveling claims with kind skepticism, stating, "Zabou, you were there long before."[9] Zabou is knowable as a Malian alone. Still, Zabou knows herself to be a *Ginen* ("*pitou pitou se neg Ginen mwen ye*"). She directly descends from the Haitian revolutionary subjects I argued are absented from the archive of Caribbean cultural thought.[10] Sissako is not creating art within this archive, but like the Haitian rebel in the Caribbean classics of the Revolution studied in *Haiti and the Revolution Unseen*, his Haitian rebel is similarly denied presence as a *Ginen*. The question is why? Why is Zabou unknowable as the *Ginen* Haitian she claims to be? Why is the *Ginen* rebel perpetually out of place, of but not stably within the space of the work inspired by the Revolution?

These questions subtend *Haiti and the Revolution Unseen*, which sought to alter the genealogy of the Haitian revolutionary subject in the annals of Caribbean cultural thought to include a *Ginen* understanding of the Haitian rebel. This understanding invites cognizance of *Ginen* philosophies of freedom and their impact in Saint Domingue and Haiti. These philosophies questioned the legitimacy of colonial power and produced a glitch in the colonial world order, a lingering sense that another world is possible, another life in reach, and another way of being human viable. This glitch has made the *Ginen* revolutionist untimely, of and yet unsuitable to the space and time memorialized in art inspired by the Revolution or in literatures that depict the Revolution. In other words, the world of the Haitian Revolutionist text housing the *Ginen* rebel or the work inspired by the Revolution that has a *Ginen* rebel is still colonized, but the rebel herself shows that there is a place and time where the text's world could be radically different. The rebel shows this because she is an African who exists on the outside of the colonial project. Indeed, whether the Haitian revolutionist is symbolically invoked and identifiable as an African Haitian or *Ginen* as in *Timbuktu*, or whether this revolutionary is unimaginable as an African as in *Drums and Colours*, the kinds of Africans these persons represent are, to borrow from Trinidadian Canadian writer Dionne Brand, of "another place, not here."[11] They are disruptively African and thought past by characters and/or creators of Haitian Revolutionist art because the opposition they name to the colonial project is untenable to the colonized world.

This is evident in Walcott's pageant *Drums and Colours*, where the *Ginen* revolutionist is untimely because she signifies the Haitian rebel and yet cannot be the Haitian rebel because she is African. Of importance here is how the concerted invocation and then disavowal of the African in the eighteenth-century Caribbean of the Revolution in Walcott's pageant is telling of a common approach to the Revolution found in canonical Caribbean Haitian Revolutionist literatures. In this approach, the African is thought past to get to the modern twentieth-century Caribbean, a space that is uniformly regarded as peopled with many kinds of persons except Africans, or that is peopled with Black persons who do not know themselves as Africans, being alienated from themselves. Recall that Walcott writes the following in *Drums and Colours* in the voice of the racially ambiguous, maroon leader Emmanuel Mano, "oh God, but it's hard sometimes to love one another; if you get on like a beast, bind him hand and foot. I can't have no runction in this place. He getting on like some mad Haitian rebel."[12] Mano says this in exasperation when a new Black recruit (a runaway captive) attempts to assault another new recruit (a white colonist) because of the latter's race. Mano refuses to be party to racist separatism and accepts the white recruit into his band of Black, East Indian, and Chinese maroons because "the times" prevented self-reflection. He states, "sometimes the times so bad a man don't have time to think properly."[13] But his Black recruit now has the "time" to think as a member of his multi-racial army, and he still chooses retributive Black power, a choice that mirrors, for Walcott, the Haitian Revolutionary conduct of Haiti's first rulers, the renowned Caribbean-born revolutionists Dessalines and Henry Christophe. In the preceding scene, Christophe (apprehensively) and Dessalines (enthusiastically) await the start of "a new age, the black man's time to kill."[14]

This reductive depiction of Christophe's and Dessalines's bloodlust would have viewers/readers of the pageant believe that colonizers are the sole source of political knowledge and conduct in the eighteenth-century Caribbean, even as Africans exist in Walcott's dramatization of the period. Mano is from Accompong, a Jamaican maroon community started by Africans. He calls to mind the immensity of African political power in the eighteenth century. His racially ambiguous complexion, however, displaces this African reference as he also invokes the transformation of Africans into something less visibly African—and thus more culturally and racially Caribbean in Walcott's imagining. Mano's subordinate describes him thusly: "know as Cadjoe, sometimes John Orr, sometimes Fédon, and various multicoloured aliases."[15] Mano's "multicolouredness" signals a Caribbean where "sex [is] the great republic," as the maroon general Yu remarks.[16] The forced and consensual relations of the region's many peoples have created new kinds of persons, neither Black, White, nor Asian. The vast numbers of these new peoples, who are key characters in the pageant, help Walcott showcase the Caribbean "as a syncretizing locus [with] disparate energies, ethnicities and cultures."[17]

Still, Mano's "multi-colouredness" can only denote the modern Caribbean as Walcott envisions because of African resistance. The Caribbean for Walcott and other influential Caribbean writers of the Revolution is enunciated through the African and the resistance of Africans, hence Walcott's decision to racially democratize the members of Mano's maroon band. Walcott gets around the important living presence of Africans in the Caribbean in the eighteenth century onward by excising the African and Indigenous person from the modern twentieth-century Caribbean. Both appear in part one of the pageant, titled "CONQUEST," set in Europe and the Caribbean, but neither appears as a character in part two of the pageant, titled "REBELLION," which is set exclusively in the Caribbean. In this portion, rebellion is signaled first through the Haitian Revolution, and through the anticipated birth of Haiti thereafter, which is to say, rebellion begets something new politically that neither Africans nor Indigenous peoples can signify but that accords with the pageant's purpose in its moment.[18]

Like Walcott, the foundational writers studied here—Alejo Carpentier, C. L. R. James, Aimé Césaire, and Édouard Glissant—also think past the African in their celebrated writings of the Revolution, and the Indigenous Haitian revolutionist is altogether unthought, though this rebel is very present in the cultural complex of *Ginens* as an ancestor revolutionist. This thinking past begets a conception of the Caribbean as a space that exists without African and Indigenous peoples. I stress Africans here because my focus is on the Haitian Revolution and its overwhelmingly African agents. Carpentier, for instance, thinks alongside Walcott and imagines the Caribbean as syncretic by romanticizing its multi-racial peoples. In the prologue to *The Kingdom of This World*, he thinks past the African Haitian revolutionaries who inspired his project to get to the modern Americas, and instead he celebrates the Caribbean and Latin America for "the fecund racial mixtures it enabled."[19] Africans are also thought past in James's history of the Revolution, *The Black Jacobins*: they do not fit his Caribbean, where the violence of acculturation is mediated through a masculinist aspiration to become the proudly Black male variant of the English gentleman. James invents a new kind of Black man but strips him of the politicized cultural singularity (i.e., African-ness) that could take him beyond the West. Africans do not fit Césaire's and Glissant's distinct Caribbean either, the former via the racially affirming and inventive politics of *négritude*, the latter via the equally inventive politics of cross-cultural relations. Each writer assumes that the Caribbean person is acculturated into the West, Césaire because of alienation from Blackness and Glissant because Blackness has become a site of colonial relation. Each thus writes the Revolution with the heavy hand of French colonialism on their homeland and thinks the modern Caribbean as a space determined by Black radical striving that transforms French revolutionary traditions (Césaire), or they conceive the Caribbean as modern because it is a politically potent mélange of French and Antillean culture and its cultural realities (Glissant). The question worth asking of Walcott and each of the canonical writers studied here is why celebrate the Caribbean as an inventive space of distinction (be it through creole syncretism and cross-cultural relations (Walcott, Carpentier, Glissant) or affirmative Black genius (Césaire and James) if the Caribbean is forever imagined as inevitably following the path of the West but with a twist? This twist is either resistant acculturation or creolization into the same onto-epistemic reality; in whatever variant, it is a dead end.

The ambition of this book is to resist dead-end options and expand scholarly conversations about the anticolonial politics animating the classics studied here. This expansion requires foregrounding the cultural thought of *Ginens* themselves, as showcased through their philosophies and texts oriented by their knowledges (like Edwidge Danticat's stories). It also demands resisting understanding Haiti and the Haitian revolutionary through an idea of the Caribbean as modern because Africans can no longer be identified as African due to racial alienation or cultural syncretism / cross-cultural relations. An understanding of the modern Caribbean in this fashion confounds awareness of how Africa is not simply a continent whose cultures are present in retained traditions in the Caribbean, but it is also knowable as a political praxis, as Haiti shows.

The new world-building actions of *Ginen* revolutionists around their politicized use of Africa as an imaginary demonstrates that political power resides in thought as it does action. It resides in a critical response to colonial power—*Sa blan dit?* (what did the white say?)—and the resolve to think and act beyond this power. This thinking and acting did not make Haitian revolutionists into non-Africans or creoles, persons acculturated into the West or determined by the West, but into different kinds of Africans. Indeed, Haitians exist because their *bossale* and Africanized captive ancestors knew themselves outside of French cultural thought, and they secured Haiti because of their distinct African way of knowing, which is what captivated Walcott, James, Carpentier, Césaire, and Glissant. Each are drawn to the absolutist, nonconformist spirit of African resistance. So even when these writers of Caribbean classics of the Revolution perceive Haitian Revolutionists with their eyes wide shut to their resistant African sense of self, their Haitian Revolutionist texts are so constituted by the decolonial imagination of these persons that *Ginens* still resonate loudly as they were in the texts via the resistant behaviors of characters written as their betters, as the better kind of Haitian rebel. These sublimated rebels are constellations in a larger universe of thought that maps Haiti beyond the colony. They signal *Ayiti Ginen*'s resistant futurism, the way it is factually here (in the now of the twentieth century and onward) but also of "another place, not here."

This elsewhere is what Haiti promises colonized peoples, and it is this Haiti-specific elsewhere that Sissako invokes. *Timbuktu* suggests that the promise of a future that is evocative of "another place, not here" lies beyond Africa and resides in Haiti. Indeed, the existence of "another place," one that is "not here" yet, is needed to disrupt thinking past the quotidian violence that is affecting Mali. Zabou signifies this critical disruption. She is key to Sissako's critique of colonial power and how it has arbitrarily divided Africa. This critique accounts for his concerted attention to land and space in the film. His attention to both suggests that the jihadist occupation is not about religious extremism. More pressingly, it is about the nonexistence of an "open system" of relation, one "based upon movements, networks, nodes, and hierarchies."[20] The absence of this "system" is directly tied to the Berlin Conference (1884–1886), which arbitrarily divided Africa for Western colonial interests.[21] Emizet F. Kisangani writes that "over much of Africa, colonialism froze societies within fixed boundaries even when the dynamic quality of ethnic groups did not fit well into the rigidity of these new boundaries."[22] Avoidable catastrophes like famine, soil erosion, and a scarcity of water occurred in time because of these boundaries.[23] These crises, in turn, bore forced migration and conflict as hostilities arose between "different cultural entities," who were grouped together "without any commonalities . . . to create the colonial states."[24] In the postcolonial moment, these conflicts continued. Kisangani writes that when "any cultural group" "attempt[ed] to break away from these colonial entities" (i.e., the postcolonial nation state), they were "viewed as . . . outlaw[s]" by the "state system," which "accepted colonial boundaries with almost sacrosanct respect."[25] This complicated history is why Sissako refuses to demonize the jihadists in the film, as their lives and that of the average Malian are marked by the fact that there are now no "alternatives in the evolution of hierarchical development" in Mali and the Sahel but those proposed by nineteenth-century Western colonialists.[26] In other words, an "alternative" system of free "movements, networks, nodes, and [navigable] hierarchies" is an impossibility because the region has been mapped and remained mapped for colonial power alone.[27]

Zabou, however, names an alternative in Haiti that is of the film's present but yet is unstable and disruptive to this present. She states, "Time doesn't matter. The earthquake is my body, the cracks, it's me! Cracked pine from head to toe and vice versa, my arms, my back, and my face, cracked. What is time? I am cracked."[28] How can "time" matter when there is no space and no place to be open, to enact new modalities of being?[29] How can one exist sanely in the time of the colony and its derivative the postcolony? Zabou chooses to incarnate disaster itself—"the earthquake is my body"—and in doing so imbues the film with an "otherwise," with "perspectives and frameworks not based in . . . western rationality," the very kind that bore the Berlin Conference.[30] Her presence calls for questioning, for a radical thinking about the actions of jihadists, the Malians under their rule, and their absent state leaders. It calls too for a reconsideration of relations and for a new way of being Malian that Haiti names as possible because of its very existence, which is to say, Zabou is an alarm and clarion call to action, hence the resistance that attends her movements in the film. She is emblematic of the disobedient questioning that each writer studied in *Haiti and the Revolution Unseen* enacts with their literatures.

In closing with an imagined Haiti, embodied in Zabou, I hope to expose the existence of an irreparable tear in the fabric of colonial being that *Ginens* made, and that Haiti's significations proliferate for persons outside of Haiti. My intent with *Haiti and the Revolution Unseen* was to show how this tear outwardly manifests as a critical skepticism, a desire to appraise colonial power and ask *Sa blan dit? Timbuktu* stages this ask and stops viewers from thinking past the quotidian violence affecting Mali. This thinking past encourages reductive reasoning that conceives the violence of the 2012 jihadist invasion as simply occurring because Tuaregs are barbaric, the Malian state indifferent, the Black African ethnic peoples of the nation and Sahel are weak. Zabou checks this reasoning. She is there to disrupt a narrative of resigned complicity as well as a narrative of racist/ethnic bigotry. She is there to create a context in which to think novelly, so as to build the nation and the Sahel region differently. The point is to shift thinking and introduce new possibilities for being into the world.

This is Haiti's purpose in this long colonial moment, and in the year 2024 where Kenyans serve alongside imperial occupiers of Haiti as police officers in the nation, where contemporary African geopolitical relations to Haiti seem to prove the colonial lie that *depi nan Ginen, nèg rayi nèg*, it is important to remember the disruptive importance of *Ginen* resistance.[31] *Ginen* resistance not only begot a new world in Haiti, but it also continues to point toward distinct ways of being human, which Zabou captures. In the scene where she invokes the 2010 earthquake, she throws a small fabric bundle to Abdelkrim, the jihadist who spoke directly to her and questioned her time-traveling abilities, and says to him, "This will give you luck," to which he says, "Thank you," as he unties the charm or *wanga*.[32] Later in the film when two persons accused of adultery are stoned to death, Abdelkrim begins to dance like a graceful chicken, miming a *Gonaïves* possessed as Zabou watches content.³³ His body is no longer beholden to his rationalities and thus to his reasoning for joining the jihad/anti-state movement. It moves freely. He touches the ground, takes handfuls of dirt and becomes again a *moun*, a plain person.³⁴

Moun in Kreyòl-speaking regions does not refer to "the individual" but to a "presence," as the Martinican writer Monchoachi contends.³⁵ He writes that "an individual is a representation while a person is a presence. To get to 'individual,' you have to go down the ladder of the species to the bottom rung. A person, as a person, is irrevocable."³⁶ *Ginen* captives internalized this conception and insisted on being human plainly, without colonial modernity's "ladder of . . . species."³⁷ This insistence is what has made the *Ginen* revolutionary *and* Haiti untimely. Haiti is neither of the colonizing West or the (de)colonizing Africa, a space under colonial subjection but with polities (and devoted subjects) willing to move in the world as colonizers. Haiti subsists as a plus, a preposition that exceeds its formative influences because it disrupts how those influences can be known and how each can individually know themselves. It is a disruptor of norms, of the rationalities that reason the terror that was the Berlin Conference, coercive jihad as a response to state violence, the postcolonial state's existence as the colony and the contemporary African's rebirth as an occupying police officer in Haiti. It disrupts to invite thinking toward. Carole Boyce Davies writes that "we see in each encounter with Haiti what it means to be human in the world."³⁸ To know Haitians differently as *Ginens*—indeed, to know Haiti differently as *Ayiti Ginen* (the new world *bossales* invented) and as *Ayiti Ginen+* (the discoverable uncharted world within reach of all colonized peoples)—invites perceiving the world and ourselves differently. *Haiti and the Revolution Unseen* shows that the story of Haiti's revolutionary origins expresses how big the world is, how expansive, on the one hand, is our capacity to be human distinctly, and how copious, on the other, is our speculative ability to envision and resistantly enact our worlds anew. To know this is to be "cracked" in the time of the colony, but potentially whole in the time to come.³⁹

Appendix

Ancestral Homage for Revolutionaries

This homage was posted on the Haitixchange, a now defunct online forum for Haitians in Haiti and in the Diaspora. I was an active member during its duration and came across this homage, which was authored by an unnamed forum member. The translated version is by Johanne Castera.

I. Kreyòl Original

August 14 - August 21
Se nan jou sa yo ... Nan jou sa yo, yo di zansèt nou komanse òganize. Se nan jou sa yo te di zansèt nou yo pran pou yo mobilize. Se nan jou sa yo te di zansèt nou yo te pran pou yo ini.

Eske Ou kwè sa vre???

Depi lane 1492 jiska 1791 te rive ... kè yo tap boule, kè yo tap mande Jistis. Ou kwè nou deja bliye yo?

Chef Kaonabo ...	Nou pa bliye
Chef Hatuey ...	Nou pa bliye
Chef Manicatoex ...	Nou pa bliye
Chef Cotubanama ...	Nou pa bliye

Chef Henri . . .	Nou pa bliye
Chef Tamayo . . .	Nou pa bliye
Fanm Anakaona . . .	Nou pa bliye
Padre Jean . . .	Nou pa bliye
Makandal . . .	Nou pa bliye
Nèg Teyselo . . .	Nou pa bliye
Nèg Santiago . . .	Nou pa bliye
Cola Janm koupe . . .	Nou pa bliye
Polydor . . .	Nou pa bliye
Nèg (Sim) Don Pedre . . .	Nou pa bliye
Etienne Daty . . .	Nou pa bliye
Ductaque . . .	Nou pa bliye
Pierre Mondongue . . .	Nou pa bliye
Jospeh Flaville . . .	Nou pa bliye
Agnès . . .	Nou pa bliye
Jeannot . . .	Nou pa bliye
Nèg Kandi . . .	Nou pa bliye
Nèg Halaou . . .	Nou pa bliye
Nèg Bébé . . .	Nou pa bliye
Bélisaire . . .	Nou pa bliye
Guimbeau . . .	Nou pa bliye
Nèg Pierrot . . .	Nou pa bliye
Nèg Makaya . . .	Nou pa bliye
Pierre Michel . . .	Nou pa bliye
Paul Lafrance . . .	Nou pa bliye
Barthélemy . . .	Nou pa bliye
Zéphirin . . .	Nou pa bliye
Jan Kina . . .	Nou pa bliye
Dieudonne . . .	Nou pa bliye
Nèg Pompée . . .	Nou pa bliye
Jean Baptiste le grand . . .	Nou pa bliye
Malouba . . .	Nou pa bliye
Nèg Boukman . . .	Nou pa bliye
Nèg Jan franswa . . .	Nou pa bliye
Nèg Biasou . . .	Nou pa bliye
Nèg Titus . . .	Nou pa bliye

Jean Jacques Sully . . .	Nou pa bliye
Giles Bambara . . .	Nou pa bliye
Lanmou Deranse . . .	Nou pa bliye
Sanon Loup . . .	Nou pa bliye
Petit Noel . . .	Nou pa bliye
Jacques Tellier . . .	Nou pa bliye
Nèg Kanga . . .	Nou pa bliye
Nèg San Souci . . .	Nou pa bliye
Va malheureux. . . .	Nou pa bliye
Henriette Sen Mak . . .	Nou pa bliye
Suzanne . . .	Nou pa bliye
Mari Jan . . .	Nou pa bliye
E tout sa nou pa site yo . . .	Nou pap janm bliye nou.

II. English Translation

August 14–August 21

On these days . . . On these days they said our ancestors begin to organize. On these days they said our ancestors mobilized themselves. On these days they said our ancestors began to unite themselves.

Do you believe that's true???

Ever since 1492 until 1791 arrived . . . their hearts were on fire, their hearts demanded Justice. Do you think we've already forgotten them?

Chief Kaonabo . . .	We haven't forgotten
Chief Hatuey . . .	We haven't forgotten
Chief Manicatoex . . .	We haven't forgotten
Chief Cotubanama . . .	We haven't forgotten
Chief Henri . . .	We haven't forgotten
Chief Tamayo . . .	We haven't forgotten
Anacaona . . .	We haven't forgotten
Father Jean . . .	We haven't forgotten
Makandal . . .	We haven't forgotten
Nèg Teyselo . . .	We haven't forgotten
Nèg Santiago . . .	We haven't forgotten

Cola Janm koupe ...	We haven't forgotten
Polydor ...	We haven't forgotten
Nèg (Sim) Don Pedre ...	We haven't forgotten
Etienne Daty ...	We haven't forgotten
Ductaque ...	We haven't forgotten
Pierre Mondongue ...	We haven't forgotten
Joseph Flaville ...	We haven't forgotten
Agnès ...	We haven't forgotten
Jeanot ...	We haven't forgotten
Nèg Kandi ...	We haven't forgotten
Nèg Halaou ...	We haven't forgotten
Nèg Bébé ...	We haven't forgotten
Bélisaire ...	We haven't forgotten
Guimbeau ...	We haven't forgotten
Nèg Pierrot ...	We haven't forgotten
Nèg Makaya ...	We haven't forgotten
Pierre Michel ...	We haven't forgotten
Paul Lafrance ...	We haven't forgotten
Barthélemy ...	We haven't forgotten
Zéphirin ...	We haven't forgotten
Jan Kina ...	We haven't forgotten
Dieudonne ...	We haven't forgotten
Nèg Pompée ...	We haven't forgotten
Jean Baptiste le grand ...	We haven't forgotten
Malouba ...	We haven't forgotten
Nèg Boukman ...	We haven't forgotten
Nèg Jan franswa ...	We haven't forgotten
Nèg Biasou ...	We haven't forgotten
Nèg Titus ...	We haven't forgotten
Jean Jacques Sully ...	We haven't forgotten
Giles Bambara ...	We haven't forgotten
Lanmou Deranse ...	We haven't forgotten
Sanon Loup ...	We haven't forgotten
Petit Noel ...	We haven't forgotten
Jacques Tellier ...	We haven't forgotten
Nèg Kanga ...	We haven't forgotten

Nèg San Souci . . .	We haven't forgotten
Va malheureux . . .	We haven't forgotten
Henriette Sen Mak . . .	We haven't forgotten
Suzanne . . .	We haven't forgotten
Mari Jan . . .	We haven't forgotten
And all whom we don't know . . .	We haven't forgotten.

Notes

Introduction

Epigraph. *Agwe Tawoyo*, There's a time when they'll see us. *Agwe Tawoyo* is a *lwa* or spirit of the sea, who served as the guardian of the Africans who crossed the Atlantic during the slave trade.

1. See Kenya Downs, "Despite Reports, Haiti Not Joining the African Union," PBS News, May 20, 2016, https://www.pbs.org/newshour/world/despite-reports-haiti-not-joining-the-african-union.
2. Carolyn E. Fick, *The Making of Haiti: The Saint Domingue Revolution from Below* (Knoxville: University of Tennessee Press, 1990), 25.
3. Carolyn E. Fick, "From Slave Colony to Black Nation: Haiti's Revolutionary Inversion," in *New Countries: Capitalism, Revolutions, and Nations in the Americas, 1750–1870,* ed. John Tutino (Durham, NC: Duke University Press, 2017), 140.
4. As "units of production [whose existence] represented an investment that, once amortized, had already yield[ed] its profit," African-born captives were regarded as depreciated goods upon purchase, see Fick, *The Making of Haiti*, 27. The majority of new arrivals worked on sugar plantations and lived for a mere "five to eight" years because colonists actively sought to extract all of their labor power even if that meant ending their lives. Fick, "From Slave Colony," 140. See also Crystal Eddins's discussion of captive death in Saint Domingue in *Rituals, Runaways, and the Haitian Revolution: Collective Action in the African Diaspora* (Cambridge: Cambridge University Press, 2021), 88–94.
5. Michel-Rolph Trouillot, *Stirring the Pot of Haitian History*, trans. and ed. Mariana Past and Benjamin Hebblethwaite (Liverpool: Liverpool University Press, 2021), 16.
6. Trouillot, *Stirring the Pot*, 16, 52–53.
7. Trouillot, *Stirring the Pot*, 16.
8. Eddins, *Rituals, Runaways*, 2.

9. Fouchard, *The Haitian Maroons: Liberty or Death* (New York: Edward W. Blyden Press, 1981), 104.
10. Eddins, *Rituals, Runaways*, 2. For the counter-plantation system, see Jean Casimir, *The Haitians: A Decolonial History* (Chapel Hill: University of North Carolina Press, 2020).
11. Casimir, *The Haitians*, 281. The counter-plantation, according to Casimir, is a system of resistance that touched all aspects of life in Saint Domingue and later Haiti. It included "gender relations [and] family [and it engendered] the creation of the *lakou*, indivisible collective property, Vodou temples, rural markets, garden-towns, leisure, crafts, [and] the arts," *The Haitians*, 351. For a succinct discussion of the *"lakou"* and its significance to post-independence Haiti, see Brandon R. Byrd and Chelsea Stieber, introduction to *Haiti for the Haitians*, eds. Brandon R. Byrd and Chelsea Stieber (Liverpool: Liverpool University Press, 2023), 4–5. For the *"lakou"* and decoloniality, see Beaudelaine Pierre, "Thinking Decoloniality through Haitian Indigenous Ecologies," *Hypatia: A Journal of Feminist Philosophy* 35, no. 3 (Summer 2020): 393–409.
12. Trouillot, *Stirring the Pot*, 56. Bold in original.
13. Fouchard, *The Haitian Maroons*, 104.
14. Fouchard, *The Haitian Maroons*, 104, 105.
15. Vastey, *Réflexions sur une lettre de Mazères, ex-colon français, . . . sur les noirs et les blancs, la civilisation de l'Afrique, le Royaume d'Hayti, etc.* (Sans Souci: L'Imprimerie Royale, 1816), 31. Vastey details his radicalization as an Africanization in *À Mes Concitoyens*. There he describes having to run into the woods to safeguard his life near the Revolution's end. Napoleonic France had issued a mandate to liquidate all adults who were African and African descended in Saint Domingue, even those like Vastey who were fighting in the French colonial army. Faced with certain death, Vastey enters the woods and finds *bossales*, who he expects to be hateful toward him, but he is stunned to receive a warm welcome and is transformed thereafter. He writes, "the bosom of [his] maternal roots" usurped the genomic significance of his white father, as the "fathers, mothers, brothers [and] friends" he inherited when among the Africans extended such "paternal tenderness" that they became his father, occasioning his transformation into an African. See *À mes concitoyens* (Cap-Henry: P. Roux, imprimeur du Roi, 1815), 18.
16. Eddins, *Rituals, Runaways*, 58. See Casimir, *The Haitians*, 9.
17. Eddins, *Rituals, Runaways*, 58.
18. Some of their works include Casimir, *The Haitians*; Anibal Quijano and Michael Joseph Ennis, "Coloniality of Power, Eurocentrism, and Latin America," *Nepantla: Views from South* 1 (2000): 533–80; Catherine E. Walsh, "Shifting the Geopolitics of Critical Knowledge: Decolonial Thought and Cultural Studies 'Others' in the Andes," in *Globalization and the Decolonial Option*, ed.

W. Mignolo and A. Escobar (New York: Routledge, 2010); María Lugones, *Pilgrimages/Peregrinajes: Theorizing Coalition Against Multiple Oppressions* (Lanham, MD: Rowman and Littlefield, 2003); Walter Mignolo, "The Geopolitics of Knowledge and the Colonial Difference," *South Atlantic Quarterly* 101, no. 1 (Winter 2002): 58–96; Nelson Maldonado-Torres, "On the Coloniality of Being: Contributions to the Development of a Concept," *Cultural Studies* 21, no. 2–3 (March/May 2007): 240–70; and Sylvia Wynter, "Beyond Miranda's Meanings: Un/silencing the 'Demonic Ground' of Caliban's Woman," in *Out of Kumbla: Caribbean Women and Literature*, ed. Carole Boyce Davies and Elaine Savory Fido (Trenton: African World Press, 1990), 355–71.

19. Wynter, "Beyond Miranda's Meanings," 364.
20. Perez, *Eros Ideologies: Writings on Art, Spirituality, and the Decolonial* (Durham, NC: Duke University Press, 2018), 7.
21. Catherine E. Walsh, "Pedagogical Notes from the Decolonial Cracks," Hemispheric Institute, Oct. 23, 2013, https://hemisphericinstitute.org/en/emisferica-11-1-decolonial-gesture/11-1-dossier/pedagogical-notes-from-the-decolonial-cracks.html.
22. Nwokocha, *Vodou en Vogue: Fashioning Black Divinities in Haiti and the United States* (Chapel Hill: University of North Carolina, 2023), 13–14.
23. Nwokocha, *Vodou en Vogue*, 13–14.
24. Anonymous, "Sou Lamné," trans. Erol Josué and Laurent Dubois, in *The Haiti Reader: History, Culture, Politics*, eds. Laurent Dubois, Kaiama L. Glover, Nadève Ménard, Millery Polyné, and Chantalle F. Verna (Durham, NC: Duke University Press, 2020), 15.
25. Wynter asserts that "our present system of knowledge is based on the premise that the human is, like all purely biological species, a natural organism; or, the human is defined biocentrically and therefore exists, as such, in a relationship of pure continuity with all other living beings (rather than in one of both continuity and discontinuity)." This premise categorizes human difference as natural, as biological; because of this categorization, narratives of the flesh (or race) are used to understand identity, politics and resistance to colonial violence. Wynter states that if an epistemic shift occurred away from biocentricism, "humans [could be] conceptualized as hybrid beings" as "*bios* and *mythoi*." Under this formula, "you [could not] classify human individuals, as well as human groups, as naturally selected (i.e., eugenic) and naturally dysselected (i.e., dysgenic) beings." In other words, you could not rely on race (via the flesh) to understand identity, politics and resistant anticolonial behaviors. I favor the possibility of a new understanding of the human that Wynter outlines as viable, and I do so because such an understanding would better illuminate the importance and novelty of Ginen revolutionary action and thought. See Sylvia Wynter and Katherine McKittrick, "Unparalleled Catastrophe for

Our Species?: Or, to Give Humanness a Different Future: Conversations" in *Sylvia Wynter: On Being Human as Praxis*, ed. Katherine McKittrick (Durham, NC: Duke University Press, 2015), 16–17. Emphasis in original.
26. Anonymous, "Sou Lamné," 13. The Kreyòl reads, "*Yo pwan de pie nou, yo enchenen de ponyet nou, yo lage nou anba kal*" and "*gen yon tan ya we nou.*"
27. Walcott, "Drums and Colours," *Caribbean Quarterly* 38, no. 4 (December 1992), 122.
28. Fick, *The Making of Haiti*, 17, 18.
29. *Gen des couleur libre* is often referenced without the *"libre,"* a convention this book will follow from this point on.
30. Casimir, *The Haitians*, 13.
31. Fick, *The Making of Haiti*, 20.
32. Casimir, *The Haitians*, 13.
33. Singh, "A Schizophrenic Metaphor? Disciplining Creoleness," *Transforming Anthropology* 20, no. 2 (2012): 173; emphasis in original.
34. Allen, "Creole: The Problem of Definition," in *Questioning Creole: Creolisation Discourses in Caribbean Culture*, ed. Verene A. Shepherd and Glen L. Richards (Kingston, Jamaica: Ian Randle Publishers, 2002), 50.
35. Allen, "Creole," 50.
36. Fick, *The Making of Haiti*, 18.
37. Casimir, *The Haitians*, 13.
38. Fick, *The Making of Haiti*, 20.
39. Casimir, *The Haitians*, 13; Fick, *The Making of Haiti*, 21.
40. Eddins, *Rituals, Runaways*, 81; Fick, *The Making of Haiti*, 21.
41. Trouillot, *Stirring the Pot*, 100.
42. Mocombe, *The Vodou Ethic and the Spirit of Communism: The Practical Consciousness of the African People of Haiti* (Lanham, MD: University Press of America, 2016), 110.
43. Casimir, *The Haitians*, 13; Fick 20. The emancipated's identification with *gens de couleurs* was sociocultural according to Casimir and Mary Claypool, who state, "Among the enfranchised, the stratum of free blacks distinguished itself: they did not consider themselves *American colonists* [a term *gens de couleurs* gave themselves to establish their right to govern Saint Domingue and Haiti thereafter] and would not be considered as such. Yet in the absence of a relationship of consanguinity with the colonists, their belonging to this privileged class [of the free] owed itself to the acquisition and display of ideological and cultural affinities." See Jean Casimir and Mary Claypool, "Going Backwards Toward the Future," *The Global South* 6, no. 1 (Spring 2012): 175.
44. Mocombe, *The Vodou Ethic*, 110.
45. Allen, "Creole," 50.
46. Jean Casimir, Eglantine Colon, and Michelle Koerner, "Haiti's Need for a Great South," *The Global South* 5, no. 1 (2011): 21.
47. Walcott, "Drums and Colours," 122.

48. Walcott, "Drums and Colours," 87.
49. Walcott, "Drums and Colours," 121.
50. Walcott, "Drums and Colours," 104.
51. Walcott, "Drums and Colours," 122.
52. The Africans in question include the play's first "Mano," who is described as an African king. See "Drums and Colours," 25. There are other "Manos" thereafter in the pageant whose person reflects the specific circumstances of the period in which they lived. Whoever bears the name "Mano" in the performance is always a leader, however. This narrative detail speaks to the political circumstances of the pageant's authorship. It was commissioned by the short-lived West Indian Federation (1958–1962) to bolster support for its governance. Mano, the non-African or the "multicoloured" maroon, is a political charlatan and evocative of a distinctly Caribbean style of anticolonial nationalist governance that, Walcott argues, Haiti names and heralds. See Walcott, "Drums and Colours," 87. Mano cries out in exasperation, "oh God, but it's hard sometimes to love one another" and yet fails to actually love the Black maroon recruit, who he harshly disciplines; and he overly loves the white planter maroon, who he absolves quickly for his participation in slavery. See Walcott, "Drums and Colours," 122. He cares for neither and yet is at the helm of maroon resistance and the Caribbean political community to come, a storyline that speaks to Walcott's critique of the expanding and corrupt power of Caribbean anticolonial nationalists in his moment.
53. Walcott, "Drums and Colours," 122.
54. Walcott, "Drums and Colours," 122.
55. Glissant also writes that Victor Schoelcher's "very lively biography" on Louverture was also indispensable and brought "together all the essential information about this heroic figure." See Glissant, "Preface to the Present Edition," *Monsieur Toussaint*, trans. J. Michael Dash and Édouard Glissant (Boulder, CO: Lynne Rienner Publishers, 2005), 15.
56. See *Monsieur Toussaint: A Play*, trans. Joseph G. Forester and Barbara Franklin (Washington, DC: Three Continents Press, 1981), 24. All in-text citations are from this text.
57. Glissant, *Monsieur Toussaint*, 25.
58. Glissant, *Monsieur Toussaint*, 25, 32.
59. This point is detailed in Chapter 1.
60. Fouchard, *The Haitian Maroons*, 347; Eddins, *Rituals, Runaways*, 179.
61. "*Neg*" is a Black person, friend, or more broadly person.
62. See Katherine McKittrick, *Dear Science and Other Stories* (Durham, NC: Duke University Press, 2021), 38.
63. McKittrick, *Dear Science*, 38.
64. *Ginen*'s various meanings and its association with ancestral spirits (*lwa*) is discussed more extensively later in the introduction.

65. McKittrick, *Dear Science*, 38-39
66. McKittrick, *Dear Science*, 39; emphasis in original.
67. The claim that *Ginen yo tout koulé* (*Ginens*, here ancestor spirits, come in all colors) does not denote equality as understood within colonial modernity's political traditions. Its meanings are rooted within Vodou's system of thought and is taken from the song, "Loumandja" by the Haitian band *Lakou Mizik*. The song critiques Haiti's occupation by new colonizers, the US, and it resists how Haitians are subjugated in their own homes because of the racist logic underwriting the US's imperial presence in Haiti. See Lakou Mizik, "Loumandja," track 5 on *HaitiaNola* (Cumbancha, 2019), Spotify. This logic is the brainchild of colonial modernity, which says "men are born and remain free and equal in rights" but qualifies this equality through race because "social distinctions may be founded . . . upon the general good." See "The Declaration of the Rights of Man – 1789," August 26, 1789, Avalon Project, Yale Law School, https://avalon.law.yale.edu/18th_century/rightsof.asp. *Ginen* culture affords ancestors and guiding spirits the volition to freely change their physical appearance. It does so precisely to resist the racist logic of colonial modernity, which qualifies its notions of equality to say that *koulè nou pa djowo* (literally, "our color cannot be divine," figuratively, the color of Black peoples is not within the principles of the cosmos and therefore it cannot be determined by their agency and singular perception). See Lakou Mizik, "Loumandja," which prefaces the line "Ginen yo tout koulé" with "Yo di koulè nou pa djowo" (they said our color cannot be divine). *Djowo* is untranslatable as a single term; it references the *lwa* (ancestral spirit) Jobolo Bosou and that *lwa*'s many physical manifestations. My translation of *djwowo*'s meanings stresses agency and perception because the point here is that the *lwa* decide what their physical appearance will be and mean on their own terms within the scope of what the cosmos allows. Their appearance is not bound to the dictates of colonizers; how then can their peoples' appearance be bound to their notions as well given that the Black countenance of the Haitian majority is valid in the cosmos? When one takes into consideration the ease with which the *lwa* change appearances and the consistency of their personalities (which do not change), it is clear that within a *Ginen* onto-epistemic framework (where ancestral spirits are key ethical and moral guides) racial identity would be a very poor signifier of politics, particularly radical decolonizing politics. *Ginen* cultural thought is emblematic of Black decolonial politics precisely because it intrinsically recognizes that if the work has not been done to intellectually displace biology (i.e., the flesh as identity) and reinvent Blackness, Brownness and/or Native-ness in terms that resist and lie outside of the biocentric model for identity outlined by the colonial project, then anticolonial politics, which is tied to and aligned with radical Black politics, radical Brown politics, and

radical Native politics, becomes colonial politics, white politics. The world will remain the colony, the West and new worlds forever un-mappable.
68. Daut, "Review of *Daring to Be Free / Dying to Be Free: Toward a Dialogic Haitian-U.S. Studies*," by Matthew J. Clavin, Millery Polyné, and Ashli White, *American Quarterly* 63, no. 2 (2011): 376.
69. Daut, "Review of *Daring*," 375.
70. The history of the Haitian Revolution has been depicted by many. Some key texts include: C. L. R. James, *The Black Jacobins: Toussaint L'Ouverture and the San Domingo Revolution* (New York: Vintage, 1989); Gabriel Debien, *Les Colons de Saint-Domingue et la Révolution: Essai sur le Club Massiac (Août 1789–Août 1792)* (Paris: Armand Colin, 1951); Thomas Madiou, *Histoire d'Haiti*, 8 vols. (Port-au-Prince: Maison Henri Deschamps, 1989 [1847–1848]); Beaubrun Ardouin, *Études sur l'histoire d'Haïti* (Port-au-Prince: Dalencourt, 1958 [1853–1865]); David P. Geggus, *Haitian Revolutionary Studies* (Bloomington: Indiana University Press, 2002); Carolyn E. Fick, *The Making of Haiti*; Laurent DuBois, *Avengers of the New World: The Story of the Haitian Revolution* (Cambridge, MA: Belknap Press of Harvard University Press, 2004); John D. Garrigus, *Before Haiti: Race and Citizenship in French Saint-Domingue* (New York: Palgrave Macmillan, 2010); Pierre Pluchon, *Toussaint Louverture: De l'esclavage au pouvoir* (Paris: Éditions de l'École, 1799) and *Toussaint Louveture: Un révolutionnarie noire d'Ancien Régime* (Paris: Fayard, 1989); Yves Benot, *La Déémeénce coloniale sous Napoléon* (Paris: La Découverte, 1992) and *La Révolution française et la fin des colonies 1789–1794* (Paris: La Découverte, 1987, 1989); Marcel Dorigny, "Aux origines: L'indépendence d'Haïti et son occultation," in *La Fracture coloniale: La société française au prisme de l'héritage colonial*, ed. Pascal Blanchard, Nicolas Bancel, and Sandrine Lemaire (Paris: La Découverte, 2005); Pascal Blanchard, *La République coloniale* (Paris: Hachette/Pluriel, 2006).
71. Fick, *The Making of Haiti*, 92.
72. Fick, *The Making of Haiti*, 97.
73. For more on the ceremony, see DuBois, *Avengers of the New World*, 99–101; Fick, *The Making of Haiti*, 92–95; and Trouillot, *Stirring the Pot*, 56–58.
74. Fick, *The Making of Haiti*, 95.
75. See Casimir, "On the Origins of the Counter-plantation System," trans. Laurent Dubois, in *The Haiti Reader: History, Culture, Politics*, ed. Laurent Dubois, Kaiama L. Glover, Nadève Ménard, Millery Polyné, and Chantalle F. Verna (Durham: Duke University Press, 2020), 63. Boukman's prayer reads, "bon Dié, zotes tendé, cache non gnou nuage." Horace Pauleus Sanon, *Histoire de Toussaint-Louverture* (Haiti: Impr. A. A. Héraux, 1932.), 1.98. For a discussion of the importance of the *lwa* of *Ginen*, Ogun in particular, to the events of *Bwa Kayïman*, see Jacob Carruthers, *Irritated Genie: An Essay on the Haitian Revolution* (Chicago: Kemetic Institute, 1985), 22–24.

76. Trouillot, *Stirring the Pot*, 90.
77. Casimir, *The Haitians*, 288–89.
78. Trouillot, *Stirring the Pot*, 76–84, 72, 124, 119–170.
79. See Fick, *The Making of Haiti*, 228. Fouchard, *The Haitian Maroons*, 356.
80. Fick, *The Making of Haiti*, 220–22.
81. For Fick's discussion of the African-born leaders, the liquidation of those in the North by Dessalines and the survival of those in the South, see Fick, *The Making of Haiti*, 231–36. See also Joan Dayan, *Haiti, History and the Gods* (Berkeley: University of California Press, 1995), 21; and Casimir, *The Haitians*, 19, 161–62.
82. Dessalines regarded the captive and free as kin to Indigenous peoples because of their united interest in ending slavery, colonialism, and white supremacy. He not only paid homage to the Indigenous for their antislavery and anticolonial resistance by renaming Saint Domingue as *Ayiti*, but he also christened his soldiers as "Incas or children of the sun" in 1802 to honor the 1780 Inca uprising in Peru. Furthermore, he adopted the title "Army of the Incas" for his armed forces and they, in turn, referred to themselves as "Sons of the Sun," later settling on the regimental title "Indigenous Army." See Dubois, *Avengers of the New World*, 299.
83. This renaming still honors the Indigenous who, for Haitians, are ancestors and comrades, which is why in the ancestor-based religion of Vodou many *lwa* (Vodou spirits) are Indigenous in origin (e.g., the *Gedes* and *Simbis*). For more on Taino survival in Vodou, see Maya Deren's *Divine Horsemen: The Living Gods of Haiti* (New York: McPherson and Company, 2004) and Karen McCarthy Brown's *Mama Lola* (Berkeley: University of California Press, 1991). In fact, so central are the Indigenous to *Ginen*'s cultural sense of self that they are included as participants in the founding ceremony of *Bwa Kayïman*. Mocombe writes, "according to Haitian oral history, at Bois Caiman or Bwa Kay-Imam (near the Imam Boukman Dutty's house), . . . leaders of the 'maroon republics,' nineteen African tribes or nations and one tribe of the Taino nation, assembled and organized a Vodou ceremony led by the oungan, Boukman Dutty, manbo Cecile Fatiman, and Edaïse to create one new nation, the Empire of Ayiti, the twenty-first tribe or nation of the ceremony, in the Americas around the Vodou religion, its ethic of democracy and communal living, and the Kreyol language." Mocombe, *The Vodou Ethic*, 99. Black decolonial politics is always relational and coalitionist, and *Ginen* cultural praxis is no different.
84. Casimir, *The Haitians*, 8.
85. Mocombe, *The Vodou Ethic*, 88.
86. Casimir, *The Haitians*, 281; also see endnote 11 of the introduction to this book.
87. Robert Farris Thompson, *Flash of the Spirit: African & Afro-American Art & Philosophy* (New York: Vintage Books, 1984), 164.

88. Conversations with religious studies scholar Eziaku Atuama Nwokocha and family members inform how this book understands *Ginen*.
89. For scholarly discussion of *Ginen*'s location and its dual signification as Africa and a divine realm, see Elizabeth McAlister, "Necroscape and Diaspora: Making Ancestors in Haitian Vodou," in *Spirit Service: Vodun and Vodou in the African Atlantic World*, ed. Timothy Landry, Eric Montgomery and Christian Vannier (Bloomington: Indiana University Press, 2022), 291, 302, 304; Karen McCarthy Brown, "Afro-Caribbean Spirituality: A Haitian Case Study," in *Vodou in Haitian Life and Culture: Invisible Powers*, ed. Claudine Michel and Patrick Bellegarde-Smith (New York: Palgrave Macmillam, 2006), 9; Joan Dayan, "Vodoun, or the Voice of the Gods," in S*acred Possessions: Vodou, Santería, Obeah, and the Caribbean*, ed. Margarite Fernández Olmos and Lizabeth Paravisini-Gebert (New Brunswick, NJ: Rutgers University Press, 2000), 17; and Kate Ramsey, *The Spirits and the Law: Vodou and Power in Haiti* (Chicago: University of Chicago Press, 2011), 7. Concerning where exactly *Ginen* is located and the divergent accounts that exist, see religious studies scholar Leslie G. Desmangles, who writes, "much as in the case of heaven, there is no agreement among Vodouisants as to the exact location of Ginen. One commonly held opinion is that it is under the sea, or under the bed of a local river. But some believe that it is located in the bowels of the earth; still others hold that it is above the sky," *The Faces of the Gods: Vodou and Roman Catholicism in Haiti* (Chapel Hill: University of North Carolina Press, 1992), 69.
90. Max Beauvoir, *Lapriyè Ginen* (Port-au-Prince: Edisyon Près Nasyonal d'Ayiti, 2008), 13.
91. Sokari Ekine, "Haiti Vodou," Visura, February 22, 2024, https://visura.co/ekine/stories/haiti-vodou#.
92. Claudine Michel, "Vodou in Haiti: Way of Life and Mode of Survival," in *Vodou in Haitian Life and Culture: Invisible Powers*, ed. Claudine Michel and Patrick Bellegarde-Smith (New York: Palgrave Macmillan, 2006) 36n26.
93. See Beaubrun, *Nan Domi: An Initiate's Journey into Haitian Vodou* (San Francisco: City Lights, 2013), 185–86.
94. Michel, "Vodou in Haiti," 36n26.
95. Michel, "Vodou in Haiti," 30.
96. Casimir, *The Haitians*, 294.
97. Eddins, *Rituals, Runaways*, 2.
98. Casimir, *The Haitians*, 294.
99. Fouchard, *The Haitian Maroons*, 104; Eddins, *Rituals, Runaways*, 20; Casimir, *The Haitians*, 294.
100. Casimir, *The Haitians*, 294.
101. Trouillot, *Stirring the Pot*, 52–53.
102. Trouillot, *Stirring the Pot*, 52–53.

103. See Casimir, *The Haitians*, 9. Casimir describes slave-making thusly: "The slave owners gained fleeting control over the Africans who were hunted and captured. But it lasted only as long as the surprise and panic created by the unbelievable experience of becoming merchandise to be trafficked. The proof is that once this initial surprise and fright had passed, the slave traders could never for a moment stop using torture or the threat of torture to terrorize their prey. The modern colonial state and its protégés took charge of making the control over the captured person permanent, and of making its conversion of a human being into merchandise seem normal and natural. By terrorizing the sufferers it had kidnapped, the French colonial empire imposed its society, way of life, language, religion, customs, history, and laws. It presented them as the only legitimate and rational forms of life, the only ones worthy of being adopted by human beings. It demanded these be embraced by those who wanted to escape the bestial condition in which its own social engineering had imprisoned them with consummate artistry;" see Casimir, *The Haitians*, 268. Both Trouillot and Casimir contend that the brutal transformation of Africans into slaves was physically violent and legislatively violent, citing "the institutionalized cruelty of the *Code Noir*," which outlined the condition and treatment of captives in French overseas colonies; Casimir, *The Haitians*, 273. See Trouillot, *Stirring the Pot*, 18.
104. Toni Pressley-Sanon, "Of Bosal and Kongo: Exploring the Evolution of the Vernacular in Contemporary Haiti," *Ufahamu: A Journal of African Studies* 41, no. 1 (2018): 56.
105. Ekine, "Haiti Vodou."
106. See Downs, "Despite Reports."
107. See Sylvia Wynter's extensive scholarship on knowledge, coloniality and new world building as articulated in these essays (among others), "Columbus and the Poetics of the *Propter Nos*," *Annals of Scholarship: An International Quarterly in the Humanities and Social Sciences* 8, no. 2 (Spring 1991): 251–86, "Columbus, the Ocean Blue, and Fables that Stir the Mind," in *Poetics of the Americas: Race, Founding and Textuality*, ed. Bainard Cohen and Jefferson Humphries (Baton Rouge: Louisiana State University Press, 1992) 141–64 and "1492: A New World View," In *Race, Discourse, and the Origin of the Americas: A New World View*, ed. Lawrence Hyatt Vera and Rex Nettleford (Washington, DC: Smithsonian Institution Press, 1995), 5–57.
108. Glissant, *Caribbean Discourse*, *Caribbean Discourse: Selected Essays*, trans. J. Michael Dash (Charlottesville: University of Virginia Press, 1989), 2n1.
109. See Chelsea Steiber, *Haiti's Paper War: Post Independence Writing, Civil War, and the Making of the Republic, 1804–1954* (New York: New York University Press, 2020), 259.
110. Armando García, "Freedom as Praxis: Migdalia Cruz's Fur and the Emancipation of Caliban's Woman," *Modern Drama* 59, no. 3 (2016), 359.

111. Walsh, "Pedagogical Notes"; emphasis in original.
112. Walsh, "Pedagogical Notes."
113. Lugones, *Pilgrimages/Peregrinajes*, 29.
114. Walsh, "Pedagogical Notes"; Avery Gordon, *Ghostly Matters: Haunting and the Sociological Imagination* (Minneapolis: University of Minnesota Press, 1997), 5.
115. Avery Gordon, *Ghostly Matters*, 5.
116. Tiffany Lethabo King, Jenell Navarro, and Andrea Smith "Beyond Incommensurability: Toward an Otherwise Stance On Black and Indigenous Relationality," in *Otherwise Worlds: Against Settler Colonialism and Anti-Blackness*, ed. Tiffany Lethabo King, Jenell Navarro, Andrea Smith (Durham, NC: Duke University Press, 2020), 8.
117. Macharia, "Not This. More That!," *The New Inquiry*, July 23, 2018, https://thenewinquiry.com/blog/not-this-more-that.
118. Refusal, as a practice and politic, has an extensive history in Black and Native communities in the Americas. I cannot address this history here but works like Tina Campt's *Image Matters: Archive, Photography and the African Diaspora in Europe* (Durham, NC: Duke University Press, 2012) and *Listening to Images* (Durham, NC: Duke University Press, 2017) as well as Audra Simpson's *Mohawk Interruptions: Political Life Across Borders of Settler States* (Durham, NC: Duke University Press, 2014) offer sound primers to Black studies and Native studies approaches to this history. For Macharia, see "Not This. More That!"
119. Casimir, "A Decolonial History of the Haitians," Lecture, Brooklyn College: Celebrating the Battle of Vertières Beyond Vertières, Friday, November 16, 2018, 18.
120. Madiou, *Histoire d'Haiti*, 1:v.
121. Casimir, *The Haitians*, xix.
122. What comes to mind is bell hooks's idea that "love is a practice of freedom," an ethic that secures liberation by channeling the critical impulses of minds and hearts; see "Love as Practice of Freedom," in *Outlaw Culture: Resisting Representations* (New York: Routledge, 2006), 248. Cherríe Moraga's consideration of bodily politics is also relevant, namely, the idea that political practices work as "theory in the flesh," shaped by desires, environments, and our capacities to feel our way toward radicalization and a liberatory politics; see *This Bridge Called My Back: Writings by Radical Women of Color* (New York: Kitchen Table, Women of Color Press, 1983) 23. Chela Sandoval's "decolonial praxis of love" is also pertinent. She defines the latter as an "attraction . . . and relation carved out of and in spite of difference." See Chela Sandoval, *Methodology of the Oppressed* (Minneapolis: University of Minnesota Press, 2000) 187. Lastly, Lugones's discussion of "playfulness" is equally applicable as she describes the latter as a loving relationality that in being open to the unknown expands how people envision and move against oppressive power; see *Pilgrimages/Peregrinajes*, 26–27

123. Madiou, *Histoire d'Haiti*, 1:v.
124. Walter Mignolo, "Coloniality: The Darker Side of Modernity," in *Modernologies: Contemporary Artists Researching Modernity and Modernism, Catalog of the Exhibit at the Museum of Modern Art, Barcelona, Spain*, ed. C. S. Breitwisser (Barcelona: MACBA, 2009), 46.
125. Lugones, *Pilgrimages/Peregrinajes*, 7.
126. The ruling terms included are Dessalines's (1804–1806), Pétion's (1807–1818), André Rigaud's (1810–1811), and Christophe's (1807–1820), coupled with the first seven years of Jean-Pierre Boyer's twenty-five-year governance (1818–1843).
127. Boyer agreed to pay a ninety-million-franc indemnity to France for their lost "properties." Today, that number would be an estimated twenty-one billion US dollars. See Alex Dupuy, "Haiti and the Indemnity Question," *University of Miami Inter-American Law Review*, 55, no.1 (December 2023): 114. This liability, as well as others incurred by the Haitian state, effectively indebted the nation and its peoples. By 1914, eighty percent of Haiti's governmental budget went to France. See Laurent Dubois, *Haiti: The Aftershocks of History* (New York: Picador Books, 2012), 8. The decision to agree to the indemnity was not unanimous and, as Casimir notes, Boyer's acceptance of it signaled a deep fracture in the revolutionary struggle. The republican faction of the creole vanguard, which Boyer belonged to, had succeeded in consolidating state power in their hands and they were eager to "maintain colonial policy" in post-independence Haiti. See Casimir, *The Haitians*, 8. This policy entailed repressing the sovereignty of the people, which necessitated viewing them as unfit to rule themselves and equally unfit to be citizens worthy of recognizable rights.
128. In the early twentieth century, artists and intellectuals from the Caribbean and the United States rethought how they knew Africa. Haiti's peasant culture, as well as Vodou-inspired folklore and dance, became an object of interest, inspiring Melville J. Herskovitz's *Life in a Haitian Valley* (New York: Knopf, 1937), James Leyburn's *The Haitian People* (New Haven: Yale University Press, 1941), Zora Neale Hurston's *Tell My Horse* (Philadelphia: J. B. Lippincott, 1938) and Katherine Dunham's *Island Possessed* (New York: Doubleday, 1969).
129. *The Black Jacobins* inspired the organizers of the 1976 Carifesta Forum, a Caribbean studies conference held in the region. The 1976 meeting was attended by writers and thinkers from throughout the Americas like Merle Hodge (Grenada), Robin Dobru (Suriname), Wilson Harris (Guyana), René Marques (Puerto Rico), Gabriel Garcia Marquéz (Columbia), Glissant (Martinique), Octavio Paz (Mexico), Césaire (Martinque), Derek Walcott (Saint Lucia), Roberto Fernández Retamar (Cuba), Sylvia Wynter (Cuba and Jamaica), Kamau Brathwaite (Barbados), George Lamming (Barbados), Nicolás Guillén (Cuba), Jan Carew (Guyana), James (Trinidad), Naipaul (Trinidad), Rex Nettleford (Jamaica), René Depéstre (Haiti), Gordon Rohlehr (Guyana), and Denis Williams (Guyana), among many others. It culminated in an edited

collection that opened with the poignant sentence, "History is the angel with whom all we Caribbean Jacobs have to wrestle, sooner or later, if we hope for a blessing." Jamaican novelist John Hearne authored this line and, with it, called attention to both the conference's subject matter (history) and to the importance of Haiti (via James) to the Caribbean's sense of self. See John Hearne, "Singular and Collective Securities: An Introduction to Carifesta Forum," in *Carifesta Forum: An Anthology of 20 Caribbean Voices*, ed. John Hearne (Kingston: Institute of Jamaica, 1976), vii.

130. See Maryse Condé, "Sketching a Literature from the French Antilles: From Negritude to Creolite," in *Sisyphus and Eldorado: Magical and Other Realisms in Caribbean Literature*, ed. Timothy Reiss (Trenton, NJ: African World Press, 2002), 222.

131. Following the fiscal deterioration occasioned by the indemnity and other debts incurred by the Haitian state, the state became politically unstable. A series of coups was used as pretext by the United States to invade the nation and stabilize a politically fraught situation. The US would seize control of the nation's treasury, create infrastructure for its commercial interests and place Haitian politicians more amenable to their oversight into positions of power. These actions would shift the course of Haiti's trajectory and most notably lead to the dispossession of the folk majority. The US would not only revise Haiti's constitution to allow foreigner ownership of Haitian land, but it paved the way for US corporations to buy land; both actions displaced rural peoples. This displacement began in earnest during the Occupation but was compounded in the years after the rise of the Duvaliers, father François Duvalier (1957–1971), and then son, Jean Claude (1971–1986). It was under Jean Claude's regime that the folk would begin to leave Haiti in 1972 by boat for the US. Middle- to upper-class Haitians had already begun to leave by plane in the 1950s under his father's rule. For more on US imperialism and Haitian migration by sea, see Paul Farmer, *The Uses of Haiti* (Monroe, ME: Common Courage Press, 1994).

132. Aimé Césaire, "Notebook of a Return to the Native Land," in *Aime Cesaire: The Collected Poetry*, trans. Clayton Eshleman and Annette Smith (Berkeley: University of California Press, 1983), 47.

133. Morrison, "Playing in the Dark: Whiteness and the Literary Imagination," in *Racism in America: A Reader* (Cambridge, MA: Harvard University Press, 2020), 9.

134. Walsh, "Pedagogical Notes."

135. *Chapô ba*, "hats off."

136. Yomaira C. Figueroa-Vásquez, *Decolonizing Diasporas: Radical Mappings of Afro-Atlantic Literature* (Evanston, IL: Northwestern University Press, 2020), 15.

137. Wynter, "The Pope Must Have Been Drunk, the King of Castile a Madman," in *The Reordering of Culture: Latin America, The Caribbean and Canada in the*

Hood, ed. Alvina Ruprecht and Celicia Taiania (Ottawa: Carleton University Press, 1995), 35.
138. Nelson Maldonado-Torres, "The Topology of Being and the Geopolitics of Knowledge: Modernity, Empire, Coloniality," *City* 8, no. 1 (2004): 10.
139. Maldonado-Torres, "The Topology of Being," 10.
140. Maldonado-Torres, "The Topology of Being," 10.
141. James reimagines Louverture as Hamlet-like in *The Black Jacobins*. He also draws from Enlightenment discourse's interest in the idea of an avenging Black Spartacus when writing his history. I discuss the consequences of James's likening of Louverture to Hamlet and his reading of the Revolution through Enlightenment thought in Chapter 1 of this book. For a thorough examination of Louverture's figuration as a Black Spartacus in Caribbean cultural production, see Grégory Pierrot's *The Black Avenger in Atlantic Culture* (Athens: University of Georgia Press), 2019.
142. Nelson Maldonado-Torres, "On the Coloniality of Being," 243.
143. Lisa Lowe, *The Intimacies of Four Continents* (Durham, NC: Duke University Press, 2015), 6.
144. Carpentier, *The Kingdom of This World*, 184.
145. McKittrick, *Dear Science*, 38.
146. McKittrick, *Dear Science*, 44.
147. McKittrick, *Dear Science*, 44.
148. McKittrick, *Dear Science*, 46.
149. McKittrick, *Dear Science*, 46.
150. See McKittrick, *Dear Science*, 46. What comes to the mind is the closing scene of the film and the promise of the return of T'Challa, the deceased Black Panther, through his son who is named after Louverture and who resides hidden in plain sight in Haiti.
151. McKittrick, *Dear Science*, 41.
152. Figueroa, *Prophetic Visions of the Past*, 23.
153. Figueroa, *Prophetic Visions of the Past*, 23. See Víctor Figueroa, *Prophetic Visions of the Past*; J. Michael Dash, *The Other America: Caribbean Literature in a New World Context* (Charlottesville: University of Virginia Press, 1998); Mariana Past, "Toussaint on Trial in 'Ti Difé Boulé Sou Istoua Ayiti,' or the People's Role in the Haitian Revolution," *Journal of Haitian Studies* 10, no. 1 (2004): 87–102; Deborah Jensen, *Beyond the Slave Narrative: Politics, Sex, and Manuscripts in the Haitian Revolution* (Liverpool: Liverpool University Press, 2012); Joan Dayan, *Haiti, History, and the Gods*; Nick Nesbitt, *Universal Emancipation: The Haitian Revolution and the Radical Enlightenment* (Charlottesville: University of Virginia Press, 2008); and Paul B. Miller, "Enlightened Hesitations: Black Masses and Tragic Heroes in C. L. R. James's *The Black Jacobins*," *MLN* 116, no. 5 (2001): 1069–90.

154. Cedric J. Robinson, *Black Marxism: The Making of the Black Radical Tradition* (Chapel Hill: University of North Carolina Press, 2000), 171.
155. See VèVè Clark, "Haiti's Tragic Overture: Statecraft and Stagecraft in Plays by Glissant, Trouillot, and Césaire." Unpublished paper read at the Annual Meeting of the Caribbean Studies Association, Basse Terre, St. Kitts-Nevis, May 28–31, 1984; Jeremy Matthew Glick, *The Black Radical Tragic: Performance, Aesthetics, and the Unfinished Haitian Revolution* (New York: New York University Press, 2016); Karen Salt, *The Unfinished Revolution: Haiti, Black Sovereignty and Power in the Nineteenth-Century Atlantic World* (Liverpool: Liverpool University Press, 2019); and Tammie Jenkins, *The Haitian Revolution, the Harlem Renaissance, and Caribbean Négritude: Overlapping Discourses of Freedom and Identity* (New York: Lexington Books, 2021).
156. Doris L. Garraway, "'Légitime Defense': Universalism and Nationalism in the Discourse of the Haitian Revolution," in *Tree of Liberty: Cultural Legacies of the Haitian Revolution in the Atlantic World*, ed. Doris L. Garraway (Charlottesville: University of Virginia Press, 2008), 63–65.
157. See Garraway, *The Libertine Colony: Creolization in the Early French Caribbean* (Durham, NC: Duke University Press, 2005), Daut, *Tropics of Haiti*; Valerie Kaussen, *Migrant Revolutions: Haitian Literature, Globalization, and U.S. Imperialism* (Lanham, MD: Lexington Books, 2008); Charles Forsdick, "The Traveling Revolutionary: Situating Toussaint Louverture," in *Reinterpreting the Haitian Revolution and Its Cultural Aftershocks*, ed. Martin Munro and Elizabeth Walcott-Hackshaw (Kingston: University of West Indies Press, 2006), 150–67; Chris Bongie, *Friends and Enemies: The Scribal Politics of Post/Colonial Literature* (Liverpool: Liverpool University Press, 2009); Elizabeth Walcott-Hackshaw and Martin Munro, *Reinterpreting the Haitian Revolution and Its Cultural Aftershocks* (Kingston: University of the West Indies Press, 2006), John Patrick Walsh, *Free and French in the Caribbean: Toussaint Louverture, Aimé Césaire, and Narratives of Loyal Opposition* (Bloomington: Indiana University Press, 2013); Chelsea Stieber, *Haiti's Paper War*; and A. James Arnold "Recuperating the Haitian Revolution in Literature: From Victor Hugo to Derek Walcott," in *Tree of Liberty: Cultural legacies of the Haitian Revolution in the Atlantic World*, ed. Doris L. Garraway (Charlottesville: University of Virginia Press, 2008).
158. Philip Kaisary, *The Haitian Revolution in the Literary Imagination: Radical Horizons, Conservative Constraints* (Charlottesville: University of Virginia Press, 2014); Victor Figueroa's *Prophetic Visions of the Past: Pan-Caribbean Representations of the Haitian Revolution* (Columbus: Ohio State University Press, 2015); and Jeremy Matthew Glick's *The Black Radical Tragic*.
159. Stieber, *Haiti's Paper War*, 259.
160. Stieber, *Haiti's Paper War*, 259.
161. Daut, *Tropics of Haiti*; and Arnold, "Recuperating."

162. Michel-Rolph Trouillot's keystone anthropological work on the Revolution in *Silencing the Past: Power and the Production of History* importantly outlines the long tradition of "silencing" (or trivializing) the Revolution in the West. The literary scholarship of Sibylle Fischer in *Modernity Disavowed: Haiti and the Cultures of Slavery in the Age of Revolution* (Durham, NC: Duke University Press, 2004) and Daut in *Tropics of Haiti* respectively addresses the custom of disavowing the formative influence of its "radical politics of anti-slavery" to Western modernity and the racialist sense-making practices that dominated discussions of the Revolution during the revolutionary moment.

163. Casimir, *The Haitians*, 256.

164. Republican *affranchis* were mostly from the South of Saint Domingue, an area where "the mulattoes [*gens de couleur*] . . . were slave-holding property owners, and . . . were . . . more numerous than the whites." More strikingly, the "slave population [in the South had a] near-total absence of mulatto slaves," unlike the North of Saint Domingue, which is to say, Blackness immediately denoted a captive status in the region. Because of the region's distinct demographics, captives there could more readily "see . . . that the mulatto owners were no less a class enemy than their white masters," which did not bode well for new class relations in independent Haiti. See Fick, *The Making of Haiti*, 153. For more on the tensions between captives and *affranchis* of the South see Fick, *The Making of Haiti*, 185–86, 187–88.

165. Leslie Manigat, *Éventail d'Histoire Vivante d'Haïti: Des préludes à la révolution de Saint Domingue jusqu' à nos jours* (1789–2007), 5 vols. (Port-au-Prince: Collection du CHUDAC, 2001), 1:311. See also Casimir, *The Haitians*, 270. Republican revolutionists were "primarily former [André] Rigaudins from the South who had fought against Toussaint in the War of Knives, among them Alexandre Pétion, Nicolas Geffrard, Laurent Férou, Jean-Louis François, Elie Gérin, Guy Joseph Bonnet, Bruno Blanche, David Troy, Yayou, and Guillaume Vaval," writes Stieber; see *Haiti's Paper War*, 23–24. André Rigaud was born in Saint Domingue to a captive African mother and a French colonist, but he was raised primarily in France. Trouillot writes that when he returned to Saint Domingue, he "got involved in the camp of mulatto plantation owners, and from then on, never stopped defending the *ancien libres* and the new French government." See Trouillot, *Stirring the Pot*, 99–100. In other words, he "never stopped defending" *affranchis* with means, *gens de couleur* primarily, and the first republic of France (1792–1804). His forces fought against Louverture's northern armies during the "War of the South," otherwise known as the "War of Knives," which was waged between June 1799 and July 1800 with Louverture prevailing. For more on this conflict, see Trouillot, *Stirring the Pot*, 91–117, and Fick, *The Making of Haiti*, 199–203. What bears stressing here is that Rigaudins "believed that the interests of the Republic (the new government in France) were joined to the interests of the *ancient libres* in Saint Domingue." Trouillot, *Stirring the*

Pot, 100. This conviction explains why "many *ancient libres* threw themselves into the French camp, into the camp of the revolution's enemy," after the battle's end and Rigaud absconded to France. Trouillot, *Stirring the Pot*, 114. They maintained this conviction after the battle's end because "France had given them an education. The French Revolution had made them equal to whites, and the Republic had given them ranks," writes Trouillot, and "so long as France didn't bother them in the South [of Saint Domingue], they were shouting: Long Live France." See *Stirring the Pot*, 100.

166. See Casimir, *The Haitians*, 70. Many who left after the Revolution returned to Haiti between 1815 and 1816, when the South of Haiti was governed as a republic, and they were joined by other "traveling republican revolutionaries from all nations," notably, Símon Bolívar. See Stieber, *Haiti's Paper War*, 94–98.

167. See Jean Casimir and Mary Claypool, "Going Backwards Toward the Future: From Haiti to Saint Domingue," *The Global South* 6, no. 1 (Spring 2012): 184. *Affranchi* revolutionists who had fought for the French faced enslavement and death as the Revolution intensified alongside captive people fighting to realize Haiti. Yet even with this experience, many remained republicans and French oriented. The previously mentioned *gens de couleur*, Vastey, who reinvented himself as an African, does not describe Haiti's first liberal democratic president, the mixed-race *gens de couleur* Pétion, as a "Haytian ... despite of himself" because Pétion is the political rival of the Black revolutionist-turned-monarch Christophe, who Vastey serves as scribe; rather, he describes him thusly because Pétion had not radically shifted his thinking and his allegiances to the African and Africanized peoples of Haiti, yet he served as their leader (in the South). Pétion was not the only republican revolutionary like this. It took the republican leaders of the South of Saint Domingue, an area which remained a republican stronghold throughout Dessalines's rule, significantly longer to agree to cede the Revolution's control to Dessalines. The Congress of Archaie united the creole vanguard under Dessalines in May of 1803, joining Louverture's former generals with Rigaud's. But it was not until July of 1803 that the Southern region agreed to join Dessalines. Dessalines labeled them "mauvais indigènes" or "bad Haitians," because of their reluctance to join him and because of their political maneuverings against him during his tenure as emperor. See Madiou, *Histoire d'Haiti*, 3:276. Vastey, in turn, builds from Dessalines to suggest that Pétion is a "Haytian ... despite of himself" because of his republican politics. For Vastey's slight against Pétion, see *An Essay on the Causes of the Revolution and Civil Wars of Hayti: Being a Sequel to the Political Remarks upon Certain French Publications and Journals Concerning Hayti*, trans. William Hamilton (Exeter: Western Luminary Office, 1823) 161.

168. The republican rebellion against Dessalines began on October 6, 1806, with a staged insurrection in the South. It was led by Pétion, Gérin, Yayou, Vaval, and Bonnet and culminated eleven days later with his death. Two Haitis would

initially exist in the period of civil war that followed Dessalines's liquidation: in 1807, Christophe presided over the north and Pétion the south. Three years into Pétion's rule, Rigaud returns to Haiti from France and leads a secessionist movement that expropriated territory from Pétion in 1810. He would independently govern this territory for a year until his death in 1811. Pétion reseized this territory and in 1812 created a liberal democratic republic (in theory) and named himself president (for life). Christophe adopted a constitutional monarchy with hereditary transmission of power in 1811 and would govern this region until 1820. When Pétion died in 1818, Boyer became president of the republican south; he later united Haiti under his command in 1820 following Christophe's suicide and ruled Haiti as a republic.

169. Republicans were reformists, who thought they could work within the colonial system, which meant they did not question its beliefs. This resulted in an unthinking anti-African sensibility. They were so Eurocentric and prejudiced against Africans that their descendants in Haiti's twentieth-century elite regarded the term "African" as "the most humiliating insult." See Jean Price Mars, *Ainsi parla l'oncle* (Haiti: Imprimerie De Compiegne, 1954), ii. It is true that their resistance against slavery and white supremacy resulted in practical efforts to see the rights of man extended to Africans. (One need only recall Pétion's aid of arms and soldiers to the republican revolutionist Símon Bolívar. He agreed to assist Bolívar only if Bolívar agreed to abolish slavery and return any African captives seized in the Caribbean to Haiti, where they would be freed.) But it is also true that that they "based their demands for civil and political rights on the *Code Noir*" and thus on the colonial right to conquer the vanquished other. See Casimir, *The Haitians*, 198, 62. They "didn't demand rights for Africans" when in power, writes Casimir, "given that they were planning on trampling those of the Haitian masses in a similar way," 198.

170. Casimir, *The Haitians*, 198, 64; Trouillot, *Stirring the Pot*, 100.
171. Dayan, *Haiti, History and the Gods*, 19.
172. Pierrot, *Black Avenger*, 126.
173. Walsh, "Pedagogical Notes." Supporters of Dessalines varied in class and race. They included Juste Chanlatte, who served as Dessalines's scribe, and prominent *affranchis*, former captives as well as French clergymen. Stieber names the following persons: "Louis Félix Mathurin Boisrond Tonnerre, Louis Laurent Bazelais, Jean-J. Dominque Diaquoi (Diaquoi Aînè), . . . Carbonne[,] Alexis Dupuy, Jean-Jacques Chaéron, Joseph Balthazar Inginac, François Capois (Cappoix), Corneille Brelle . . . Etienne Victor Mentor and Charles Victor Rouanez." See Steiber, *Haiti's Paper War*, 24.
174. Stieber, *Haiti's Paper War*, 5.
175. Stieber, *Haiti's Paper War*, 5. This *Ginen* idea meant that the African's condition of freedom was of the utmost importance to Dessalines. The African could not simply be free from slavery but he felt that she must also have the

means to thrive in freedom. He famously stated, "And the poor blacks whose fathers are in Africa . . . will they have nothing," and went on to ensure they had something by confiscating the land from his political peers, who had amassed plantations throughout the Revolution. Historian Louis Janvier confirms his commitment to improving the lived existence of Africans when writing that Dessalines "wanted to make the genuine independence of the peasant possible by making him an owner of land." See Janvier, *Les Constitutions d'Haiti (1801–1885)* (Paris: Marpon et Flam-marion, 1886), 1: 43. Dessalines is quoted in J.C Dorsainvil, *Manuel d'histoire d'Haïti* (Port-au-Prince: Procure des Frères de l'instruction chrétienne, 1934), 147. See Trouillot, *Stirring the Pot,* for a discussion of the creole vanguard's practice of seizing land throughout the Revolution, 83–86; and see Casimir for the Fanonian nature of Dessalines's style of governance, *The Haitians,* 17.

176. As proponents of political liberalism, republicans stressed "individual rights, political equality and the active contestation of any arbitrary government" (save their own). See Stieber, *Haiti's Paper War,* 4. They regarded any governmental control of "individual rights" as despotic. Dessalines and his supporters were weary of rights discourse, which was overwhelmingly used by colonists to support their right to enslave Africans and the African descended in Saint Domingue. What's more, they viewed political liberalism and rights discourse as a colonial inheritance, one that was given to them and tied to an epistemological framework that could not denote the specific nature of their liberation effort. They astutely realized that liberalism could not realize a political project conducive to safeguarding their liberation as a collective from the colonizer's return in thought or by way of physical occupation. They chose, instead, to stress collectivism under a leader who could ensure that liberty was protected for all Haitians, not simply the moneyed or propertied, as is often the case in states that adhere to political liberalism.

177. Stieber, *Haiti's Paper War,* 1.
178. Stieber, *Haiti's Paper War,* 49.
179. Stieber, *Haiti's Paper War,* 4–10, 259.
180. Carpentier does not explicitly engage republicanism in his novella. However, he does excise Dessalines from the post-independence period that he treats extensively; he also maligns Christophe's governance in that period. These choices intimate Carpentier's understanding of a successful Haitian Revolution as necessarily being "a radical, liberal universal revolution," to borrow from Stieber, because of who among the Revolution's vanguard he foregrounds, absents, or acknowledges. Stieber, *Haiti's Paper War,* 1. Furthermore, the fact that Louverture makes a passing appearance in the novella, when the Revolution is on the horizon and full of promise, corroborates the republican subtext of the narrative, as Louverture is the face of a republican understanding of the Revolution for persons outside of Haiti.

181. Dessalines's concern for the suffering and rights of Africans was echoed by his successor in northern Haiti, Christophe. He and his renowned secretary, Vastey, "believed that it was impossible to speak about the rights of Haitians while ignoring that of Africans," which resulted in legislation that protected the African peoples of post independent Haiti. See Casimir, *The Haitians*, 198. For more on Christophe and republican indifference to *Ginen* suffering, see Casimir, *The Haitians*, 168, 196, 204, and 316. Yet like Dessalines, Christophe is routinely depicted as a maniacal despot, a reading that ignores how concern for Africans yielded decolonizing thought and action.
182. See Walcott, "What the Twilight Says," in *What the Twilight Says: Essays* (New York: Farrar, Straus & Giroux, 1998), 11.
183. See Lambert, *Comrade Sister: Caribbean Feminist Revisions of the Grenada Revolution* (Charlottesville: University of Virginia Press, 2020).
184. See Forsdick, "The Traveling Revolutionary"; Aravamudan, *Tropicopolitans: Colonialism and Agency, 1688–1804* (Durham, NC: Duke University Press, 1999); Miller, "Enlightened Hesitations"; Nesbitt, *Universal Emancipation*; Jenson, *Beyond the Slave Narrative*; and Daut, *Tropics of Haiti*.
185. See Casimir, *The Haitians*; and Casimir, Colon, and Koerner, "Haiti's Need for a Great South," *The Global South* 5, no. 1 (2011): 14–36; Neelam Srivastava, "Anticolonial Violence and the 'Dictatorship of the Truth' in the Films of Gillo Pontecorvo: An Interview," *Interventions: International Journal of Postcolonial Studies* 7, no. 1 (2005), 97–106; and Neelam Srivastava, *Italian Colonialism and Resistances to Empire, 1930–1970* (London: Palgrave Macmillan UK, 2018).
186. See Dayan, *Haiti, History and the Gods*; and Jana Evans Braziel, "Re-membering Défilée: Dédée Bazile as Revolutionary Lieu de Mémoire," *Small Axe* 9, no. 2 (2005): 57–85.
187. Mariame Kaba, *We Do This 'til We Free Us: Abolitionist Organizing and Transforming Justice* (Chicago: Haymarket Books, 2021), 26–27.

Chapter 1

1. See Michel-Rolph Trouillot, *Silencing the Past: Power and the Production of History* (Boston: Beacon Press, 1995). 156.
2. For more on the discredited asset, see Marc Prigg, "Shipwreck Found Off Haiti Was NOT the Santa Maria, the Ship Columbus Used to Discover the Americas," *Daily Mail*, October 6, 2014, http://www.dailymail.co.uk/sciencetech/article-2782747/Shipwreck-Haiti-NOT-Santa-Maria-ship-Columbus-used-discover-Americas.html.
3. See Columbus's famous letter to the financier of his first voyage, Luis de Santángel. See "Letter to Santangel" in *The Voyages of Christopher Columbus, Being the Journals of his First and Third, and the Letters Concerning his First and Last Voyages, to Which is Added the Account of his Second Voyage Written by*

Andres Bernaldez, trans. and ed. Cecil Jane (London: Argonaut Press, 1930). http://eada.lib.umd.edu/text-entries/columbus-letter-to-santangel.
4. Manthia Diawara, director. *Edouard Glissant: One World in Relation*. K'a Yelema Productions, 2010. 51 mins. https://video-alexanderstreet-com.libproxy.temple.edu/watch/edouard-glissant-one-world-in-relation, 4:06 to 6:43.
5. Diawara, *Edouard Glissant*, 5:56 to 6:03.
6. Diawara, *Edouard Glissant*, 5:56 to 6:03.
7. Lambert, *Comrade Sister*, 4.
8. Lambert, *Comrade Sister* 4.
9. David Scott, "The Re-enchantment of Humanism: An Interview with Sylvia Wynter," *Small Axe* 8 no. 2 (2000), 174.
10. Scott, "The Re-enchantment of Humanism," 174.
11. Scott, "The Re-enchantment of Humanism," 174.
12. Scott, "The Re-enchantment of Humanism," 174.
13. Diawara, *Édouard Glissant*, 6:08 to 6:43.
14. Diawara, *Édouard Glissan*, 6:35.
15. Glissant, *Caribbean Discourse: Selected Essays*, trans. J. Michael Dash, 2n1.
16. Diawara, *Édouard Glissant*, 6:43.
17. Glissant, *Poetics of Relation*, trans. Betty Wing (Ann Arbor: University of Michigan Press, 2006), 9.
18. Glissant, *Caribbean Discourse*, 2n1.
19. Maldonado-Torres, "On the Coloniality of Being," 245; emphasis in original.
20. Maldonado-Torres, "On the Coloniality of Being," 245; emphasis in original.
21. Diawara, *Édouard Glissant*. 6:03 to 6:43; emphasis added.
22. Casimir, *The Haitians*, 186.
23. Scott, "The Re-enchantment of Humanism," 174.
24. "We have not forgotten."
25. James, *The Black Jacobins*, 196–97.
26. James, *The Black Jacobins*; emphasis added.
27. Carolyn E. Fick, *The Making of Haiti*, 162. Hazareesingh, *Black Spartacus: The Epic Life of Toussaint Louverture* (New York: Farrar, Straus and Giroux, 2020), 99.
28. Trouillot, *Stirring the Pot*, 58; emphasis in original. Trouillot writes that the popular call, *"koupe tèt boulé kay,"* "was like the former maroons' rallying cry [of freedom, which erupted in collective contestations in 1691, 1703, 1704, 1775 and 1778], but instead of freedom meaning flight, for slaves in 1791, in the North especially [where Louverture rose in prominence], freedom meant fighting," 58; emphasis in original.
29. Trouillot, *Stirring the Pot*, 58.
30. Trouillot, *Stirring the Pot*, 56. Casimir, *The Haitians*, 256.
31. Hazareesingh, *Black Spartacus*, 68. The South and West areas of Saint Domingue had fewer large-scale plantations and were not as densely populated with captive peoples, in particular African-born captives. These factors

and its mountainous topography meant that marronage remained a better option versus fighting for a longer period of time. See Trouillot, *Stirring the Pot*, 59–60. However, even as that was the case, captives in the South and West did organize themselves and created important antislavery resistance movements, which historian Carolyn E. Fick extensively details in *The Making of Haiti*, see 137–203.

32. Trouillot, *Stirring the Pot*, 50. See also Hazareesingh's discussion of the captive populace's absorption of republican ideas, *Black Spartacus*, 75–76.
33. Trouillot, *Stirring the Pot*, 50. For African martial experience and its importance to the success of the Revolution, see John Thornton's essay, "'I Am the Subject of the King of Congo': African Political Ideology and the Haitian Revolution," *Journal of World History* 4, no. 2 (1993): 181–214.
34. Trouillot, *Stirring the Pot*, 56. For Casimir's discussion of the radicalism inherent in Kreyòl and Vodou, see *The Haitians*, 212, 228, 256, 297, 304. For Hazareesingh's discussion, see *Black Spartacus*, 68–69, 62–65.
35. Hazareesingh, *Black Spartacus*, 99.
36. Hazareesingh, *Black Spartacus*, 62. See also Fouchard, *The Haitian Maroons*, 321.
37. Hazareesingh, *Black Spartacus*, 64.
38. Trouillot, *Stirring the Pot*, 64.
39. Trouillot, *Stirring the Pot*, 81.
40. The rebel leaders Trouillot cites Louverture as abandoning include Jean-François and George Biassou, who "stayed in the Spanish camp" when Louverture and his group left. They framed their resistance in particularistic terms, as a means to secure liberation for themselves, their families, their soldiers and their soldiers' families alone. Trouillot, *Stirring the Pot*, 81.
41. Trouillot, *Stirring the Pot*, 81.
42. Trouillot, *Stirring the Pot*, 90.
43. Trouillot, *Stirring the Pot*, 90.
44. Trouillot, *Stirring the Pot*, 90.
45. James, *The Black Jacobins*, 198.
46. Madison Smartt Bell, *Toussaint Louverture* (New York: First Vintage Books, 2008), 83. Hazareesingh, *Black Spartacus*, 59.
47. Debien, "A propos du trésor de Toussaint Louverture," *Revue de la société d'histoire et géographie d'Haïti* 17, no. 62 (1946), 35.
48. Stewart King, "Toussaint L'Ouverture before 1791: Free Planter and Slave-Holder," *Journal of Haitian Studies* 3/4 (1997), 67–69.
49. Bell, *Toussaint Louverture*, 83.
50. Bell, *Toussaint Louverture*, 83.
51. Philippe Girard, *Toussaint Louverture: A Revolutionary Life* (New York: Basic Books, 2016) 24, 28.
52. Girard, *Toussaint Louverture*, 24.
53. Trouillot, *Stirring the Pot*, 100.

54. Trouillot, *Stirring the Pot*, 100. For more on Girard's conservative reading of the general, see Charles Forsdick and Christian Høgsbjerg, *Toussaint Louverture: A Black Jacobin in the Age of Revolutions* (London: Pluto Press, 2017), 7–10.
55. Bell, *Toussaint Louverture*, 78–79.
56. Forsdick and Høgsbjerg, *Toussaint Louverture*, 34.
57. Bell, *Toussaint Louverture*, 87.
58. See Carol Anderson, *White Rage: The Unspoken Truth of Our Racial Divide* (New York: Bloomsbury, 2016). Bell composed his biography during Obama's first election year in 2008 and Girard's during his second term as president (2013–2017). Historian Carol Anderson cites the Obama political moment as telling of the anti-Black conservatism or "white rage" that she argues follows Black social gains in the United States, since it engendered widespread anti-Blackness in political punditry, popular discourse, and academic production about Black peoples in and outside of the United States.
59. For more on Louverture's early life and his brief stint as an owner of captive persons see Forsdick and Høgsbjerg, *Toussaint Louverture*, 25; Philippe Girard, *Toussaint Louverture*, 54–55; and Hazareesingh, *Black Spartacus*, 44–69.
60. Forsdick and Høgsbjerg, *Toussaint Louverture*, 42.
61. Forsdick and Høgsbjerg, *Toussaint Louverture*, 24.
62. Girard, *Toussaint Louverture*, 44.
63. Hazareesingh, *Black Spartacus*, 60.
64. Alladan references "Toussaint's ancestral ethnic group" and it denotes the "African kingdom" of Allada located in present day Benin. See Hazareesingh, *Black Spartacus*, 20.
65. Hazareesingh, *Black Spartacus*, 51–55, 60.
66. Hazareesingh, *Black Spartacus*, 51.
67. Hazareesingh, *Black Spartacus*, 65.
68. Hazareesingh, *Black Spartacus*, 66.
69. Marlene L. Daut, *Baron de Vastey and the Origins of Black Atlantic Humanism* (New York: Palgrave Macmillan, 2017), 11.
70. Daut, *Baron de Vastey*, 11.
71. In 1798, Louverture began issuing edits "confin[ing] the blacks to the plantations under rigid penalties." He would release additional "proclamations" that James describes as "the propaganda of a dictatorship" in January and October of 1800 once he secured absolute dominion over the island of Hispaniola with the defeat of the Spanish, the pacification of the French, and the ousting of the British. See James, *The Black Jacobins*, 242, 247.
72. Girard, *Toussaint Louverture*, 24, 28.
73. Girard and Donnadieu, "Toussaint before Louverture: New Archival Findings on the Early Life of Toussaint Louverture," *The William and Mary Quarterly* 70, no. 1 (January 2013), 43, Girard, *Toussaint Louverture,* 72–3, Hazareesingh, *Black Spartacus*, 67.

74. James, *The Black Jacobins*, 197.
75. James, "Lectures on *The Black Jacobins*," *Small Axe* 8, no. 2 (2000), 108, 107.
76. James, "Lectures," 109.
77. James, "Lectures, 106; emphasis in original.
78. James, "Lectures," 106.
79. James, "Lectures," 108–9.
80. James, "Lectures,"106.
81. James, "Lectures," 73.
82. James, "Lectures," 84.
83. James, "Lectures," 84.
84. James, "Lectures," 84.
85. See the groundbreaking 1979 book by Michele Wallace, *Black Macho and the Myth of the Superwoman* (New York: Dial Press, 1979).
86. Belinda Edmondson, *Making Men: Gender, Literary Authority, and Women's Writing in Caribbean Narrative* (Durham, NC: Duke University Press, 1999), 30.
87. Edmondson, *Making Men*, 1.
88. Edmondson, *Making Men*, 5.
89. Edmondson, *Making Men* 6, 5.
90. Edmondson, *Making Men* 6.
91. Froude, *The English in the West Indies, or, The Bow of Ulysses* (London: Longmans, Green, and Co., 1888), 325.
92. Jonathan Connolly broadly outlines the revolt and its underlining causes when writing, "On October 11, 1865, a group of black Jamaicans armed with cutlasses and sticks approached the colonial courthouse at Morant Bay, on the southeastern side of the island. Their immediate grievance was the attempted arrest, the day before, of Paul Bogle, a Native Baptist preacher and social activist in the nearby community of Stony Gut. A set of social and political concerns also underlay their protest: increased taxation, widespread poverty, a lack of political representation, and a legal system dominated by planters' interests." See Connolly, "Re-Reading Morant Bay: Protest, Inquiry, and Colonial Rule," *Law and History Review* 41 (2023), 193–94. These "concerns" were the product of the crown's abandonment. The English freed the captives of Jamaica in 1838, compensated planters for their lost property and left captives to fend for themselves, while burdening them through "taxation" and policing.
93. Scott, "The Re-enchantment of Humanism," 174
94. James, *The Black Jacobins*, 198.
95. James, "Lectures," 73.
96. McKittrick, *Dear Science*, 44.
97. McKittrick, *Dear Science*, 46
98. James, *The Black Jacobins*, 198.
99. James, *Beyond the Boundary* (Durham, NC: Duke University Press, 2013), 7.
100. Makalani, "'West Indian Through and Through, and Very British': C. L. R. James's *Beyond a Boundary*, Coloniality, and Theorizing Caribbean Independence,"

in *Marxism, Colonialism, and Cricket: C. L. R. James's Beyond a Boundary*, ed. David Featherstone, Christopher Gair, Christian Høgsbjerg, and Andrew Smith (Durham, NC: Duke University Press, 2018), 92.
101. See Makalani, "'West Indian Through and Through,'" 90, 92, 96–98.
102. Makalani, "'West Indian Through and Through,'" 97.
103. Makalani, "'West Indian Through and Through,'" 98.
104. James, *The Black Jacobins*, 90.
105. James, *The Black Jacobins*, 91.
106. James, *The Black Jacobins*, 91.
107. James, *The Black Jacobins*, 91.
108. James, *The Black Jacobins*, 25.
109. Forsdick, "The Traveling Revolutionary," 151.
110. Daut, *Tropics of Haiti*, 50. For a thorough discussion of the "Enlightenment literacy narrative of the Haitian Revolution," see Daut, *Tropics of Haiti*, 49–72.
111. Deborah Jenson, *Beyond the Slave Narrative: Politics, Sex, and Manuscripts in the Haitian Revolution* (Liverpool: Liverpool University Press, 2012), 49.
112. Jenson, *Beyond the Slave Narrative*, 47.
113. Aravamudan, *Tropicopolitans: Colonialism and Agency, 1688–1804* (Durham, NC: Duke University Press, 1999), 303.
114. See James, *The Black Jacobins*, 24–25.
115. See Paul B. Miller, "Enlightened Hesitations," 1077.
116. Edmondson, *Making Men*, 6.
117. Edmondson, *Making Men*, 8.
118. James, *The Black Jacobins*, 260.
119. James, *The Black Jacobins*, 291.
120. James, *The Black Jacobins*, 290.
121. James, *The Black Jacobins*, 288.
122. See Kara Rabbitt, "C. L. R. James's Figuring of Toussaint Louverture: *The Black Jacobins* and the Literary Hero," in *C. L. R. James: His Intellectual Legacies*, ed. Selwyn R. Cudjoe and William E. Cain (Amherst: University of Massachusetts Press, 1995), 123.
123. See James, *The Black Jacobins*, 291.
124. James, "Lectures," 84.
125. See Hazareesingh, *Black Spartacus*, 33, 65, 109.
126. Troulliot, *Stirring the Pot*, 158; emphasis in original.
127. Troulliot, *Stirring the Pot*, 160; emphasis added.
128. Mariana F. Past, "Twin Pillars of Resistance: Vodou and Haitian Kreyòl in Michel-Rolph Trouillot's *Ti difé boulé sou istoua Ayiti* [Stirring the Pot of Haitian History]," *Latin American Literary Review* 48, no. 97 (2021), 46.
129. James, "Lectures," 107.
130. See Caitlin Schiller, "Ben Horowitz's Top 5 Books on Management," *Blinkest Magazine*, Sep. 16, 2014, https://www.blinkist.com/magazine/posts/ben-horowitzs-top-5-books.

131. See Alyssa Goldstein Sepinwall, "Beyond *The Black Jacobins*: Haitian Revolutionary Historiography Comes of Age," *Journal of Haitian Studies*, 23 no. 1 (2017), 5.
132. Sepinwall, "Beyond The Black Jacobins," 5.
133. See Stuart Hall, "David Scott," *BOMB Magazine*, no. 90 (Winter 2005), https://bombmagazine.org/articles/2005/01/01/david-scott.
134. Hall, "David Scott." For the saliency of the Grenadian Revolution to Scott's thoughts on anticolonial revolution, see his book *Omens of Adversity: Tragedy, Time, Memory and Justice* (Durham, NC: Duke University, 2014).
135. Scott's argument in *Conscripts of Modernity: The Tragedy of Colonial Enlightenment* (Durham, NC: Duke University Press, 2004) builds on his earlier *Refashioning Futures: Criticism after Postcoloniality* (Princeton, NJ: Princeton University Press, 1999). He also reiterates his argument in the essay "Tragedy's Time: Postemancipation Futures, Past and Present," in *Rethinking Tragedy*, ed. Rita Felski (Baltimore, MD: John Hopkins University Press, 2008), 199–217. I paraphrase and quote from each of these texts when addressing *Conscripts of Modernity*.
136. Scott, *Refashioning Futures*, 26.
137. For a nuanced reading of James's revision to the 1963 edition of *The Black Jacobins*, see Rachel Douglas, *Making the Black Jacobins: C. L. R James and the Drama of History* (Durham, NC: Duke University Press, 2019), 102–32.

   For the formative influence of Steiner's representation of tragedy and romance to Scott's work see Scott, *Conscripts of Modernity*, 134–35, and Scott's article, "Tragedy's Time," 201. In addition to Steiner, Scott is also heavily influenced by Hayden White and his theory of historical narration via emplottment. White also corroborates, for Scott, Steiner's reading of tragedy and romance with his definitions of the genres; see "Tragedy's Time," 201. Scott also draws heavily from Hegel's scattered readings concerning tragedy, in particular, his idea of "tragic conflict." The latter involves, as he writes, "world-Historical collision between irreconcilable social temporal orders;" see "Tragedy's Time," 211, and *Conscripts of Modernity*, 12, 156, 167.
138. Wynter, "No Humans Involved: An Open Letter to My Colleagues," *Forum H.H.I. Knowledge for the 21st Century* 1, no. 1 (Fall 1994), 49.
139. See Rita Felski, "Introduction," in *Rethinking Tragedy*, ed. Rita Felski (Baltimore, MD: John Hopkins University Press, 2008), 4.
140. Rita Felski, "Introduction," 3.
141. James, "Notes on Hamlet," in *The C. L. R. James Reader*, ed. Anna Grimshaw (Oxford: Blackwell, 1992), 243–44, quoted in Scott, "Tragedy's Time," 212.
142. James, "Notes on Hamlet," 243–44, quoted in Scott, "Tragedy's Time," 212.
143. Scott, "Tragedy's Time," 212.
144. Scott, "Tragedy's Time," 212; Chris Bongie, *Friends and Enemies: The Scribal Politics of Post/Colonial Literature* (Liverpool: Liverpool University Press, 2009) 265.

145. Bongie, *Friends and Enemies*, 266.
146. For more on tragedy's supremacist origins, see Nicole Loraux's *Mourning Voice: An Essay on Greek Tragedy*, trans. Elizabeth Trapnell Rawlings (Ithaca, NY: Cornell University Press, 2002), and *Mothers in Mourning*, trans. Corinne Pache (Ithaca, NY: Cornell University, 1998). Olga Taxidou, *Tragedy, Modernity and Mourning* (Edinburgh: Edinburgh University Press, 2004) is also generative.
147. Fischer, *Modernity Disavowed*, 23.
148. See Bongie, *Friends and Enemies*, 266. For his provocative reading of Scott's excision of Dessalines from tragic consequence, see 266–67.
149. Rabbitt, "C. L. R. James's Figuring,"128.
150. This idea of "sovereign peoples" is borrowed from Casimir who writes that the Haitian people, in the revolutionary moment and now, are sovereign peoples like all peoples the world over: they "do not need any help in expressing and asserting their own principles" for existence. See *The Haitians*, 1.
151. I cite from the latest scenic version of the play, Édouard Glissant, *Monsieur Toussaint: A Play*, trans. J. Michael Dash (Boulder, CO: Lynne Rienner Publishers, 2005). For context about Glissant's political activities concerning decolonization and their significance to the play's many iterations see the generative essay by Sarah J. Townsend, "The Spectral Stage of Édouard Glissant's *Monsieur Toussaint*," *Modern Drama* 61, no. 4 (Winter 2018) 61, 4.
152. See the preface to Glissant, *Monsieur Toussaint*, 15. Glissant also cites the influence of French politician and abolitionist Victor Schœlcher's *Vie de Toussaint Louverture*, a book that influenced both James's and Césaire's presentation of Louverture.
153. See Louverture's April 1803 handwritten statement found upon his death at the Fort de Joux prison, which reads, "Arresting me arbitrarily, without hearing me out or telling me why, taking all my possessions, pillaging my whole family in general, seizing my papers and keeping them, putting me on board a ship, sending me off naked as an earthworm, spreading the most atrocious lies about me, and after that, I am sent to the depths of this dungeon, isn't this like cutting off someone's leg and saying 'walk,' isn't this like cutting out someone's tongue and saying 'talk,' isn't this burying a man alive?" Quoted in Deborah Jenson, "From the Kidnapping(s) of the Louvertures to the Alleged Kidnapping of Aristide: Legacies of Slavery in the Post/Colonial World," *Yale French Studies* 107 (2005), 162. Jenson's translation.
154. McKittrick, *Dear Science*, 44.
155. Glissant, *Caribbean Discourse*, 2.
156. Glissant, *Caribbean Discourse*, 2.
157. Glissant, *Caribbean Discourse*, 2.
158. Glissant, *Caribbean Discourse*, 168.
159. Glissant, *Monsieur Toussaint*, 29.

160. Glissant, *Monsieur Toussaint*, 56.
161. Glissant, *Monsieur Toussaint*, 62.
162. Glissant, *Monsieur Toussaint*, 35.
163. Glissant, *Monsieur Toussaint*, 63.
164. Glissant, *Monsieur Toussaint*, 56, 96.
165. Glissant, *Monsieur Toussaint*, 96.
166. The Moyse of historic fact would not discipline laborers who rejected Louverture's draconian labor polices, which included returning to work on former plantations manned by the very slave drivers or planters who brutalized the newly liberated. For more on Moyse, see *The Black Jacobins*, 257, 275–79, 284, 359. See also Trouillot, *Stirring the Pot*, 144–54.
167. Glissant, *Monsieur Toussaint*, 82.
168. Glissant, *Monsieur Toussaint*, 116.
169. Glissant, *Caribbean Discourse*, 2.
170. Jonathan B. Monroe, "Composite Cultures, Chaos Wor(l)ds: Relational Poetics, Textual Hybridity, and the Future of Opacity," in *Tradition, Trauma, Translation: The Classic and the Modern*, ed. Timothy Mathews and Jan Parker (New York: Oxford University Press, 2011), 156.
171. Glissant, *Caribbean Discourse*, 2.
172. Glissant, *Caribbean Discourse*, 168.
173. James, *The Black Jacobins*, 198.
174. James, "Lectures on The Black Jacobins," 110.
175. On Dessalines and republicanism see the introduction to this book and Chelsea Stieber's book, *Haiti's Paper War*.
176. See Raj Chetty, "The Tragicomedy of Anticolonial Overcoming: Toussaint Louverture and *The Black Jacobins* on Stage," *Callaloo* 37, no. 1 (2014): 85.
177. Natalie Melas, "Comparative Noncontemporaneities: C. L. R. James and Ernst Bloch," in *Theory Aside*, ed. Jason Potts and Daniel Stout (Durham, NC: Duke University Press, 2014), 65.
178. Glissant, *Caribbean Discourse*, 168.

Chapter 2

1. Alejo Carpentier, *The Kingdom of This World*, trans. Harriet De Onis (New York: Farrar, Straus and Giroux, 1957), 116.
2. Figueroa, *Prophetic Visions of the Past*, 164.
3. Walsh, "Pedagogical Notes."
4. Honor and respect, Father Dessalines, Father Toussaint, Father Christophe, Father Pétion, Father Vastey, and all major heroes of our independence. . . . We have not forgotten.
5. The homage is provided in full in the appendix.

6. Paravisini-Gebert, "The Haitian Revolution in Interstices and Shadows: A Rereading of Alejo Carpentier's *The Kingdom of This World*," *Research in African Literatures* 35, no. 2 (2004): 117, 118.
7. Ali Tal-mason, "Voyage to the Marvelous: A Traveler's Guide to *The Kingdom of This World*," *Cambridge Journal of Postcolonial Literary Inquiry* 7, no. 1 (2020): 52.
8. Katerina Gonzalez Seligmann, *Writing the Caribbean in Magazine Time* (New Brunswick, NJ: Rutgers University Press, 2021), 91, 89.
9. Seligmann, *Writing the Caribbean*, 91.
10. This history and its significance to the novella's storyline is discussed in greater length in the essay "Mucho Woulo: Black Freedom and *The Kingdom of This World*," and it will be returned to briefly in this chapter. See Natalie M. Léger, "Mucho Woulo: Black Freedom and *The Kingdom of This World*," in *Racialized Visions: Haiti and the Hispanic Caribbean*, ed. Vanessa K. Valdés (Albany: State University Press of New York, 2020).
11. The effort to naturalize kinship with revolutionary Haiti that I align with Carpentier was but one part of a larger scholarly effort put forth by Cuban thinkers in the 1900s to establish their cultural distinction from Western Europe. Literary critic Roberto González Echevarría writes that for Cuban scholars and artists establishing difference from Western Europe especially "meant embracing the cultural heritage of Afro-Cubans," an advent that led to the Afro-Cuban movement in Cuban arts and letters; see *Alejo Carpentier: The Pilgrim at Home* (Austin: University of Texas Press, 1990), 43. This 1920s movement had fallen out of favor by the time Carpentier composed *The Kingdom of This World* in 1943, but it is clear that it nonetheless influenced Carpentier's writings about Haiti and the Black population of Cuba. See his ethnomusicological study, *Music in Cuba*, and first novel, *Ecué-Yamba-O*. Echevarría accordingly writes that Carpentier extensively read the work of Ramiro Guerra y Sánchez (*Sugar and Society in the Caribbean* [1927]) and Fernando Ortiz Fernández (*Afro-Cuban Underworld: Black Sorcerers (Notes for a Study of Criminal Ethnology* [1906] among other texts), "two men who left a lasting impression on Carpentier and all Cuban intellectuals" thereafter and whose "object of earnest study" was Cuba's Black population." Echevarría, *Alejo Carpentier*, 44.
12. Lois Parkinson Zamora and Wendy B. Faris, "Introduction: Daiquiri Birds and Flaubertian Parrot(ie)s," in *Magical Realism: Theory, History, Community*, ed. Lois Parkinson Zamora and Wendy B. Faris (Durham, NC: Duke University Press, 1995), 6.
13. Kramer, "Marvelous Realism in the Caribbean: A Second Look at Jacques Stephen Alexis and Alejo Carpentier," *Atlantic Studies* 11, no. 2 (2014): 225.
14. Seligmann, *Writing the Caribbean*, 89–99.

15. Annaliese Hoehling, "Minoritarian 'Marvelous Real': Enfolding Revolution in Alejo Carpentier's *The Kingdom of This World*," *Journal of Postcolonial Writing* 54, no. 2 (2018): 255.
16. See McKittrick, *Dear Science*, 46.
17. See Wynter's articles "1492: A New World View"; "Columbus, the Ocean Blue and 'Fables That Stir the Mind'"; and "Columbus and the Poetics of the *Propter Nos*."
18. The Haitian maxim *tout moun se moun* broadly translates as "all persons are persons." It addresses the ethics of the West's colonial conception of the human, which has long questioned the actuality of Black humanity.
19. See Wynter, "Columbus and the Poetics," 271; and Wynter, "The Pope Must Have Been Drunk," 29–34. For detailed overview of her argument, see "Unsettling the Coloniality of Being/Power/Truth/Freedom: Towards the Human, After Man, Its Overrepresentation—An Argument," *CR: The New Centennial Review* 3, no. 3 (Fall 2003): 257–337.
20. This project is most clearly seen in Wynter's Columbus essays, which are treated later in the chapter: "1492: A New World View," "Columbus, the Ocean Blue, and 'Fables that Stir the Mind,'" and "Columbus and the Poetics of the *Propter Nos*," and in her essay on Blackness in the Iberian imaginary, "The Eye of the Other," which this chapter also addresses. See "The Eye of the Other" in *Blacks in Hispanic Literature: Critical Essays*, ed. Miriam DeCosta-Willis (Port Washington, NY: Kennikat Press, 1977), 8–19.
21. See Wynter, "The Pope Must Have Been Drunk," 29–34.
22. Wynter, "The Pope Must Have Been Drunk," 35.
23. Glissant, *Caribbean Discourse*, 2n1.
24. See Fanon, *Black Skins, White Masks* (New York: Grove Press, 1967), 11.
25. See Christina Sharpe, *In the Wake: Blackness and Being* (Durham, NC: Duke University Press, 2016).
26. Following the Spanish-American War in 1898, the Platt Amendment was issued by the US stipulating how American troops would vacate Cuba. The amendment also delineated the neocolonial conditions that would ensure US dominance in Cuba up until 1959.
27. Echevarría, *Alejo Carpentier*, 42.
28. Echevarría, *Alejo Carpentier*, 43.
29. Yanick Hume situates Cuba's pre-revolutionary desire to be a modern republic as a push to embody "an idea of modernity" tied to the United States, which stood in sharp contradistinction to the idea of modernity Cuba's ruling elite imagined Haiti exemplified; see Hume, "Performing Haiti: Casa del Caribe and the Popularisation of Haitian Heritage Communities in Cuba," *Caribbean Quarterly* 62 no. 1 (2016) 41; 41–43.
30. Echevarría, *Alejo Carpentier*, 42.
31. Hume, "Performing Haiti," 42. The planter class of colonial Cuba had long turned to the slave trade to derive the manpower needed for the colony's full

commitment to plantation industries (like sugar and coffee) following the collapse of Saint Domingue. The abolition of the slave trade and the rising interference of the United States in Cuban colonial and later national affairs, after independence in 1902, necessitated a new pool of labor that was both cost efficient and that could act as "army reserve of labor," against a Cuban workforce seeking greater economic equity; see Pedro Serviat, "Solutions to the Black Problem," in *Afro-Cuba: An Anthology of Cuban Writing on Race, Politics, and Culture*, ed. Pedro Pérez Sarduy and Jean Stubbs (New York: Ocean Press, 1992), 80. This reserve was predominantly derived from Haiti and Jamaica, with the largest migrants arriving from Haiti.

32. Hume, "Performing Haiti," 42.
33. Serviat, "Solutions to the Black Problem," 80. For more on the Haitian migrant labor in Cuba, see Barry Carr, "Identity, Class, and Nation: Black Immigrant Workers, Cuban Communism, and the Sugar Insurgency, 1925–1934," *Hispanic American Historical Review* 78, no.1 (1998): 83–116; Marc McLeod, "Undesirable Aliens: Race, Ethnicity, and Nationalism in the Comparison of Haitian and British West Indian Immigrant Workers in Cuba, 1912–1939," *Journal of Social History* 31, no. 3 (1998): 599–623; Matthew Casey, "From Haiti to Cuba and Back: Haitians' Experiences of Migration, Labor, and Return, 1900–1940" (PhD diss., University of Pittsburgh, 2012).
34. Hume, "Performing Haiti," 42.
35. See Serviat for the "propaganda campaign" that depicted Haitian and Jamaican migrants as "inferior." "Solutions to the Black Problem," 80.
36. Serviat, "Solutions to the Black Problem," 80. "1790 in Haiti" refers to Haiti's revolution, 1912 to Cuba's one and only "race war." See Pérez Sarduy and Stubbs, "Introduction," 8. Rafael Duharte Jiménez writes that Black Cubans who had participated in the war for independence discovered soon thereafter that "the republic they helped create turned its back on them." The Independent Colored Movement (Independientes de Color), organized by Evaristo Estenoz and Pedro Ivonnet, sought a political intervention, which would result in full and equal inclusion in the republic. However, a political intervention was not possible because their movement was deemed a "race war" against whites and condemned by the new national government. Consequently, when the movement turned to limited military engagement, the government deployed its armed forces and "over 3000 black [Cubans, movement soldiers and unaffiliated peasants, were] brutally massacred in the Oriente countryside by the republican army." See Rafael Duharte Jiménez, "The 19th Century Black Fear," in *Afro-Cuba: An Anthology of Cuban Writing on Race, Politics, and Culture*, ed. Pedro Perez Sarduy and Jean Stubbs (New York: Ocean Press, 1992), 45.
37. A pro-US Cuban government accepted the neocolonial conditions outlined in the Platt Amendment and the ratification that followed, which gave Cuban

sugar preferential treatment within the US market, in order to strengthen its economy. Little thought was given to the predominately Black laborers who would be exploited within the sugar industry for the national economy's growth.

38. This is discussed at length in Léger, "Mucho Woulo: Black Freedom and *The Kingdom of This World*."
39. In the Prologue, Carpentier offers the following spelling for the pre-Haitian revolutionary figure, "Mackandal," whereas in the novella, he uses "Macandal." This discussion of Carpentier's Haitian writings defers to contemporary Haitian linguistics and uses "Makandal." This chapter also defers to contemporary Haitian Kreyòl spelling of *lwa* for Vodou spirits as opposed to Carpentier's *loa*.
40. Carpentier, *The Kingdom of This World*, 10.
41. Carpentier, *The Kingdom of This World*, 184.
42. Wynter has written extensively about the biocentric nature of colonial modernity. See Wynter, "Unsettling the Coloniality of Being," for one reading.
43. Carpentier, *The Kingdom of This World*, 184.
44. See Wynter, "The Eye and the Other," 10.
45. Carpentier, *The Kingdom of This World*, 4–5.
46. Carpentier, *The Kingdom of This World*, 4–5.
47. Carpentier, *The Kingdom of This World*, 6.
48. Carpentier, *The Kingdom of This World*, 7.
49. Avery Gordon, *Ghostly Matters*, 5.
50. Carpentier, *The Kingdom of This World*, 8.
51. Carpentier, *The Kingdom of This World*, 8–9.
52. Carpentier, *The Kingdom of This World*, 8.
53. The Dauphin of France (literally, the "dolphin of France") is the heir to the French crown. Ti-Noël references this heir when mentioning the "puling prince" who is named after a "dolphin." See Carpentier, *The Kingdom of This World*, 8–9.
54. Carpentier, *The Kingdom of This World*, 8.
55. Casimir, *The Haitians*, 287.
56. Casimir, *The Haitians*, 287.
57. Carpentier, *The Kingdom of This World*, 9; emphasis added.
58. Carpentier, *The Kingdom of This World*, 9.
59. Carpentier, *The Kingdom of This World*, 10.
60. Carpentier, *The Kingdom of This World*, 10.
61. Carpentier, *The Kingdom of This World*, 10.
62. See Trouillot, *Silencing the Past*, 73.
63. Trouillot, *Silencing the Past*, 73.
64. Jean Jacques Dessalines, "The Haitian Declaration of Independence," in *The Haiti Reader: History, Culture, Politics*, edited by Laurent Dubois, Kaiama L.

Glover, Nadève Ménard, Millery Polyné, and Chantalle F. Verna (Durham, NC: Duke University Press, 2020).
65. See Casimir, "A Decolonial History of the Haitians" (lecture, Brooklyn College, Brooklyn, NY, November 16, 2018); emphasis in original. Throughout this chapter, I cite from an unpublished print copy of the lecture.
66. Carpentier, *The Kingdom of This World*, 1.
67. Carpentier, *The Kingdom of This World*, 1.
68. Wynter, "1492: A New World View," 18; Wynter, "Columbus, the Ocean Blue," 151.
69. Lope de Vega, *The Discovery of the New World by Christopher Columbus: A Comedy in Verse*, trans. Frieda Fligelman (Berkley: Gillick Press, 1950), 13.
70. Wynter, "Columbus, the Ocean Blue," 151.
71. Wynter, "Columbus, the Ocean Blue," 155.
72. Wynter, "Columbus, the Ocean Blue," 155, 158.
73. Wynter, "Columbus, the Ocean Blue," 158. Wynter borrows from Robert Pirsig when referencing a "root expansion in thought." See Robert Pirsig, *Zen and the Art of Motorcycle Maintenance: An Inquiry into Values* (New York: Morrow, 1974), 74.
74. Wynter, "Columbus and the Poetics," 255.
75. The "he" is deliberate here: this was a conversation among men, for men.
76. de Vega, *The Discovery of the New World*, 47. In the scene in question, a Native woman happens upon a Spanish seaman when in flight from her captor, a soon to be reformed and Christianized Native chieftain. Upon securing the Spaniard's protection, she asks for this seaman's name, receives his surname, and then inquires if it is "noble." In reply, he offers the aforesaid response, "all Spanish are" and when asked immediately thereafter if he would "use violence on" her, he replies un-ironically, "never."
77. Wynter, "1492," 9.
78. Wynter, "The Eye of the Other," 9.
79. Perhaps de Vega obscures this devaluation in order to present this new-found equality as a worthwhile development. He does, however, have his misgivings concerning the new humans that the noble Spanish typify. These misgivings appear in his attention to the pitfalls of gold lust among *some* Spanish seamen, who never appear in his play. Indeed, not one European (least of all Columbus) mistreats Native peoples in his drama because of their desire for gold, despite the fact that material aggrandizement drove Native and African enslavement in the Caribbean. His attention to gold lust versus slavery allows him to subsume the violent barbarisms of Columbus's (and his crew's) wealth-seeking actions into an abstract examination of the wayward Christian. This abstract assessment of Christian impiety does not take into consideration that people died and continue to die so that Western Europeans

could lay claim to a superior cultural sensibility predicated on living as human equals among a world populated by lesser peoples.

80. Wynter denotes the human's figuration under Christian humanism as Man$_1$ and the human's articulation under our secular, biocentric, humanism as Man$_2$.
81. Following Copernicus's challenge to the tenets of medieval astronomy concerning the sun's unmoving position within the atmosphere, Wynter maintains that "the earth itself could now be perceived as unified," see "Columbus and the *Proper Nos*" 263. In other words, Copernicus's scientific findings (with that of the Portuguese's much earlier discovery of Africa in 1441) furthered the epistemological veracity of Columbus's challenge to the knowledge dictates of his moment as upheld by Scholasticism, particularly his emphasis on geography's homogeneousness.
82. de Vega, *The Discovery of the New World*, 47; Bench Ansfield, "Sylvia Wynter: What Does It Mean to Be Human," in *Sylvia Wynter: On Being Human as Praxis*, ed. Katherine McKittrick (Durham, NC: Duke University Press, 2015), 124. I would also add the aspiring aristocratic, men (like Columbus) who strived to attain the socio-political prominence and economic security of the aristocracy.
83. Wynter, "Beyond Miranda's Meanings," 364.
84. Wynter, "Beyond Miranda's Meanings," 364.
85. See Wynter, "The Re-enchantment of Humanism," 146.
86. Carpentier, *The Kingdom of This World*, 1.
87. See Katherine McKittrick, *Demonic Grounds: Black Women and the Cartographies of Struggle* (Minneapolis: University of Minnesota Press, 2006), xi.
88. Carpentier, *The Kingdom of This World*, 87.
89. Ada Ferrer, *Freedom's Mirror: Cuba and Haiti in the Age of Revolution* (New York: Cambridge University Press, 2014), 4
90. Ada Ferrer, *Freedom's Mirror*, 17.
91. Ada Ferrer, *Freedom's Mirror*, 17.
92. Ada Ferrer, *Freedom's Mirror*, 224.
93. Ada Ferrer, *Freedom's Mirror*, 38.
94. Carpentier, *The Kingdom of This World*, 87.
95. Carpentier, *The Kingdom of This World*, 87, 86.
96. Carpentier, *The Kingdom of This World*, 65–69. Boukman convened the meeting at *Bwa Kayïman* and served as the first of the Revolution's many leaders. This chapter uses the contemporary spelling of the famed insurgent's name.
97. Carpentier, *The Kingdom of This World*, 74, 77.
98. Carpentier, "On the Marvelous Real," trans. Tanya Huntington and Lois Parkinson Zamora, in *Magical Realism: Theory, History, Community*, ed. Lois Parkinson Zamora and Wendy B. Faris (Durham, NC: Duke University Press, 1995), 83, 87.
99. Sandra H. Ferdman, "Conquering Marvels: The Marvelous Other in the Texts of Christopher Columbus," *Hispanic Review* 62, no. 4 (Autumn 1994), 488.

100. Carpentier, *The Kingdom of This World*, 1.
101. Stephen Greenblatt, "Marvelous Possessions," in *The Greenblatt Reader*, ed., Michael Payne (Malden, MA: Blackwell Publishing, 2005), 97.
102. Greenblatt, "Marvelous Possessions," 97–98.
103. Greenblatt, "Marvelous Possessions," 95.
104. Columbus, "Letter to Santángel," in *The Voyages of Christopher Columbus, Being the Journals of His First and Third, and the Letters Concerning His First and Last Voyages, to Which Is Added the Account of His Second Voyage Written by Andres Bernaldez*, trans. and ed., Cecil Jane (London: Argonaut Press, 1930), no pagination.
105. Columbus, "Letter to Santángel."
106. Columbus, "Letter to Santángel."
107. Wynter, "1492," 9.
108. Leo Wiener, *Africa and the Discovery of America* (Philadelphia: Innes & Sons, 1922), 25.
109. Wynter, "The Eye of the Other," 10.
110. Wiener, *Africa and the Discovery of America*, 26.
111. Wynter, "The Eye of the Other," 13.
112. Wynter, "The Eye of the Other," 12; emphasis in original.
113. Wynter, "The Eye of the Other," 10.
114. Wynter, "The Eye of the Other," 10.
115. Wynter, "The Eye of the Other," 11.
116. Wynter, "The Eye of the Other," 10.
117. Wynter, "The Eye of the Other," 10.
118. Wiener, *Africa and the Discovery of America*, 26.
119. Wynter, "Columbus, the Ocean Blue," 158.
120. de Vega, *The Discovery of the New World*, 47.
121. Greenblatt, "Marvelous Possessions," 94.
122. Greenblatt, "Marvelous Possessions," 94. The Indigenous are also justly subject to slavery for Columbus because they symbolically look like Africans in his mind's eye being cannibals and thus monsters, which are a variant of the devils associated with Islam. Columbus notes in his letter to Santángel that the Indigenous do not look like Africans but is also clear to state that their appearance is not in the least bit Western European. He writes: "In these islands I have so far found no human monstrosities, as many expected, but on the contrary the whole population is very well formed, nor are they negroes as in Guinea, but their hair is flowing and they are not born where there is intense force in the rays of the sun." They are different, neither African or Western European, and yet wholly familiar, made legible as idolaters via the imperialist alchemy of a nascent racial capitalism that charges the marvelous with the ability to perceive the monsters that reside within "the very well formed." It is hardly insignificant that Columbus dismisses the possibility of

monsters in the Indies and yet goes on to describe monsters, invoking the lie of Native cannibalism to produce idolaters and thus willing slaves where they did not exist. He writes, "As I have found no monsters, so I have had no report of any, except in an island 'Quaris,' . . . which is inhabited by a people who are regarded in all the islands as very fierce and who eat human flesh;" see Columbus, "Letter to Santángel."

123. See Carpentier, "On the Marvelous Real in America" written in 1967, and "The Baroque and the Marvelous Real" from 1975. Alejo Carpentier, "The Baroque and the Marvelous Real (1975)," trans. Tanya Huntington and Lois Parkinson Zamora, in *Magical Realism: Theory, History, Community*, ed. Lois Parkinson Zamora and Wendy B. Faris (Durham, NC: Duke University Press, 1995), 89–108.

124. Alejo Carpentier, "Prologue to *The Kingdom of This World* (1949)," trans. Alfred Mac Adam, *Review: Literature and Arts of the Americas* 26, no. 47 (1993): 30; Carpentier, "On the Marvelous Real," 87.

125. Piranesi was an eighteenth-century Italian engraver whose peculiar artistry inspired the surrealists, European artists who were contemporaries of Carpentier and who were extensively critiqued by him in his delineation of "the marvelous real." Carpentier's chief grievance with the surrealists concerned their inability to truthfully describe the sterility of their own lived realities. He writes in the prologue that they "were very much affected by imaginary tyrannies without ever having suffered a one" and they relished in invoking the magical in a region that had long forsook the lived actuality of magic; see Carpentier, "On the Marvelous Real," 87, 86. Unlike the surrealists who needed to invent what did not exist in order to derive meaning from their existence, Carpentier argues that hemispheric Americans artists and laymen were firmly grounded in their real and the wondrousness that lie therein.

126. Carpentier, "Prologue (1949)," 30.

127. Carpentier, "On the Marvelous Real," 86.

128. Carpentier, "On the Marvelous Real," 85–86; Carpentier, "Prologue (1949)," 29.

129. Carpentier, "The Baroque," 104.

130. Carpentier, "On the Marvelous Real," 85.

131. Kramer, "Marvelous Realism in the Caribbean," 221.

132. Kramer, "Marvelous Realism in the Caribbean," 221.

133. Carpentier, "On the Marvelous Real," 83, 87. The other cultural aspects that Carpentier highlights in the prologue include Europeans who searched for El Dorado well into the French Revolution. "On the Marvelous Real," 87. These are activities that are not invented by regional peoples but are adopted behaviors that add to the region's marvelousness because they accentuate the irreality shaping how the region is thought and lived by Americans and others.

134. Carpentier, *The Kingdom of This World*, 119–25.

135. Carpentier, *The Kingdom of This World*, 176. Following independence in 1804 and the assassination of then emperor, Dessalines, in 1806, Haiti was divided into three polities before settling into a kingdom in the north and a republic in the southwest. In 1820, it was unified as a liberal democratic republic by former revolutionary general, Jean-Pierre Boyer.
136. Capentier, *The Kingdom of This World*, 178.
137. See Philip Kaisary, *The Haitian Revolution*, 175.
138. See Léger, "Mucho Woulo."
139. I have argued in both the journal article, "Faithless Sight: Haiti in *The Kingdom of this World*," *Research in African Literatures*, 45, no. 1 (Spring 2014), 85–106, and the chapter "Mucho Woulo" that Carpentier's grim portrayal of post-revolutionary Haiti does not signify that the Haitian Revolution was a failed endeavor. Indeed, the Revolution, for Carpentier, remains a worthwhile feat notwithstanding post-revolutionary Haiti because of its ideational value for hemispheric Americans, hence his theory of the marvelous real.
140. Carpentier, *The Kingdom of This World*, 116–17.
141. Laurent Dubois, *Haiti: The Aftershocks of History* (New York: Picador Books, 2012), 21.
142. See Echevarría, *Alejo Carpentier*, 133 and Paravisini-Gebert, "The Haitian Revolution," 116–17.
143. See the prologue, and in particular, the line "The reader must be warned that the story he is going to read is based on an extremely rigorous documentation which not only respects the historical truth of the events, the names of the characters (even the minor ones), of the places, and even the streets but which hides under its apparently non-chronological facade, a minute collation of dates and chronologies." Carpentier, "Prologue (1949),"31.
144. See Chapter 3 for a discussion this kind of tyranny and its importance to Caribbean writing of the Revolution.
145. Casimir, "A Decolonial History"; emphasis in original.
146. Casimir writes that "a new world was built in Haiti after 1804" in *The Haitians*, see 330. I think alongside him here and find that with respect to the Haitian state, it bears stating (to quote Casimir again) that "the power the [Haitian] state had at its disposal [post the Revolution] allowed it *only to label* the components of the universe within its reach in a manner conducive to the eradication of the world created by the former captives from any official concern. This maneuver, *which did not overly prepare a possible reactivation of the plantation or an analogous economic system*, authorized the state to blame the workers (supposedly entangled in archaic traditionalism) for the failure of large-scale plantation agriculture." See Casimir and Claypool, "Going Backwards Toward the Future," 182; emphasis added. Haiti's *Ginen* peoples have always risen to demand another way of being outside of the plantation

economy favored by the creolized Haitians at the helm of Haiti and their colonial overlords. For a contemporary take on their resistance, see Jesus Ruiz, "A Sense of History: Lessons from Haiti's New Political Uprising," *Weaver News*, March 2, 2021: https://www.weavenews.org/stories/2021/3/3/a-sense-of-history-lessons-from-haitis-new-political-uprising. Robert Fatton Jr. offers a thorough accounting of the predatory logic of Haitian politicians and geopolitical powers in "Haiti: The Saturnalia of Emancipation and the Vicissitudes of Predatory Rule," *Third World Quarterly* 27, no. 1 (2006): 115–33.

147. See Carpentier, *The Harp and the Shadow: The Beatification of Christopher Columbus: A Novel*, trans. Thomas Christensen and Carole Christensen (San Francisco: Mercury House, 1990), 159. Carpentier describes Columbus when a ghost as "the Invisible One" and when Columbus meets another deceased Genoan mariner, Andrea Doria, Carpentier also describes this spirit as an "Invisible One," 155.

148. Regarding Carpentier's critique of Latin American and Caribbean artists, consider his discussion of the composer's musical career and "The Young Wise Men" scene of *The Lost Steps*. The scene involves a Native poet, a Black painter, and a white musician from Los Altos and shows how they are blindly devoted to Western European cultural traditions to the detriment of their own cultural art, which Carpentier is clear to indicate they know nothing about; see Lois Park Zamora, *The Lost Steps*, trans. Harriet De Onis (Minneapolis: University of Minnesota Press, 2001), 71–74.

Chapter 3

1. Maryse Condé, "Aimé Césaire and America," trans. Richard Philcox, *Black Renaissance / Renaissance Noire* 5, no. 3 (2004): 159.
2. Condé, "Aimé Césaire and America," 157.
3. See Alex Dupuy, "Haiti and the Indemnity Question," 114.
4. Following Jean Jacques Dessalines's assassination on October 6, 1806, Haiti would be divided into two polities: in 1807, Henry Christophe presided over the north and Alexandre Pétion the south. Three years into Pétion's rule, André Rigaud returned to Haiti from France and led a secessionist movement that expropriated territory from Pétion in 1810. He would independently govern this territory as a republic for a year until his death in 1811. Pétion re-seized this territory and in 1812 created a republic in a now united south. Concerning the indemnity and the political decisions regarding it made in a divided Haiti, Alex Dupuy writes, "In 1814, France sent envoys to Haiti to demand that King Henry Christophe, who controlled the north of Haiti, and President Alexandre Pétion, who controlled the south and west, resubmit to French sovereignty. Christophe had that envoy arrested and jailed. Pétion, on the other hand, offered to pay an indemnity to France to compensate the

former colonial property owners in return for France's official recognition of Haiti's independence. Jean-Pierre Boyer succeeded Pétion as president of the Republic of Haiti in 1818 and of the whole of Haiti in 1820 after Christophe's death by suicide.... Boyer... offered to pay an indemnity to France [in 1824] ... for the same reason his predecessor did in 1814." Dupuy contends that "Both presidents [agreed to pay the indemnity] to solve two problems simultaneously: the recognition of Haiti's independence [which France officially acknowledged in 1825] and to settle once and for all the property question in the interest of the Haitian ruling class." See "Haiti and the Indemnity Question," 112–13, 120. For more on the property question, see Chapter 4 of this book.

5. Casimir, Colon, and Koerner, "Haiti's Need for a Great South," 21. See also Casimir, *The Haitians*, 270.
6. Casimir, Colon, and Koerner, "Haiti's Need for a Great South," 21.
7. Of the free Blacks' relation to the oligarchy, Casimir tellingly writes, "Among the enfranchised, the stratum of free blacks distinguished itself: they did not consider themselves *American colonists* [a term used by the *gens de couleurs* for themselves], and would not be considered as such. Yet in the absence of a relationship of consanguinity with the colonists, their belonging to this privileged class [of the traditional oligarchy] owed itself to the acquisition and display of ideological and cultural affinities." See Casimir and Mary Claypool. "Going Backwards Toward the Future," 175.
8. Trouillot, *Stirring the Pot*, 8.
9. Manigat, *Éventail d'histoire*, 1:311.
10. Condé, "Aimé Césaire and America," 157.
11. Fick, *The Making of Haiti*, 248.
12. Fick, *The Making of Haiti*, 248.
13. See Chapter 1 for a discussion of the political power of Northern captives and how Louverture was beholden to this power.
14. For Carpentier's depiction of each governance, see *The Kingdom of This World*, 105–50, 169–70. Concerning Christophe's rule and that of Boyer's predecessor and mentor, Pétion, Casimir and Claypool write, "The fundamental difference between Christophe's authoritarian regime and Pétion's liberal one would lay in the meaning of economic recovery for one or the other sector of the 1804 oligarchy. In the kingdom of the North, a conquering state implanted and imposed the material foundations for the economy with the iron fist from large planters and the enthusiasm of *nouveaux riches* in the process of building their preeminence. In the southern Republic, the state comforted the traditional oligarchy [*affranchis* and their allies in the Revolution] by ratifying the legitimacy of the law of conquest and by preserving the primacy of the natural sons of the French Metropole. In both cases, the employment policies hardly differed and the conceptions of political and economic life coincided broadly

with that of the European bourgeoisie." See "Going Backwards Toward the Future," 186. For Pétion's agricultural codes see Casimir, *The Haitians*, 164.

15. Recall that early in the novella, insects and amphibians heed Makandal's call and offer their poisonous talents in the fight against the whites in pre-revolutionary Haiti. In post-revolutionary Haiti, nature also discloses the first signs of the country's internal disintegration, with an "evil tree" and barren fields signifying the disunion brewing between the people within Christophe's realm. See Capentier, *The Kingdom of This World*, 35, 102–3.

16. Despite political hostilities from abroad, the early Haitian states found innovative ways to contend with Western European empires and surrounding nations; see Julia Gaffield, *Haitian Connections in the Atlantic World: Recognition After Revolution* (Chapel Hill: University of North Carolina Press, 2015), 182–96. Still, non-recognition was disastrous for the states as "it limited the ability of Haitian leaders to negotiate, treat, and connect with their counterparts in the Atlantic World." Gaffield's conclusion outlines this very well. Robin Blackburn offers another important perspective, highlighting how fear of Haiti shaped political interaction with colonial powers; see "The Force of Example" in *The Impact of the Haitian Revolution in the Atlantic World*, ed. David Geggus (Columbia: University of South Carolina, 2001), 15–20.

17. Casimir, Colon, and Koerner, "Haiti's Need for a Great South," 28.

18. Condé, "Aimé Césaire and America," 157.

19. For post-revolutionary Haiti and the Atlantic World, see Gaffield, *Haitian Connections*. For discussions of Haiti and geopolitical politics in Carpentier's moment, see Brenda Gayle Plummer, *Haiti and the Great Powers, 1902–1915* (Baton Rouge: Louisiana State University Press, 1988); Hans Schmidt's *The United States Occupation of Haiti, 1915–1934* (New Brunswick, NJ: Rutgers University Press, 1995); and Mary Renda, *Taking Haiti: Military Occupation and the Culture of US Imperialism 1915–1940* (Chapel Hill: University of North Carolina Press, 2001). Peter Hudson offers a superb accounting of Wall Street, banking and US financial interests in Haiti prior to and during the 1915 US Occupation. See Peter Hudson, "Financial Occupations," in *Bankers and Empire: How Wall Street Colonized the Caribbean* (Chicago: University of Chicago Press, 2018), 81–116. Lastly, Raphael Dalleo's monograph on the profound influence of the 1915 US Occupation of Haiti on contemporaneous Caribbean anticolonial writing and politics situates Carpentier in a Caribbean intellectual milieu that ought to have nurtured a more thoughtful analysis of post-revolutionary Haiti. See Raphael Dalleo, *American Imperialism's Undead: The Occupation of Haiti and the Rise of Caribbean Anticolonialism* (Charlottesville: University of Virginia Press, 2016).

20. Condé, "Aimé Césaire and America," 157.

21. See Kaisary, *From Havana to Hollywood: Slave Resistance in the Cinematic Imaginary* (New York: State University of New York Press, 2024), 37.

22. Lamming's essay collection *The Pleasures of Exile* (Ann Arbor: University of Michigan Press, 1992) addresses how the Caribbean writer can establish literary authority. The collection opens with reference to the republic of Haiti, moves to a reading of *The Tempest* as a metaphor for colonial relations and devotes a chapter to the Haitian Revolution, a set of interests that outlines the importance of Haiti and its revolutionary past to the work of thinking through the Columbian narrative of discovery.
23. Hurley, "Césaire's 'Toussaint Louverture': A Revolution in Question," *Présence Africaine*, no. 169 (2004): 203.
24. Paul Breslin and Rachel Ney, "Introduction: The Challenge of Aimé Césaire's *The Tragedy of King Christophe*" in *Tragedy of King Christophe* (Evanston, IL: Northwestern University Press, 2015), xli; emphasis in original.
25. The homage relays the Revolution's opening as happening on August 21, but Fick and other historians of the Revolution write that it began on August 22. See Fick, *The Making of Haiti*, 91, 92.
26. Povinelli, *Economies of Abandonment: Social Belonging and Endurance in Late Liberalism* (Durham, NC: Duke University Press, 2011), 191. Keguro Macharia's thought provoking use of Povinelli in "Not This. More That!" inspired my work here.
27. Césaire, *Toussaint Louverture: La révolution française et al problème colonial* (Paris: Présence Africaine, 1961), 21–22. The French reads, "Saint-Domingue est le premier pays des temps modernes à avoir posé dans la réalité et à avoir proposé à la réflexion des hommes, et cela dans toute sa complexité, sociale, économique, raciale, le grand problème que le xx siècle s'essouffle à résoudre: le problème colonial."
28. Kevin Q. Warner also reads *The Tragedy of King Christophe* with attention to Césaire's political life in his essay "De l'écrivan devenu leader politique: À la recherche d'un héros antillais," in *Soleil éclaté*, ed. Jacqueline Leiner (Tübinger: Gunter Narr, 1984), 421–31.
29. For more scholarly considerations of Césaire's visit to Haiti, see Maximilien Laroche, "Aimé Césaire et Haiti," in *Césaire 70*, ed. Mbwil a Mpaang Ngal and Martin Steins (Paris: Silex, 1984), 91–107; Henock Trouillot, "La présence d'Aimé Césaire en Haïti," in *Soleil éclaté*, ed. Jacqueline Leiner (Tübingen: Gunter Narr, 1984), 405–12; Charles Forsdick, "Haiti and Departmentalization: The Spectral Presence of Toussaint Louverture," *International Journal of Francophone Studies* 11, no. 3 (Nov 2008): 327–44, DOI: https://doi.org/10.1386/ijfs.11.3.327_1; Michelle Kendall, "Co-opting Haitian History in Martinican Theatre," *Journal of Haitian Studies* 19, no. 1 (2013): 185–97; and Walsh, *Free and French*, 107–16.
30. Dayan, "Out of Defeat: Aimé Césaire's Miraculous Words," *Boston Review*, September-October 2008, http://www.bostonreview.net/colin-dayan-out-of-defeat-aime-cesaire.

31. Alex Gil, "La découverte de l'Ur-text de *El les chiens se taisent*" in *Aimé Césaire à l'oeuvre* (Paris: Éditions des archives contemporaines), 145–56. See also Gil's English translation of the play ......*And the Dogs Were Silent* / ......*Et les chiens se taisaient* (Durham, NC: Duke University Press, 2024).
32. Casimir, Colon, and Koerner, "Haiti's Need for a Great South," 24.
33. Casimir and Claypool, "Going Backwards Toward the Future," 186. The failure of the oligarchy to institute plantation labor and the resistance of the peasant population is discussed by Casimir and Claypool in detail. They write: "If, since 1789, and in an accelerated fashion since the ceremony of Bois Caïman, the French colonial administration was unable to ensure the smooth operation of the plantation economy, if Toussaint Louverture had to overcome extraordinary difficulties to militarize and reorganize it, and if the French expeditionary army lost almost 40,000 hardened soldiers in the anti-revolutionary battle, one cannot help but wonder what factors would make the Haitian oligarchy believe it could succeed where its predecessors had lamentably tried and even failed," 184.
34. See Casimir and Claypool, "Going Backwards Toward the Future," 187.
35. Madiou, *Histoire d'Haiti*, 2:176.
36. Casimir, Colon, and Koerner, "Haiti's Need for a Great South," 24.
37. See "Going Backwards Toward the Future," where Casimir and Claypool write, "Before 1915, the list of leaders coming from popular classes included the Pierrots and the Soulouques, born of the dregs of slave society, and the Nord Alexises, the Antoine Simons, the Mérisier Janises, the Jean Jumeaux, and other illiterates from the provinces and rural society of Haiti. After 1915, such characters, incapable of expressing themselves in metropolitan French, were barred from the apex of society. The capillarity initiated by Toussaint Louverture's social mobility ended in 1915 to the great satisfaction of the French oriented Haitians," 188. For more on the disastrous effects of the occupation, see Casimir, *The Haitians*, 382–83.
38. See Michel-Rolph Trouillot, *State Against Nation* (New York: Monthly Review Press, 1990), 133.
39. Gil, "Introduction: The Making," 14. Gary Wilder briefly referenced the speech and writes that Césaire spoke before an audience of "1500" people. See Gary Wilder, *Freedom Time: Negritude, Decolonization, and the Future of the World* (Durham, NC: Duke University Press, 2015), 108. For the Césaire quote directly, see Kora Véron and Thomas A. Hale, *Les écrits d'Aimé Césaire, biobibliographie commentée (1913–2008)* (Paris: Honoré Champion, 2013), 76–77.
40. "Á Haïti, j'ai surtout vu ce qu'il ne fallait pas faire! Un pays qui avait prétendument conquis sa liberté, qui avait conquis son indépendance et que je voyais plus miserable que la Martinque, colonie française! Les intellectuels faisaient de 'l'intectualism', ils écriaient des poèmes, ils prenaient des positions sur telle ou telle question, mais sas rapport avec le people lui-même.

C'était tragique, et cela pouvait très bien nous arriver aussi, à nous Martiniqauis." Césaire and Vergès, *Nègre je suis, nègre je resterai* (Paris: Michel Albin SA, 2005), 56. For English translation, see Césaire and Vergès, *Resolutely Black: Conversations with Françoise Vergès*, trans. Mathew B. Smith (Cambridge: Polity Press, 2020), 32.

41. See *The Haitians*, 41.
42. Fick, *The Making of Haiti*, 25.
43. Césaire and Vergès, *Nègre je suis*, 56; Césaire and Vergès, *Resolutely Black*, 32. The racism of the first US occupation did occasion an intellectual turn to the folk as evidenced by Jean Price-Mars's influential work *Ainsi parla l'oncle*, among other important *Ginen*-inspired writings produced during and after the invasion in Haiti.
44. Walsh, *Free and French*, 113.
45. Césaire and Vergès, *Nègre je suis*, 56; Césaire and Vergès, *Resolutely Black*, 32.
46. For more on colonialism's ties with republicanism, see Nicolas Bancel, Pascal Blanchard, and Françoise Vergès, *La République coloniale: Essai sur une utopie* (Paris: Armand Colin, 2003) and Gary Wilder, *The French Imperial Nation-State: Negritude and Colonial Humanism between the Two World Wars* (Chicago: University of Chicago Press, 2005).
47. Nelson Maldonado-Torres, "On the Coloniality of Being," 245; emphasis in original.
48. Césaire and Vergès, *Nègre je suis*, 56; Césaire and Vergès, *Resolutely Black*, 32.
49. Gil, "Introduction: The Making," 14. For the Césaire quote directly, see Véron and Hale, *Les écrits d'Aimé Césaire*, 76–77.
50. Stieber, *Haiti's Paper War*, 16.
51. See also Gil, "Introduction: The Making," 22.
52. Stieber, *Haiti's Paper War*, 16, 154.
53. The latter included the affluent and the aspirationally affluent "Alexandre Pétion, Nicolas Geffrard, Laurent Férou, Jean-Louis François, Elie Gérin, Guy Joseph Bonnet, Bruno Blanche, David Troy, Yayou, and Guillaume Vaval," writes Chelsea Stieber. See *Haiti's Paper War*, 23–24.
54. Stieber, *Haiti's Paper War*, 16.
55. Césaire and Vergès, *Resolutely Black*, 29. For the French original, see Césaire and Vergès, *Nègre je suis*, 52.
56. Gil, "Introduction: The Making," 14. For the Césaire quote directly, see Véron and Hale, *Les écrits d'Aimé Césaire*, 76–77.
57. Casimir and Claypool, "Going Backwards Toward the Future," 182.
58. Casimir and Claypool, "Going Backwards Toward the Future," 184.
59. Casimir and Claypool, "Going Backwards Toward the Future," 184.
60. Republican revolutionists and future leaders of Haiti, like Pétion, had named themselves *habitant Américain* (American colonists) during the revolutionary struggle. They took this identification to mean that they were the rightful

settlers and owners of the land, and as such, the superiors of the self-liberated in post-independence Haiti. *Ginens* responded by appropriating the designation of *habitant* (colonist) for themselves. See Casimir, Colon, and Koerner, "Haiti's Need for a Great South," 19–20; Casimir and Claypool, "Going Backwards Toward the Future," 173; and Casimir, *The Haitians*, 310. They did so, firstly, to name themselves as the nation's true stewards, and secondly, to resist the republicans attempt to constitute them as servile laborers (or "cultivators") from 1807 onward. Casimir, Colon, and Koerner, "Haiti's Need for a Great South," 19, 20; and Casimir, *The Haitians*, 165. As the nineteenth century progressed, the *Ginen* peasantry went on to radically define themselves as outsiders, *moun andeyo*, persons who exist on the outside of Haiti's (oligarchically driven, Western-facing) socio-political order. For more on "moun andeyo," see Gérard Barthélémy's influential *L'univers rural haïtien: Le pays en dehors* (Paris: L'Harmattan, 1990).

61. Casimir and Claypool, "Going Backwards Toward the Future," 184.
62. Patrice Louis, *Conversation avec Aimé Césaire* (Paris: Arléa, 2007), 64.
63. René Depestre, "Truer than Biography: Aimé Césaire Interviewed by René Depestre," *Savacou* 5 (1971): 77.
64. Gil, "Introduction: The Making," 23; emphasis in original..
65. Césaire, ...*And the Dogs Were Silent*, 82; emphasis in original.
66. Césaire, ...*And the Dogs Were Silent*, 82; emphasis in original.
67. Gil, "Introduction: The Making," 27.
68. Cesaire, ...*And the Dogs Were Silent*, 48.
69. Walsh, *Free and French*, 109.
70. Walsh, *Free and French*, 110.
71. Césaire, *Toussaint Louverture*, 344.
72. Césaire and Vergès, *Nègre je suis*, 56; Césaire and Vergès, *Resolutely Black*, 32.
73. Césaire and Vergès, *Nègre je suis*, 52.
74. Hurley, "'Toussaint Louverture,'" 203; Paul Breslin and Rachel Ney, "Introduction: The Challenge," 209.
75. Césaire and Vergès, *Nègre je suis*, 52. When speaking before the Constituent Assembly of France in 1946 about the living conditions of impoverished French overseas workers, Césaire states: "in a country where salaries are abnormally low and the cost of living approaches that in France, the worker [from the Antilles and Réunion] is at the mercy of sickness, injury, and age without any guarantees accorded to him." Césaire, qtd. in Wilder, *Freedom Time*, 109–10. Worse yet, he states that "almost no effort has been made to assure workers from the Antilles and Réunion an economic and social status that is in harmony with the political status they have enjoyed for a century" as French subjects. Césaire, qtd. in Wilder, *Freedom Time*, 109–10.
76. James, "Lectures," 108–9.

77. James cannot make sense of Haiti as *Ayiti Ginen* either, but his willingness to reimagine the Revolution and rewrite it with the captives foregrounded suggests to me that perhaps one day he could recognize the critical salience of a *Ginen* interpretation of the Revolution and of Haiti.
78. Forsdick, "Haiti and Departmentalization," 333; emphasis in original.
79. Césaire discusses his initial support for departmentalization and disenchantment in the introduction he penned for *Les Antilles décolonisées* by Daniel Guérin (Paris, Présence Africaine, 1956), 9–17. For thorough engagements with Césaire's pursuit of departmentalization, see Nick Nesbitt, "Aimé Césaire and the Logic of Decolonization," in *Caribbean Critique: Antillean Critical Theory from Toussaint to Glissant* (Liverpool: Liverpool University Press, 2013), 86–117; Nesbitt, "Departmentalization and the Spirit of Schoelcher," *L'esprit créateur* 47 no. 1 (2007), 32–43; Wilder, *Freedom Time*, 106–32; Walsh, *Free and French*, 120–21, and Yarimar Bonilla, *Non-Sovereign Futures: French Politics in the Wake of Disenchantment* (Chicago: University of Chicago Press, 2015), 20–24.
80. Nesbitt, "Departmentalization," 32.
81. Nesbitt, "Departmentalization," 32.
82. Nesbitt, "Departmentalization," 32.
83. Wilder, *Freedom Time*, 110.
84. Nesbitt, "Departmentalization," 37.
85. Césaire, *Notebook of a Return to the Native Land*, 27; Césaire and Vergès, *Nègre je suis*, 56.
86. Césaire and Vergès, *Nègre je suis*, 56; emphasis added.
87. Césaire and Vergès, *Nègre je suis*, 56, 52.
88. Lambropoulos, *The Tragic Idea* (London: Gerald Duckworth, 2006), 10.
89. Lambropoulos, *The Tragic Idea*, 8.
90. Césaire, *Toussaint Louverture*, 103. The French reads, "A l'occasion de la question coloniale, la Revolution francaise avait commence il s'affronter elle-meme, et, en se confrontaut avec les principes dont elle etait nee, il se cliver, done a se definer."
91. Lambropoulos, *The Tragic Idea*, 10.
92. Nesbitt, "Departmentalization," 33.
93. Moten, *In the Break: The Aesthetics of the Black Radical Tradition* (Minneapolis: University of Minnesota Press, 2003), 94.
94. Moten, *In the Break*, 94.
95. "On a présenté Christophe comme un homme ridicule, un personnage qui passait son temps à singer les Français. On a mis l'accent sur cet aspect, bien réel, mais moi aussi je suis un nègre, et ce nègre n'avait pas qu'un côté 'singe'. Dans ce singe, il y avait une pensée profonde, une angoisse réelle; j'ai voulu transpercer le grotesque pour trouver le tragique." Césaire and Vergès, *Nègre je suis*, 57.

96. Glick, *The Black Radical Tragic*, 271.
97. Césaire, "Culture and Colonization," trans. Brent Hayes Edwards, *Social Text* 28, no. 2 (2010), 140, 139; emphasis in original.
98. Césaire, "Culture and Colonization," 140, 139; emphasis in original.
99. Césaire, "Culture and Colonization," 139.
100. Césaire, "Culture and Colonization," 140; emphasis in original.
101. Césaire, "Culture and Colonization," 142.
102. Césaire, "Culture and Colonization," 140.
103. Césaire and Vergès, *Nègre je suis*, 52.
104. Césaire, "Culture and Colonization," 140; 141.
105. Casimir, *The Haitians*, xix.
106. Casimir, *The Haitians*, xix; Césaire, "Culture and Colonization," 142.
107. McKittrick, *Dear Science*, 46,142.
108. Césaire, "Letter to Maurice Thorez," trans. Chike Jeffers, *Social Text* 28, no. 2 (2010), 149.
109. Césaire, "Culture and Colonization," 140; emphasis in original; Glick, *The Black Radical Tragic*, 271.
110. Césaire, "Culture and Colonization," 140; emphasis in original.
111. George Yancy, "The Perils of Being a Black Philosopher," *New York Times*, April 4, 2016, https://opinionator.blogs.nytimes.com/2016/04/18/the-perils-of-being-a-black-philosopher.
112. Dash, *Edouard Glissant* (Cambridge: Cambridge University Press, 1995), 6.
113. Césaire, *Toussaint Louverture*, 304.
114. "Il y a beaucoup de moi dans ce livre sur Toussaint Louverture." See Césaire and Vergès, *Nègre je suis*, 54.
115. Forsdick, "Haiti and Departmentalization," 339.
116. Forsdick, "Haiti and Departmentalization," 339.
117. Walsh, *Free and French*, 122.
118. Gil, "Introduction: The Making," 12.
119. Wilder, *Freedom Time*, 194.
120. Wilder, *Freedom Time*, 172.
121. Wilder, *Freedom Time*, 195.
122. Wilder, *Freedom Time*, 195.
123. Louverture is not a bedsheet/cover! This phrasing is tied to the following Vodou song for the *lwa* Gede Nibo, which came to mind: *Gede Nibo nou pa dra. Si nou te dra nou t'ap kouvri pou yo* (Gede Nibo we are not a sheet. If we were, we would cover for them).
124. The play was first published serially, an act per year (1961, 1962, and 1963), in the journal *Présence Africaine*; it was later published by *Présence Africaine* in its entirety in 1963 and substantially amended in 1970. The 1969 English translation by Ralph Manheim is an acting version of the play. The translation I use here by Paul Breslin and Rachel Ney corresponds to the revised 1970 edition.

125. See Bonilla, *Non-Sovereign Futures*, 20–28.
126. For more on Dessalines's anticolonial politics and governance see Deborah Jensen's *Beyond the Slave Narrative* and Chelsea Stieber's *Haiti's Paper War*.
127. Stieber, *Haiti's Paper War*, 1.
128. Stieber, *Haiti's Paper War*, 16.
129. Victor-Emmanuel Roberto Wilson and Jacqueline Van Baelen, "The Forgotten Eighth Wonder of the World," *Callaloo* 15, no. 3 (1992): 852.
130. Wilson and Baelen, "The Forgotten Eighth Wonder," 852.
131. Césaire, *The Tragedy of King Christophe*, 40.
132. Césaire, *The Tragedy of King Christophe*, 40.
133. Césaire, *The Tragedy of King Christophe*, 38.
134. Césaire, *The Tragedy of King Christophe*, 37.
135. Césaire, *The Tragedy of King Christophe*, 37.
136. Césaire, *The Tragedy of King Christophe*, 28.
137. Césaire, *The Tragedy of King Christophe*, 16.
138. Césaire, *The Tragedy of King Christophe*, 28.
139. Césaire, *The Tragedy of King Christophe*, 42.
140. Césaire, *The Tragedy of King Christophe*, 42.
141. Césaire, *The Tragedy of King Christophe*, 28.
142. Césaire, *The Tragedy of King Christophe*, 38.
143. Césaire, *The Tragedy of King Christophe*, 38.
144. Maurya Wickstrom, *Fiery Temporalities in Theatre and Performance: The Initiation of History* (New York: Bloomsbury Methuen Drama, 2018), 102.
145. Wickstrom, *Fiery Temporalities*, 102.
146. Césaire, *The Tragedy of King Christophe*, 38.
147. See Micheal Hanchard, "Afro-Modernity: Temporality, Politics, and the African Diaspora," in *Alternative Modernities*, ed. Dilip Parameshwar Gaonkar (Durham, NC: Duke University Press, 2001), 272–98.
148. Césaire, *The Tragedy of King Christophe*, 42.
149. Césaire, *The Tragedy of King Christophe*, 42.
150. Césaire, *The Tragedy of King Christophe*, 42; emphasis in original.
151. Edward Said, "The Quest for Gillo Pontecorvo," in *Reflections on Exile and Other Literary and Cultural Essays* (London: Granta, 2001), 283.
152. Kaisary describes the film as a "rare and radical bird [because it] strived to break free of the constraints imposed by its genesis in a Hollywood studio environment to communicate a stunning and radical message of Black insurrection as a liberatory historical force;" see *From Havana to Hollywood*, 3. Forsdick and Høgsberg also positively regard the movie and contend that it comes "the closest to recognizing the revolutionary spirit of the enslaved men, women, and children who made the Haitian Revolution." See Forsdick and Høgsbjerg, "Sergei Eisenstein and the Haitian Revolution: 'The Confrontation Between Black and White Explodes Into Red,' *History Workshop Journal*

78, no. 1 (2014),157. Davis emphasizes "the historical achievement of" the film and argues that this "achievement" lies in "its successful experiment in telling specific and general stories at the same time;" see Davis, *Slaves on Screen: Film and Historical Vision* (Cambridge: Harvard University Press, 2000), 52. Lastly, Mellen asserts that the film "sounded a paean to the glory and moral necessity of revolution;" see Mellen, "A Reassessment of Gillo Pontecorvo's Burn!" *Cinema*, no. 32 (1972), 47.

153. For the film's release, see Carlo Celli, *Gillo Pontecorvo: From Resistance to Terrorism* (Latham, MD: Scarecrow Press, 2005), vii. Celli also describes *Queimada!* as Pontecorvo's "most undervalued film." Celli, *Gillo Pontecorvo*, 89. Stevenson critiques Pontecorvo for his presentation of captives as unintelligent since the Black leading man is prodded into revolting by the film's white male lead; see Stevenson, "Filming Black Voices and Stories: Slavery on Americas Screens," *Journal of the Civil War Era* 8, no. 3 (2018), 508. Sepinwall finds the movie's presentation of African dance and women of mixed ancestry wanting because it reinforces racial stereotypes. See Sepinwall, *Slave Revolt on Screen: The Haitian Revolution in Film and Video Games* (Jackson: University Press of Mississippi, 2021) 34. Ella Shohat and Robert Stam's critique relates to the casting of a Hollywood star (Marlon Brando) as the lead. A novice actor is the star's counterpart, which for Shohat and Stam has the effect of creating the context for "the scales of spectatorial fascination" to be tipped "in favor of the colonizer." See Shohat and Stam, *Unthinking Eurocentrism: Multiculturalism and the Media* (New York: Routledge, 2014), 188. Lastly, Stone finds fault with the film's "patronizing psychological assumption" about the ineffectuality of Black agency and self-autonomy, which Stone argues "did not appear in *The Battle of Algiers*." See Stone, "Last Battle: Gillo Pontecorvo's Burn!" *Boston Review* 29, no. 2 (April/May 2004). https://bostonreview.net/articles/alan-stone-last-battle.

154. Avery Gordon, *Ghostly Matters*, 5.

155. Aimé Césaire, *Discourse on Colonialism* (New York: Monthly Review Press, 2000), 39.

156. Pontecorvo's first movie addresses the plight of an impoverished fisherman (*La grande strada Azzurra*; 1957) and is his least political film. This film, like his second on the holocaust (*Kapo*; 1960), are focused on Western Europe much as his last film (*Orgo*; 1979), which concerns Basque resistance during Francisco Franco's fascist rule of Spain. His remaining two pictures are set outside of Western Europe: his third and most famous film takes place in Algeria and concerns the Algerian Revolution (*The Battle of Algiers*; 1961) and his fourth picture, which I treat here, is loosely based on captive uprisings in the Caribbean and Latin America (*Queimada!*; 1969). Davis writes that "Pontecorvo, together with scriptwriters Solinas and Franco Giorgio Arloria, put together events from Brazil, Saint-Domingue, Jamaica, Cuba, and elsewhere" to accurately portray captive resistance in film; see Davis, *Slaves on Screen*, 44. Taken together, his

oeuvre links the genocidal actions of Hitler in Germany and Franco in Spain to the genocidal destruction of the ally nation of France wrought in its colonial territory of Algeria while fighting Nazi Germany in World War II. They show Pontecorvo's awareness of how the rise of fascism in Europe was inextricably linked to the long existent colonial project pursued and maintained by more powerful Western European nations. Indeed, that Mussolini attempted to expand Italy's colonial possessions when in power likely cemented his recognition of the ties that bind fascism to colonial power. For more on Italy and colonialism, see Neelam Srivastava, who writes that Italy's invasion of Ethiopia in 1935 was Mussolini's attempt to "build up Italian colonial possessions at a time in which colonialism was beginning its decline and anti-imperialist movements were developing in various parts of the European empires." Srivastava, *Italian Colonialism and Resistance of Empire, 1930–1970* (London: Palgrave Macmillan UK, 2018), 15. For more on how the Italo-Ethiopian war acted as a catalyst for anti-fascist and anticolonial resistance movements on the eve of World War II, see Srivastava, *Italian Colonialism*, 204–11.

157. Pontecorvo's attention to colonial violence in *Queimada!* and *The Battle of Algiers* was shaped by his reading of Frantz Fanon's anticolonial writings, which likely accounts for why he showcases the transformative effects of violence undertaken by the colonized. See Neelam Srivastava, "Anticolonial Violence and the 'Dictatorship of the Truth' in the Films of Gillo Pontecorvo: An Interview," *Interventions: International Journal of Postcolonial Studies* 7, no. 1 (2005): 97–106.

158. *Queimada!*, directed by Gillo Pontecorvo (United Artists, 1969), 2:07:00–2:08:30. https://youtu.be/cF5mhZDXoKc.

159. Césaire, "Culture and Colonization," 140; emphasis in original.

160. *Queimada!*, 39:07–39:22.

161. *Queimada!*, 39:23–39:52.

162. *Queimada!*, 35:15–37:90.

163. *Queimada!*, 37:30–37:57.

164. *Queimada!*, 39:10–39:14.

165. *Queimada!*, 39:23–39:52.

166. *Queimada!*, 39:07–39:22.

167. Someruelos to Secretario de Estado, July 28, 1810, in AGI, Estado, leg. 12, exp. 51, quoted in Ada Ferrer, *Freedom's Mirror: Cuba and Haiti in the Age of Revolution* (New York: Cambridge University Press, 2014), 259.

168. Someruelos to Secretario de Estado, July 28, 1810, in AGI, Estado, leg. 12, exp. 51, qtd. in Ferrer, *Freedom's Mirror*, 259.

169. *Queimada!*, 39:23–39:52.

170. *Queimada!*, 1:18:50–1:19:15.

171. *Queimada!*, 1:18:50–1:19:15.

172. *Queimada!*, 1:00:49–1:01:05.

173. *Queimada!*, 1:01:06–1:01:07
174. *Queimada!*, 2:06:03–2:06:14.
175. Césaire, "Culture and Colonization," 140, 141.
176. Aimé Césaire, *A Tempest*, trans. Richard Miller (New York: Theater Communications Group, 2002), 62.
177. Césaire, *A Tempest*, 63.
178. Césaire, *A Tempest*, 65, 66.
179. Césaire, *A Tempest*, 67.
180. Ralph Korngold's 1944 biography of Louverture espouses this rumor as does Madison Smartt Bell's 2007 biography; see Korngold, *Citizen Toussaint* (Boston: Little, Brown and Company, 1944) and Bell, *Toussaint Louverture*, 78–79.

Chapter 4

1. *Chapo ba, respè pou yo* directly translates as "hats off, respect for them," but figuratively resonates as I have translated it here. I am grateful to Kellie Carter Jackson and our ongoing conversations concerning Trouillot's *Silencing the Past* for bringing the importance of this contention to my attention.
2. And all whom we don't know. . . . We haven't forgotten.
3. After securing Haitian independence in 1804, Dessalines is said to have declared: "I have avenged America." See Laurent Dubois's aptly titled *Avengers of the New World*, and Lysuis Salomon's commemorative utterance thirty-nine years following Dessalines' death: "Avenger of the black race, liberator of Haiti, founder of independence, Emperor Dessalines! today is your glory, the sun today burns for you as radiantly as it did in 1804." See Joan Dayan, *Haiti, History, and the Gods*, 27. C. L. R. James famously reads Toussaint as a "figure of enlightenment," which I address in Chapter 1. See *The Black Jacobins: Toussaint L'Ouverture and the San Domingo Revolution* (New York: Vintage, 1989), 288.
4. Dayan, *Haiti, History and the Gods*, 6.
5. Jana Evans Braziel, "Re-membering Défilée: Dédée Bazile as Revolutionary Lieu de Mémoire," *Small Axe* 9, no. 2 (2005), 60.
6. See Edwidge Danticat, *Krik? Krak!* (New York: Vintage Contemporaries, 1996), 27.
7. In *Brother, I Am Dying*, a family memoir that recounts her uncle's detention and later death in Immigration and Naturalization Services (INS) custody, Danticat reveals that her uncle's name is "Joseph Nosius," 76; her uncle's grandchildren are named "Maxime, Nozial . . . [and] Joseph." See *Brother, I Am Dying* (New York: Vintage Books, 2007), 171. She also has another uncle named "Franck" and a cousin named "Maxo," 247, 25.
8. "Kitchen poets" is a designation borrowed from the Bajan-American writer Paule Marshall and is meant to underscore how Bajan women, as Haitian women, are overdetermined, at home and abroad, by two kitchens: that at the

nape of the neck (signaling their race) and that where one cooks (signaling their gender). See Paule Marshall, "From the Poets in the Kitchen," *Callaloo* 2 no. 2 (2001), 627–33.

9. Danticat, *Krik? Krak!*, 222. Both hair braiding and cooking are micropractices that religious studies scholar Elizabeth Perez persuasively demonstrates "hold the chief ingredients for the survival of Black Atlantic religions," as "elders [within Santeria, as Vodou] regard [them] as a prelude to eventual initiation." See Elizabeth Perez, *Religion in the Kitchen: Cooking, Talking, and the Making of Black Atlantic Traditions* (New York: New York University Press, 2016) 15.
10. Danticat, *Krik? Krak!*, 224, 219, 221, 222, 224.
11. Danticat, *Krik? Krak!*, 221.
12. Danticat, *Krik? Krak!*, 221.
13. Danticat, *Krik? Krak!*, 222; Marshall, "From the Poets," 630.
14. Marshall, "From the Poets," 630.
15. Marshall, "From the Poets," 630; Danticat's entire oeuvre is driven by this refutation. See her novels *Claire of the Sea Light* (New York: Vintage Books, 2013); *Behind the Mountains* (New York: Orchard Press, 2002); *Eight Days: A Story of Haiti* (New York: Orchard Press, 2010); *Breath, Eyes, Memory* (New York: SoHo, Press 1994); *Farming of Bones* (New York: SoHo Press, 1998); *The Dew Breaker* (New York: Knopf, 2004); her travel narrative *After the Dance: A Walk Through Carnival Jacmel, Haiti* (New York: Penguin, 2002); her family memoir *Brother, I Am Dying* (New York: Vintage Books, 2007); her short-story collection *Everything Inside: Stories* (New York; Knopf, 2020); and her essay collection *Create Dangerously* (New York: Vintage, 2010).
16. The phrase "development as progress" refers to a twenty-first-century understanding of progress derived from María Josefina Saldaña-Portillo's *The Revolutionary Imagination in the Americas and the Age of Development* (Durham, NC: Duke University Press, 2003). Whereas the Enlightenment and the Age of Revolution reveals that progress is the means by which existence can be remade anew, laying the foundation for a free liberal democratic existence through revolution, following World War II when much of the world was in upheaval due to decolonization movements and the communist peril, Saldaña-Portillo suggests that revolution itself (be it liberal democratic or socialist) was a threat to the very existence progress-as-revolution valorized.
17. Sigmund Freud, "Mourning and Melancholia," *Collected Papers* (London: Hogarth Press, 1953) 152–70.
18. David L. Eng and David Kazanjian, "Introduction: Mourning Remains," in *Loss: Politics of Mourning* (Berkeley: University of California Press, 2003) 4.
19. Freud, "Mourning and Melancholia," 155, 166.
20. Eng and Kazanjian, "Introduction," 6.
21. Eng and Kazanjian, "Introduction," 4.
22. Casimir, *The Haitians*, 294.

23. Casimir, *The Haitians*, 287.
24. This system names the institutions and mechanisms by which the rural majority or Ginen folk resisted the oligarchic state and imperialism. It includes "gender relations, family, the creation of the lakou [communal courtyard], indivisible collective property, Vodou temples, rural markets, garden-towns, leisure, crafts, [and] the arts." See Casimir, *The Haitians*, 351.
25. See Angela Naimou, *Salvage Work: U.S. and Caribbean Literatures amid the Debris of Legal Personhood* (New York: Fordham University Press, 2015), 103.
26. For personal details of her life, see Jean Fouchard, *La Méringue: Danse nationale d'Haïti* (Montreal: Eds. Leméac, 1974) 77–80; and Octave Petit, "Défilée-La-Folle," *Revue de la Société d'Histoire et de Géographie d'Haïti* 3, no. 8 (October 1932), 3.
27. See Petit, "Défilée-La-Folle," 4, 5, 6; and Dayan, *Haiti, History, and the Gods*, 44.
28. See Dayan, *Haiti, History and the Gods*, 40.
29. Dayan, *Haiti, History and the Gods*, 40; and Casimir, *The Haitians*, 324.
30. Casimir, *The Haitians*, 13.
31. Casimir, *The Haitians*, 324.
32. Casimir, *The Haitians*, 324.
33. Trouillot, *Stirring the Pot*, 127.
34. Chelsea Stieber outlines who these oligarchs were in *Haiti's Paper War*, 22, 24.
35. See Jean Jacques Dessalines, "The Haitian Declaration of Independence," in *The Haiti Reader: History, Culture, Politics*, ed. Laurent Dubois, Kaiama L. Glover, Nadève Ménard, Millery Polyné, and Chantalle F. Verna (Durham, NC: Duke University Press, 2020), 24.
36. Casimir, *The Haitians*, 218–19.
37. Janvier, *Constitutions d'Haiti (1801–1885)* (Paris: Marpon et Flammarion, 1886), 31–32.
38. For more on Dessalines's politics, see Deborah Jensen's *Beyond the Slave Narrative: Politics, Sex, and Manuscripts in the Haitian Revolution* (Liverpool: Liverpool University Press, 2012); Chelsea Stieber's *Haiti's Paper War*, and Casimir's *The Haitians: A Decolonial History*.
39. Casimir, *The Haitians*, 219.
40. Pétion governed the entirety of the south until the mixed-race *gens de couleur* and staunchly republican revolutionist André Rigaud returned to Haiti from France after a brief stay in the United States. Rigaud appropriated a portion of Pétion's territory in 1810 and governed it until his death in 1811. After Rigaud's passing, Pétion re-assumed control of the entire south.
41. Casimir, *The Haitians*, 199.
42. Casimir, *The Haitians*, 168, 169.
43. In "Going Backwards Toward the Future," Casmir and Mary Claypool write, the "kingdom of the North [operated as] a conquering state [that] implanted and imposed the material foundations for the economy with the iron fist from

large planters and the enthusiasm of *nouveaux riches* in the process of building their preeminence." See "Going Backwards Toward the Future," 186. For more about Christophe's infrastructural efforts to alleviate Ginen suffering, see Casimir, *The Haitians*, 168, 196, 204, and 316.
44. Casimir, *The Haitians*, 165.
45. Casimir, *The Haitians*, 165.
46. Ardouin, *Études sur l'histoire d'Haïti*, 4:36.
47. Casimir, *The Haitians*, 219; Dayan, *Haiti, History and the Gods*, 14.
48. Casimir, *The Haitians*, 214, 170 and 177. For detailed analysis of Boyer's code see 171–79. For discussion of Geffrard's code, see Casimir, *The Haitians*, 178–82.
49. Casimir, *The Haitians*, 219.
50. Casimir, *The Haitians*, 63; Leslie Manigat, *Éventail d'histoire*, 2:27.
51. Casimir, *The Haitians*, 63.
52. Casimir, *The Haitians*, 214.
53. See Casimir, *The Haitians*, 64–66.
54. Madiou, *Histoire d'Hiati*, 8:77.
55. Madiou, *Histoire d'Hiati*, 8:77.
56. Dayan, *Haiti, History, and the Gods*, 15, 27.
57. Dayan, *Haiti, History and the Gods*, 27–28.
58. Dayan, *Haiti, History and the Gods*, 27.
59. Dayan, *Haiti, History and the Gods*, 28.
60. "Elle enveloppa d'attention et de tendresse le corps inanimé de l'Empereur. Elle glissa dans un sac la tête de celui qui donna le jour à une nation. En essayant de porter sur ses épaules de femmes les restes de Dessalines, au meme moment, tel Simon de Cyrène Dauphin, un autre fou célèbre, se présenta afin d'apporter son aide a la folle." See Fouchard, *La Méringue*, 56.
61. Dayan, *Haiti, History and the Gods*, 45.
62. Jérémie qtd. in Dayan, *Haiti, History and the Gods*, 44; Petit, "Défilée-La-Folle," 7. For the French original, see Fouchard, *La Méringue*, 56.
63. Dayan, *Haiti, History and the Gods*, 40.
64. Dayan, *Haiti, History and the Gods*, 40.
65. Braziel, "Re-membering Défilée," 59.
66. Ram, "Defile," 2008, track 4 on *Gran Bwa*, Willibelle Publishing, May 16, 2016, CD.
67. *Layité* has no English equivalent and means to both *banboche* and *pran plezi*, all the while imparting the importance of a relaxed body to revelry.
68. See Aníbal Quijano, "Coloniality and Modernity/Rationality," *Cultural Studies* 21, no. 2–3 (March/May 2007), 169.
69. Sophie Mariñez calls into question whether the massacre happened at all and invites consideration of how the fraught political relations between the Dominican Republic and Haiti invented a happening that did not occur as memorialized; see her book, *Spirals in the Caribbean: Representing Violence and Connection in Haiti and the Dominican Republic* (Philadelphia: University of Pennsylvania

Press, 2024). For the reference to Dessalines's involvement in Moca cited here, see Richard L. Turtis, "A World Destroyed, A Nation Imposed: The 1937 Haitian Massacre in the Dominican Republic," *Hispanic American Historical Review*, 82, no. 3 (2002), 590, and Lester D. Langley, *The Americas in the Age of Revolution* (New Haven, CT: Yale University Press, 1998), 193. For more on the massacre, see Turits, "A World Destroyed," 633–34.

70. See Julia Gaffield, "We Have Dared to Be Free," *Public Books*, January 10, 2024, https://www.publicbooks.org/we-have-dared-to-be-free.

71. See Turits, "A World Destroyed," 599; David Nicholls, *From Dessalines to Duvalier: Race, Colour and National Independence in Haiti* (New York: Cambridge University Press, 1979), 167; Michelle Wucker, "The River Massacre: The Real and Imagined Borders of Hispaniola," Windows on Haiti, accessed March 19, 2025, http://haitiforever.com/windowsonhaiti/wucker1.shtml.

72. Turits, "A World Destroyed," 615.

73. Danticat returns to *Kout Kouto-a* in her 1998 novel *The Farming of Bones*, a narrative that more extensively deals with the traumatic aftereffects of the massacre. In the novel, Danticat also draws attention to the Haitian Revolution and its enduring significance to Haitian cultural identity by interspersing her text with references to Henry Christophe's famous citadel, La Citadelle Laferrière.

74. See Dubois, *Avengers of the New World*, 92.

75. James, *The Black Jacobins*, 88.

76. See DuBois, *Avengers of the New World*, 99; Carolyn E. Fick, *The Making of Haiti*, 92.

77. Fick, *The Making of Haiti*, 261, 91.

78. Fick, *The Making of Haiti*, 91.

79. Dubois, *Avengers of the New World*, 100; Fick, *The Making of Haiti*, 265; David P. Geggus, "The Bois Caiman Ceremony," *Journal of Caribbean History* 25 (1991), 50.

80. See Dubois, *Avengers of the New World*, 99–102; Geggus, "The Bois Caiman Ceremony"; and Léon-François Hoffmann, "Histoire, mythe et idéologie: La cérémonie du Bois-Caïman," in *Haïti: Lettres et l'être* (Toronto: Editions du GREF, 1992).

81. Dayan, *Haiti, History and the Gods*, 29. Fick, *The Making of Haiti*, 260–66.

82. For the exorcism of Boukman, see "Exorcizing Boukman: This Week in Haiti," *Haiti Progres*, 16, no. 20 (1998) 5–12, available through the World History Archives, Harford Web Publishing, http://www.hartford-hwp.com/archives/43a/520.html. For more on evangelical attacks on Vodou and the importance of *Bwa Kayiman* to these attacks, see Elizabeth McAlister, "From Slave Revolt to a Blood Pact with Satan: The Evangelical Rewriting of Haitian History," *Studies in Religion / Sciences Religieuses* 41, no. 2. (2012), 187–215.

83. Fick, *The Making of Haiti*, 102.

84. Dubois, *Avengers of the New World*, 92; James, *The Black Jacobins*, 87.

85. Dubois, *Avengers of the New World*, 92.

86. Sidney Mintz, *Sweetness and Power: The Place of Sugar in Modern History* (New York: Penguin Books, 1986), xx.
87. In *The Making of Haiti*, Fick writes, "with the advancement and expansion of Saint Domingue's sugar economy, the *petit blancs* witnessed the progressive closing off of their chances for property ownership, the one criterion that would guarantee their social integration [with wealthy whites] and satisfy their frustrated aspirations. In addition, they suffered increasing competition from the *affranchis* [free Blacks and mulattos] and even the upper-strata slaves for jobs in the trades" (18). The grim fate of the *petit blancs* led many captive persons to understand that they were not "white" in the full sense of the word, as their freedom was continually undermined by their economic hardships. Called *blanchet, faux blanc*, and *Nègre-blanc* by captives, *petit blancs* were regarded as living lives far inferior to that of the *affranchi*, the lucky among themselves and the *grand blanc* (planters, maritime bourgeoisie, and French-born bureaucrats).
88. Fouchard, *The Haitian Maroons*, 367n157.
89. Jean Casimir, *The Haitians*, 165.
90. See Robert Lacerte, "The Evolution of Land and Labor in the Haitian Revolution, 1791–1820," *The Americas* 34, no. 4 (April 1978), 459.
91. Casimir, *The Haitians*, 219.
92. Casimir, *The Haitians*, 219.
93. Casimir, *The Haitians*, 219.
94. Casimir, *The Haitians*, 219. Robert Lacerte attributes Haiti's high standard of living to the "republicanization" of land, which he argues resulted in "nearly twenty-five years of relative peace." See "The Evolution of Land and Labor in the Haitian Revolution, 1791–1820," 459. I follow Casimir, whose reading recognizes the power of *Ginen* people.
95. Casimir, Colon, and Koerner, "Haiti's Need for a Great South," 24.
96. Casimir, Colon, and Koerner, "Haiti's Need for a Great South," 24.
97. See "Going Backwards Toward the Future," where Casimir and Claypool write, "Before 1915, the list of leaders coming from popular classes included the Pierrots and the Soulouques, born of the dregs of slave society, and the Nord Alexises, the Antoine Simons, the Mérisier Janises, the Jean Jumeaux, and other illiterates from the provinces and rural society of Haiti. After 1915, such characters, incapable of expressing themselves in metropolitan French, were barred from the apex of society. The capillarity initiated by Toussaint Louverture's social mobility ended in 1915 to the great satisfaction of the French oriented Haitians" (188). For more on the disastrous effects of the occupation, see Casimir, *The Haitians*, 382–83.
98. Danticat, "A Wall of Rising Fire," 73.
99. See Elizabeth DeLoughrey, *Routes and Roots: Navigating Caribbean and Pacific Island Literatures* (Honolulu: University of Hawai'i Press, 2007), 10–11.
100. Quijano, "Coloniality and Modernity/Rationality," 169.

101. Quijano, "Coloniality and Modernity/Rationality," 169.
102. See Casimir, *The Haitians*, 39.
103. See Dayan, *Haiti, History and the Gods*, 39.
104. Dayan, *Haiti, History and the Gods*, 39.
105. Danticat, *Krik? Krak!* 43; emphasis added.
106. Danticat, *Krik? Krak!* 40.
107. Danticat, *Krik? Krak!* 40.
108. The "official" response to the massacre by the Haitian government revealed a complete disregard for both the dead and the living. Regarding *Kout Kouto-a*, Richard Lee Turits writes that "Haiti did not respond militarily to defend or avenge its compatriots. To the contrary, President [Sténio] Vincent of Haiti acted in every way possible to avoid a military conflict. It was not only the army that Vincent held back. He prohibited public discussion of the massacre and refused for a long time even to allow the church to perform masses for the dead," "A World Destroyed," 622–23.
109. Danticat, *Krik? Krak!*, 46.
110. Maya Deren, *Divine Horsemen*, 81.
111. Legend indicates that most within this regiment defected, opting to fight with the captives rather than with the French. They settled in Haiti, where their descendants remain today. In *Poland's Caribbean Tragedy*, Jan Pachonski and Reule K. Wilson argue that while some Poles did defect and some settled in Haiti, most did not. The popularity of this legend, they argue, is the result of propaganda from Dessalines (labeled the "butcher of whites") and the actions of the Poles themselves. They were often kinder to the captives and did not care for the French. See Pachonski and Wilson, *Poland's Caribbean Tragedy: A Study of the Polish Legions in the Haitian War of Independence 1802–1803* (New York: Columbia University Press, 1986), 307–317.
112. McCarthy Brown, *Mama Lola*, 229.
113. Although the occupation officially ended in 1934, US presence and influence did not cease until 1940. For more on the US Occupation of Haiti and US "modernization" efforts, see Hans Schmidt's *The United States Occupation of Haiti, 1915–1934* (New Brunswick, NJ: Rutgers University Press, 1971), 4, and Mary A. Renda's *Taking Haiti: Military Occupation and the Culture of U.S. Imperialism, 1915–1940* (Chapel Hill: University of North Carolina Press, 2001). For more on the anti-superstition campaign, see Nicholls, *From Dessalines to Duvalier*, 181–83.
114. See Sylvia Wynter, "The Pope Must Have Been Drunk," 20. For more on the first US Occupation of Haiti, see Brenda Gayle Plummer, *Haiti and the Great Powers, 1902–1915* (Baton Rouge: Louisiana State University Press, 1988); Hans Schmidt's *The United States Occupation of Haiti, 1915–1934* (New Brunswick, NJ: Rutgers University Press); and Mary Renda, *Taking Haiti: Military Occupation*

and the Culture of US Imperialism, 1915–1940 (Chapel Hill: University of North Carolina Press, 2001).
115. Turits, "A World Destroyed," 612.
116. Vodou is still considered backward by the international community and by some Haitians. An affluent character in the story "Between the Pool and the Gardenias," also in *Krik? Krak!*, expresses this sentiment when she states: "Why can't none of them [poor Haitians] get a spell to make themselves rich? It's that voodoo nonsense that's holding us Haitians back." See Danticat, *Krik? Krak!*, 95.
117. Nicholls, *From Dessalines to Duvalier*, 181–83. While witches are not a part of popular Vodou, Christian thought conflates Vodou with all things evil and thus with sorcery and witchery. A *manbò* is thought to be the same as a witch (*loupgarou*) and an *oungan* as a *bokor* (sorcerer). *Manbòs* and *oungans* are in the business of preserving and aiding life, *bokors* and *loupgarou* take and destroy lives. The former are by no means synonymous with the latter.
118. Danticat, *Krik? Krak!*, 44, 47.
119. Danticat, *Krik? Krak!*, 42, 49.
120. Danticat, *Krik? Krak!*, 49.
121. *Ginen* is a subterranean "heaven" within Vodou; see this book's introduction. Haitian lore is full of stories of persons bathing in streams, rivers or the ocean and being abruptly submerged, taken home to *Ginen*. There they learn the arts of healing and are returned in a day, week, month or year (or more) emboldened with new life vigor and the ability to work as an *oungan* or *manbò*.
122. Danticat, *Krik? Krak!*, 67.
123. Danticat, *Krik? Krak!*, 66, 68.
124. Danticat, *Krik? Krak!*, 61.
125. Danticat, *Krik? Krak!*, 61.
126. Danticat, *Krik? Krak!*, 73.
127. Danticat, *Krik? Krak!*, 73; emphasis added.
128. Danticat, *Krik? Krak!*, 73.
129. Danticat, *Krik? Krak!*, 73–74.
130. Danticat, *Krik? Krak!*, 76.
131. Danticat, *Krik? Krak!*, 56; emphasis in original.
132. Danticat, *Krik? Krak!*, 71; emphasis in original.
133. Danticat, *Krik? Krak!*, 78.
134. Danticat, *Krik? Krak!*, 54.
135. Danticat, *Krik? Krak!*, 56.
136. The Boukman of historical fact stated: "The Good Lord created the sun of which gives us light from above, who rouses the sea and makes the thunder roar—listen well, all of you—this god, hidden in the clouds, watches. He sees all that the white man does. The god of the white man calls him to commit

crimes; our god asks only good works of us. But this god who is so good orders revenge! He will direct our hands; he will aid us. Throw away the image of the god of the whites who thirsts for our tears and listen to the voice of liberty which speaks in the hearts of all of us." Fick persuasively argues that Boukman's "Good Lord" is the supreme being of the Vodou imaginary. She calls attention to the syncretism of captive society and points to how language was a creolized expression, providing new meaning to "old" words. See Fick, *The Making of Haiti*, 93.

137. Danticat, *Krik? Krak!*, 57. His recounting is described as "like the last burst of lightning out of clearing sky."
138. Danticat, *Krik? Krak!*, 57.
139. Danticat, *Krik? Krak!*, 57.
140. Danticat, *Krik? Krak!*, 94.
141. Danticat, *Krik? Krak!*, 94.
142. See Fick, *The Making of Haiti*, 266.
143. The stormy nature of the ceremonial night was a detail first added by the French surgeon Antoine Dalmas and then preserved faithfully thereafter by all other writers of the Revolution, fiction and non-fiction writers alike. See Dubois 100. Hérard Dumesle is the first Haitian writer to include this now canonical detail in his 1824 history of the Revolution, *Voyage dans le nord d'Hayti*. The passage calls to mind Danticat's rendering because of its emphasis on the collective agency and unity of the captives. Dumesle writes, "Vers le milieu du mois d'août 1791, les cultivateurs, manufacturiers et artisans deplusieurs ateliers se réunirent pendant la nuit, *au milieu d'un violent orage* dans une forêt épaisse qui couvre le sommet du morne rouge, et là formèrent le plan d'une vaste insurrection qu'ils sanctifièrent par une cérémonie religieuse." See *Voyage dans le Nord d'Hayti, ou, Revelations des lieux et des monumens historiques*. (Aux Cayes: Imp. du Gouvernement, 1824), 85; emphasis added.
144. Fick, *The Making of Haiti*, 266, 93; Danticat, *Krik? Krak!*, 56; emphasis in original.
145. Danticat, *Krik? Krak!*, 41, 34.
146. Dubois, *Avengers of the New World*, 91.
147. James, *The Black Jacobins*, 25.
148. See Paula Burnett, *Derek Walcott: Politics and Poetics* (Gainesville: University of Florida Press, 2000), 57, emphasis in original.
149. See Derek Walcott, *The Haitian Trilogy* (New York: Farrar, Straus & Giroux, 2002), 101.
150. Walcott, *The Haitian Trilogy*, 13.
151. Danticat, *Krik? Krak!*, 57.
152. Danticat, *Krik? Krak!*, 56.
153. Danticat, *Krik? Krak!*, 59.

154. Danticat, *Krik? Krak!*, 99.
155. Danticat, *Krik? Krak!*, 94.

Conclusion

1. Walcott, "Drums and Colours," 122.
2. Walcott, "Drums and Colours," 122.
3. See *Timbuktu*, 42:00 to 42:06. "I would rather be a *Ginen* person." To parallel how the Kreyòl repeats *pitou*, which can mean "would rather/rather" or "preferably/prefer," this sentence can also be translated as "it is preferable . . . yes, preferable to be a *Ginen* person."
4. *Timbuktu*, 1:08:21 to 1:08:46.
5. Before Zabou's appearance, a Black Malian woman rebuffs the Black jihadist who demands that she sell fish with gloves. Soon after, the city's Arab Imam tries to reason with the jihadist's Libyan (Arab) leader and talk him out of his jihad. Following that, a mixed-race Malian Tuaregan woman (Satima, the protagonist's wife) defies the overtures of an enamored Arab jihadist. See *Timbuktu*, 11:30 to 12:15, 15:13 to 17:08 and 17:13 to 19:35.
6. Tuaregs are a semi-nomadic group of mixed-race peoples of Berber ancestry. They are predominately Muslim and identified by some as Arabs. They reside in the Sahel region, which includes territory within the nation-states of Mali, Niger, Burkina Faso, Algeria, and Libya.
7. Tuaregs have a long history of cultural and political autonomy in the Sahel region (since the fifteenth century) and a more recent (nineteenth century onward) history of rebellion because of having lost this autonomy. Their rebellion has been waged primarily against European colonizers (France mostly), Black African and Arab African postcolonial political leaders, and the United States (e.g., the war on terror). The 2012 jihadist invasion of northern Mali that began on January 16 was part of a Tuaregan resistance movement, which sought to free Tuaregs from the postcolonial state of Mali and the colonial project of the West. Emizet F. Kisangani writes that Mali, post independence, was first led by the "Black African ethnic groups" who had access to education under the French, who colonized Mali in 1892 and named it French Sudan; see Kisangani, "The Tuaregs' Rebellions in Mali and Niger and the U.S. Global War on Terror," *International Journal of World Peace* 29, no. 1 (March 2012), 70. "Black African ethnic groups" continued to govern Mali and openly discriminated against Tuaregs who were, for some, former overlords. Tuaregs were once slavers of Black Africans in the precolonial moment and some Tuaregs detested being governed by former captives. The charged history between Mali's racially and ethnically distinct peoples, coupled with the postcolonial Malian state's acceptance of the borders Western European imperial powers

had allotted to Mali and the nations in the Sahel at the Berlin Conference (1884–1886) set Tuaregs at odds with the state and Black Malians, as Tuaregs were effectively dispossessed of their former standing and way of life, having limited mobility and limited access to arable land; see Kisangani, "The Tuaregs' Rebellions," 64. Internecine conflict became a consistent feature of Malian political life as a result. The 2012 jihadist invasion led by the National Movement for the Liberation of Azawad was one iteration of this conflict. Azawad sought to create an independent nation for Tuaregs and allied with the Islamic militant group Ansar Dine, another Tuareg resistance movement. The latter imposed the strict sharia law that the film depicts. The 2012 jihadist invasion ended with the military intervention of the French in September 2013, though the conflict continued. For an exhaustive discussion of Sahel, the interethnic conflicts in the region and the colonial project, see the entirety of Kisangani's essay, "The Tuaregs' Rebellions in Mali."

8. *Timbuktu*, 19:37 to 20:00.
9. *Timbuktu*, 1:08:47 to 1:08:53.
10. *Timbuktu*, 42:00 to 42:06.
11. See Dionne Brand, *In Another Place, Not Here* (New York: Grove Press, 2000).
12. Walcott, "Drums and Colours," 122.
13. Walcott, "Drums and Colours," 121.
14. Walcott, "Drums and Colours," 104.
15. Walcott, "Drums and Colours," 119.
16. Walcott, "Drums and Colours," 124.
17. Harold N. McDermott, "Towards 'that republic in which complexions do not matter': Derek Walcott's *Drums and Colours* Fifty Years On," *Anthurium: A Caribbean Studies Journal* 11, no. 2 (2014): 6. Mano's mixed-race ancestry and Walcott's multi-racial understanding of the Caribbean dramatizes Walcott's concerns with appeasing the short lived West Indian Federation (1958-1962). The government of the Federation financed the pageant, and it did so to elicit enthusiasm for the Federation among distinct Anglophone Caribbean polities. The racially and culturally varied peoples of these polities were unconvinced of their cultural similarity to neighboring Caribbean territories, those who were slated to be a part of the Federation and those not; the Federation reasoned that if the people knew their history as a region, they would support a collectivist government. Mano's color also facilitates Walcott's critique of the "clean-face browns from Babylon," to quote Barbadian poet Kamau Brathwaite. The "clean-face brown['s]" forebear is not just the colonist, for Walcott, but also the Haitian revolutionist turned political leader who uncritically mimes the colonist. As the archetype of the "clean-face browns," Mano represents a new age of Caribbean leadership. This age has moved from the colonial predation of the sixteenth, seventeenth, and eighteenth centuries, ventured past the Black power politics of Haiti in the eighteenth and nineteenth centuries,

and settled into the brown bourgeois politics of performative inclusivity in the twentieth century. See Edward Kamau Brathwaite, *The Arrivants: A New World Trilogy* (New York: Oxford University Press, 1973), 74-5.
18. For more on the play and its ties to the West Indian Federation (1958-1962), see Joe Kraus, "Through Loins and Coins: Derek Walcott's Weaving of the West Indian Federation," *Callaloo* 28, no. 1 (2005): 60–74.
19. See Alejo Carpentier, prologue to *The Kingdom of This World*, trans. Pablo Medina (New York: Farrar, Straus and Giroux, 2017), xx.
20. Kisangani, "The Tuaregs' Rebellions," 64.
21. Kisangani, "The Tuaregs' Rebellions," 64.
22. Kisangani, "The Tuaregs' Rebellions," 63, 62-65.
23. Kisangani, "The Tuaregs' Rebellions," 63, 62-65.
24. Kisangani, "The Tuaregs' Rebellions," 64.
25. Kisangani, "The Tuaregs' Rebellions," 64.
26. Kisangani, "The Tuaregs' Rebellions," 64.
27. Kisangani, "The Tuaregs' Rebellions," 64.
28. *Timbuktu*, 1:08:56 to 1:09:15.
29. *Timbuktu*, 1:08:56 to 1:09:15.
30. Walsh, "Pedagogical Notes"; see also *Timbuktu*, 1:08:56 to 1:09:15.
31. The saying *depi nan Ginen, nèg rayi nèg* translates as "since Africa, Black people have betrayed other Black people." It is often used to suggest that Haitians can never get along and they never have. The Revolution suggests otherwise, *combite* suggests otherwise, *sòl* suggests otherwise, how easily Haitians banded together in times of crisis (e.g., the 2010 earthquake) and sociopolitical protest (e.g., the 2024 canal building initiatives) all suggest otherwise. *Combite* is a type of solidarity work that often takes place in rural areas. *Sòl* "is a group money-saving method that works on a (usually short-term) rotating cycle." For more on *sòl*, see Smelanda Jean-Baptiste, "Sòl, and How Traditionally-African Economies Persevered Through Colonialism," *Woy Magazine*, January 23, 2020, https://woymagazine.com/2020/01/23/sol-traditionally-african-economies-persevered-colonialism. For the United Nations–supported and US-funded security mission that has deployed more than four hundred Kenyan police officers in Haiti since June of 2024, see Nate Koury, "Imperialism Comes to Haiti with a Black Face," Liberation, June 26, 2024, https://www.liberationnews.org/imperialism-comes-to-haiti-with-a-black-face; Sobukwe Shukura, "Imperialism in Black Face," Africa Is a Country, March 2024, https://africasacountry.com/2024/03/imperialism-in-black-face; and Ju-Hyun Park, "The Kenyan-Led 'Multilateral' Invasion of Haiti Is a Smokescreen for US Imperialism," The Real News Network, October 18, 2023, https://therealnews.com/the-kenyan-led-multilateral-invasion-of-haiti-is-a-smokescreen-for-us-imperialism, among others.
32. *Timbuktu*, 1:08:50 to 1:08:58.

33. *Timbuktu*, 1:10:30 to 1:12:53.
34. See Casimir, "A Decolonial History."
35. Monchoachi, "Let Yourself Be Told," trans. Kavita Ashana Singh, *Small Axe* 18, no. 3 (November 2014): 111.
36. Monchoachi, "Let Yourself Be Told," 111.
37. Monchoachi, "Let Yourself Be Told," 111.
38. Carole Boyce Davies, *Caribbean Spaces: Escapes from Twilight Zones* (Urbana: University of Illinois, 2013), 159.
39. *Timbuktu*, 1:08:56 to 1:09:15.

Bibliography

Allen, Carolyn. "Creole: The Problem of Definition." In *Questioning Creole: Creolisation Discourses in Caribbean Culture*, edited by Verene A. Shepherd and Glen L. Richards. Kingston, Jamaica: Ian Randle Publishers, 2002.

Anderson, Carol. *White Rage: The Unspoken Truth of Our Racial Divide*. New York: Bloomsbury, 2016.

Anonymous. "Sou Lamné." Trans. Erol Josué and Laurent Dubois. In *The Haiti Reader: History, Culture, Politics*, edited by Laurent Dubois, Kaiama L. Glover, Nadève Ménard, Millery Polyné, and Chantalle F. Verna. Durham, NC: Duke University Press, 2020.

Ansfield, Bench. "Sylvia Wynter: What Does It Mean to Be Human." In *Sylvia Wynter: On Being Human as Praxis*, edited by Katherine McKittrick. Durham, NC: Duke University Press, 2015.

Aravamudan, Srinivas. *Tropicopolitans: Colonialism and Agency, 1688–1804*. Durham, NC: Duke University Press, 1999.

Ardouin, Beaubrun. *Études sur l'histoire d'Haïti*. Port-au-Prince: Dalencourt, 1958 [1853–1865].

Arnold, A. James. "Recuperating the Haitian Revolution in Literature: From Victor Hugo to Derek Walcott." In *Tree of Liberty: Cultural legacies of the Haitian Revolution in the Atlantic World*, edited by Doris L. Garraway. New World Studies. Charlottesville: University of Virginia Press, 2008.

Bancel, Nicolas, Pascal Blanchard, and Françoise Vergès, *La République coloniale: Essai sur une utopie*. Paris: Armand Colin, 2003.

Barthélemy, Gérard. *Le pays en dehors: Essai sur l'univers rural haïtien*. Haiti: H. Deschamps, 1989.

Beaubrun, Mimerose. *Nan Domi: An Initiate's Journey into Haitian Vodou*. San Francisco: City Lights, 2013.

Beauvoir, Max. *Lapriyè Ginen*. Port-au-Prince: Edisyon Près Nasyonal d'Ayiti, 2008.

Bell, Madison Smartt. *Toussaint Louverture*. New York: First Vintage Books, 2008.

Bellegarde-Smith, Patrick and Claudine Michel. "Danbala/Ayida as Cosmic Prism: The Lwa as Trope for Understanding Metaphysics in Haitian Vodou and Beyond." *Journal of Africana Religions* 1, no. 4 (2013): 458–87.

Benot, Yves. *La Déémeénce coloniale sous Napoléon*. Paris: La Découverte, 1992.
Benot, Yves. *La Révolution française et la fin des colonies, 1789–1794*. Paris: La Découverte, 1989.
Bogues, Anthony. *Empire of Liberty: Power, Desire, and Freedom*. Hanover, NH: Dartmouth College Press, 2010.
Bongie, Christopher. "Chroniques de la francophonie triomphante." In *Tree of Liberty: Cultural Legacies of the Haitian Revolution in the Atlantic World*, edited by Doris Garraway. Charlottesville: University of Virginia Press, 2008.
Bongie, Christopher. *The Colonial System Unveiled*. Translated and edited by Chris Bongie. Liverpool: Liverpool University Press, 2015.
Bongie, Christopher. *Friends and Enemies: The Scribal Politics of Post/Colonial Literature*. Liverpool: Liverpool University Press, 2009.
Bongie, Christopher. "'Monotonies of History': Baron de Vastey and the Mulatto Legend of Derek Walcott's 'Haitian Trilogy.'" *Yale French Studies* 107 (2005): 70–107.
Bonilla, Yarimar. *Non-Sovereign Futures: French Caribbean Politics in the Wake of Disenchantment*. Chicago: University of Chicago Press, 2015.
Boyce Davies, Carole. *Caribbean Spaces: Escapes from Twilight Zones*. Urbana: University of Illinois Press, 2013.
Boyce Davies, Carole, and Elaine Savory-Fido. "Introduction: Woman and Literature in the Caribbean: An Overview." In *Out of Kumbla: Caribbean Women and Literature*, edited by Carole Boyce Davies and Elaine Savory-Fido. Trenton, NJ: African World Press, 1990.
Blackburn, Robin. "The Force of Example." In *The Impact of the Haitian Revolution in the Atlantic World*, edited by David Geggus. Columbia: University of South Carolina Press, 2001.
Blanchard, Pascal. *La République colonial*. Paris: Hachette/Pluriel, 2006.
Brand, Dionne. *In Another Place, Not Here*. New York: Grove Press, 2000.
Brathwaite, Edward Kamau. *The Arrivants: A New World Trilogy*. New York: Oxford University Press, 1973.
Braziel, Jana Evans. "Defilee's Disaporic Daughters: Revolutionary Narratives of *Ayiti* (Haiti), *Nancho* (Nation), and *Dyaspora* (Diaspora) in Edwidge Danticat's *Krik? Krak!*" *Studies in the Literary Imagination* 37, no. 2 (Fall 2004): 77–96.
Braziel, Jana Evans. "Re-membering Défilée: Dédée Bazile as Revolutionary *Lieu de Mémoire*." *Small Axe* 9, no. 2 (2005): 57–85.
Breslin, Paul. *Nobody's Nation: Reading Derek Walcott*. Chicago: University of Chicago Press, 2001.
Breslin, Paul, and Rachel Ney. "Introduction: The Challenge of Aimé Césaire's *The Tragedy of King Christophe*." In *The Tragedy of King Christophe* by Aimé

Césaire, translated and edited by Paul Breslin and Rachel Ney. Evanston, IL: Northwestern University Press, 2015.
Byrd, Brandon R., and Chelsea Stieber. "Introduction." In *Haiti for the Haitians*, edited by Brandon R. Byrd and Chelsea Stieber. Liverpool: Liverpool University Press, 2023.
Burnett, Paula. *Derek Walcott: Politics and Poetics*. Gainesville: University of Florida Press, 2000.
Campt, Tina. *Image Matters: Archive, Photography and the African Diaspora in Europe*. Durham, NC: Duke University Press, 2012.
Campt, Tina. *Listening to Images*. Durham, NC: Duke University Press, 2017.
Carpentier, Alejo. "The Baroque and the Marvelous Real (1975)." Translated by Tanya Huntington and Lois Parkinson Zamora. In *Magical Realism: Theory, History, Community*, edited by Lois Parkinson Zamora and Wendy B. Faris. Durham, NC: Duke University Press, 1995.
Carpentier, Alejo. *The Harp and the Shadow: The Beatification of Christopher Columbus: A Novel*. Translated by Thomas Christensen and Carole Christensen. San Francisco: Mercury House, 1990.
Carpentier, Alejo. *The Kingdom of This World*. Translated by Harriet De Onis. New York: Farrar, Straus and Giroux, 1957.
Carpentier, Alejo. *The Lost Steps*. Translated by Harriet De Onis. Minneapolis: University of Minnesota Press, 2001.
Carpentier, Alejo. "On the Marvelous Real in America." Translated by Tanya Huntington and Lois Parkinson Zamora. In *Magical Realism: Theory, History, Community*, edited by Lois Parkinson Zamora and Wendy B. Faris. Durham, NC: Duke University Press, 1995.
Carpentier, Alejo. "Prologue to *The Kingdom of This World* (1949)." Translated by Alfred Mac Adam. *Review: Literature and Arts of the Americas* 26, no. 47 (1993): 28–32.
Carpentier, Alejo. Prologue to *The Kingdom of This World*. Translated by Pablo Medina. New York: Farrar, Straus and Giroux, 2017.
Carr, Barry. "Identity, Class, and Nation: Black Immigrant Workers, Cuban Communism, and the Sugar Insurgency, 1925–1934." *Hispanic American Historical Review* 78, no. 1 (1998): 83–116.
Carruthers, Jacob H. *The Irritated Genie: An Essay on the Haitian Revolution*. Chicago: Kemetic Institute, 1985.
Casey, Matthew. "From Haiti to Cuba and Back: Haitians' Experiences of Migration, Labor, and Return, 1900–1940." PhD diss., University of Pittsburgh, 2012.
Casimir, Jean. "A Decolonial History of the Haitians," Lecture. Brooklyn College: Celebrating the Battle of Vertières Beyond Vertières. Friday, November 16, 2018.

Casimir, Jean. *The Haitians: A Decolonial History*. Chapel Hill: University of North Carolina Press, 2020.

Casimir, Jean. "On the Origins of the Counter-plantation System." Translated by Laurent Dubois. In *The Haiti Reader: History, Culture, Politics*, edited by Laurent Dubois, Kaiama L. Glover, Nadève Ménard, Millery Polyné, and Chantalle F. Verna. Durham, NC: Duke University Press, 2020.

Casimir, Jean, and Mary Claypool. "Going Backwards Toward the Future: From Haiti to Saint-Domingue." *The Global South* 6, no. 1 (Spring 2012): 172–92.

Casimir, Jean, Eglantine Colon, and Michelle Koerner. "Haiti's Need for a Great South." *The Global South* 5, no. 1 (2011): 14–36. https://doi.org/10.2979/globalsouth.5.1.14.

Celli, Carlo. *Gillo Pontecorvo: From Resistance to Terrorism*. Latham, MD: Scarecrow Press, 2005.

Césaire, Aimé. ......*And the Dogs Were Silent* / ......*Et les chiens se taisaient*. Translated and edited by Alex Gil. Durham, NC: Duke University Press, 2024.

Césaire, Aimé. "Culture and Colonization." Translated by Brent Hayes Edwards. *Social Text* 28, no. 2 (Summer 2010): 127–44.

Césaire, Aimé. "Letter to Maurice Thorez." Translated by Chike Jeffers. *Social Text* 28, no. 2 (Summer 2010): 145–52.

Césaire, Aimé. "Notebook of a Return to the Native Land." In *Aime Cesaire, The Collected Poetry*, translated by Clayton Eshleman and Annette Smith. Berkeley: University of California Press, 1983.

Césaire, Aimé. *A Tempest*. Translated by Richard Miller. New York: Theater Communications Group, 2002.

Césaire, Aimé. *Toussaint Louverture: La révolution française et al problème colonial*. Paris: Présence Africaine, 1961.

Césaire, Aimé. *The Tragedy of King Christophe*. Translated by Paul Breslin and Rachel Ney. Evanston, IL: Northwestern University Press, 2015.

Césaire, Aimé. *Discourse on Colonialism*. Translated by Joan Pinkham. New York: Monthly Review Press, 2000.

Césaire, Aimé, and Françoise Vergés. *Resolutely Black: Conversations with Françoise Vergès*. Translated by Matthew B. Smith. Cambridge: Polity Press, 2020.

Césaire, Aimé, and Françoise Vergés. *Nègre je suis, nègre je resterai: Entretiens avec Françoise Vergès*. Paris: Michel Albin SA, 2005.

Charles, Carolle. "Gender and Politics in Contemporary Haiti: The Duvalierist State, Transnationalism, and the Emergence of a New Feminism (1980-1990)." *Feminist Studies* 21, no. 1 (1995): 135–64.

Chetty, Raj. "The Tragicomedy of Anticolonial Overcoming: Toussaint Louverture and *The Black Jacobins* on Stage." *Callaloo* 37, no. 1 (2014): 69–88.

Clark, VèVè. "Haiti's Tragic Overture: Statecraft and Stagecraft in Plays by Glissant, Trouillot, and Césaire." Unpublished paper read at the Annual

Meeting of the Caribbean Studies Association, Basse Terre, St. Kitts-Nevis, May 28–31, 1984.
Cole, Hubert. *Christophe, King of Haiti.* New York: The Viking Press, 1967.
Columbus, Christopher. "The Journal of the First Voyage." https://archive.org/details/journalofhisfirsoocoluuoft.
Columbus, Christopher. "Letter to Santangel." In *The Voyages of Christopher Columbus, Being the Journals of his First and Third, and the Letters Concerning his First and Last Voyages, to Which is Added the Account of his Second Voyage Written by Andres Bernaldez.* Translated and edited by Cecil Jane. London: The Argonaut Press, 1930. http://eada.lib.umd.edu/text-entries/columbus-letter-to-santangel.
Conde, Maryse. "Aimé Césaire and America." Translated by Richard Philcox. *Black Renaissance/Renaissance noire* 5, no. 3 (2004): 152–61.
Conde, Maryse. "Sketching a Literature from the French Antilles: From Negritude to Creolite." In *Sisyphus and Eldorado: Magical and Other Realisms in Caribbean Literature*, edited by Timothy Reiss. Trenton, NJ: African World Press, 2002.
Connolly, Jonathan. "Re-Reading Morant Bay: Protest, Inquiry, and Colonial Rule." *Law and History Review* 41 (2023): 193–216. doi:10.1017/S0738248022000578
Dalleo, Raphael. *American Imperialism's Undead: The Occupation of Haiti and the Rise of Caribbean Anticolonialism.* Charlottesville: University of Virginia Press, 2016.
Danticat, Edwidge. *Krik? Krak!* New York: Vintage Contemporaries, 1996.
Danticat, Edwidge. *Brother, I am Dying.* New York: Vintage Books, 2007.
Danticat, Edwidge. *Claire of the Sea Light.* New York: Vintage Books, 2013.
Danticat, Edwidge. *Behind the Mountains.* New York: Orchard Press, 2002.
Danticat, Edwidge. *Eight Days: A Story of Haiti.* New York: Orchard Press, 2010.
Danticat, Edwidge. *Breath, Eyes, Memory.* New York: SoHo Press, 1994.
Danticat, Edwidge. *Farming of Bones.* New York: SoHo Press, 1998.
Danticat, Edwidge. *The Dew Breaker.* New York: Knopf, 2004.
Danticat, Edwidge. *After the Dance: A Walk Through Carnival Jacmel, Haiti.* New York: Penguin, 2002.
Danticat, Edwidge. *Everything Inside: Stories.* New York; Knopf, 2020.
Danticat, Edwidge. *Create Dangerously.* New York: Vintage, 2010.
Dash, J. Michael. *The Other America: Caribbean Literature in a New World Context.* Charlottesville: University of Virginia Press, 1998.
Dash, J. Michael. "Roundtable: Writing, History, and Revolution." *Small Axe* 9, no. 2 (2005): 189–99.
Dash, J. Michael. "The Theater of the Haitian Revolution/The Haitian Revolution as Theater." *Small Axe* 9, no. 2. (2005): 16–23.

Dash, J. Michael. *Édouard Glissant*. Cambridge: Cambridge University Press, 1995.
Daut, Marlene L. *Baron de Vastey and the Origins of Black Atlantic Humanism*. New York: Palgrave Macmillan, 2017.
Daut, Marlene L. Review of *Daring to Be Free / Dying to Be Free: Toward a Dialogic Haitian-U.S. Studies*, by Matthew J. Clavin, Millery Polyné, and Ashli White. *American Quarterly* 63, no. 2 (2011): 375–89.
Daut, Marlene L. *Tropics of Haiti: Race and the Literary History of the Haitian Revolution in the Atlantic World, 1789–1865*. Liverpool: Liverpool University Press, 2015.
Davis, Natalie Zemon. *Slaves on Screen: Film and Historical Vision*. Cambridge, MA: Harvard University Press, 2000.
Dayan, Colin (Joan). "Erzulie: A Women's History of Haiti." In *The Woman, the Writer and Caribbean Society*, edited by Helen Pyne-Timothy. Los Angeles: Center for Afro-American Publication, UCLA 1998.
Dayan, Colin (Joan). *Haiti, History, and the Gods*. Berkeley: University of California Press, 1995.
Dayan, Colin (Joan). "Vodoun, or the Voice of the Gods." In *Sacred Possessions: Vodou, Santería, Obeah, and the Caribbean*, edited by Margarite Fernández Olmos and Lizabeth Paravisini-Gebert. New Brunswick, NJ: Rutgers University Press 2000.
de Vega, Lope. *The Discovery of the New World by Christopher Columbus: A Comedy in Verse*. Translated by Frieda Fligelman. Berkley: Gillick Press, 1950.
Debien, Gabriel. *Les Colons de Saint-Domingue et la Révolution: Essai sur le Club Massiac (Août 1789–Août 1792)*. Paris: Armand Colin, 1951.
Debien, Gabriel. "A propos du trésor de Toussaint-Louverture." *Revue de la société d'histoire et géographie d'Haïti* 17, no. 62 (1946): 30–40.
"Declaration of the Rights of Man – 1789." August 26, 1789. Avalon Project, Lillian Goldman Law Library, Yale Law School, © 2008. https://avalon.law.yale.edu/18th_century/rightsof.asp.
DeLoughrey, Elizabeth. *Routes and Roots: Navigating Caribbean and Pacific Island Literatures*. Honolulu: University of Hawai'i Press, 2007.
Depestre, René. "Truer than Biography: Aimé Césaire Interviewed by René Depestre." *Savacou* 5 (1971): 77–86.
Desmangles, Leslie Gérald. *The Faces of the Gods: Vodou and Roman Catholicism in Haiti*. Chapel Hill: The University of North Carolina Press, 1992.
Dessalines, Jean Jacques. "The Haitian Declaration of Independence." In *The Haiti Reader: History, Culture, Politics*, edited by Laurent Dubois, Kaiama L. Glover, Nadève Ménard, Millery Polyné, and Chantalle F. Verna. Durham, NC: Duke University Press, 2020.
Deren, Maya. *Divine Horsemen: The Living Gods of Haiti*. New York: McPherson and Company, 2004.

Diawara, Manthia, director. *Edouard Glissant: One World in Relation*. K'a Yelema Productions, 2010. 51 mins. https://video-alexanderstreet-com.libproxy.temple.edu/watch/edouard-glissant-one-world-in-relation.

Dorigny, Marcel. "Aux origines: L'indépendance d'Haïti et son occultation." In *La Fracture coloniale: La société française au prisme de l'héritage colonial*, edited by Pascal Blanchard, Nicolas Bancel, and Sandrine Lemaire. Paris: La Découverte, 2005.

Dorsainvil, Justin Chrysostome. *Manuel d'histoire d'Haïti*. Port-au-Prince: Procure des Frères de l'instruction chrétienne. 1934.

Douglas, Rachel. *Making the Black Jacobins: C. L. R. James and the Drama of History*. Durham, NC: Duke University Press, 2019.

Dubois, Laurent. *Avengers of the New World: The Story of the Haitian Revolution*. Cambridge, MA: Belknap Press of Harvard University Press, 2004.

Dubois, Laurent. *Haiti: The Aftershocks of History*. New York: Picador Books, 2012.

Dumesle, Hérard. *Voyage dans le Nord d'Hayti, ou, Revelations des lieux et des monumens historiques*. Aux Cayes: Imp. du Gouvernement, 1824.

Dunham, Katherine. *Island Possessed*. New York: Doubleday, 1969.

Dupuy, Alex. *Haiti in the World Economy: Class, Race and Underdevelopment since 1700*. Boulder, CO: Westview Press, 1989.

Dupuy, Alex. *Haiti in the New World Order: The Limits of Democratic Revolution*. Boulder, CO: Westview Press, 1997.

Dupuy, Alex. "Haiti and the Indemnity Question." *University of Miami Inter-American Law Review* 55, no. 1 (December 2023): 112–21.

Durrant, Sam. *Postcolonial Narrative and the work of Mourning*, Albany: State University of New York, 2004.

Dussel, Enrique. *The Invention of the Americas: Eclipse of "the Other" and the Myth of Modernity*. Translated by Michael D. Barber. New York: Continuum Publishing Company, 1995.

Echevarría, Roberto González. *Alejo Carpentier: The Pilgrim at Home*. Austin: University of Texas Press, 1990.

Eddins, Crystal. *Rituals, Runaways, and the Haitian Revolution: Collective Action in the African Diaspora*. Cambridge: Cambridge University Press, 2021.

Edmondson, Belinda. *Making Men: Gender, Literary Authority, and Women's Writing in Caribbean Narrative*. Durham, NC: Duke University Press, 1999.

Eng, David L., and David Kazanjian. "Introduction: Mourning Remains." In *Loss: Politics of Mourning*, edited by David L. Eng and David Kazanjian. Berkeley: University of California Press, 2003.

Fanon, Franz. *Black Skin White Masks*. New York: Grove Press, 1967.

Fanon, Franz. *The Wretched of the Earth*. New York: Grove Press, 1963.

Farmer, Paul. *Aids and Accusation: Haiti and the Geography of Blame*. Berkeley: University of California Press, 1992.

Farmer, Paul. *The Uses of Haiti*. Monroe, ME: Common Courage Press, 1994.
Fass, Simon M. *The Political Economy of Haiti: The Drama of Survival*. New Brunswick, NJ: Transactions Publishers, 1990.
Fatton, Robert, Jr. *Haiti's Predatory Republic: The Unending Transition to Democracy*. Boulder, CO: Lynne Rienner, 2002.
Fatton, Robert, Jr. "Haiti: The Saturnalia of Emancipation and the Vicissitudes of Predatory Rule." *Third World Quarterly* 27, no. 1 (2006): 115–33.
Felski, Rita. "Introduction." In *Rethinking Tragedy*, edited by Rita Felski. Baltimore, MD: John Hopkins University Press, 2008.
Ferdman, Sandra H. "Conquering Marvels: The Marvelous Other in the Texts of Christopher Columbus." *Hispanic Review* 62, no. 4 (Autumn 1994): 487–96.
Ferrer, Ada. *Freedom's Mirror: Cuba and Haiti in the Age of Revolution*. New York: Cambridge University Press, 2014.
Ferrer, Ada. "Haiti, Free Soil, and Antislavery in the Revolutionary Atlantic." *American Historical Review* 117, no. 1 (February 2012): 40–66.
Fick, Carolyn E. "From Slave Colony to Black Nation: Haiti's Revolutionary Inversion." In *New Countries: Capitalism, Revolutions, and Nations in the Americas, 1750–1870*, edited by John Tutino. Durham, NC: Duke University Press, 2017. https://doi.org/10.1215/9780822374305.
Fick, Carolyn E. "Dilemmas of Emancipation: From the Saint Domingue Insurrections of 1791 to the Emerging Haitian State." *History Workshop Journal* 46 (1998): 1–16.
Fick, Carolyn E. *The Making of Haiti: The Saint Domingue Revolution from Below*. Knoxville: University of Tennessee Press, 1990.
Figueroa, Victor. "The Kingdom of Black Jacobins: C. L. R. James and Alejo Carpentier on the Haitian Revolution." *Afro-Hispanic Review* 25, no. 2 (Fall 2006): 55–71.
Figueroa, Victor. *Prophetic Visions of the Past: Pan-Caribbean Representations of the Haitian Revolution*. Columbus: Ohio State University Press, 2015.
Figueroa-Vásquez, Yomaira C. *Decolonizing Diasporas: Radical Mappings of Afro-Atlantic Literature*. Evanston, IL: Northwestern University Press, 2020.
Fischer, Sibylle. *Modernity Disavowed: Haiti and the Cultures of Slavery in the Age of Revolution*. Durham, NC: Duke University Press, 2004.
Forsdick, Charles. "Haiti and Departmentalization: The Spectral Presence of Toussaint Louverture." *International Journal of Francophone Studies*. 11 no. 3 (November 2008): 327–44. DOI: https://doi.org/10.1386/ijfs.11.3.327_1.
Forsdick, Charles. "The Traveling Revolutionary: Situating Toussaint Louverture." In *Reinterpreting the Haitian Revolution and Its Cultural Aftershocks*, edited by Martin Munro and Elizabeth Walcott-Hackshaw. Kingston: University of West Indies Press, 2006.
Forsdick, Charles, and Christen Høgsbjerg. *The Black Jacobins Reader*. Durham, NC: Duke University, 2017.

Forsdick, Charles, and Christen Høgsbjerg. *Toussaint Louverture: A Black Jacobin in the Age of Revolutions*. London: Pluto Press, 2017.

Forsdick, Charles, and Christian Høgsbjerg. "Sergei Eisenstein and the Haitian Revolution: 'The Confrontation Between Black and White Explodes into Red.'" *History Workshop Journal* 78, no. 1 (2014): 157–85.

Fouchard, Jean. *The Haitian Maroons: Liberty or Death*. New York: Edward W. Blyden Press, 1981.

Fouchard, Jean. *La Méringue: Danse nationale d'Haïti*. Montreal: Eds. Leméac, 1974.

Fraser, Cary. *Ambivalent Anti-colonialism: The United States and the Genesis of West Indian Independence, 1940–1964*. Westport, CT: Greenwood Press, 1994.

Freud, Sigmund. "Mourning and Melancholia." In *Collected Papers*, edited by James Strachey. London: Hogarth Press, 1953.

Froude, James Anthony. *The English in the West Indies, or, The Bow of Ulysses*. London: Longmans, Green, and Co., 1888.

Gaffield, Julia. "We Have Dared to Be Free." *Public Books*, January 10, 2024. https://www.publicbooks.org/we-have-dared-to-be-free.

Gaffield, Julia. *Haitian Connections in the Atlantic World: Recognition after Revolution*. Chapel Hill: University of North Carolina Press, 2015.

Gaonkar, Dilip Parameshwar, ed. *Alternative Modernities*. Durham, NC: Duke University Press, 2001.

García, Armando. "Freedom as Praxis: Migdalia Cruz's Fur and the Emancipation of Caliban's Woman." *Modern Drama* 59, no. 3 (2016): 343–62.

Garraway, Doris L. *The Libertine Colony: Creolization in the Early French Caribbean*. Durham, NC: Duke University Press, 2005.

Garraway, Doris L. "'Légitime Defense': Universalism and Nationalism in the Discourse of the Haitian Revolution." In *Tree of Liberty: Cultural Legacies of the Haitian Revolution in the Atlantic World*, edited by Doris L. Garraway. Charlottesville: University of Virginia Press, 2008.

Garrigus, John D. *Before Haiti: Race and Citizenship in French Saint-Domingue*. New York: Palgrave Macmillan, 2010.

Geggus, David P. "The Bois Caiman Ceremony." *Journal of Caribbean History* 25 (1991): 41–57.

Geggus, David P. *Haitian Revolutionary Studies*. Bloomington: Indiana University Press, 2002.

Gil, Alex. "La découverte de l'Ur-text de *El les chiens se taisent*." *Aimé Césaire à l'oeuvre*, edited by Marc Cheymol and Philippe Ollé-Laprune. Paris: Éditions des Archives Contemporaines, 2010.

Girard, Philippe. *Toussaint Louverture: A Revolutionary Life*. New York: Basic Books, 2016.

Girard, Philippe, and Jean-Louis Donnadieu. "Toussaint before Louverture: New Archival Findings on the Early Life of Toussaint Louverture." *The William and Mary Quarterly* 70, no. 1 (January 2013): 41–78.

Glick, Jeremy Matthew. *The Black Radical Tragic: Performance, Aesthetics, and the Unfinished Haitian Revolution.* New York: New York University Press, 2016.
Glissant, Édouard. *Monsieur Toussaint: A Play.* Translated by Joseph G. Forester and Barbara Franklin. Washington, DC: Three Continents Press, 1981.
Glissant, Édouard. *Caribbean Discourse: Selected Essays.* Translated by J. Michael Dash. Charlottesville: University of Virginia Press, 1989.
Glissant, Édouard. *Poetics of Relation.* Translated by Betty Wing. Ann Arbor: The University of Michigan Press, 2006.
Glissant, Édouard. *Monsieur Toussaint: A Play.* Translated by J. Michael Dash. Boulder, CO: Lynne Rienner Publishers, 2005.
Gordon, Avery. *Ghostly Matters: Haunting and the Sociological Imagination.* Minneapolis: University of Minnesota Press, 1997.
Greenblatt, Stephen. "Marvelous Possessions." In *The Greenblatt Reader*, edited by Michael Payne. Malden, MA: Blackwell Publishing 2005.
Guérin, Daniel. *Les Antilles décolonisées.* Paris: Présence Africaine, 1956.
Hall, Stuart. "David Scott," *BOMB Magazine*, no. 90 (Winter 2005), https://bomb-magazine.org/articles/2005/01/01/david-scott.
Hanchard, Micheal. "Afro-Modernity: Temporality, Politics, and the African Diaspora." In *Alternative Modernities*, edited by Dilip Parameshwar Gaonkar (Durham, NC: Duke University Press, 2001).
Hawkes, Sophie. "The Drama of Liberation: A Comparative Study of Aimé Céaire's Theater; A Translation of Césaire's ......*And the Dogs Were Silent.*" PhD diss. New York University, 1987.
Hazareesingh, Sudhir. *Black Spartacus: The Epic Life of Toussaint Louverture.* New York: Farrar, Straus and Giroux, 2020.
Hearne, John, "Singular and Collective Securities: An Introduction to Carifesta Forum." In *Carifesta Forum: An Anthology of 20 Caribbean Voices*, edited by John Hearne. Kingston: Institute of Jamaica, 1976.
Herskovitz, Melville J. *Life in a Haitian Valley.* New York: Knopf, 1937.
Hoehling, Annaliese. "Minoritarian 'Marvelous Real': Enfolding Revolution in Alejo Carpentier's *The Kingdom of This World*," *Journal of Postcolonial Writing* 54, no. 2 (2018): 254–57.
Hoffmann, Léon-François. "Histoire, mythe et idéologie: La cérémonie du Bois-Caïman," *Haïti: lettres et l'être.* Toronto: Editions du GREF, 1992.
hooks, bell. "Love as a Practice of Freedom." In *Outlaw Culture: Resisting Representations.* New York: Routledge, 2006.
Hudson, Peter. *Bankers and Empire: How Wall Street Colonized the Caribbean.* Chicago: University of Chicago Press, 2018.
Hume, Yanick. "Performing Haiti: Casa del Caribe and the Popularisation of Haitian Heritage Communities in Cuba." *Caribbean Quarterly: A Journal of Caribbean Culture* 62, no. 1 (2016): 39–68.

Hurbon, Laënnec. *Comprende Haïti: Essai sur l'état, la nation, la culture*. Paris: Les Éditions Karthala, 1987.
Hurbon, Laënnec. *Culture et dictacture en Haïti: L'imaginarie sous contrôle*. Paris: L'Harmattan, 1979.
Hurbon, Laënnec. "Vodou: A Faith for Individual, Family, and Community from Dieu dans le Vaudou Haïtien." *Callaloo* 15, no. 3 (1992): 787–96.
Hurley, Anthony E. "Césaire's 'Toussaint Louverture': A Revolution in Question." Présence Africaine, no. 169 (2004): 199–209. http://www.jstor.org/stable/43617188.
Hurston, Zora Neale. *Tell My Horse*. Philadelphia: J. B. Lippincott, 1938.
Jackson, Shona N. *Creole Indigeneity: Between Myth and Nation in the Caribbean*. Minneapolis: University of Minnesota Press, 2012.
James, C. L. R. *The Black Jacobins: Toussaint L'Ouverture and the San Domingo Revolution*. New York: Vintage, 1989.
James, C. L. R. *Beyond the Boundary*. Durham, NC: Duke University Press, 2013.
James, C. L. R. "Lectures on *The Black Jacobins*." *Small Axe* 8, no. 2 (2000): 65–112.
James, Selma. "*The Black Jacobins*, Past and Present." In *The Black Jacobins Reader*, edited by Charles Forsdick and Christian Høgsbjerg. Durham, NC: Duke University, 2017.
Janvier, Louis. *Les Constitutions d'Haiti (1801–1885)*. Paris: Marpon et Flammarion, 1886.
Jenkins, Tammie. *The Haitian Revolution, the Harlem Renaissance, and Caribbean Négritude: Overlapping Discourses of Freedom and Identity*. New York: Lexington Books, 2021.
Jenson, Deborah. *Beyond the Slave Narrative: Politics, Sex, and Manuscripts in the Haitian Revolution*. Liverpool: Liverpool University Press, 2012.
Jenson, Deborah. "From the Kidnapping(s) of the Louvertures to the Alleged Kidnapping of Aristide: Legacies of Slavery in the Post/Colonial World." *Yale French Studies* 107 (2005): 162–86.
Jiménez, Rafael Duharte. "The 19th Century Black Fear." In *Afro-Cuba: An Anthology of Cuban Writing on Race, Politics, and Culture*, edited by Pedro Perez Sarduy and Jean Stubbs. New York: Ocean Press, 1992.
Kaba, Mariame. *We Do This 'til We Free Us: Abolitionist Organizing and Transforming Justice*. Chicago: Haymarket Books, 2021.
Kaisary, Philip. *From Havana to Hollywood: Slave Resistance in the Cinematic Imaginary*. New York: State University of New York Press, 2024.
Kaisary, Philip. *The Haitian Revolution in the Literary Imagination: Radical Horizons, Conservative Constraints*. Charlottesville: University of Virginia Press, 2014.
Kaisary, Philip, and Mariana Past. "Haiti, Principle of Hope: Parallels and Connections in the Works of C. L. R. James, Derek Walcott, Aimé Césaire, and Édouard Glissant." *Atlantic Studies* 17, no. 2 (2019): 260–80. doi:10.1080/14788810.2019.1666633.

Kaussen, Valerie. *Migrant Revolutions: Haitian Literature, Globalization, and U.S. Imperialism*. Lanham, MD: Lexington Books, 2008.

Kendall, Michelle. "Co-opting Haitian History in Martinican Theatre," *Journal of Haitian Studies* 19, no. 1 (2013): 185–97.

King, Stewart. "Toussaint L'Ouverture before 1791: Free Planter and Slave-Holder." *Journal of Haitian Studies* 3/4 (1997): 66–71. http://www.jstor.org/stable/41715043.

King, Tiffany, Jenell Navarro, and Andrea Smith. "Beyond Incommensurability: Toward an Otherwise Stance on Black and Indigenous Relationality." In *Otherwise Worlds: Against Settler Colonialism and Anti-Blackness*, edited by Tiffany Lethabo King, Jenell Navarro, Andrea Smith. Durham, NC: Duke University Press, 2020.

Kisangani, Emizet F. "The Tuareg's Rebellions in Mali and Niger and the U.S. Global War on Terror." *International Journal of World Peace* 29, no. 1 (March 2012): 59–97.

Korngold, Ralph. *Citizen Toussaint*. Boston: Little, Brown and Company, 1944.

Kramer, Nicholas Michael. "Marvelous Realism in the Caribbean: A Second Look at Jacques Stephen Alexis and Alejo Carpentier." *Atlantic Studies* 11, no. 2 (2014): 220–34.

Kraus, Joe. "Through Loins and Coins: Derek Walcott's Weaving of the West Indian Federation." *Callaloo* 28, no. 1 (2005): 60–74.

Lacerete, Robert. "The Evolution of Land and Labor in the Haitian Revolution, 1791–1820." *The Americas* 34, no. 4 (April 1978): 449–59.

Laguerre, Michael. *The Military and Society in Haiti*. Knoxville: University of Tennessee Press, 1993.

Lakou Mizik. "Loumandja." *HaitiaNola*. Cumbancha, 2019. Spotify.

Langley, Lester D. *The Americas in the Age of Revolution, 1750–1850*. New Haven, CT: Yale University Press, 1998.

Lambert, Laurie. *Comrade Sister: Caribbean Feminist Revisions of the Grenada Revolution*. Charlottesville: University of Virginia Press, 2020.

Lambropoulos, Vassilis. *The Tragic Idea*. London: Gerald Duckworth, 2006.

Lamming, George. *The Pleasures of Exile*. Ann Arbor: University of Michigan Press, 1992.

Laroche, Maximilien. "Aimé Césaire et Haiti." In *Césaire 70*, edited by Mbwil a Mpaang Ngal and Martin Steins. Paris: Silex, 1984.

Laroche, Maximilien. "The Founding Myths of the Haitian Nation." *Small Axe* 9, no. 2 (2005): 1–15.

Lawless, Robert. *Haiti's Bad Press*. Rochester: Schenkman Books, 1992.

Léger, Natalie M. "Faithless Sight: Haiti in the Kingdom of This World." *Research in African Literatures* 45, no. 1 (Spring 2014): 85–106.

Léger, Natalie M. "Mucho Woulo: Black Freedom and *The Kingdom of This World*." In *Racialized Visions: Haiti and the Hispanic Caribbean*, edited by Vanessa K. Valdés. Albany: State University Press of New York, December 2020.

Lemoine, Patrick. *Fort-Dimanche Dungeon of Death*. Bloomington: Trafford Publishing, 1999.
Leyburn, James. *The Haitian People*. New Haven, CT: Yale University Press, 1941.
Loraux, Nicole. *Mothers in Mourning*. Translated by Corinne Pache. Ithaca, NY: Cornell University, 1998.
Loraux, Nicole. *Mourning Voice: An Essay on Greek Tragedy*. Translated by Elizabeth Trapnell Rawlings. Ithaca, NY: Cornell University Press, 2002.
Lowe, Lisa. *The Intimacies of Four Continents*. Durham: Duke University Press, 2015.
Lugones, María. n.d. "Indigenous movements and decolonial feminism." Unpublished paper. https://wgss.osu.edu/sites/wgss.osu.edu/files/LugonesSeminarReadings.pdf.
Lugones, María. *Pilgrimages/Peregrinajes: Theorizing Coalition Against Multiple Oppressions*. Lanham, MD: Rowman and Littlefield, 2003.
Macharia, Keguro. *Frottage: Frictions of Intimacy across the Black Diaspora*. New York: New York University Press, 2019.
Macharia, Keguro. "Not This. More That!" *The New Inquiry*, July 23, 2018.
Madiou, Thomas. *Histoire d'Haiti*. 8 vols. Port-au-Prince: Maison Henri Deschamps, 1989 [1847–48].
Madureira, Luís. *Cannibal Modernities: Postcoloniality and the Avant-Garde in Caribbean and Brazilian Literature*. Charlottesville: University of Virginia Press, 2005.
Makalani, Minkah. "'West Indian Through and Through, and Very British': C. L. R. James's *Beyond a Boundary*, Coloniality, and Theorizing Caribbean Independence." In *Marxism, Colonialism, and Cricket: C. L. R. James's Beyond a Boundary*, edited by David Featherstone, Christopher Gair, Christian Høgsbjerg, and Andrew Smith. Durham, NC: Duke University Press, 2018. https://doi.org/10.1215/9781478002550-005.
Maldonado-Torres, Nelson. "On the Coloniality of Being: Contributions to the Development of a Concept." *Cultural Studies* 21, no. 2-3 (March/May 2007): 240–70.
Maldonado-Torres, Nelson. "The Topology of Being and the Geopolitics of Knowledge: Modernity, Empire, Coloniality." *City* 8, no. 1 (2004): 29–56.
Manigat, Leslie. *Éventail d'histoire vivante d'Haïti: Des préludes à la révolution de Saint Domingue jusqu' à nos jours (1789–2007)*. 5 vols. Port-au-Prince: Collection du CHUDAC, 2001.
Mariñez, Sophie. *Spirals in the Caribbean: Representing Violence and Connection in Haiti and the Dominican Republic*. Philadelphia: University of Pennsylvania Press, 2024.
Marshall, Paule. "From the Poets in the Kitchen." *Callaloo* 24, no. 2 (2001): 627–33.
McAlister, Elizabeth. "From Slave Revolt to a Blood Pact with Satan: The Evangelical Rewriting of Haitian History." *Studies in Religion / Sciences Religieuses* 41, no. 2 (2012): 187–215.

McAlister, Elizabeth. "Necroscape and Diaspora: Making Ancestors in Haitian Vodou." In *Spirit Service: Vodun and Vodou in the African Atlantic World*, edited by Timothy Landry, Eric Montgomery and Christian Vannier. Bloomington: Indiana University Press, 2022.

McCarthy Brown, Karen. "Afro-Caribbean Spirituality: A Haitian Case Study." In *Vodou in Haitian Life and Culture: Invisible Powers*, edited by Claudine Michel and Bellegarde-Smith. New York: Palgrave Macmillam, 2006.

McCarthy Brown, Karen. *Mama Lola: A Vodou Priestess in Brooklyn*. Berkeley: University of California Press, 1991.

McDermott, Harold N. "Towards 'that republic in which complexions do not matter': Derek Walcott's *Drums and Colours* Fifty Years On." *Anthurium: A Caribbean Studies Journal* 11 no. 2 (2014): 1–13. DOI: 10.33596/anth.269

McKittrick, Katherine. *Dear Science and Other Stories*. Durham, NC: Duke University Press, 2021.

McKittrick, Katherine. *Demonic Grounds: Black Women and the Cartographies of Struggle*. Minneapolis: University of Minnesota Press, 2006.

McLeod, Marc. "Undesirable Aliens: Race, Ethnicity, and Nationalism in the Comparison of Haitian and British West Indian Immigrant Workers in Cuba, 1912–1939." *Journal of Social History* 31, no. 3 (1998): 599–623.

Melas, Natalie. "Comparative Noncontemporaneities: C. L. R. James and Ernst Bloch." In *Theory Aside*, edited by Jason Potts and Daniel Stout. Durham, NC: Duke University Press, 2014

Mellen, Joan. "A Reassessment of Gillo Pontecorvo's *Burn!*" *Cinema*, no. 32 (1972): 38–47.

Michel, Claudine. "Vodou in Haiti: Way of Life and Mode of Survival." In *Vodou in Haitian Life and Culture: Invisible Powers*, edited by Claudine Michel and Patrick Bellegarde-Smith. New York: Palgrave Macmillan, 2006.

Mignolo, Walter. *The Darker Side of Western Modernity: Global Futures, Decolonial Options*. Durham, NC: Duke University Press, 2011.

Mignolo, Walter. "Coloniality: The Darker Side of Modernity." In *Modernologies: Contemporary Artists Researching Modernity and Modernism, Catalog of the Exhibit at the Museum of Modern Art, Barcelona, Spain*, edited by C. S. Breitwisser. Barcelona: MACBA, 2009.

Mignolo, Walter. "Delinking: The Rhetoric of Modernity, the Logic of Coloniality and the Grammar of De-coloniality." *Cultural Studies* 21, no. 2-3 (March/May 2007): 449–514.

Mignolo, Walter. "Foreword: Thinking Decoloniality beyond One Nation-One State." In *The Haitians: A Decolonial History*, by Jean Casimir. Chapel Hill: University of North Carolina Press, 2020.

Mignolo, Walter. "The Geopolitics of Knowledge and the Colonial Difference." *South Atlantic Quarterly* 101, no. 1 (Winter 2002): 58–96.

Miller, Paul B. "Enlightened Hesitations: Black Masses and Tragic Heroes in C. L. R. James's *The Black Jacobins*." *MLN* 116, no. 5 (Dec. 2001): 1069–90.

Mintz, Sidney. *Sweetness and Power: The Place of Sugar in Modern History*. New York: Penguin Books, 1986.

Mocombe, *The Vodou Ethic and the Spirit of Communism: The Practical Consciousness of the African People of Haiti*. Lanham, MD: University Press of America, 2016.

Monchoachi. "Let Yourself Be Told." Translated by Kavita Ashana Singh. *Small Axe* 18, no. 3 (November 2014): 107–14.

Monroe, Jonathan B. "Composite Cultures, Chaos Wor(l)ds: Relational Poetics, Textual Hybridity, and the Future of Opacity." In *Tradition, Trauma, Translation: The Classic and the Modern*, edited by Timothy Mathews and Jan Parker. New York: Oxford University Press, 2011.

Moraga, Cherríe, and Gloria Anzaldúa. *This Bridge Called My Back: Writings by Radical Women of Color*. New York: Kitchen Table, Women of Color Press, 1983.

Morrison, Toni. "Playing in the Dark: Whiteness and the Literary Imagination." In *Racism in America: A Reader*. Cambridge, MA: Harvard University Press, 2020. https://doi.org/10.4159/9780674251656-004.

Moten, Fred. *In the Break: The Aesthetics of The Black Radical Tradition*. Minneapolis: University of Minnesota Press, 2003.

Munro, Martin, and Elizabeth Walcott-Hackshaw, eds. *Reinterpreting the Haitian Revolution and its Cultural Aftershocks*. Kingston, Jamaica: University of the West Indies Press, 2006.

Naimou, Angela. *Salvage Work: U.S. and Caribbean Literatures amid the Debris of Legal Personhood*. New York: Fordham University Press, 2015.

Nesbitt, Nick. *Caribbean Critique: Antillean Critical Theory from Toussaint to Glissant*. Liverpool: Liverpool University Press, 2013.

Nesbitt, Nick. *Universal Emancipation: The Haitian Revolution and the Radical Enlightenment*. Charlottesville: University of Virginia Press, 2008.

Nesbitt, Nick. "Departmentalization and the Logic of Decolonization." *L'esprit créateur* 47 no. 1 (2007): 32–43.

Nesbitt, Nick. "Troping Toussaint, Reading Revolution." *Research in African Literature* 35, no. 2 (Summer 2004): 18–33.

Nicholls, David. *From Dessalines to Duvalier: Race, Colour and National Independence in Haiti*. New York: Cambridge University Press, 1979.

Nwokocha, Eziaku Atuama. *Vodou en Vogue: Fashioning Black Divinities in Haiti and the United States*. Chapel Hill: University of North Carolina, 2023.

N'Zengou-Tayo, Marie-Jose. "Children in Haitian Popular Imagination as Seen by Edwidge Danticat and Maryse Conde." In *Winds of Change: Transforming Voices of Caribbean Women Writers and Scholars*, edited by Adele S. Newman and Linda Strong-Leek. New York: Peter Lang Publishing Company, 1998.

N'Zengou-Tayo, Marie-Jose. "'Famn Sa Poto Mitan': Haitian Women, the Pillar of Society." *Feminist Review* 59 (1998): 118–42.

Pachonski, Jan, and Reuel K. Wilson. *Poland's Caribbean Tragedy: A Study of the Polish Legions in the Haitian War of Independence 1802-1803*. New York: Columbia University Press, 1986.

Pauléus Sannon, Horace. *Histoire de Toussaint-Louverture*. Haiti: Impr. A. A. Héraux, 1932.

Paravisini-Gebert, Lizabeth. "The Haitian Revolution in Interstices and Shadows: A Re-reading of Alejo Carpentier's *The Kingdom of This World*." *Research in African Literatures* 35, no. 2 (Summer 2004): 114–27.

Past, Mariana F. "Twin Pillars of Resistance: *Ti difé boulé sou istoua Ayiti* [Stirring the Pot of Haitian History]." *Latin American Literary Review* 48, no. 97 (2021): 39–49.

Past, Mariana F. "Toussaint on Trial in 'Ti Difé Boulé Sou Istoua Ayiti,' or the People's Role in the Haitian Revolution." *Journal of Haitian Studies* 10, no. 1 (2004): 87–102. http://www.jstor.org/stable/41715238.

Past, Mariana F. "Reclaiming the Haitian Revolution: Race, Politics and History in Twentieth Century Caribbean Literature." PhD diss., Duke University, 2006.

Perez, Elizabeth. *Religion in the Kitchen: Cooking, Talking, and the Making of Black Atlantic Traditions*. New York: New York University Press, 2016.

Pérez, Laura E. *Eros Ideologies: Writings on Art, Spirituality, and the Decolonial*. Durham, NC: Duke University Press, 2018.

Pérez Sarduy, Pedro, and Jean Stubbs. "Introduction: The Rite of Social Communion." In *Afro-Cuba: An Anthology of Cuban Writing on Race, Politics, and Culture*, edited by Pedro Pérez Sarduy and Jean Stubbs. New York: Ocean Press, 1993.

Petit, Octave. "Défilée-La-Folle." *Revue de la Société d'Histoire et de Géographie d'Haïti* 3, no. 8 (October 1932): 1-21.

Pierre, Beaudelaine. "Thinking Decoloniality through Haitian Indigenous Ecologies." *Hypatia: A Journal of Feminist Philosophy* 35, no. 3 (Summer 2020): 393–409.

Pierrot, Grégory. *The Black Avenger in Atlantic Culture*. Athens: University of Georgia Press. 2019.

Pirsig, Robert. *Zen and the Art of Motorcycle Maintenance: An Inquiry into Values*. New York: Morrow, 1974.

Pluchon, Pierre. *Toussaint Louverture: De l'esclavage au pouvoir*. Paris: Éditions de l'École, 1979.

Pluchon, Pierre. *Toussaint Louveture: Un révolutionnarie noire d'Ancien Régime*. Paris: Fayard, 1989.

Plummer, Brenda Gayle. *Haiti and the Great Powers, 1902–1915*. Baton Rouge: Louisiana State University Press, 1988.

Pontercorvo, Gillo, director. *Queimada!* United Artists, 1969. 2 hr. 09 min. Posted by Maynard G. Krebs to YouTube, March 18, 2021. https://youtu.be/cF5m-hZDXoKc.
Pressley-Sanon, Toni. "Of Bosal and Kongo: Exploring the Evolution of the Vernacular in Contemporary Haiti." *Ufahamu: A Journal of African Studies* 41, no. 1 (2018): 47–64. http://dx.doi.org/10.5070/F7411042303.
Pontiero, Giovanni. "'The Human Comedy' in El Reino de Este Mundo." *Journal of Interamerican Studies and World Affairs* 4, no. 12 (1970): 528–38.
Poon, Angelia. "Re-Writing the Male Text: Mapping Cultural Spaces in Edwidge Danticat's *Krik? Krak!* and Jamaica Kincaid's *A Small Place.*" *Jouvert: A Journal of Postcolonial Studies* 4, no. 2 (Winter 2000), https://legacy.chass.ncsu.edu/jouvert/v4i2/anpoon.htm.
Povinelli, Elizabeth, *Economies of Abandonment: Social Belonging and Endurance in Late Liberalism*. Durham, NC: Duke University Press, 2011.
Price Mars, Jean. *Ainsi parla l'oncle: Essais d'ethnographie*. Haiti: Imprimerie De Compiegne, 1954.
Quijano, Aníbal. "Coloniality and Modernity/Rationality." *Cultural Studies* 21, no. 2-3 (March/May 2007): 168–78.
Quijano, Aníbal, and Michael Joseph Ennis. "Coloniality of Power, Eurocentrism, and Latin America." *Nepantla: Views from South* 1 (2000): 533–80.
Rabbitt, Kara. "C. L. R. James's Figuring of Toussaint Louverture: *The Black Jacobins* and the Literary Hero." In *C. L. R. James: His Intellectual Legacies*, edited by Selwyn R. Cudjoe and William E. Cain. Amherst: University of Massachusetts Press, 1995.
Racine, Jean. *Phèdre*. Translated by Margaret Rawlings. London: Faber and Faber, 1961.
RAM. "Defile." 2008. Track 4 on *Gran Bwa*. Willibelle Publishing, May 16, 2016. Spotify.
Ramsey, Kate. *The Spirits and the Law: Vodou and Power in Haiti*. Chicago: University of Chicago Press, 2011.
Renda, Mary. *Taking Haiti: Military Occupation and the Culture of US Imperialism 1915–1940*. Chapel Hill: University of North Carolina Press, 2001.
Robaina, Tomás Fernández. "The 20th Century Black Question." In *Afro-Cuba: An Anthology of Cuban Writing on Race, Politics, and Culture*, edited by Pedro Pérez Sarduy and Jean Stubbs. New York: Ocean Press, 1993.
Robinson, Cedric J. *Black Marxism: The Making of the Black Radical Tradition*. Chapel Hill: University of North Carolina Press, 2000.
Said, Edward. "The Quest for Gillo Pontecorvo." In *Reflections on Exile and Other Literary and Cultural Essays*. London: Granta, 2001.
Saldaña-Portillo, María Josefina. *The Revolutionary Imagination in the Americas and the Age of Development*. Durham, NC: Duke University Press, 2003.

Salt, Karen. *The Unfinished Revolution: Haiti, Black Sovereignty and Power in the Nineteenth-Century Atlantic World*. Liverpool: Liverpool University Press, 2019.

Sandoval, Chela. *Methodology of the Oppressed*. Minneapolis: University of Minnesota Press, 2000.

Seligmann, Katerina Gonzalez. *Writing the Caribbean in Magazine Time*. New Brunswick, NJ: Rutgers University Press, 2021.

Sepinwall, Alyssa Goldstein. "Beyond *The Black Jacobins*: Haitian Revolutionary Historiography Comes of Age." *Journal of Haitian Studies* 23, no. 1 (2017): 4–34.

Sepinwall, Alyssa Goldstein. *Slave Revolt on Screen: The Haitian Revolution in Film and Video Games*. Jackson: University Press of Mississippi, 2021.

Serviat, Pedro. "Solutions to the Black Problem." In *Afro-Cuba: An Anthology of Cuban Writing on Race, Politics, and Culture*, edited by Pedro Pérez Sarduy and Jean Stubbs. New York: Ocean Press, 1993.

Schmidt, Hans. *The United States Occupation of Haiti, 1915–1934*. New Brunswick, NJ: Rutgers University Press, 1971.

Scott, David. *Conscripts of Modernity: The Tragedy of Colonial Enlightenment*. Durham, NC: Duke University Press, 2004.

Scott, David. *Refashioning Futures: Criticism after Postcoloniality*. Princeton, NJ: Princeton University Press, 1999.

Scott, David. "The Theory of Haiti: *The Black Jacobins* and the Poetics of Universal History." *Small Axe* 18, no. 3 (2014): 35-51.

Scott, David. "Tragedy's Time: Postemancipation Futures, Past and Present." In *Rethinking Tragedy*, edited by Rita Felski. Baltimore, MD: John Hopkins University Press, 2008.

Scott, David. "The Re-Enchantment of Humanism: An Interview with Sylvia Wynter." *Small Axe* 8 no. 2 (2000): 119-207.

Simpson, Audra. *Mohawk Interruptions: Political Life Across Borders of Settler States*. Durham, NC: Duke University Press, 2014.

Singh, Kavita Ashana. "A Schizophrenic Metaphor? Disciplining Creoleness." *Transforming Anthropology* 20, no. 2 (2012): 172–85.

Sharpe, Christina. *In the Wake: On Blackness and Being*. Durham, NC: Duke University Press, 2016.

Shaw, Donald. *Alejo Carpentier*. Boston: Twayne, 1985.

Shea, Renee H. "The Dangerous Job of Edwidge Danticat: An Interview." *Callaloo* 19, no. 2 (1996): 382–89.

Sissako, Abderrahmane, director. *Timbuktu*. Cohen Media Group, 2014. 1 hr. 36 mins.

Smith, Faith. *Creole Recitations: John Jacob Thomas and Colonial Formations in the Late Nineteenth-Century Caribbean*. Charlottesville: University of Virginia Press, 2002.

Smith, Matthew J. "H.G. and Haiti: An Analysis of 'Land of Revolutions (1911).'" *Journal of Caribbean History* 44, no. 2 (2010): 1–18.
Smith, Matthew J. *Red & Black: Radicalism, Conflict, and Political Change, 1934–1957*. Chapel Hill: University of North Carolina Press, 2009.
Srivastava, Neelam. "Anticolonial Violence and the 'Dictatorship of the Truth' in the Films of Gillo Pontecorvo: An Interview." *Interventions: International Journal of Postcolonial Studies* 7, no. 1 (2005): 97–106.
Srivastava, Neelam. *Italian Colonialism and Resistances to Empire, 1930–1970*. London: Palgrave Macmillan UK, 2018.
St. John, Spenser. *Hayti; or, the Black Republic*. London: Smith, Elder, & Co., 1889.
Stevenson, Brenda. "Filming Black Voices and Stories: Slavery on Americas Screens." *Journal of the Civil War Era* 8, no. 3 (2018): 488–520.
Stieber, Chelsea. *Haiti's Paper War: Post Independence Writing, Civil War, and the Making of the Republic, 1804–1954*. New York: New York University Press, 2020.
Stone, Alan. "Last Battle: Gillo Pontecorvo's *Burn!*" *Boston Review* 29, no. 2 (April/May 2004). https://bostonreview.net/articles/alan-stone-last-battle.
Tal-mason, Ali. "Voyage to the Marvelous: A Traveler's Guide to *The Kingdom of This World*." *Cambridge Journal of Postcolonial Literary Inquiry* 7, no. 1 (2020): 50–68.
Taxidou, Olga. *Tragedy, Modernity and Mourning*. Edinburgh: Edinburgh University Press, 2004.
Thompson, Robert Farris. *Flash of the Spirit: African and Afro-American Art and Philosophy*. New York: Vintage Books, 1984.
Thornton, John K. "I Am the Subject of the King of Congo: African Political Ideology and the Haitian Revolution." *Journal of World History* 4, no. 2 (1993): 181–214.
Townsend, Sarah J. "The Spectral Stage of Édouard Glissant's *Monsieur Toussaint*." *Modern Drama* 61, no. 4 (Winter 2018): 501–25.
Trouillot, Henock. "La présence d'Aimé Césaire en Haïti." In *Soleil éclaté: Mélanges offerts à Aimé Césaire à l'occasion de son soixante-dixième anniversaire par une équipe internationale d'artistes et de chercheurs*, edited by Jacqueline Leiner. Tübingen: Gunter Narr, 1984.
Trouillot, Michel-Rolph. *Haiti: State Against Nation*. New York: Monthly Review Press, 1990.
Trouillot, Michel-Rolph. "North Atlantic Universals: Analytical Fictions, 1492–1945." *South Atlantic Quarterly* 101, no. 4 (2002): 839–58.
Trouillot, Michel-Rolph. "The Odd and the Ordinary." *Cimarrón* 2, no. 3 (1990): 3–12.
Trouillot, Michel-Rolph. *Silencing the Past: Power and the Production of History*. Boston: Beacon Press, 1995.

Trouillot, Michel-Rolph. *Stirring the Pot of Haitian History*. Translated and edited by Mariana Past and Benjamin Hebblethwaite. Liverpool: Liverpool University Press, 2021.

Turtis, Richard Lee. "A World Destroyed, A Nation Imposed: The 1937 Haitian Massacre in the Dominican Republic." *Hispanic American Historical Review* 82, no. 3 (2002): 613–35.

Vastey, Pompée Valentin de. *An Essay on the Causes of the Revolution and Civil Wars of Hayti: Being a Sequel to the Political Remarks upon Certain French Publications and Journals Concerning Hayti*. Translated by William Hamilton. Exeter: Western Luminary Office, 1823.

Vastey, Pompée Valentin de. *Reflexions on the Blacks and Whites: Remarks upon a Letter Addressed by M. Mazères, a French Ex-Colonist, to J. C. L. Sismonde de Sismondi . . .* Translated by William Hamilton. London: J. Hatchard, 1817.

Vastey, Pompée Valentin de. *Réflexions sur une lettre de Mazères, ex-colon français, . . . sur les noirs et les blancs, la civilisation de l'Afrique, le Royaume d'Hayti, etc.* Sans Souci: L'Imprimerie Royale, 1816.

Vastey, Pompée Valentin de. *À Mes Concitoyens*. Cap-Henry: P. Roux, imprimeur du Roi, 1815.

Vega-González, Susana. "(Dis)Locations of Oppression: Redemptive Forces in Edwidge Danticat's *Krik? Krak!*" *Irish Journal of American Studies* 11/12 (2002/2003): 47–60.

Vega-González, Susana. "Sites of Memory, Sites of Mourning and History: Danticat's Insights into the Past." *Revista Estudios Ingleses* 17 (2004): 6–24.

Véron, Kora, and Thomas A. Hale. *Les écrits d'Aimé Césaire, biobibliographie commentée (1913-2008)*. Paris: Honoré Champion, 2013.

Walcott, Derek. "Antilles: Fragments of Epic Memory." In *What the Twilight Says: Essays*. New York: Farrar, Straus & Giroux, 1998.

Walcott, Derek. "The Caribbean: Culture or Mimicry?" In *Critical Perspectives on Derek Walcott*, edited by David Hamner. Boulder: Three Continental Press, 1997.

Walcott, Derek. "Drums and Colours." *Caribbean Quarterly* 38, no. 4 (December 1992), 22–135. https://www.jstor.org/stable/23050378.

Walcott, Derek. "The Figure of Crusoe." In *Critical Perspectives on Derek Walcott*, edited by David Hamner. Boulder: Three Continental Press, 1997.

Walcott, Derek. *The Haitian Trilogy*. New York: Farrar, Straus & Giroux, 2002.

Walcott, Derek. "History and Picong . . . in the Middle Passage." In *Critical Perspectives on Derek Walcott*, edited by David Hamner. Boulder: Three Continental Press, 1997.

Walcott, Derek. "The Muse of History." In *What the Twilight Says: Essays*. New York: Farrar, Straus & Giroux, 1998.

Walcott, Derek. "What the Twilight Says." In *What the Twilight Says: Essays*. New York: Farrar, Straus & Giroux, 1998.

Wallace, Michele. *Black Macho and the Myth of the Superwoman.* New York: Dial Press, 1979.
Walsh, Catherine E. "Pedagogical Notes from the Decolonial Cracks." Hemispheric Institute, Oct. 23, 2013. https://hemisphericinstitute.org/en/emisferica-11-1-decolonial-gesture/11-1-dossier/pedagogical-notes-from-the-decolonial-cracks.html.
Walsh, Catherine E. "Shifting the Geopolitics of Critical Knowledge: Decolonial Thought and Cultural Studies 'Others' in the Andes." In *Globalization and the Decolonial Option*, edited by W. Mignolo and A. Escobar. New York Routledge, 2010.
Walsh, John Patrick. *Free and French in the Caribbean: Toussaint Louverture, Aimé Césaire, and Narratives of Loyal Opposition.* Bloomington: Indiana University Press, 2013.
Warner, Kevin Q. "De l'écrivan devenu leader politique: À la recherche d'un héros antillais." In *Soleil eclaté: Mélanges offerts à Aimé Césaire*, edited by Jacqueline Leiner. Tübinger: Gunter Narr, 1984.
Wickstrom, Maurya. *Fiery Temporalities in Theatre and Performance: The Initiation of History.* London: Bloomsbury Publishing, 2018.
Wiener, Leo. *Africa and the Discovery of America.* Philadelphia: Innes & Sons, 1922.
Wilder, Gary. *Freedom Time: Negritude, Decolonization, and the Future of the World.* Durham, NC: Duke University Press, 2015.
Wilder, Gary. *The French Imperial Nation-State: Negritude and Colonial Humanism between the Two World Wars.* Chicago: University of Chicago Press, 2005.
Wilson, Victor-Emmanuel Roberto, and Jacqueline Van Baelen. "The Forgotten Eighth Wonder of the World." *Callaloo* 15, no. 3 (Summer 1992): 849–56.
Wynter, Sylvia. "1492: A New World View." In *Race, Discourse, and the Origin of the Americas: A New World View*, edited by Lawrence Hyatt Vera and Rex Nettleford. Washington, DC: Smithsonian Institution Press, 1995.
Wynter, Sylvia. "Beyond Miranda's Meanings: Un/silencing the 'Demonic Ground' of Caliban's Woman.'" In *Out of Kumbla: Caribbean Women and Literature*, edited by Carole Boyce Davies and Elaine Savory Fido. Trenton, NJ: African World Press, 1990.
Wynter, Sylvia. "Columbus, the Ocean Blue and 'Fables That Stir the Mind': To Reinvent the Study of Letters." In *Poetics of the Americas: Race, Founding and Textuality*, edited by Bainard Cohen and Jefferson Humphries. Baton Rouge: Louisiana State University Press, 1992.
Wynter, Sylvia. "Columbus and the Poetics of the *Propter Nos*." *Annals of Scholarship* 8, no. 2 (Spring 1991): 251–86.
Wynter, Sylvia. "The Eye of the Other." In *Blacks in Hispanic Literature: Critical Essays*, edited by Miriam DeCosta-Willis. Port Washington, NY: Kennikat Press, 1977.

Wynter, Sylvia. "No Humans Involved: An Open Letter to My Colleagues." *Forum H. H. I. Knowledge for the 21st Century* 1, no. 1 (Fall 1994): 42–73.

Wynter, Sylvia. "The Pope Must Have Been Drunk, The King of Castile a Madman: Culture as Actuality, and the Caribbean Rethinking Modernity." In *The Reordering of Culture: Latin America, the Caribbean and Canada in the Hood*, edited by Alvina Ruprecht and Celicia Taiania. Ottawa: Carleton University Press, 1995.

Wynter, Sylvia. "Unsettling the Coloniality of Being/Power/Truth/Freedom: Towards the Human, after Man, Its Overrepresentation—An Argument." *CR: The New Centennial Review* 3, no. 3 (Fall 2003): 257–337.

Wynter, Sylvia, and Katherine McKittrick. "Unparalleled Catastrophe for Our Species?: Or, to Give Humanness a Different Future: Conversations." In *Sylvia Wynter: On Being Human as Praxis*, edited by Katherine McKittrick. Durham, NC: Duke University Press, 2015.

Young, J. C. Robert. *White Mythologies*. New York: Routledge, 2004.

Zamora, Lois Parkinson, and Wendy B. Faris. "Introduction: Daiquiri Birds and Flaubertian Parrot(ie)s." In *Magical Realism: Theory, History, Community*, edited by Lois Parkinson Zamora and Wendy B. Faris. Durham, NC: Duke University Press, 1995. https://doi.org/10.1515/9780822397212-002.

Index

Page numbers in *italic* refer to figures.

abolition(ist)/(ism), 23, 38, 48, 51, 64, 90, 93, 108, 169
Accau, Jacques, 215, 216, 225
affranchi
  class, 7–9, 42, 42, 152, 175
  as creoles, 8, 9, 42, 148, 214, 224, 227
  gens du coleur libre, 18, 110–11, 146, 158
  generals, 7, 9, 18–19, 177, 214, 224
  revolutionists, 19, 42, 68, 148, 152, 227
Africa, 1–7, 9, 10–13, 16, 17–28, 26, 29, 31, 38, 40, 42, 52–58, 61, 62, 66, 67, 68, 71, 72, 73, 75, 76, 91, 92, 97, 99, 100, 103, 104, 109, 113–17, 120, 124–25, 131–34, 137, 140, 146, 148, 158, 159, 160, 163–65, 170, 174, 189, 202, 207, 209, 212, 222, 223, 231, 234, 242, 249–50, 253–59
African Union (AU), 1, 23, 249
Africanized, 6, 10, 12, 13, 16, 17, 18, 19, 24, 40, 54, 100, 103, 113, 117, 146, 174, 256
agriculture
  agricultural code, 212, 215, 221, 225
  and *bossale* ethic, 20
  and Boyer, 215
  as coloniality and Cuba, 109–10
  and Danticat, 214–15, 224–26
  and Haitian Revolution, 17–18
  and Pétion, 214–15, 224
Allada, 67. *See also* Arada
Allen, Carolyn, 8
Americas
  person from Hemispheric, 120, 137, 138, 184, 221
  region, 52, 60, 89, 101, 102, 104, 105, 111, 117, 125, 126, 127, 130, 134, 135, 136, 137, 138, 143, 144, 152, 153, 170, 189, 198, 203, 207, 227, 244, 255
ancestors
  bossale, 5
  and capitalism, 158
  connection, 12
  deities, 3
  and *Ginen*, 20–23, 54, 99–100, 159–63, 239, 243, 254, 256, 263
  Haitian, 1
  and Haitian Revolution, 155, 199, 202, 204, 227, 223, 263
  and Louverture, 59, 67
  service to, 8
  and slavery, 176
  veneration, 144, 220–21
  and Vodou, 17, 21, 208, 226–28, 230–31, 240, 243

351

Antilles, 17, 30, 95, 175, 177, 182, 255
Arab, 250–51
Arada, 23, 67, 113
Aravamudan, Srinivas, 38, 47, 79
Ardouin, Beaubrun Alexis, 161, 215
armies
  armée indigène, 9, 68, 148, 211
  and Danticat, 206
  Dominican, 220
  French, 61, 71, 149, 151, 220
  Haitian, 8–9, 17, 61, 96, 129, 148, 159, 208, 210, 220, 223, 225, 251
  in *Queimada!*, 189, 190
  US, 156, 225
  in Walcott's *Drums and Colours*, 9, 253
Arnold, A. James, 41
artists/art
  Black artists and Black peoples, 96
  Caribbean, 28–29, 45, 59, 76–77, 103, 104, 135–38, 144, 153
  Césaire as, 152
  and Citadelle, 134–35
  and decolonial politics, 13
  First International Congress of Negro Writers and Artists, 169
  and *Ginen*, 32, 35, 155–56
  Haitian revolutionary, 13, 15, 28, 32, 39, 40, 41, 44, 45, 48–9, 55, 63, 67, 77, 99, 103, 153, 197–98, 200, 203–4, 211, 252
  and Louverture, 67, 76–78
  and marvelous, 104, 135
  and tragedy, 85
  and women, 206–7
Asia, 71, 254
Ayiti Ginen (Africa Haiti)
  and Césaire, 152, 163, 165, 168
  and Dessalines, 43
  and French colonial rule, 23, 57
  and *Ginen*, 16, 19, 25, 28, 33–35, 51, 58, 81, 113, 141, 150, 256, 259
  Haiti, 246
  as Haitian identity, 3, 33–35, 51, 58, 256
  and Louverture, 82
Ayiti Ginen+, 249, 259

Bahamas, 123
Baraka, Amiri, 170
Baril, Jacques Junior, 1, 23
Bayon de Libertat, 66–67, 77
Bazile, Marissainte Dédée, 204, 211. *See also* Défilée (Défilée-la-folle)
Beaubrun, Mimerose, 20
Bell, Madison Smartt, 64–66, 69, 75, 83
Bénech, Gilles, 19
Biassou, George, 17, 18, 66
biocentric, 6, 14, 107, 125. *See also* biology
biology, 6, 14–15, 112, 115, 116, 118, 162. *See also* biocentric
Bissol, Léopold, 168
Black
  colonial man, 81, 86, 89, 255
  culture(s), 96, 113, 115, 117, 136, 138, 143, 144, 159, 163, 171–72, 186, 210
  decolonial politics, 14–15, 107, 108
  and Dessalines, 96
  hemispheric American, 99, 138
  inventors, 76, 152, 255
  knowledge and knowing, 36–38, 43, 75, 90
  liberation, 58, 64, 67, 75, 77, 89, 95, 108, 126, 147, 151, 152, 166, 221
  Native and, 56, 59, 69, 75, 100, 135, 144
  person/people, 14–15, 36–38, 51, 55, 56, 58, 65, 66, 70, 72, 73, 75, 76, 77, 93, 96, 102, 104, 110, 114, 117, 119, 126–27, 128, 129, 137–38, 140, 142, 144, 155, 166, 170,

171–73, 176, 180–85, 188, 193, 194, 195, 197, 200, 215, 221, 246, 253
philosophies and *Queimada!*, 188, 195, 200
philosophies/thought, 96, 188
power politics, 9, 71, 79, 107, 110, 185, 186, 253
radical politics, 83, 255
Radicalism, 38–39, 169–71
resistance, 74, 77, 129, 199, 223, 246
self-love/care, 27, 67. 69, 156, 209
thinking as new world making, 120
vengeance, 192, 194
Black studies, 2, 14–16, 20, 25, 32, 38–40, 75–76, 87, 97, 98, 101, 102, 151
Blackness
  anti-Blackness, 8, 47, 56, 63, 66, 74, 89, 102, 107, 108–11, 117, 121, 130, 134, 137, 142, 150, 156, 158, 166, 180, 194, 204, 215
  and Black knowledge, 36
  Carpentier, 102, 107, 108–11, 117, 120–21, 130, 134, 137, 142
  Césaire, 156, 166, 170, 173, 177, 180–81, 184, 192, 194, 255
  Danticat, 204, 215–16, 234
  and Dessalines, 213
  as expansive, 5
  and Haiti, 108, 118, 234
  and historical initiative (Césaire), 171–73, 190
  James (and masculinity), 73–74, 79–83
  and labor, 112, 116
  lived Blackness, 100, 184
  McKittrick, 14–15, 36
  Wynter, 6, 108
blancs, 65, 224
Bonaparte, Napoléon, 70–71, 94, 99, 161, 169, 232

Bongie, Chris, 86, 87
bossale
  African, 2–6, 61, 67, 100, 140, 146, 256, 259
  and decolonial, 4
  and epistemology, 20–21, 25–28
  as *Ginen*, 21–23, 25–27, 209
  inventor, 259
  as revolutionists, 17–19
  See also captives: African
Boukman (Zamba Boukman or Boukman Dutty), 17, 61, 66, 129–30, 210, 221, 222–24, 229–30, 233, 239, 240–42, 243–44, 246–49, 260, 264
Boyer, Jean-Pierre, 18, 29, 42, 111, 150, 162, 215
Brand, Dionne, 252
Braziel, Jana Evans, 50, 204, 218
Bullet, 17
Bwa Kaïyman, 17, 18, 66, 111, 129, 156, 207, 222, 223, 241–42

Caliban, 154, 198–200
cannibalism, 112, 117, 118, 135
canon
  Caribbean writing on Haitian Revolution, 6, 11, 15–16, 19, 34, 35, 45, 50, 54, 60, 91, 92, 94, 98, 102, 154, 202, 204, 205, 210, 227, 244, 246, 248, 254
  and masculinist tradition of writing Caribbean resistance, 46, 54, 55–59, 60, 86, 89, 90, 245, 246, 248
  and republicanism, 40–46
  writers, 14–16, 253
  writing with and against, 38–40
capitalism, 21, 24, 38, 83, 107, 125, 155, 156, 157, 159, 160, 161, 162, 186, 188, 191, 223, 224
captives
  African, 2, 3, 12, 16, 17, 21, 22, 117, 140, 209 (*see also bossale*)

captives (*continued*)
  Africanized, 16, 54, 117
  Black and Native, 56, 59, 69, 75, 100, 135, 144
  creole, 17–18, 21–22, 24, 111
  and Cuba, 128–31
  forbear/ancestor, 5, 20, 23, 162, 256
  Ginen, 46, 58, 99, 103, 112, 120, 130, 136, 146, 149, 159, 169, 180, 200, 209, 224, 228, 233, 243, 245
  liberation, 12
  majority, 2, 14, 37, 45, 63, 67, 86, 117, 119, 129, 140, 148, 156, 174, 180, 184, 189, 207, 210, 222–24, 227, 244
  note on terminology, 3
  person(s), 2–4, 5, 8, 9, 12, 14, 16, 17, 18, 19, 21–22, 23, 24, 26–27, 28, 32, 37, 45–46, 58, 61–64, 65, 66–67, 78, 79, 86, 87, 88, 94, 96, 99, 102, 103, 105, 111–18, 119, 120, 126, 127–30, 139, 140, 141, 148, 158, 163, 166, 173, 180, 189, 191, 192, 195, 196, 199, 209, 211, 214, 244, 246, 253
  resistance, 129
  revolutionist, 54, 102, 103, 118, 242, 243
Caribbean studies, 15–16, 32, 38–39, 84, 88, 99, 102, 151
Caribbean writers, 73, 92, 154
Carpentier, Alejo
  "Baroque and the Marvelous Real, The," 103
  and Black knowing, 37, 47–48, 104, 111–18, 126–27, 137–38, 255
  and Columbus, 47–48, 104, 121–27, 131–35, 143–44
  and de/anticolonial politics, 14, 30–32, 39, 55–59, 102, 254–55
  and *Ginen* thought, 44, 47, 111–18, 137–38
  Harp and the Shadow, The, 47, 103, 142–44
  Kingdom of This World, The, 15, 30, 46–47, 97–110, 115, 133, 136–40, 143, 147, 252
  Lost Steps, The, 47, 103, 142–43
  and Louverture, 98
  and the marvelous, 31, 37, 47, 102–6, 120–21, 128–38, 142, 144–45, 150, 151
  1943 visit to Haiti, 127
  "On the Marvelous Real in America," 103
  and scholarship of the Haitian Revolution, 39–40, 47–48, 254–55
  white Cuban, 14, 101–2, 110
cartography, 23, 33, 126, 152
Casimir, Jean
  and *bossales*, 2–4, 20–22, 26–27
  and counter-plantation system, 2, 20, 210
  and *Ginen*, 20–23, 26, 62, 115, 141, 148, 162, 209–10, 212, 225, 228
  and Saint Domingue, 7–8, 42, 49, 62, 115, 119, 141, 147–48, 158, 162, 209, 212, 213–15, 225, 228
  and Vodou, 115, 209
Césaire, Aimé
  And the Dogs Were Silent (play and poem), 147, 158, 164, 166, 175
  "Culture and Colonization," 49, 169, 171–73
  and de/anticolonial politics, 14, 30–32, 39, 55–59, 102, 254–55
  Discourse on Colonialism, 161, 188
  Haitian laborers, 162, 165–66, 168, 172
  "Letter to Maurice Thorez," 49, 169, 171–72
  and Louverture, 164, 166, 169, 174–77, 199, 200, 201
  négritude, 30, 153, 164, 165, 255

1944 visit to Haiti, 157–66, 167–71, 173, 176, 177, 187, 190
Notebook, The, 164
as poet, 11, 157
republicanism, 11, 33, 44, 49, 90, 152, 157, 161, 160–66, 167, 173, 175, 177, 180, 198
speech to First International Congress of Negro Writers and Artists, 169
Tempest, A, 49, 152–53, 197–200
Toussaint Louverture: The French Revolution and the Colonial Problem, 10–11, 64, 90, 147, 160, 164–65, 166, 169, 174, 175
and tragedy, 167–73
Tragedy of King Christophe, The, 15, 30–31, 48–49, 147, 152–53, 157, 170, 177–87, 187, 190, 197, 198, 200
Chetty, Raj, 97
Chinese, 9, 253
Christianity
and Columbus, 121–26, 126–33, 131–35
resistance to, 244
and Vodou, 82, 116, 128–31
and the West, 107
Christophe, Henry
affranchi, 9, 18
army of, 18–19
bloodlust, 10, 253
and Citadelle, 135–37, 178–84, 245–46
as colonizer, 9–10, 138–41
creole revolutionist, 18, 45, 59, 98, 99–100, 203, 214, 228, 253
Drums and Colours, 9–10, 13, 253
fall of, 111, 150, 161, 170, 179, 215
and forced labor, 44, 138, 179
and gender, 203
Grenada, 9
Henri Christophe: A Chronicle in Seven Scenes, 98–99, 245
"International Writers Conference in Dublin," 245–46
king of Haiti, 68, 88, 98, 111–12, 135, 138–40, 144, 155, 157, 174–84, 190, 197, 210–11, 214, 221, 224, 241–42
Kingdom of this World, The, 98, 111–12, 135, 138–40, 144
Louverture and *Tragedy of King Christophe, The*, as veiled Republican, 177–78
Madame Christophe and *Tragedy of King Christophe, The*, 177–78
and plantation industry, 158, 214, 224
Raft-keepers and *Tragedy of King Christophe, The*, 180–83
and tragedy, 30, 170–71
Tragedy of King Christophe, The, 15, 31, 49, 147, 150–51, 154–55, 167, 175, 179–80, 184, 187, 194, 197
"What the Twilight Says," 45
Citadelle, the (La Citadelle Laferriere), 135–37, 138, 178–84, 245–46
civilization
and Black people, 140–41, 155, 199
and Césaire, 154, 163, 172, 182, 188, 190, 198
and colonial project, 49, 138, 154, 188, 199
and *Ginen*, 156, 160
and Haiti, 24, 41, 43, 158, 160, 170
and Indigenous peoples, 132
and James's Louverture, 96
and music in *The Lost Steps*, 143
and *Queimada!*, 155, 188, 190–97
and West, 23, 41, 43, 155, 157, 163, 172, 188
Claypool, Mary, 42, 158
Clifford, Barry, 52–53

Colon, Eglantine, 147, 158
colonial
    administration/state, 7, 17, 18, 34
    colonialism, 15, 18, 29, 32, 34, 35,
        69, 78, 81, 94, 113, 118, 125, 136,
        141, 153, 156, 157, 165, 167–68,
        171, 172, 176, 178, 184, 186, 189,
        190, 192, 193, 194, 197, 209, 210,
        250, 255, 257
    coloniality, 32, 34, 60, 76, 110, 155,
        156, 221, 228
    colonist/colonialist/colonizer, 45,
        53, 68, 87, 129, 193, 197, 198,
        221, 224, 227, 238, 257
    and conquest, 161, 213
    context, 27, 73, 108
    and Cuba, 128–30
    culture(s), 19, 65, 91, 116, 159,
        161, 171
    as descriptor, 8, 10, 13, 59, 60, 64,
        97, 102, 110, 142, 165, 207, 208,
        209, 221, 223, 255, 258
    and desire, 44
    difference, 25, 27 (*see also* Mignolo,
        Walter)
    and direction/movement, 23, 33,
        179, 194
    and discourse, 5, 62, 118
    divisions, 35
    doublespeak, 164
    encounter, 69, 110, 153–54, 155,
        157, 188, 197, 198, 199
    and the English, 73
    existence, 95, 207
    and exploitation, 141, 154, 169, 194
    imagination, 83
    impossible, 28
    indoctrination, 209, 213, 225
    inheritance, 34
    inspired, 44
    knowledge/thought, 4, 14, 24, 25, 33,
        34, 36, 46, 57, 58, 83, 112–13, 117
    and labor, 148, 165–66
    law, 168, 212, 214–15
    and masculinity, 100
    mimic, 10, 34
    modernity, 4, 6, 14, 33, 36, 46, 47,
        56, 59, 66, 69, 85, 112, 117, 199,
        207, 209, 211, 237, 239, 259
    moment, 45, 46, 66, 109, 116, 185,
        258
    neocolonialism, 48, 83, 102, 105,
        108–10, 153, 167, 171, 172, 189,
        190, 192, 198, 200, 226, 233
    norms, 3, 7, 45, 114, 160, 211
    and oblivion, 91
    ontology, 15, 48, 56, 100, 103, 108,
        129, 155, 181, 186, 199, 227, 228,
        238, 258
    order, 2, 8, 25, 39, 59, 68, 75, 86, 89,
        102, 104, 108, 110, 120, 125, 129,
        139, 141, 144, 145, 154, 173, 176,
        177, 193, 201, 212, 238
    past, 25, 176, 203
    politics, 47, 60
    power(s), x, 4, 5, 10, 14, 15, 17, 19,
        24, 27, 30, 32, 33, 35, 45, 46, 53,
        54, 56, 84, 87, 89, 90, 91, 94, 104,
        119, 125, 145, 149, 156, 163, 164,
        171, 172, 180, 181, 185, 188, 189,
        194, 197, 204, 209, 213, 221, 226,
        227, 228, 235, 252, 256, 257, 258
    present, 45, 49, 57, 85, 87, 88, 97,
        115, 157, 179, 184, 188, 199, 248
    problem, 157, 176
    project, x, 13, 15, 23, 28, 32, 36, 42,
        49, 60, 89, 99, 101, 103, 110, 111,
        119, 154, 156, 173, 187, 197, 198,
        210, 212, 249, 252
    and race, 59, 172, 173
    reasoning, 45, 142, 182
    resistance, 59
    rule, 5, 14, 23, 35, 48, 61, 87, 112,
        139, 150, 151, 175, 183, 189, 193,

199, 204, 217, 218
society, 8, 10, 22, 128, 222
subject, 35, 91, 174
subordination, 31, 108, 110, 172, 176, 197, 207, 212, 259
and time, 49, 155
and tragedy, 85–87, 168–71
trope, 117–18
and tyranny, 53, 93
understanding, 28, 162, 188
and US, 73
violence, 188
West, 118, 127, 157, 161, 217, 219
world, 13, 46, 105, 106, 115, 126, 127, 129, 139, 154, 157, 192, 197, 252
world system, 33
colony
as existence, 201
beyond the, 13, 32, 34, 46, 48, 49, 62, 77, 86, 87, 97, 102, 115, 130, 152, 153, 155, 157, 173, 177, 178, 179, 181, 182, 186, 190, 194, 197, 197–201, 256
Columbus, Christopher
Beatification of Christopher Columbus, The, 103
canonization of, 143
The Kingdom of this World, 47–48, 104–5, 120–22, 143–44
as colonial signifier, 49, 52–59, 60, 95, 105–6, 136, 137, 140, 161, 205
Discovery of the New World by Christopher Columbus, The, 120–21, 123–24
and Haitian leadership, 53
hawk's bells, 132–34
letter to Santangel, 131–32
and the marvelous, 31, 128, 131–32, 134
and "new world," 23, 47
and Christian Imperialism, 131, 131–35

and Scholasticism, 105, 107–8, 122–23, 125–27
communism, 20, 154, 167, 169, 172, 173
Condé, Maryse, 30, 147, 151
Congo, 3, 12, 23
Conscripts of Modernity, 46, 54, 83–89
Copernicus, 107
Cortez, Hernán, 137
creole
as Africanized, 3, 17, 99
and *affranchi*, 5, 8–9, 148
colonist, 189
definition of, 7–8
generals, 12, 19, 44–46, 67, 100, 149, 202, 207, 245–46
and *Ginen*, 19–24, 43–44, 100
language and Césaire, 162, 164
"mad Haitian rebel," 6, 10, 249, 253
person, 2–5, 10, 67, 100, 141, 202, 249, 256.
Walcott, 6–7, 9–10, 249, 253–55
in *Queimada!*, 189–99
revolutionists as, 6–7, 9, 10–17, 19, 34, 37, 39, 45–47, 49, 148, 214, 227, 228, 236, 224, 233, 254
See also captive
Creolization
drama of, 91, 95
syncretism, 225
Cuba
Black Cubans, 109–10, 128–28, 137, 193–94
Haitians in, 109–10
Junta Central, 193
Kingdom of This World, The, 108–11, 128–31, 137
Platt Amendment, 101
Santiago, 128–30
US colonialism and, 28, 101–2, 109–10
white Cubans, 14, 101–2, 110
cultivator, 214–15

dance, 184, 233, 243–44, 259
Danticat, Edwidge
　"Between the Pool and the
　　Gardenias," 241
　and Boukman, 221–23, 229–30, 233,
　　239–41
　"Children of the Sea," 205, 235, 241
　and Cultural Europeanisation, 219–29
　and Défilée-Dantò, 233, 235, 236,
　　244
　and Défilée-la-folle, 211, 217–19,
　　220, 223, 230, 232, 233, 240
　and Dessalines, 211–17, 218–19, 221,
　　233
　and Gallifet sugar plantation, 222,
　　223, 244–46
　and gender, 49–50, 204, 206, 218–19,
　　241–24
　and Haitian cultural praxis, 16, 50, 255
　and Haitian diaspora, 205
　Krik? Krak!, 205–6, 240
　and melancholia, 208
　"Nineteen Thirty-Seven," 15, 50,
　　204, 211, 219–21, 226–27, 230–36,
　　240–41, 244, 248
　and otherwise existence, 37, 253
　and Vodou, 49, 207–10, 227, 228,
　　229–36, 240–44
　"Wall of Rising Fire, A," 15, 50, 204,
　　207, 221–26, 236–40, 242, 246–48
Dash, J. Michael, 174
Dauphin Simon de Cyrene, 217
Daut, L. Marlene, 16, 41, 47, 68, 79
Davis, Natalie Zemon, 188
Dayan, Colin, 50, 157, 204, 216, 223, 229
de Mézy M. Lenormand, 111, 112–16,
　　128–29, 139
de Vega, Lope, 120–25
Debien, Gabriel, 64
decolonial
　analysis, 33, 104, 155, 169, 171, 219
　change, 97, 156

　choice, 185
　as descriptor, 4, 5, 15, 16, 18, 23,
　　115, 120, 141, 156, 229
　difference, 156, 210, 218
　and direction, 100, 181, 199
　ethics, 48, 105, 141
　existence, 166, 248
　future, 33, 35, 108, 248
　and *Ginen*, 195, 209, 217, 219
　governance, 179
　ground, 155
　horizon, 13, 28
　imagination, 14, 24, 31, 256
　liberation, 152, 198
　nature, 5, 14, 15, 102, 126, 130, 142,
　　200, 204
　plan, 195
　politics, 14, 15, 39, 107
　possible, 28, 116
　praxis, 86, 108, 126
　present, 157, 186, 210
　program, 200
　project, 108
　query, 186
　resistance, 50
　self, 142, 209
　striving, 50, 199
　thought, 23, 27, 28, 31, 32, 46, 50,
　　93, 99, 100, 103, 107, 111, 118,
　　119, 126, 150, 155, 180, 197, 200
　time, 156, 185
　tradition, 180
　and tragedy, 87
　world, 48, 105, 141, 146, 169
decolonial studies, 2, 4, 24, 27, 57
Defile, 211, 218, 219–20, 230–32, 233–
　　35, 238, 241, 243, 248
Défilée (Défilée-la-folle), 50, 204, 210–
　　11, 214, 217–19, 220, 223, 230,
　　232, 233, 240
Défilée-Dantò, 233, 235, 236, 244
défilez, 50, 219, 238

Delores, José
  and Colombia, 189
  Evaristo Márquez as, 189
  in *Queimada!*, 189–91, 193–97, 199–200
demonic ground, 4, 107, 120–27, 137, 138
Depestre, René, 163
Dessalines, Jean Jacques
  alleged bloodlust, 10, 60, 95, 251
  armies of, 18, 68, 220
  assassination of, 161, 178, 211, 216, 220
  as avenger, 203
  and Citadelle, 135, 178
  compared to colonizers, 9–10
  creole revolutionist, 59, 87, 99–100, 111, 149, 203, 212, 227, 228, 250
  Danticat and, 211–17, 218–19, 221, 233
  former captive, 19
  and *Ginen*, 41–45, 118–20, 141, 186, 212–14
  and Haitian Independence, 19, 41–42, 118–20, 141, 213
  and James, 96
  and *koupe tèt boulé kay*, 62
  and Louverture, 69
  as military genius, 120
  Monsieur Toussaint, 94, 95
  politics, 41–45, 178
  post-revolution, 99, 150, 159, 161, 175, 213
  and republicanism, 41–45, 161, 164, 217
  and revolutionary record, 229
  and Vodou, 229
  in Walcott, 9, 13, 45, 98
Dominican Republic, 18, 29, 206, 211, 219–21, 226, 230, 233–35, 241
Du Bois, W. E. B, 73, 170
Dubois, Laurent, 139–40, 223

Duvalier, François, 30, 53, 82, 162, 233
Duvalier, Jean-Claude, 30, 52–53

East Indian, 9, 253
Eddins, Crystal, 2–4, 8, 21
Edmondson, Belinda, 73, 80
elites
  and Césaire, 160, 168–73
  and Columbus, 123–224
  Cuban, 109–10
  and liberation, 42
  political, 9, 35, 42, 43, 148, 153, 159, 160, 168–73, 190, 209, 211, 212, 214, 216, 225
  in *Queimada!*, 189–99
  and tragedy, 85
  See also oligarchy
emancipation, 7–8, 61–63, 84, 126, 138, 148, 184, 189, 212, 224
England
  in Carpentier, 116
  in Haiti, 17
  language, 49, 54, 174
  and masculinity, 255
  in *Queimada!*, 154–55, 189, 190, 192, 194
  Victorian masculinity, 73–74, 79
Enlightenment, the
  Haiti as critique of, 24
  James, Louverture, and, 32, 45, 47, 60, 77, 79–82, 87, 203, 245
  and republicanism, 42–43, 92, 95, 241
epistemology
  Afro-Caribbean, 93
  and Black knowing, 35–37, 75, 90, 104
  bossale, 5–6, 20–21
  and Carpentier, 103, 104, 106, 121–23, 125, 128, 130, 136, 142
  and difference, 26, 33, 115, 117
  and *Ginen*, 6, 21–28, 44, 88, 103–6, 119, 120, 128, 207

epistemology (*continued*)
  and masculinist tradition of writing Caribbean resistance, 46
  and tragedy, 87
  and violence, 75
  and West, 34, 58, 75, 91, 92, 95, 97, 104, 107, 113, 117
  and Wynter, 105, 106, 107, 122, 124, 125
Eveline, 230, 238, 241

Fanon, Frantz, 4, 106–7
Faris, Wendy B., 104
Fatiman, Cécile, 17, 222–23, 242
Ferrand, Jean-Louis, 220
Ferrer, Ada, 128–29
Fick, Carolyn E., 1, 4, 7–8, 17, 149, 223
Figueroa, Víctor, 33, 39–40, 99
Figueroa-Vásquez, Yomaira C., 32
Fischer, Sibylle, 41, 87
Forsdick, Charles, 47, 65, 79, 167, 175, 188
Fouchard, Jean, 2–4, 21, 217, 224
France
  ambassadors, 113, 158
  colonialism, 2–8, 17–19, 21–23, 60–63, 118–21, 139–40, 141–42, 147–48, 161, 174, 209–10, 212, 214–15, 217, 218, 222, 223–24, 227, 244, 246, 253, 256–57
  culture, 7–8, 26, 54, 159
  Duvalier in, 53
  education, 7
  epistemology, 88
  and Guadeloupe, 177
  Haitian indemnity to, 29, 147, 150
  Haitian relationship to, 40–41, 147
  Houphouët Boigny Act, 167
  James and, 11, 80–81
  Lamine Gueye Act, 167
  and Louverture, 61, 63, 64–70, 78, 90, 94–95
  National Assembly, 167
  Overseas Departments, 167–68, 174
  plans to invade Haiti, 18, 61, 135, 178, 220
  surrealism, 135, 137, 158
  and World War II, 167
French Revolution
  and colonial right to conquest, 161
  Directory, 12, 61, 63, 70
  egalitarianism, 164
  First Republic of France, 44, 163–65, 169
  Haitian Revolution as extension of, 42–44
  James and, 32–33
  and Louverture, 80–81, 90
  and republicanism, 11, 32, 90, 157, 160–66
  and tragedy, 169
Froude, James Anthony, 74
Fulah, 113

Gairy, Eric, 84
García, Armando, 24
Garraway, Doris L., 38
Geffrard, Guillaume Fabre Nicolas, 212
Geggus, David, 222
gender
  and Columbus, 55–58
  and Haitian revolutionists, 203–5, 217
  and the human, 55–56, 75, 124
  and Louverture, 46–47, 59–60, 69, 77–83
  masculinist tradition of writing, 46, 54–60, 83, 86, 88–89, 90, 177, 203–4, 245–48, 255
  and tragedy, 87
  Victorian masculinity, 72–73, 79
  white masculinity, 58, 82
  womanhood, 55

genocide, 57, 118, 125, 139, 147, 168, 176, 186, 209, 211, 220
Gil, Alex, 159, 163, 164, 175
Ginen
  as African, 16, 19, 26–27, 54
  as ancestral spirit or *lwa*, 16, 17
  anti-, 16, 41, 154, 245
  captives, 46, 58, 99, 103, 112, 130, 136, 146, 149, 159, 169, 180, 195, 200, 209, 224, 228, 233, 243, 244, 245, 259
  cartographic genius, 23–24
  and civilization, 156, 160
  and Columbus, 58
  and creoles, 19–23, 43–44, 99, 253
  culture, 33, 44, 45, 46, 50, 59, 62, 67, 69, 116, 159, 186, 207, 223, 246, 250, 254
  and Danticat, 50
  as descriptor, 154, 167, 187, 207, 217, 229
  and Dessalines, 41–45, 213–19
  and epistemology, 6, 20, 88, 103–6
  ethic, 48, 105, 113, 148, 228
  Ginen-making, 19–23
  Guinea Africa (*Lafrik Ginen*), 20, 236
  Haitians, 3, 13, 16–17, 19, 23, 25, 33–34, 35, 36, 37, 41, 46, 48, 50–51, 54–55, 69, 75, 77, 86, 99, 102, 105, 106, 141, 145, 147, 150–52, 159, 160, 162–63, 173, 176, 186, 187, 193, 195, 197, 200, 209, 212–19, 221, 224, 225, 226, 227, 229, 233, 242, 246, 248, 249, 251, 252, 256, 258, 259
  and human, 107, 118–20, 127, 128
  as identity, 117
  inventor, 25, 26, 33, 49, 58, 103, 136, 163, 209
  and Louverture, 47, 54, 59, 66–67, 70, 77, 79, 81–82, 86, 95, 97
  and Makandalism, 62
  and marvelous, 127–31
  new world builders, 33, 47, 49, 103, 107, 120, 128, 149, 166, 256
  notes on terminology, 16, 19–21, 62
  philosophies of freedom, x, 155–56, 243, 252, 255
  politics, 49, 62, 213, 216, 218, 221
  praxis, 4, 6, 14, 35–36, 37, 38, 44, 46, 48, 54, 103, 113, 121, 136, 203
  refusal, 25, 41, 47, 54, 58, 60, 99, 109, 139, 177, 194
  and republicanism, 16, 41–45, 151–52, 154, 160, 185
  resistance, 86, 118, 130, 186, 187, 226, 228, 246, 258
  revolutionist, 32, 33, 34, 46, 47–51, 54–55, 58–59, 70, 74, 100, 103, 105–6, 111, 118, 120, 123, 125, 126, 136, 141, 144, 149, 155, 181, 184, 202, 243, 247, 250, 252, 256, 259
  sèvi Ginen (*Ginen yo*), 20
  and sovereignty, 16, 47, 27, 89, 119, 172, 209, 211
  thought, 14, 24, 28, 33, 41, 47, 54, 58, 88, 90, 94, 103, 105, 111–20, 127, 128, 156, 157, 172, 228, 252, 255
  un-*Ginen*, 12
  as unseen, 34–38, 46–49, 71, 73, 96, 200
  and Vodou, 16, 17, 20–22, 82, 106, 115, 138, 207–9
  Zabou as, 249–50, 251–52
  See also *Ayiti Ginen* (Africa Haiti); *Ayiti Ginen*+
Girard, Philippe, 65–66, 69, 75, 83
Glissant, Édouard
  and Africa, 11–12, 52, 56, 254
  and Black knowing, 37, 90–91
  Caribbean Discourse: Selected Essays, 56–57, 91, 95

Glissant, Édouard (*continued*)
  and Caribbean studies, Black studies, and postcolonial studies, 39
  and Caribbean tradition of writing resistance, 55–58, 90–91
  and de/anticolonial politics, 14, 30–32, 39, 55–59, 102, 256
  Édouard Glissant: One World in Relation, 55, 95
  and *Ginen(s)*, 15, 34, 37, 39, 41, 54, 255
  and Louverture, 11–13, 37, 46, 60, 90–95
  Monsieur Toussaint, 11–13, 15, 31, 45, 54, 89
  multiplicity, 55–58, 97
  Poetics of Relation, 57
  and republicanism, 32–33, 41, 45, 46, 90–95
  and the West, 23, 56–57, 91–92
Goman, 19
Gordon, Avery, 25, 113
Greenblatt, Stephen, 131, 134
Grenada, 9, 46, 69, 84
grief, 208, 240–44
Guadeloupe, 30, 147, 177
Guy, 210, 221, 226–28, 236–38, 239, 240, 246–48
Guyane, 168

habitant, 225
Haiti
  abolitionist project, 23–24
  Anti-Superstition Campaign of 1941–1942, 233–35
  as banana republic, 48, 105
  Cacos Resistance, 29
  in Caribbean, Black, postcolonial, and Haitian studies, 38–40
  Césaire, departmentalization and, 167–77
  Constitution, 41, 142, 213
  as decolonial possible, 28
  as demonic ground, 4, 107, 121–27, 137, 138
  early history defined (1804–1820), 29, 178
  as failed state (trope), 101
  and forced labor (*see* indentureship; plantation)
  as idea, 16, 29, 32, 152, 154, 156, 186, 187, 188, 201
  Kout Kout-a (1937 Dominican massacre of Haitians), 211, 219–21, 226, 241
  language of (*see* Kreyòl)
  manufactured ills, 151, 221
  as new world, 23, 25, 28, 41, 48, 58, 139, 142, 145, 146, 163, 258, 259
  1915 US Occupation (*see* United States)
  peasants, 34, 94, 123, 162–63, 183, 195, 214
  as place and principle, 160, 165
  political leaders (*see specific leaders*)
  post-revolutionary Haiti, 28–29
  revolutionary Haiti defined, 28–29
  spirituality (*see* Vodou)
  2010 earthquake, 251, 257, 258
  See also Indigenous peoples
Haitian Revolution (1791–1804)
  African leaders (*see specific leaders*)
  armée indigène, 9, 68, 148, 211, 213
  Battle of *Vertieres*, 119
  as Caribbean fight, 147
  Cultural Europeanisation, 219, 227
  defined, 23–24
  generals (*see specific generals*)
  historical overview, 17–19
  lore, 233
  male focus, 210

as new world building, 47, 104–5, 121
opening stages (*Set Jou*; August 14–21, 1791), 17, 66, 100, 148, 156, 219
revolutionists (*see* captives; creole; *Ginen*)
War of Independence, 18, 71
Haitian studies, 15, 17, 32, 38, 40, 98, 102, 151
Halaou, 19, 262, 264
Hazareesingh, Sudhir, 62, 64, 67
Hegel, G. W. F., 6
Hoehling, Annaliese, 104
Hoffmann, Léon-François, 222
Høgsbjerg, Christian, 65, 188
hooks, bell, 27
Horowitz, Ben, 83
hot-air balloons, 221, 226, 227, 236–38, 241
Hurley, E. Anthony, 153
Hyppolite, Florvil, 216

idolatry, 121, 125, 132
imaginary
 Africa as, 23, 25, 256
 Caribbean cultural, 29, 46, 89, 152, 153, 154, 177, 198
 English, 73
 spiritual, 243
 United States, 73
 Vodou, 50, 207, 208–10, 243
imperialism, 29, 38, 65, 107, 151, 175, 176
indentureship, 214, 224, 226. *See also* plantation
Indigenous peoples
 Africans and, 10, 132–33, 134, 254
 anti-Native, 134, 204
 Black and, 56, 59, 69, 75, 100, 135, 144
 Caliban as, 198

and *Ginen*, 19, 58
and Latin America, 137
Lost Steps, The, 142
marronage, 10
the marvelous and Columbus, 132–35
and modern Caribbean, 10, 254
and Revolution, 19, 100, 202, 231
subjugation, 69, 121, 124, 134
International Monetary Fund, 146
Islam
 and Christian Imperialism, 134
 and *Timbuktu* (film), 249–51, 257, 258–59
Italy, 15, 152, 154

Jacqueline, 231, 235, 241
Jamaica, 10, 17, 46, 54, 56, 69, 74, 83, 84, 98, 105, 233, 253
James, C. L. R.
 and Black colonial man, 80–82, 86, 255
 Black Jacobins, The, 11, 15, 29–30, 31, 46, 54–55, 70–85, 95–97, 255
 Black knowing, 37, 75–77
 and Caribbean imaginary, 29–30, 43, 54
 and de/anticolonial politics, 14, 30–32, 39, 55–59, 102, 254–55
 French Revolution and/or Enlightenment, 11, 32, 35, 41, 46–47, 60, 79–80, 90
 and *Ginen*, 15, 33, 37, 74, 77, 166, 254
 and Haitian Revolution, 54, 70–72, 96, 222, 253, 255
 lectures on *The Black Jacobins*, 70–73, 81, 95–96, 163, 171
 and Louverture, 33, 37, 46, 60, 63–64, 76–83, 86, 88, 96, 98
 masculinist tradition of writing Caribbean resistance, 55, 74–75, 77–84
 Victorian masculinity, 73–74, 80

Jean-Francois, 17
Jensen, Deborah, 47
Jérémie, Joseph, 217
Jew, 154
Josephine, 219, 230–31, 235, 236, 240, 241, 248

Kaba, Mariame, 51
Kaisary, Philip, 39–40, 139, 153, 188
Kidane, 250
King, Stewart, 64
King, Tiffany Lethabo, 25
Koerner, Michelle, 147, 158
Korngold, Ralph, 65
Kramer, Nicholas Micheal, 104, 137
Kreyòl, 2, 20, 62, 67, 120, 141, 234, 250, 259, 261

labor
  in Carpentier's writing, 137
  in Césaire's writing, 179–82
  and Cuba and Haiti, 109–10
  and racialization, 214–15
Lafrik Ginen (Guinea Africa), 20
Lamartinère, Mar Jan (Marie-Jeanne), 204
Lambert, Laurie, 46, 55
Lambropoulos, Vassilis, 168–69
Lamming, George, 73, 153
land
  and Dessalines, 213–14
  and freedom, 224
  promised, 132, 135
  as property
  uncharted, 226–27
Le Goff, Jacques, 131
Leclerc, Charles, 70, 151, 224
Legba, 12, 93
Lescot, Élie, 159, 233, 234, 238
Lherison, Justin, 216
liberalism
  and Boyer, 150
  and Dessalines, 178

French republicanism, 11, 60, 68, 90, 161, 170
  and Haitian republicanism, 42–44, 68, 148, 161
  and Louverture, 90, 92
  and *Queimada!*, 191
  and tragedy, 85, 170
  and *Tragedy of King Christophe, The*, 180
Lili, 221, 226, 236–38, 240–41, 243, 247–49
Little Guy, 211, 221–22, 238–40, 242, 244, 246–48
Louverture, Suzette Simon, 204
Louverture, Toussaint
  Black Jacobins, The, 64, 70–77, 77–82, 96
  as Black Spartacus, 34, 45, 79
  Conscripts of Modernity, 83–89
  deportation, 18, 63, 70, 91
  early life and family, 66–67
  as exceptional, 46, 77–83, 85
  as *Ginen*, 46–47, 66–67, 74, 77, 79, 81–83, 86
  as Hamlet, 33, 80, 83, 87, 97–98
  and masculinity, 55, 59, 63, 83, 74–83, 89
  as mimic, 65, 69, 63, 74, 83, 85, 88
  1797 letter, 61, 70
  personal ambition, 64–70, 75, 83, 96
  Queimada!, 190, 193, 199
  and republicanism (*see* republicanism)
  Toussaint Louverture, 10–11, 64, 89, 145, 158–63, 166, 171–72
  as tragic figure, 11, 60, 80–81, 85–89
Lowe, Lisa, 35
Lugones, María, 3, 24, 25, 27, 28
Lumumba, Patrice, 170
lwa, 14, 18, 20–21, 22, 207, 208, 209, 229, 231–34, 235–36, 239–45, 247–48

Mabille, Pierre, 158
Macaïa, 12–13, 19, 92–94
Macharia, Keguro, 25
Madiou, Thomas, 227, 158, 216
Makalani, Minkah, 76
Makandal, François
    Makandalism, 62, 67, 78, 82
    personage, 11–13, 62, 67, 112, 114–15, 136, 137, 262, 264
    talisman, 82, 201
Maldonado-Torres, Nelson, 4, 34, 58
Mali, 249–52, 256–58
Mama Dio, 11–13
Manigat, Leslie, 42
Manley, Michael, 84
Mano, Emmauel, 9–10, 253–54
maroon
    marronage, 2, 18, 22
    person, 2–3, 9, 10, 11, 12, 17, 62, 76, 111, 129, 224, 253–54
Martinique, 11, 54, 98, 106, 137, 147, 157, 159, 160–67, 171, 173–77, 178, 187, 190, 259
Martino, 194
marvelous, the
    Carpentier and, 31, 32, 37, 47, 103–4, 106, 120, 121, 127, 135–38
    and Columbus, 118, 131–35
    and *Ginen*, 127–31
    and Haiti, 126–28, 130–31
    as political, 104
Marxism, 53, 71, 83, 88
Massacre River, 220
Masson, André, 137
Mauritius, 248
McKittrick, Katherine, 14, 36, 75, 127
Melas, Natalie, 97
Mellen, Joan 188
Michel, Claudine, 20, 21
Mignolo, Walter, 4, 27
migrants, 73, 109–10, 139
Miller, Paul B., 47, 80
Mocombe, Paul C., 8, 20

Molina, Rafael Leónidas Trujillo, 220, 233–34, 238
Monchoachi, 259
Monnerville, Gaston, 168
Monroe, Jonathan B., 94
Monroe Doctrine, 29
Moraga, Cherríe, 27
Morrison, Toni, 30
Moten, Fred, 169
moun, 118–20, 125, 127, 128, 141, 162–63, 228, 259
moun andeyo, 163
Moyse, 93–94, 97
music (songs)
    mizik rasin (root music), 223
    musicians, 20, 143
    in *Queimada!*, 198–99
    "Sou Lamné," 1, 5–6
    and Vodou, 79, 128, 223, 250
Mussolini, Benito, 158

Nagos, 113
Naimou, Angela, 210
Naipaul, V. S., 73
Native people. *See* Indigenous people
Navarro, Jenell, 25
Nesbitt, Nick, 47, 167
North America
    experience, 163
    imperialism, 88, 154
    person, 85, 99, 143, 172, 203
    place, 102, 142, 204, 227
North Atlantic Treaty Organization, 146
Nwokocha, Eziaku Atuama, 5

oligarchy
    békés, 161, 168
    as descriptor, 148, 226, 231, 235, 246
    Haitian, 142, 148, 149, 152, 158, 159, 162, 221, 224, 225, 227, 228, 229

oligarchy (*continued*)
    Haitians and Haiti imagined as, 35, 166, 186
    and predation, 225
    reading, 218
    Revolution cast as, 245
    See also elites
onto-epistemic, 6, 120, 125, 130, 136, 163, 255
ontology
    Carpentier and, 105, 111, 115–17, 126, 129, 136
    and colonial power, 56, 185, 199
    and decolonial thought, 4, 27, 48, 56, 106, 111, 141, 213
    Wynter and, 106, 123, 133
otherwise, 24–25, 31, 37, 43, 51, 57, 99, 111, 119, 146, 156, 192, 195, 204, 227, 233, 236, 257
    imagine, 25, 113, 188

Pamphile de Lacroix, 71
Pan-Africanism, 38, 222
Paravisini-Gebert, Lizabeth, 101, 140
Past, Mariana F., 82
Pérez, Laura E., 4
Pétion, Alexandre, 9, 18, 42, 59, 100, 111, 178, 181, 183 193, 214–15, 224, 228
planetary, 23, 24, 28, 35, 104, 124
plantation
    in Carpentier's writing, 109–10, 128
    and Césaire, 157–59, 172
    and Christophe, 158, 214, 224
    in Glissant's writing, 93
    and Louverture, 69, 84
    and marronage, 18
    See also agriculture
poetry
    kitchen poets, 206, 231
    poems, 147, 160, 168, 170, 175
    poetics, 158, 164, 167
    poets, 6, 11, 98, 157, 163, 169, 245, 249
    See also specific works and individuals
Pontecorvo, Gillo, 15, 37, 48, 49, 152–57, 187–200. See also *Queimada!*
Popo, 113
Portugal, 124, 134, 154, 194, 192
postcolonial studies, 15–16, 32, 38–39, 84, 87, 98, 102
Povinelli, Elizabeth, 146, 156
praxis
    Africa, 13, 256
    and Black decolonial politics, 15
    Carpentier and cultural, 108–20
    critical, 90, 108
    and *Ginen* (*see Ginen*)
    Haiti, 152, 178
    and Vodou, 240
Prieur, Petit-Noël, 19
property. *See* land
Prospero, 198–99
Puerto Rico, 28

Queimada!, 15, 48–49, 152, 153, 154, 188–99
Quijano, Aníbal, 3, 228

Rabbitt, Kara M., 81, 88
race
    anti-Blackness, 8, 22, 5 63, 66, 74, 45, 89, 107, 117, 121, 130, 134, 156, 167, 204
    and anxiety, 109
    and biology, 14, 110–11 (*see also* biocentric)
    capitalism, 38
    and Carpentier, 47, 48, 108–11, 121, 255
    and Césaire, 167, 176, 179–81, 255
    collective/person, 27, 49, 51, 89, 105, 125, 140, 144, 180, 199
    colonial project/order, 32, 47, 108,

143, 177, 204
and Columbus, 47, 120–27, 131–35
and Cuba, 108–10
and enslavement, 136
and gender, 56, 75 (*see also* Louverture, Toussaint)
Ginen, 5–6, 25–28 (*see also Ginen*)
and Glissant, 56–58, 91, 95
and Haiti, 47, 108, 137, 142, 150, 156, 215, 234
innocence, 140
and James, 72–83
mixed-raced, 5–10, 17–18, 66, 99, 100, 148, 159, 173, 176, 190, 214, 215, 217, 222, 253, 225
multi-racial, 9, 190, 253, 254
and Pontecorvo, 156, 194
and post-independence Haiti, 213–16
race science, 41
racial tropics, 41
racism, 4, 5, 34, 48, 68, 74, 75, 101, 102, 109, 111, 117, 123, 126, 136, 137, 129, 140, 149, 150, 157, 166, 168, 170, 171, 192, 194, 195, 197, 205, 212, 213, 215, 253, 258
and separatism, 9, 173, 253
social construct, 9, 38, 47, 74, 110, 121, 155, 165, 169, 206, 219, 238, 250, 253
solidarity, 2, 24
and subjection, 195, 234
supremacy, 47, 60, 90, 141
and *Timbuktu* (film), 250
and time, 185, 187
and uplift, 179, 182, 184
See also Blackness; white supremacy; whiteness
racialization
and Blackness, 47, 180, 181
and *bossales*, 2
civilization, 196
and colonial project, 47, 48, 56, 74, 75, 103, 105, 110, 121, 137, 186, 187, 210, 212
and Cuba, 100–102
Haitian Constitution, 118–20, 213
and labor, 166, 214–16
lived experience of, 14, 31, 47, 115, 118, 170, 173, 184
and religion (*see* Columbus, Christopher; race: and Columbus)
and struggle for liberation, 100, 254
tragedy, 85, 168–71
and Vodou, 5–6, 14
Raimond, Julien, 68
RAM, 218
Raynal, Guillaume-Thomas, 78–80, 245
Régnier, Nicolas, 19
republicanism
and canon, 40–46
and Césaire (*see* Césaire)
and gender, 50
and *Ginen*, 147–48, 152, 157–66, 213–17
Haitian, 32, 49, 68, 161 (*see* republicanism and canon)
and indemnity, 147
and Louverture, 11, 59, 60–63, 90–96, 169
and post-revolutionary Haiti, 148–49, 159–60, 161–62, 173–74, 213–17
in *Queimada!*, 191–92
Revolution of 1946, 158–59
Rigaud, André, 18, 68
rituals, 2, 5, 241
Riviere-Hérard, Charles, 215–16
Robespierre, Maximilien, 61, 161
Robinson, Cedric, 38
Rodney, Walter, 84
Roman Catholicism, 2, 67, 82, 130, 131–35, 207, 230–35, 242–43, 244
Roosevelt Corollary, 29
Rosario, 143

sa blan dit, 5 6, 113, 256, 258
Said, Edward, 188
Saint Domingue
  affranchi (*see affranchi*)
  colony, 1–3, 7–8, 9, 12, 17–19, 21–28, 45, 53, 58, 61–62, 66, 69–70, 71, 82, 87, 90, 93, 94, 96, 99, 105, 114, 116–19, 121, 128–30, 139–42, 149, 152, 156, 159–60, 162, 173, 180–82, 183, 195, 200, 207, 209, 210, 212, 214, 222–23, 227–28, 233, 244–45, 246, 252
  gens de couleur libre (*see affranchi*)
  Le Cap, 18, 110, 112, 222
  northern Saint Domingue, 17–18, 61–63, 67, 78, 79, 88, 149, 150, 222, 242
  1768 ordinance, 8
  south and western Saint Domingue, 17–19, 41, 62–63, 149
Saint James, 130
Saint Lucia, 6, 98, 245, 249
Saint-Méry, Moreau, 3
Salomon, Lysius, 216
Sanchez, Teddy, 191–92
Sandoval, Chela, 27
Sans Souci, Jean-Baptiste, 19, 263, 265
Sans-Souci palace, 138, 139
savagery, 73, 110, 132, 160, 204
Scott, David, 46, 54, 60, 83–89, 98
Seabrook, William, 101
Seligmann, Katerina Gonzalez, 101, 104
Sepinwall, Alyssa Goldstein, 82, 188
Sharpe, Christina, 107
Shohat, Ella, 188
Simon-Baptist, Suzanne, 66, 204
Singh, Kavita Ashana, 7
Sissako, Abderrahmane, 249, 252, 256, 257. *See also Timbuktu* (film)
slavery
  apologists/supporters of, 39, 45, 61, 64, 68, 70, 71

bonded person (enslaved), 45, 46, 62, 64, 67, 78–79, 96, 115, 117–19, 124, 126, 128, 129, 133, 139, 162, 222, 223, 227 (*see also* captives)
chattel, 1, 3–6, 7–12, 16, 17–21, 22–27, 42, 45, 52, 55, 61, 63–67, 78, 81, 98, 99–100, 103, 112–13, 117–18, 120, 124, 126, 129–30, 132, 133–37, 156, 168, 169, 180, 183, 184–86, 189–93, 194, 209, 218, 220, 224, 250
and Christian imperialism (*see* Columbus, Christopher)
class/collective, 62, 128
colony, 17, 154, 189, 198
critique of, 15
driver (*commandeurs*), 17, 222
holding past, 109–10
and indigenous peoples, 124, 132–35
and latifundia, 124, 133–34
neo-, 168
and racialization, 131–33, 134
raiders, 220
resistance to, 21–23, 25–28, 56, 57, 64, 129, 154, 189, 239
ship, 179–80
slavers, 39, 45, 56, 57, 68, 78, 111, 113, 114, 119, 149, 181, 211
trade, 123, 132
Smith, Andrea, 25
Someruelos, 193
Sonthonox, Léger-Félicité, 61, 224
South Africa, 1
sovereignty
  of dispossessed, 153, 222
  food, 214
  of *Ginens*, 27–28, 89, 119, 158, 172, 211–12, 214, 225, 227
  and Haiti, 5, 29, 52, 146
  head of state, 114, 178
  and Louverture in *Conscripts of Modernity*, 175

and postcolonial statecraft in *The Tragedy of King Christophe*, 179, 184
and republicanism, 161
Spain
  language, 54
  nation, 17–18, 58, 107, 112, 114, 119–22, 129–32, 135, 185, 190, 217, 230
Spanish-American War, 100
Stam, Robert, 188
Steiner, George, 85
Stevenson, Brenda, 188
Stieber, Chelsea, 23–24, 44
Stone, Alan, 188
sugar, 17, 94, 109, 128, 154–55, 189, 190, 221–23, 226, 236, 244, 247
surrealism, 135, 137, 158
Sylla, 19

Taino, 100, 202
Tal-mason, Ali, 101
Timbuktu (film), 249–52, 256, 258
time
  beyond the colony, 49
  and Césaire, 152, 157, 179, 182, 186–88, 198
  of colony, 48, 93, 116, 155, 157, 185, 199, 259
  and *Drums and Colours*, 9, 253
  fixation on, 179, 184
  and *Ginens*, 49, 50, 241
  new (decolonial) existence in, 155, 156, 158
  of oligarchs, 186
  of possibility (Revolution), 186
  problem of, 48, 158
  as progressive, 49, 154–55, 179, 184, 188
  in *Queimada!*, 48, 182–83, 194–95, 197
  racial, 185
  and resistance, 6
  tragedy and time, 86
  in *Timbuktu* (film), 250–52, 257–58
  unmoored in, 157
Ti-Noël, 111–18, 129–30, 139
tout moun se moun, x, 25–28, 42, 69, 105, 113, 119–20, 128, 141–42, 243
tragedy, 11, 30, 31, 60, 80–81, 84–90, 97, 168–70, 173. *See also* Césaire, Aimé: *Tragedy of King Christophe, The*
Trinidad, 11, 53, 76, 98, 252
Trouillot, Michel-Rolph, 2, 4, 8, 18, 22, 41, 52, 61–65, 82, 117, 148, 174, 202, 212
Tuaregs, 250–51, 258

United Nations, 151
United States
  Black experience in, 170, 206
  Black power and Civil Rights movement, 71, 106
  and colonial project, 204
  and Cuba, 101–2, 108–10
  in Haiti, 146, 151, 153, 166, 158, 211, 221, 224–25
  imperialism, 28, 30, 172, 225
  1915 occupation of Haiti, 29, 158–59, 225, 233
  1916 occupation of Dominican Republic, 233
  post-revolutionary Haiti, 29
  prisons in Haiti and the Dominican Republic, 233
  and white rage, 66
unseen, the
  collectivism, 60–70
  Défilée, 219
  defined, 33–35, 54
  Ginen as, 45, 54
  Haiti and Haitians, 43, 49, 50, 138–44, 151, 152, 165, 187, 200, 215

unseen, the (*continued*)
  Louverture as, 47, 60, 69, 74, 97
  new world, 31–35
  reading for, 35–38
untimely, 252, 259

Vastey, Jean Louis, 3, 45, 68, 87, 100, 181
Venezuela, 137
Vergès, Raymond, 168
Vodou
  anba dlo, 20
  and Carpentier, 101, 116, 130
  chants, 79
  condemnation of, 116, 233
  Dantò, 232–33
  ethic, 20
  Ezili, 232
  Freda, 232
  and *Ginen*, 20–22, 78, 207, 209–10
  imaginary, 50, 207–9, 240, 243
  lòt bò dlo, 20
  and Louverture, 67, 79, 82
  and Makandal, 62, 111
  manbò, 11, 17, 20, 222–23, 250
  Marasa, lè (twins), 209
  and marvelous, 127, 130, 135–37
  and *Mistè, lè* (mystery) 208
  Mò, lè (dead), 208
  Ogoun (Fai), 12, 93, 128–30
  oungan, 20, 111, 222
  Petro, 130
  practitioners of, 234
  Rada, 128
  and resistance, 2, 5, 17, 21, 62, 78, 111, 130, 207, 223, 227–30, 232, 241, 242, 244
  and root music (*mizik rasin*), 223
  Siren, La, 232
  "Sou Lamné," 1, 5
  thought, 207
  and time, 92
  and Wynter, 106
  See also Bwa Kayiman; *lwa*

Walcott, Derek
  "citadels" and "cathedrals," 245–46
  Drums and Colours, 6–7, 9–10, 13, 249, 252–54
  Henri Christophe: A Chronicle in Seven Scenes, 98–99, 245
  International Writers Conference, 245
  slave kings, 45
  and Victorian discourse, 73
Walker, William, 189–97, 199
Walsh, Catherine E., 4, 24
Walsh, John Patrick, 164, 174
West, the
  abolition of, 48, 58, 90, 93, 106, 107, 108, 116, 141, 190
  anti-West, 12, 42, 193
  beyond the, x, 4, 27, 31, 32, 43, 58, 103, 106, 111, 114, 119, 255
  Carpentier and, 112–18, 126–31, 135–38, 140, 142–44
  and Césaire, 38, 167–87, 197
  colonizer(s), 88, 113
  and Columbus, 54–56, 103, 120–27, 131–35, 144
  countries, 82
  culture, 82, 86, 88, 91, 114, 117, 125, 138, 144, 150, 161, 162, 171, 186, 190, 219, 227, 228, 229, 233, 244, 246
  and Dessalines, 43–44, 212–17
  epistemology/thought, 88, 89, 91, 97, 112, 113, 126, 133, 168, 170, 189, 229
  and gender, 56, 75
  and *Ginen*, 23, 28, 34, 41, 43, 47, 54, 58, 60, 101, 187, 193, 213–14, 246
  Glissant and, 11–13, 23, 55–57, 91, 94, 105

Haiti as place beyond, 4, 23, 48, 53, 125, 259 (*see also* demonic ground)
and Haitian elites, 148, 160, 171–73, 186, 200, 212–17, 221, 224–25, 227–28, 233, 234
and Haitian republicanism, 43–44, 161
hemisphere, 105, 107, 116, 121–22, 132, 137, 142, 227
and the human, 56, 119–20, 124–25, 126–27, 143–44 (*see also* Wynter, Sylvia)
imperialism, 42, 88–89, 113, 126, 150, 154, 190, 226, 244, 256
and James, 75, 255
and Louverture, 11–12, 13, 36, 45, 47, 60, 69, 74–93, 97
and marvelous (*see* Carpentier, Alejo)
modernity, 84, 127 (*see also* colonial: modernity)
ontology, 91, 93, 113, 127, 136, 138, 213–14, 227
outside of, 10, 54, 82, 90, 94, 117, 120, 125, 143, 176, 233
place, 95, 113, 117, 118, 120, 121, 124, 126, 127, 131, 134, 135, 137, 142, 144, 145, 155, 157, 166, 177, 179, 184, 186, 187, 188, 189, 194, 197, 201, 203, 204, 208, 217, 223, 226, 238, 245, 255
power(s), 88, 189, 228, 257 (*see also* colonial: power(s))
and racism (*see* race)
rationality, 24, 31, 34, 99, 111, 127, 257
resisting, 137, 138, 153
and sameness, 26, 229
and Scholasticism (*see* Columbus, Christopher)
and slavery, 124
story of, 88
and tragic, 81, 168–70
transformation of, 76–77
and unseen, 33
and Westernization, 11, 45, 54, 80–81, 166, 171, 203–4, 225, 229, 240, 244, 249, 255, 256
white peoples of, and hemispheric American descendants, 85, 99, 102, 105, 119, 122, 123, 126, 128, 131, 134, 135, 136, 137, 140, 141, 144, 154, 155, 171, 181, 184, 189
as white supremacist, 89, 114, 116
and Wynter, 106–7, 122–23, 124
See also colonial: project
West Indies, 74, 78, 86, 174
white supremacy
and colonial project, 152, 157, 171, 181, 182
and creole revolutionists, 45
and Cuba, 110
and gender, 56
and *Ginens*, 119
and Haiti, 96, 125, 156
Haitian Revolution combats, 108
in *Queimada!*, 192, 193, 194
and republicanism, 42
and scholarly work on Louverture, 60, 63, 65, 68, 74, 89
and tragedy, 168
and the West, 114, 130, 140, 141, 151, 180
whiteness
acting in, 99
Carpentier's investment in, 141
and Césaire's critique of Haitian elites, 172
colonial project, 27, 111
conditional, 101, 102
cultural, 109
Lost Steps, The, 143
and Louverture, 60, 68, 83, 89, 90

whiteness (*continued*)
   outside of, 14, 38, 111
   perceptual, 117
Wickstrom, Maurya, 185
Wiener, Leo, 132–33
Wilder, Gary, 175–76
Williams, Patricia J., 25
Williams, Raymond, 170
world, new, 15, 120, 121, 127, 176

World Bank, 146
Wynter, Sylvia, 4, 6, 36, 48, 55–56, 75, 85, 105–8, 112, 122–26, 133

Young, Assad, 236

Zabou, 249–52, 256–59
Zamora, 104

www.ingramcontent.com/pod-product-compliance
Lightning Source LLC
Chambersburg PA
CBHW051205300426
44116CB00006B/443